Private Truths, Public Lies

Private Truths, Public Lies

The Social Consequences of Preference Falsification

Timur Kuran

Harvard University Press
Cambridge, Massachusetts
London, England

First Harvard University Press paperback edition, 1997

Library of Congress Cataloging-in-Publication Data

Kuran, Timur.
    Private truths, public lies : the social consequences of
preference falsification / Timur Kuran.
       p. cm.
    Includes index.
    ISBN 0-674-70757-5 (cloth)
    ISBN 0-674-70758-3 (pbk.)
    1. Social influence.   2. Truthfulness and falsehood—Social
aspects.   3. Knowledge, Theory of.   4. Public opinion.   I. Title.
HM259.K87   1995
303.3'4—dc20   94-47969

To my parents,
Aptullah Kuran and Sylvia Stockdale Kuran,
for the gift of curiosity

Contents

Preface

While in the thick of writing this book, I sent a segment on the fall of East European communism to a Czech scholar I had met at a conference. He wrote back that he found the argument sufficiently compelling to wonder whether I myself had experienced totalitarian rule. I replied that I had spent my life in Turkey and the United States, countries that have spared themselves the ravages of totalitarianism.

The question deserved a more thoughtful answer. I have lived under governments tolerant of criticism, though the principle of free speech is interpreted more broadly and enforced more consistently in the United States than in Turkey. In both countries the press features debates on a host of matters, and criticisms of official policies enjoy wide circulation. Contrast this openness and competition with a totalitarian system, where the government systematically persecutes dissenters. Fearful of official reprisals, potential critics refrain from saying what they think, from revealing their misgivings about government policies, from calling for reforms. It is this dimension of insincerity—of what the East Europeans characterize as "living a lie"—that prompted my Czech reader's inquiry. He wanted to know how, unless I had first-hand experience with totalitarianism, I could appreciate the significance, much less understand the dynamics, of "preference falsification"—the act of misrepresenting one's wants under perceived social pressures.

But despotic government is not the only source of fear, the only obstacle to overt and candid discourse. A more basic factor is public opinion. For one thing, despotism is unsustainable without at least the tacit consent of public opinion. For another, public opinion is itself a determinant of people's willingness to reveal their innermost selves. Even in democratic societies, where the right to think, speak, and act freely enjoys official protection, and where tolerance is a prized virtue, unorthodox views can evoke enormous hostility. In the United States, for instance, to defend the sterilization of poor women or the legalization of importing ivory would be to raise doubts about one's civility and morality, if not one's sanity. To be sure, time and again the courts have ruled that unpopular views, no matter how outrageous, are protected by the law. Yet a person may be free under the law to enunciate despised views without enjoying the same esteem, in the eyes of others, as people with widely accepted views. However strictly enforced, freedom of speech does not insulate people's reputations from their expressed opinions.

Precisely because people who express different opinions do get treated differently, individuals normally tailor their expressions to the prevailing social pressures. Their adjustments vary greatly in social impact. At one extreme are harmless, and possibly beneficial, acts of politeness, as when one tells a friend wearing a garish shirt that he has good taste. At the other are acts of spinelessness on issues of general concern, as when a politician endorses a protectionist measure that he recognizes as harmful to most of his constituents. The pressures generating such acts of insincerity need not originate from the government. Preference falsification is compatible with all political systems, from the most unyielding dictatorship to the most libertarian democracy.

To return to my colleague's inquiry, one does not have to live under a tyrannical regime to commit and observe acts of preference falsification. Nor need one know the history of communism to sense that such acts have important consequences. Thus my own point of departure was not communist repression but the taboos of contemporary American politics. I had just immersed myself in modern political economy, having spent my student years studying economic development and microeconomic theory. It struck me as a weakness of the literature that it generally failed to recognize, let alone explain and interpret, that some issues are more open to discussion, and some viewpoints better tolerated, than others. For the evidence, one did not have to go beyond college campuses: many free-speech advocates who were quick to condemn the McCarthyism of the 1950s were promoting efforts to deny a public forum to speakers whose views they found offensive, such as eugenicists and representatives of the Palestine Liberation Organization.

My first two essays on preference falsification, technical pieces drafted in 1983 and published four years later in *Public Choice* and the *Economic Journal,* sought to bring realism to the economic theory of politics through insights from sociology and psychology. As my thinking progressed, it became apparent that preference falsification touches every area of social thought. Accordingly my research expanded in scope and became increasingly interdisciplinary.

This book thus offers a theory that synthesizes approaches and findings from social-scientific traditions that have developed more or less separately. In the tradition of economics, the theory incorporates the concepts of optimization and equilibrium. Like political science, it assigns to political pressure groups a key role in collective decision making. As in sociology, it treats humans as social beings—creatures who learn from one another, care about others, and worry about what others think of them. Finally, along with various branches of psychology, it recognizes that the mind has limitations and that it is a seat of tensions. In keeping with its hybrid origins, the theory yields propositions embodying observations now sequestered in disparate fields of inquiry.

All these disciplines, along with philosophy, have provided insights into the phenomenon I am calling preference falsification. I try in this book to reconcile and unite these insights. Specifically, I seek to provide an integrated account of the role of preference falsification in guiding, distorting, stabilizing, constraining, and changing the social order, including the knowledge that undergirds it. More than the individual mechanisms I describe and analyze—preference falsification as a source of rigidity, as a shaper of ideology, as a cradle of surprise—the book's theoretical significance lies in the linkages it posits among the particular mechanisms.

A book purporting to analyze a universal social process must justify its claim to generality by testing its thesis in diverse contexts. It must connect facts previously treated as unrelated by identifying common patterns in geographically distinct, temporally removed, culturally specific events. I have therefore woven three case studies into the argument. They involve India's caste system, communist rule in Eastern

Europe, and racial affirmative action in the United States. In each of these studies the focus is on linking diverse facts. The same logic runs through each set of explanations, demonstrating the theory's generality. The case studies were chosen because of their social significance and because they offer striking illustrations of the book's theoretical claims.

Had I focused on a single case the added detail might have enhanced the book's standing in the eyes of some, but the theory's generality would have remained poorly demonstrated. The book might have given the impression that its relevance is limited to a single culture, society, or historical episode. There are vast differences, of course, between the cultures of India and Eastern Europe, between a system of segregation and a political regime, between an ancient religion and a modern secular ideology. But one can recognize such differences without overlooking the similarities. In fact, the study of differences may benefit from the identification of universal social processes that account for them. Where differences fascinate, says Stephen Jay Gould, generalities instruct. Anyone who has seen a tiger and a leopard knows that one is striped and the other spotted. It is a general theory, the theory of natural evolution, that accounts for the origins and stability of this intriguing difference.

We live in an age of escalating intellectual balkanization, a time when professional scholars can scarcely keep up with developments in their chosen specialties, let alone trends in other specialties and disciplines. For nonscholars the problem is even less manageable. The growing integration of the world economy is compounding the need for nonlocal knowledge, yet as individuals we all remain terribly constrained in our capacity to process information. There exists an acute need, then, for broad syntheses, for tools of conceptualization, for studies that identify hidden patterns. It is in this spirit that the present work was composed. I have sought to illuminate a universal phenomenon. The examples are of interest in their own right, but the book's main objective is to develop a simple framework for thinking about the mechanics, dynamics, and consequences of preference falsification.

Because preference falsification is an act that conceals information on the forces behind social trends, readers may wonder whether the theory has any predictive value, and also whether it furnishes refutable implications. I will answer these questions head on, but only after the argument has been developed in full. I ask the reader to judge the theory initially by its internal coherence and plausibility, trusting that questions of measurement, testability, and predictive potential will receive attention in due course.

To immerse oneself in the study of a particular phenomenon inevitably raises one's awareness of its manifestations in daily life. In this case, I found myself increasingly conscious of human hypocrisy and insincerity. I began seeing the signs of preference falsification everywhere: in faculty meetings, at social gatherings, watching political debates, in the press, in my students' exam books. I also became increasingly self-conscious as I noticed it in my own behavior. Fortunately, my preoccupation with the darker side of human nature was not without reward. I became more sensitized to the independent streak in the human character, to the spirit that gives one the courage to say "no" when the pressures of the moment demand a "yes." With a heightened appreciation for the complexity of the human personality, for the tensions we all endure in trying to mediate between our needs for social approval and those for self-assertion, I gained more respect for the nonconformist, the pioneer, the innovator, the dissident, even the misfit. It is my hope that the reader will come to share in this appreciation.

In writing *Private Truths, Public Lies,* I benefited from the assistance of many organizations and individuals. While it would be impractical to name them all, I cannot omit mentioning those who made the most significant contributions.

I owe an immense debt of gratitude to Wendy Kuran, my wife, who has been not only an unfailing source of emotional sustenance but also an exacting critic of my various drafts. Among my colleagues in the economics department at the University of Southern California, I am particularly indebted to Richard Day, Richard Easterlin, Peter Gordon, and Jeffrey Nugent. When, as a young assistant professor, curiosity led me beyond the conventional boundaries of economics, their enthusiasm created an environment in which I could pursue my interests freely. Over the years I have also benefited from their knowledge, advice, and friendship. Outside my own university,

I received encouragement and support from James Buchanan, Albert Hirschman, Mancur Olson, and Thomas Schelling, each an author of seminal works that have profoundly influenced my thinking.

As the project advanced, many scholars contributed their time to evaluating drafts of my chapters, pointing out errors and helping me clarify concepts. I am especially grateful to Lee Alston, Anjum Altaf, Arjun Appadurai, Randall Bartlett, Young Back Choi, Metin Coşgel, Dipak Gupta, Andrea Halpern, Robert Higgs, Sheila Ryan Johansson, William Kaempfer, Daniel Klein, Michael Krauss, Mark Lichbach, Glenn Loury, Thomas Miceli, Vai-Lam Mui, Raaj Sah, Ekkehart Schlicht, Wolfgang Seibel, and Bruce Thompson. Along the way, several of my graduate students made helpful comments; I am particularly indebted to Tolga Köker and Enrico Marcelli. When the manuscript was at an advanced stage of completion, Michael Aronson, my editor at Harvard University Press, offered sound editorial judgment that led to numerous additional improvements, both substantive and expositional. And Elizabeth Gretz, my manuscript editor, skillfully refined the text.

I also benefited from several generous research grants. The National Science Foundation supported my early theoretical papers, and the Earhart Foundation the book's chapters on India and Eastern Europe. The National Endowment for the Humanities provided a fellowship that enabled me to spend the 1989–90 academic year at the Institute for Advanced Study in Princeton, a scholar's paradise. Two other research centers granted me the privileges of a visiting scholar: in 1991, the Center for Economic Research and Graduate Education at Charles University in Prague, and in 1992, the Indian Statistical Institute in New Delhi.

A number of my chapters draw on materials published in provisional form. An earlier version of Chapter 2 appeared as "Private and Public Preferences," *Economics and Philosophy,* 6 (April 1990): 1–26. Parts of Chapter 5 were included in "Mitigating the Tyranny of Public Opinion: Anonymous Discourse and the Ethic of Sincerity," *Constitutional Political Economy,* 4 (Winter 1993): 41–78. Chapters 10 and 11 build on "The Unthinkable and the Unthought," *Rationality and Society,* 5 (October 1993): 473–505. Scattered portions of Chapters 7, 15, and 16 are based on "Now Out of Never: The Element of Surprise in the East European Revolution of 1989," *World Politics,*

44 (October 1991): 7–48. Some segments of Chapter 16 draw on "Sparks and Prairie Fires: A Theory of Unanticipated Political Revolution," *Public Choice*, 61 (April 1989): 41–74. And parts of Chapter 19 have appeared in "The Inevitability of Future Revolutionary Surprises," *American Journal of Sociology*, 100 (May 1995): 1528–1551, © 1995 by The University of Chicago, all rights reserved. I would like to thank the publishers of these articles for permission to use them here.

I wish, finally, to extend my thanks to Neşe Kanoğlu, Feisal Khan, and Jason MacInnes, for enthusiastic research assistance; to Gautam Bose, Helena Flam, Shubhashis Gangopadhyay, David Lipps, Sanjay Subrahmanyam, and Peter Voss, for useful discussions and help with establishing contacts; to Herbert Addison, Colin Day, Peter Dougherty, and Jack Repcheck, for fruitful advice and valuable encouragement at various stages of my work; to Robert Manchin of Gallup-Hungary, Elisabeth Noelle-Neumann of the Allensbach Institute in Germany, and Ivan Tomek of the Public Opinion Research Institute in the Czech Republic, for putting at my disposal some important surveys; to Ruth Wallach, for helping with translations from Slavic languages; and to Joan Walsh, for drawing the figures.

Los Angeles
November 1994

I

Living a Lie

1

The Significance of Preference Falsification

Imagine that a person in a position to alter your career invites you to a party at his home. When you arrive at the party, the talk of the moment seems to be about the living room's pale neutral colors, the latest trend in interior decoration. The look does not appeal to you, but you would rather not say so, lest your host be hurt. Feeling pressured to say something, you compliment his "sophisticated taste." A while later you find yourself in a conversation on wasteful development projects in Latin America. Someone pompously asserts that under socialism there would be no waste. Although you find the claim preposterous, you let it go unchallenged, to avoid sparking a divisive debate.

With the advancing hour, you get bored and start itching to leave. A voice inside objects that it would be imprudent to be the first to make a move. So you stay on, hoping that somebody else will comment on the late hour and signal a readiness to depart, giving you an opportunity to slip out without becoming the focus of attention. At long last someone stands up to leave, and to your secret delight, the party unravels. Thanking your host for a "marvelous evening," you head for the door, grateful that it was not you who initiated the exodus.

Your evening contained several instances of *preference falsification*, the act of misrepresenting one's genuine wants under perceived social pressures. In admiring the bland decor, remaining silent on Latin America, delaying your departure, and stating that you had a delightful time, you conveyed impressions at odds with your private thoughts and desires, at least partly to avoid disapproval. On each occasion, you faced a choice between openness and concealment, between self-assertion and social accommodation, between maintaining your integrity and protecting your image. There were always good reasons to opt for insincerity, advantages that outweighed the benefits of being uncompromisingly and assertively truthful.

Preference Falsification as a Specific Form of Lying

Why introduce a complicated term like preference falsification? Wouldn't "lying" do? While always a form of lying, preference falsification is a more specific concept. Consider a person who, as a soldier, followed orders to massacre unarmed civilians. Years later, he denies taking part in the crime. If he was personally opposed to the atrocity, and participated solely to avoid being court-martialed for disobedience, his lie about his involvement does not misrepresent his sentiment toward his victims. Given that he felt no antagonism toward them, he would not be falsifying a preference. Preference falsification aims specifically at manipulating the perceptions others hold about one's motivations or dispositions, as when you complimented your host to make him think that you shared his taste.

Nor is preference falsification synonymous with "self-censorship," the suppression of one's potentially objectionable thoughts. In this instance, preference falsification is the broader concept. Had you merely kept quiet during the discussion about the decor, that would have been self-censorship. In pretending to like it, you went beyond self-censorship. You deliberately projected a contrived opinion.

Two other common terms with which preference falsification has close affinity are "insincerity" and "hypocrisy." I will sometimes use them where the context leaves no room for ambiguity, just as I will refer occasionally to lying. But no such term is sufficiently precise for the topic at hand. What gets falsified may be a preference, one's knowledge, or a value. For analytical clarity, it will often be essential to distinguish among various forms of falsification.

A phrase that captures the meaning of preference falsification exactly is "living a lie." It was developed by East European dissidents during their long winter of communist dictatorship, because they, too, found their existing vocabulary inadequate. To live a lie is to be burdened by one's lie. The source of the burden could be the guilt one suffers for having avoided social responsibility, or the anger one experiences for having failed to live up to one's personal standards, or the resentment one feels for having been induced to suppress one's individuality. Whatever the nature of the discomfort, it shows persistence. Of course, not all lying produces discomfort. The bank teller who pretends to be cooperating with a would-be robber, when she is actually buying time for the police, need not be burdened by her lie. Similarly, if you praise your host's decor only to make him feel good, without any thought of protecting your own reputation, the act is unlikely to weigh on you. You need not have to live with guilt, anger, or resentment, so the lie is not an instance of preference falsification.

If one distinguishing characteristic of preference falsification is that it brings discomfort to the falsifier, another is that it is a response to real or imagined social pressures to convey a particular preference. It is thus distinct from the strategic voting that occurs when, in a secret-ballot election, one votes for candidate B because C, one's favorite, cannot win. Strategic voting entails preference *manipulation*. But it does not involve preference *falsification*, because in a private polling booth there are no social pressures to accommodate and no social reactions to control.

Challenges Ahead

In addition to its intended effect—the regulation of others' perceptions—preference falsification may have unintended consequences. When you chose to keep silent on Latin America, you deprived your fellow guests of your personal knowledge. Had you spoken up, you might have influenced how some guests think, or will think, about Latin American development. They might have spread your thoughts to others, thus helping to increase pressure for viable reforms.

The objective of this book is to classify, connect, and explicate the unintended consequences of preference falsification. How, precisely, does preference falsification affect the mechanics of politics? How does it influence the evolution of public opinion? What are its implications for the efficiency of social policies and institutions? To what extent and by what mechanisms does it transform beliefs, ideologies, and worldviews? Finally, does it facilitate or hinder efforts to predict and control the social order?

As will become clear, some of the most striking effects of preference falsification are, in one sense or another, socially harmful. I argue that preference falsification generates inefficiencies, breeds ignorance and confusion, and conceals social possibilities. Yet preference falsification is not an unmitigated social menace. It can benefit others by suppressing the communication of knowledge that happens to be false. It can harmonize our social interactions by restraining impulses like malice, envy, and prejudice. And further, it can enhance vital social cooperation by silencing minor disagreements of opinion. There are also subtler reasons why it would be incorrect to view preference falsification in a purely negative light. These other reasons will emerge as the argument progresses, although the focus of the book is on explaining the effects of preference falsification rather than on judging them. Much of the discussion has moral implications, some of which receive attention, but I do not aim to provide a comprehensive normative analysis, and certainly not one capable of differentiating conclusively between morally justified and unjustified cases of preference falsification.[1]

Religious Dissimulation

One illustration of preference falsification involves movements aimed at fostering religious conformity. Responding to the pressures exerted by such movements, heterodox believers have often sought refuge in dissimulation. The medieval world offers some poignant examples.

Around the time of the Christian reconquest of Spain, the Church launched a persecution campaign against the country's non-Christians. It thus became increasingly unsafe to live in Spain as a practicing Jew or Muslim. Many Jews responded by fleeing abroad. But hundreds of thousands opted instead to accept baptism, resting their decision on a Judaic legal provision that allows dissimulation in times of danger. In those days, conversion was understood to imply a change not just of faith but also of lifestyle. Outwardly, therefore, the ostensible converts began to live as Christians. In the privacy of their homes, however, many continued to practice their ancestral rites, waiting for the day when they could revert to Judaism. Yet for all the precautions they took, their secret activities attracted attention. The notorious Spanish Inquisition was created to stamp out the secret practice of Judaism, which came to be known as Marranism.[2] Marranism is a form of preference falsification.

Around the time that Judaism slipped underground in Spain, Catholicism was under attack in England, where laws had been passed to make Protestantism the sole legitimate religion. Many Catholic believers started attending Protestant services, but as an act of political precaution rather than of religious faith. Some Catholic authorities encouraged the practice, arguing that dissimulation is sometimes essential for self-preservation. Others, including the pope, declared the practice of conformism illicit. One anticonformist writer suggested that Catholics who went to "false congregations" were endangering the very survival of Catholicism.[3]

Underlying this dispute among Catholic leaders is a disagreement concerning the dynamic consequences of preference falsification. In the proconformist view, preference falsification can go on indefinitely without altering the preferences being suppressed; word leaves the heart intact. In the anticonformist view, the effects of preference falsification outlive the forces behind it; word transforms the heart. The former view sanctifies accommodation. It suggests that a dissimulator may wait patiently for the danger to pass, without any weakening, no matter how long the wait, of his desire to return to the fold. By contrast, the latter view demands active resistance. Because dissimulation may give way to genuine conversion, it carries the risk of annihilation. The intuition behind the anticonformist view happens to be correct, though the risk may vary. This argument will be developed in later chapters.

A final case of religious dissimulation comes from Islam. The Sunni caliphs of the Umayyad dynasty, who began ruling the Arab empire in the late seventh century from Damascus, made it a test of Islamic devotion to insult the founders of Shi'ism. Seeing that failure to pass the test could bring great hardship, even death, the Shi'is adopted the *taqiya* doctrine, which permitted them to conceal their heterodoxy under danger, as long as they preserved it in their own hearts and minds.[4] Although the doctrine predates Islam, its justification was taken to be a verse in the Qur'an: "Whether ye conceal what is in your hearts or reveal it, Allah knows it."[5]

Every classical work of Shi'i jurisprudence stresses that *taqiya* is legitimate only under conditions of grave emergency. Over time, however, the doctrine turned into a license for general political apathy. Modern Shi'i leaders, seeing *taqiya* as a barrier to revolutionary activism, have insisted that it was never meant to rationalize passivity in the face of unjust government.[6] Significantly, the Ayatollah Khomeini, the mastermind of Iran's Islamic Revolution, launched his struggle by declaring: "The time for *taqiya* is over. Now is the time for us to stand up and proclaim the things we believe in."[7]

The modern opposition to *taqiya* highlights another theme of the book: preference falsification as a barrier to social change. Where the anticonformist writers of Catholicism saw preference falsification as an agent of transformation, contemporary Shi'i writers have considered it a source of rigidity. These two positions are by no means incompatible. Depending on various factors to be specified later, preference falsification can fuel either change or continuity.

Veiling and Its Discontents

To consider a related possibility, let us move to modern Turkey. Turkish civil libertarians, including Westernized intellectuals and self-styled progressives, reject the notion that no one should be concerned when a woman covers her head in public settings. Many favor the prohibition of veiling. The freedom to veil—a freedom taken for granted in most parts of the world—is defended primarily by Islamic fundamentalists, who tend to define individual liberties narrowly and consider modern society too permissive. Fundamentalists argue that the freedom to veil is a basic human right.

Where everyone is acting out of character, it behooves one to look for complicating factors. The complication here is a widespread perception that the freedom to veil is self-negating. Indeed, both fundamentalists and their opponents recognize that veiling on the part of some women would generate pressures to conform on those wishing to remain unveiled. Everyone senses that some veiled women would accuse their unveiled peers of breaking an ostensible religious law, prompting the latter to falsify their preferences in an effort to gain acceptance and respect. There is broad agreement, therefore, that Turkey's choice with regard to veiling is not between freedom and compulsion but, rather, between one kind of compulsion and another. Under the circumstances, civil libertarians reject the freedom to veil in order to safeguard a more precious freedom, the freedom not to veil. For their part, the fundamentalists accept the freedom not to veil, because they expect the freedom to veil to extinguish it.

As with any festering national controversy, the contending arguments are more complex and more varied than this brief account makes them seem. There are libertarians who consider the freedom to veil a basic right, and there are fundamentalists who are loath to permit the breaching of what they regard as divine law. It is significant, however, that within each camp disagreements reflect differences over the power of conformist motives. For instance, Westernized intellectuals who support the freedom to veil generally believe that the social pressures on nonveilers are unlikely to become irresistible.

An analogous controversy concerns the practice of secularism. Although secularism ordinarily entails the separation of religion from the affairs of state, in Turkey it has meant, ever since Atatürk's reforms of the 1920s, the control of religion, if not its suppression. A major justification for religious regulation has been the suspicion that Islam is incompatible with democracy. If Islam's social power were unchecked, many leaders have thought, it would drive reformist, modernist discourse underground, with fatal consequences for the country's ongoing transformation.[8] As in the veiling issue, proponents of liberal democracy have found themselves opposing religious liberties precisely to protect liberties they value more, like freedom of the press.

These Turkish controversies raise the possibility that encouraging one form of preference falsification may be the price of preventing some other form. This possibility will receive attention in chapters ahead. We shall see that it makes groups equate full freedom with their own annihilation, thinking that if they do not suppress others, others will suppress them.

Outing

In the United States, a controversy over the morality of "outing" closeted homosexuals illustrates further fears and political responses that will figure prominently in later discussions. In mid-1991, the gay-rights group Queer Nation held a press conference to announce that a senior official of the Department of Defense was a homosexual. Shortly thereafter, the *Advocate,* a gay magazine, ran a story on the official. The magazine defended its action by pointing to the Pentagon's own policy of outing gays in uniform and then discharging them. The covertly homosexual official had promoted the policy, alleged the *Advocate;* he had encouraged and helped implement discrimination against gays. Around the same time, another gay group, OutPost, covered New York with posters featuring the faces of movie stars, allegedly closeted homosexuals. The posters were inscribed "Absolutely Queer."[9]

Most newspapers refused to name the "outed" celebrities. People have a right, they maintained, to keep information about their private lives private. The gay community split. Some gays opposed outing as an infringement on the right to privacy. Others defended it as a social necessity. Though agreeing that people have a fundamental right to make their own sexual choices, the latter group insisted that individuals also have a duty to be truthful about their sexual identity, regardless of the possible personal costs. They argued that homosexuals wearing a mask of heterosexuality contribute to the oppression of fellow homosexuals by making homosexuality a badge of shame.

The debate in the gay community is about the freedom to be a *closeted* homosexual. One side grants individual homosexuals the right to falsify their sexual preferences; the other sees such preference falsification as a threat to the agenda of eradicating antihomosexual prejudice. There is also an intermediate position, which distinguishes between the "passive closet" and the "active closet." The passively closeted homosexual simply practices homosexuality discreetly, hoping to escape detection. The actively closeted homosexual tries to cover up his homosexuality through actions designed to make him appear heterosexual, as when a gay actor makes a point of being seen with promiscuous women, or when a gay official champions antihomosexual regulations.[10] The intermediate position endorses the outing of closeted homosexuals only if they are consciously benefiting from activities directly harmful to gays.[11]

This is not our first encounter with the notion that preference falsification may have socially deleterious spillover effects. We saw that it fueled bans against religious dissimulation. The new point is that the manifestations of preference falsification include punishing people whose views and needs one shares. The logic is simple. Talk being cheap, anyone can claim to be against this lifestyle or that political platform. An effective way of making such a claim credible is to participate in efforts to punish those from whom one is seeking dissociation. A closeted homosexual may become a gay basher to allay suspicions about his own private life. As the argument unfolds, we shall see that such hypocrisy is a universal, and often successful, tactic of self-protection and self-promotion.

Gay activists have long claimed that *most* gay Americans remain closeted, resting their case on the famous 1948 survey of Alfred Kinsey. As many as 10 percent of the men in Kinsey's sample reported being more or less exclusively homosexual during the preceding three years. Professional researchers of sexual behavior have regarded the sample as unrepresentative, in that it contained disproportionate numbers of sex offenders, prisoners, and recruits from Kinsey's own lectures.[12] Still, the figure slipped into the media as a settled fact—until 1993, that is, when the Battelle Human Affairs Research Center released one of the most rigorous studies ever of male sexual behavior. According to the Battelle study, only 1.1 percent of American men are exclusively homosexual, with another 1.2 percent having had homosexual sex during the past decade. Gay activists refused to give up the 10 percent figure. Even as scholars pointed out that the Battelle figures are consistent with findings from other countries, activists rushed to discredit the new study. The gay quarterly *10 Percent* announced that it would not change its name.[13]

If the gay lobby finds the Battelle study unacceptable and refuses to concede the flaws of the Kinsey survey, the reason is that it has a vested interest in the perception that homosexuals form a huge, if mostly invisible, voting bloc—just as opponents of gay rights have a vested interest in making the numerical significance of homosexuality seem vastly overstated. The gay lobby's ability to advance its objectives depends substantially on the perceived share of Americans who are overtly or covertly gay. Further on we shall see that it is a common political practice to claim that the support for one's cause is mostly hidden. Reformers and revolutionaries of every stripe have asserted that they enjoy the sympathy of a covert majority.

Leaks and Trial Balloons

A person weighing the probable consequences of an action often has reliable information to go on. For instance, a closeted lesbian in small-town America might know with near certainty that if she steps out she will face harassment. In some contexts, however, one's information about probable reactions is unreliable. A politician with a new idea may be unsure about the reception it will get. Faced with such uncertainty, he might float the idea anonymously, possibly by having a subordinate discuss it with a trusted reporter who agrees to attribute her story to "well-placed sources." Such a "trial balloon" gives the idea some exposure without requiring the politician to take personal responsibility. If the reaction is unfavorable, he can quickly dissociate himself from the idea, even join the chorus of criticism. If instead the reaction is favorable, he can claim credit and begin promoting the idea openly. The lesson here is that efforts are made to test public opinion. The efforts often prove worthwhile, because taking an unpopular position in public can be very costly. It can turn one's friends into enemies, damage one's reputation, and extinguish one's career, among other possibilities.

Other news is passed to the press because public opinion is already well known. A cabinet minister may seek to discredit another minister, or his policies, by feeding the press news certain to damage him, on condition that the source of the "leak" be left unnamed. Through the subsequent outcry, the leaker manages to hurt her opponent, but without inviting reprisals. While secretly relishing the leak's consequences, she can express outrage, even call for tough penalties on proven leakers.

News leaks are a ubiquitous feature of Washington politics. Convinced that Ronald Reagan was insufficiently active on women's issues, one of his aides leaked her own in-house report on sex discrimination to a journalist, who then asked the President at a nationally broadcast news conference why he had not acted on a report of his own administration.[14] The aide wanted to generate a public outcry that would push Reagan into action. Other Reagan aides made it a point to tip off the press about the President's disagreements with his first secretary of state, Alexander Haig.[15] Their goal was to force Haig's departure without their having to take any blame.

Politicians go to great lengths to protect themselves and their policies from inconvenient leaks. David Gergen, who served as director of communications in the first Reagan administration, recalls that aides made it a practice never to say anything controversial in a conversation where more than one other person was present. The logic of such caution is that information delivered to a single person is unlikely to be leaked, because the source of the leak would be obvious. The fear of leaks, Gergen observes, makes the number of Washington officials involved with an issue *inversely* proportional to its significance. The more significant the issue, the fewer the number—precisely because leaks become more probable and potentially more dangerous.[16]

That leaks and trial balloons play an important role in Washington politics would not have surprised Machiavelli, the arch-realist of the European Renaissance. In *The Prince* he argued that politics features many forms of deception, including insincerity.[17] The observation was not new, but earlier writers had tended to extol the virtues of sincerity. Breaking the pattern, Machiavelli insisted that insincerity is ineradicable, and on this basis, he advised the aspiring leader to be as cunning as a fox. A political player, he argued, must take on whatever appearance seems most prudent from the standpoint of acquiring and retaining power. The politician who insists on being fully open and totally honest will inevitably offend powerful groups and get outmaneuvered by more prudent rivals.

The politician's motive for wearing a socially acceptable mask did not disappear with the advent of modern democracy. We shall see that preference falsification continues to shape the political process everywhere.

The Secret Ballot, Blind Refereeing, and Secluded Negotiations

If preference falsification is as common, and its political consequences as significant, as I am suggesting, there ought to exist mechanisms for mitigating its causes. It will be instructive to consider a few.

In every modern democracy major elections and referenda are conducted by secret ballot. The rationale is to let citizens vote without intimidation. Votes taken by open ballot are considered illegitimate precisely because they may have been tainted by preference falsification.

So esteemed is the secret ballot that undemocratic regimes try to make effectively open votes seem secret. The 1979 referendum on turning Iran into an "Islamic Republic" was preceded by a campaign that threatened to brand as an infidel anyone daring to vote in the negative. Although votes would technically be anonymous, the campaign created the impression that the regime could determine the nature of any individual vote. At the polls, moreover, voters saw their identity cards stamped, fueling fears that districts with many negative votes would become the focus of interrogations and reprisals.[18] When the initiative received an approval rating of 98.2 percent, the revolutionary regime interpreted the result as an expression of overwhelming support. But the world press, sensing that millions had voted affirmatively out of fear, rightly called the referendum a sham. In effect, it declared the result biased on the grounds that voters did not *consider* their votes anonymous.

Academic promotion decisions are often made in settings designed to obviate preference falsification. Faculty asked to evaluate candidates for promotion are assured that their names, or at least the substance of their recommendations, will be kept confidential. Leaks do occur, which is why evaluations are replete with circuitous language and why experienced readers pay more attention to what is *not* being said than to what is. On the whole, however, the system undoubtedly promotes sincerity.

Scholarly journals customarily base their publication decisions on unsigned reports whose preparers are known only to the editors. As every academic writer knows, anonymous referees are notoriously quick to condemn articles that they would not dare criticize openly. Anonymity also allows referees to be sloppy and to vent their jealousies, animosities, and prejudices. But the academic community tends to consider the drawbacks of anonymity outweighed by its advantages—evidence that intellectual preference falsification is recognized as pervasive.

Academic publication lists commonly distinguish between refereed and nonrefereed publications. The latter generally enjoy less prestige, because their editors, having no anonymous reports on which to blame rejections, are thought to be less capable of upholding standards. Similar logic limits the prestige of journals that receive submissions primarily from writers with whom the editors interact on a daily basis. The editors of such "house journals" are thought to have great difficulty turning down mediocre submissions.

A final illustration comes from diplomacy. Sensitive international negotiations are often conducted in seclusion, so as to insulate the negotiators from pressures against compromise. A case in point is the Camp David Summit of 1978, which resulted in a historic peace treaty between Egypt and Israel. The final treaty was negotiated by tiny teams behind closed doors, while neither nation knew what its leaders were giving away. No daily progress reports were issued during the negotiations, lest they generate protests that would kill the chances for a settlement. The leaders on each side made concessions that they would not have wanted to defend publicly, except as the price of an accomplished treaty ending decades of hostility.[19]

The essential lesson here is that the proclivity to engage in preference falsification depends crucially on the institutional context. People who will mask their wants and beliefs in one setting will readily expose them in another. Conscious of this variation, political agents seek to manipulate the settings in which preferences are communicated. They may opt for arrangements that promote sincerity, as when the Israeli and Egyptian leaders agreed to negotiate behind closed doors. Or they may foster insincerity, as when Iran's ayatollahs made it appear risky to vote against Islamic rule. Coming chapters will show that the institutions governing the incentives for preference falsification are themselves matters of choice on which preference falsification may be rampant.

Conceptual Preview: The Social Effects of Preference Falsification

The foregoing illustrations should leave no doubt that preference falsification is a phenomenon to which political actors accord enormous significance. It should also be clear that there exist a panoply of settings where individuals find it prudent to project socially approved preferences—to act, that is, like chameleons. The settings are all ones in which people's social standing depends on their professed dispositions.

Preference falsification produces two categories of effects. First, expressed preferences have social consequences, as when women choosing to veil induce conformist responses from women who would rather stay unveiled. Second, the social climate fostered by preference falsification may transform the preferences people are trying to hide. An example would be the eventual disappearance of a religion that is practiced only in secret. In the first category of effects, individual choices shape social outcomes. The second reverses the causality: social outcomes shape individual choices. Paired together, the two categories imply a circular causal relationship between social outcomes and individual choices. They thus suggest that to identify and understand the consequences of preference falsification, one must investigate both how individuals shape social variables and how social variables shape individuals.

Where to begin the analysis? In principle, the investigation of a circular relationship can start anywhere, provided one then travels the entire circle. For our purposes, however, it is best to start with the individual's influence on social outcomes, because preference falsification is an individual act. The mechanisms by which the social effects of preference falsification shape individuals will become easier to understand once the effects themselves have been investigated systematically.[20]

The starting point of the analysis is the choice faced by an individual who must convey a preference on some issue. The issue is one where he will receive benefits or incur costs for the preference he expresses. Thus it is unlike that which he would encounter if asked to select, say, among flavors of ice cream, because that choice would not be of concern to others. In the case at hand, our individual knows that he will be judged by the preference he declares. Another important characteristic of this issue is that it will be settled through an aggregation of the relevant preferences expressed.

How will the individual choose what preference to convey? Three distinct considerations may enter his calculations: the satisfaction he is likely to obtain from society's decision, the rewards and punishments associated with his chosen preference, and finally, the benefits he derives from truthful self-expression. If large numbers of individuals are expressing preferences on the issue, the individual's capacity to influence the collective decision is likely to be negligible. In this case he will consider society's decision to be essentially fixed, basing his own preference declaration only on the second and third considerations. Ordinarily, these offer a tradeoff between the benefits of self-expression and those of being perceived as someone with the right preference. Where the latter benefits dominate, our individual will engage in preference falsification.

The preference that our individual ends up conveying to others is what I will call his *public preference*. It is distinct from his *private preference*, which is what he would express in the absence of social pressures. By definition, preference falsification is the selection of a public preference that differs from one's private preference.

Attention will be paid later on to certain determinants of the individual's private preference. At this point, however, it is simply given. Other factors that I am treating as given are the individual's susceptibility to social pressure and the satisfaction he derives from truthfulness. To treat a variable as given is not to assume, of course, that it cannot differ from individual to individual. People may bring to an issue different wants, different needs for social approval, and different compulsions to verbalize their wants.

Such possibilities imply that people can vary in their responses to prevailing social pressures. One individual may resist pressures that another chooses to accommodate through preference falsification. A related implication is that individuals can differ in terms of the incentives necessary to make them abandon one public preference for another. The switchover points define their *political thresholds*.

One more set of players needs to be introduced: pressure groups trying to get their objectives endorsed publicly. Often directed by political activists, pressure groups reward their members and exempt them from punishments they impose on others. The rewarding and punishing is done by the members themselves, so the larger a pressure group's membership, the greater the pressure it exerts. The distribution of public preferences across individuals makes up *public opinion,* and that of private preferences forms *private opinion.* The latter distribution is hidden, so insofar as people's preferences determine which political programs get implemented, it is the former distribution that pressure groups have the most immediate stake in controlling. Like-

wise, it is public opinion, and not private opinion, that determines the
rewards and punishments individuals receive for their public preferences.

Public opinion is thus a determinant of its own constituent elements,
individual public preferences. Therefore it may transform itself
through the changes it engenders in individual choices. Yet public
opinion does not change perpetually. Under common circumstances,
the transformations of public opinion will eventually produce an equilibrium. That is, public opinion will become self-reproducing. For
many sensitive issues, more than one equilibrium is possible. In such
cases which equilibrium gets established will depend on history, and
circumstances of little significance in themselves may make a crucial
difference. Once in place, a selected equilibrium will persist indefinitely, even if slightly different early circumstances would have produced a very different equilibrium. This theme receives close attention
in Chapters 2–5, which explore how public opinion emerges from the
interdependent public preference choices of individuals.

At any given equilibrium, public opinion may differ from private
opinion. In fact, the equilibrium may owe its existence and stability
largely to preference falsification on the part of people unsympathetic
to the policies it makes possible. Such disgruntled people, even if they
form a huge majority, will refrain from dissenting because of social
pressures—pressures that they themselves sustain through acts of preference falsification. One socially significant consequence of preference
falsification is thus widespread public support for policies that would
be rejected in a vote taken by secret ballot. A related consequence is
the retention of such policies, to the exclusion of alternative policies
capable of commanding stable support. The latter phenomenon,
which I call *collective conservatism,* is the subject of Chapters 6–9.

Chapters 10–14 explore how preference falsification affects private
preferences. The task requires recognizing that our private preferences
on political issues rest at least partly on beliefs shaped by *public discourse,* which consists of the suppositions, facts, arguments, and theories that are communicated publicly. We do learn, of course, from
our personal experiences, and we do think for ourselves. Yet the limitations of our cognitive powers allow us to reflect deeply and comprehensively on only a fraction of the issues on society's political
agenda. However much we might want to scrutinize every issue on

our own, we all rely heavily on public discourse, and often on its superficial elements, for the *private knowledge* that will undergird our private preferences.

Preference falsification influences public discourse. This is because to conceal our private preferences successfully we must hide the knowledge on which they rest. That is, we must reinforce our preference falsification through *knowledge falsification*. In so doing, we distort, corrupt, and impoverish the knowledge in the public domain. We conceal from others facts we know to be true and expose them to ones we consider false.

This brings us to another possible consequence of preference falsification: widespread ignorance of the status quo's disadvantages. The disadvantages may once have been appreciated quite widely. Insofar as public discourse excludes criticism of fashionable political choices, however, their shortcomings will tend to get forgotten. And in the process members of society will lose their capacity to want change. The status quo, once sustained because people were afraid to challenge it, will thus come to persist because no one understands its flaws or can imagine a better alternative. Preference falsification will have brought intellectual narrowness and ossification. When that point is reached, current preference falsification ceases to be a source of political stability. From then on, people support the status quo genuinely, because past preference falsification has removed their inclination to want something different.

Such an outcome is all the more likely on issues where private knowledge is drawn largely from others. It is less likely on matters where personal experience is the primary source of private knowledge. Two other factors influence the level of ignorance generated by preference falsification. If public opinion reaches an equilibrium devoid of dissent, individuals are more likely to lose touch with alternatives to the status quo than if dissenters keep reminding them of the advantages of change. Likewise, widespread ignorance is more likely in a closed society than in one open to outside influences.

Thus far I have outlined two major consequences of preference falsification: the persistence of unwanted social outcomes and the generation of widespread ignorance. The first of these outcomes is driven by people's need for social approval, the second by their reliance on each other for information. One involves interdependencies among individual public preferences; it does not require any interplay among private dispositions. The other involves interdependencies among private dispositions, and the interactions do not necessarily get reflected in public variables. Yet the two processes can reinforce one another. The disappearance of public dissent can make people increasingly ignorant about flaws of the status quo, and in turn, their ignorance can make them progressively less prepared to dissent. Here, then, is a manifestation of the circular causality mentioned earlier. A social outcome transforms individuals, who then strengthen the outcome's stability.

If public discourse were the only determinant of private knowledge, a public consensus in favor of some policy, once attained, would become immutable. In fact, private knowledge has other determinants, and these can undermine an attained public consensus. But the unraveling of a public consensus need not occur in tandem with the escalation of private opposition to the status quo. This theme appears prominently in Chapters 15–18, which explore how preference falsification shapes patterns of social change.

In the presence of preference falsification, private opposition may spread and intensify indefinitely without any apparent change in support for the status quo. Yet at some point the right event, even an intrinsically minor one, can make a few sufficiently disgruntled individuals reach their thresholds for speaking out against the status quo. Their switches can then impel others to add their own voices to the opposition. Public opposition can grow through a bandwagon process, with each addition generating further additions until much of society stands publicly opposed to the status quo.

The revolution will not have been anticipated, because preference falsification concealed the opposition developing under the surface. Even so, it will be easy to explain with the benefit of hindsight. One reason is that the very occurrence of the revolution lowers the personal risk of exposing the vulnerability of the prerevolutionary social order. Another reason is that the revolution creates incentives for people who had been content with the prerevolutionary order to pretend that at heart they were always revolutionaries waiting for a prudent time to speak out.

The possibility of unanticipated revolution rests critically on two factors: the imperfect observability of the criteria on which individuals base their public preferences and the interdependence of those public preferences. In combination, these factors allow small, unobserved changes in private variables to galvanize explosive changes in public opinion. By the same token, they allow private variables to undergo major changes without triggering changes in public opinion. That is, they make it possible for profound transformations to occur, and much tension to build up, in a society that appears asleep. Deceptive stability and explosive change are thus two sides of a single coin.

Disproportionate effects can also stem from other types of shocks to the social system. Suppose, for example, that government officials instructed to implement some collectively selected policy end up pursuing an alternative. Insofar as individuals derive lessons from the consequences of policies pursued, the transgression will leave an imprint on their private knowledge. Ordinarily, small policy deviations produce small effects on private knowledge, but under the right circumstances the effects on private knowledge, and ultimately on public opinion itself, will be enormous. Likewise, under certain circumstances even a huge transgression will have negligible effects on either private or public variables.

The fact that relationships among social variables follow variable rather than fixed patterns has major implications for the social order. It suggests that social evolution may feature discontinuities and inefficiencies. And it indicates, as the book's final chapter discusses, that there exist insurmountable obstacles to predicting and controlling social evolution with precision. There are techniques for identifying and measuring preference falsification, and doubtless they can be improved. But as long as people have the incentive to misrepresent what they want and know, the techniques will never attain perfection. Frequently, therefore, we will be thwarted in our attempts to manage social evolution.

This book thus provides a unified theory of how preference falsification shapes collective decisions, orients political change, sustains social stability, fuels political revolutions, distorts human knowledge, and hides political possibilities. I call the model that informs the theory the *dual preference model,* since its central feature is the duality between private and public preferences. The model incorporates a deliberately limited number of primitive concepts, most of which have already been touched upon here. My goal is to make sense of patterns and relationships found in diverse social settings as parsimoniously as possible.

2

Private and Public Preferences

When a recluse opts to have coffee with his dessert, he makes a *personal choice*. Nobody else gets involved in the decision. By contrast, the decision to build a dam is a *collective choice,* one that involves a large number of individuals. Though conceptually useful, this common distinction obscures the variability of the locus of decision. American shoppers can decide without social interference whether to buy pork chops; their counterparts in Saudi Arabia cannot. What is a personal choice in the United States is thus effectively a collective choice in Saudi Arabia, where the consumption of pork is widely considered a punishable religious offense.

Food selection is not the only context where potentially personal matters can turn into matters of collective concern. Society may regulate what people read, how they treat the flag, and whether they buckle up while driving. Diverse groups devote enormous resources to controlling choices in contexts that present no obvious impediment to allowing everyone complete personal discretion.

It is hardly surprising, then, that such efforts are commonplace in contexts where some agreement or coordination is indispensable. Whereas everyone might read a different book, one cannot build a separate dam to suit every odd taste. Nor can one create a separate air force to accommodate every perception of enemy strength. Where a good must be supplied in quantity or as a bundle to be supplied at all, people must somehow settle on an outcome that may leave some, even all, less than perfectly satisfied.[1] This is not to say that individuals must take imperfect outcomes as given. If nothing else, they can pressure others to make compromises. Consider a farmer with a stake in the site of a new railroad station. By threatening to withdraw his friendship from his neighbors supporting site A, he may make them agree to his own preferred site, B.

One may thus have rankings for the preference rankings of others, as when a farmer prefers that other farmers rank site B above site A, or that bilateral exchanges in some other society conform to his own definition of fairness. Such higher-order rankings are known as *meta-preferences,* or values. The contexts in which the rankings of others matter are hardly limited to those where economic or technological factors necessitate some form of agreement. In many contexts where an agreement is not indispensable, we get urges to regulate the lives of others, to poke our noses into matters we could leave alone, in short, to be "meddlesome."[2] Plain observation suggests that meddlesomeness is a universal human trait, and also that it drives a huge variety of potentially personal choices into the collective realm—the world of politics.

The ubiquity of meddlesomeness is traceable, says Hannah Arendt, to the division of labor. If we pursued all our activities in mutual isolation, she observes, our choices would be without significance or consequence to others.[3] Evolutionary psychologists add that early human evolution conferred an advantage on individuals who showed an interest in each other's activities. Such individuals monitored each other with greater effectiveness, so they cooperated more successfully on matters important to survival. They thus left more descendants, predisposing the human mind to meddlesomeness.[4] Today, under conditions vastly different from those faced by our hunter-gatherer ancestors, gossip is a universal pastime and soap operas have huge audiences because our minds remain adapted to taking an interest in the affairs of others.[5] Never mind whether nosiness continues to serve economic productivity or political harmony. Liberal social philosophers, including Friedrich Hayek and James Buchanan, have demonstrated that in the modern world some manifestations of meddlesomeness do great harm.[6] For the foreseeable future, however, we are stuck with a propensity to meddle in matters that we could leave alone. The basic reason, notes an anthropologist, is that modern civilization rests on "old psychology."[7] It has been about 500 generations since the rise of agriculture—by evolutionary standards too short a span for fundamental psychological readaptation. Our inherited psychology remains, therefore, essentially that which evolved during the hunter-gatherer age, a period that spanned at least 100,000 generations.

The process whereby potentially personal matters get driven into the collective realm will be analyzed further on. The purpose of this chapter is to explore, for a given issue, the process by which an individual decides to engage in preference falsification. Making no presuppositions about the issue itself, I shall simply analyze the factors that govern his pertinent public preference.

Basic Setting

Let us take a predefined issue on which a prespecified group must reach a decision. The group faces a continuum of alternatives, represented by the inclusive interval between 0 and 100. The issue could be the size of a government subsidy, or the definition of an electorate, or some person's diet. It is not necessary at this stage to distinguish between personal and collective choices. The distinction will emerge naturally in due course.

Each member of the group must first decide whether to declare a preference. The person who so decides then faces a second decision: what preference to convey. For the time being, our interest is in the mechanics of the second decision. What determines whether a particular individual advocates 20, 40, or 100?

Intrinsic Utility

Suppose that the individual is alone in a polling booth where he can vote anonymously for any option between 0 and 100. Certain that no one will know of his choice, he can support the option that in his personal estimation will yield the most favorable consequences. Clueless as to the choices others will make, he has no reason to vote strategically—to pick, for example, a second-best option when a vote for the first-best would be wasted. He weighs the expected consequences of each option for himself, his family and friends, his enemies, and the causes he cares about, concluding that 20 will make him happiest. More precisely, he identifies 20 as the option that will provide him the greatest *intrinsic utility*. This option, which he registers on the ballot in front of him, represents his private preference.

Notwithstanding national elections and referenda, we rarely register our preferences by secret ballot. In legislatures, organizations, and committees, preference canvassing is nearly always open on almost every issue that calls for some kind of decision. Consequently, most of the preferences we express in our professional and nonprofessional activities become known by others. As a rule, we register our preferences through words, actions, and gestures, not by marking some choice on a ballot behind a drawn curtain. But all that matters here is the existence of some ordering in our individual's head. If such an ordering exists, he has a private preference, regardless of how his preference is actually canvassed.

An individual may be indifferent among two or more options. For simplicity, however, I take each person's private preference to be unique. This is to say that one particular option tops any particular private ordering. The characteristic is captured by the *intrinsic utility function* depicted in Figure 2.1. The function has a single peak at $x = 20$, which is our individual's private preference. According to the

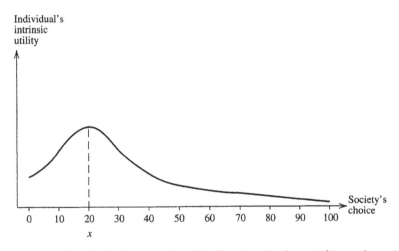

Figure 2.1 The individual's intrinsic utility function. Its shape indicates that privately he would like society to choose, from among the alternatives between 0 and 100, the option 20.

figure, he ranks options below 20 strictly according to their distance from 20, and similarly for the options above 20.

The determinants of people's intrinsic utility functions and of the corresponding private preferences will be discussed much later, beginning in Chapter 10. In the meantime, I will treat them as given. Doing so represents an analytical step, of course, not an assertion that private preferences are actually fixed. "Private" does not mean "presocial."

Reputational Utility

Imagine now that our individual steps out of the polling booth into the company of others—into what Erving Goffman would call the "field of public life" or the "realm of face-to-face interaction."[8] Someone inquires about his preference concerning the issue on which he has just voted. Will he reveal that he ranks 20 highest? His private preference being *private,* he can profess the preference of his choice. In other words, he can set his public preference, y, at any point between 0 and 100. If he chooses a public preference other than 20, he will be engaging in preference falsification.

For reasons to be discussed later, the observers of our individual may sense that he is shading the truth about his inner sentiments. But for now let me put aside this difficulty and assume that on the issue in question our individual has full control over his public preference. He may communicate his choice through such means as articulating an idea, carrying a placard, telling a joke, signing a petition, or booing a speaker. Depending on the context, even remaining silent or inactive may suffice to communicate a chosen preference.

The reason our individual might opt for preference falsification is that his public preferences influence how he is valued and treated. To maintain acceptance and respect, he must provide evidence that he accepts society's basic institutions and shares its fundamental objectives and perceptions. Insofar as he deviates from society's dominant goals, he will lose social status and endure rejection. But why do the reactions of others matter in the first place? As a "social animal," our individual derives emotional comfort from other members of his community. Without their approval, he would feel cut off and cut down. Society is also a source of physical comfort. Through participation in the social system, he gains access to goods and services that he could not possibly acquire on his own.

The individual's dependence on society and his concomitant fear of isolation have been consistent themes in social thought. But scientific confirmation had to await the rise of experimental social psychology, which focused on these phenomena from the 1930s to the 1960s.[9] The early controlled experiments established that in forming judgments and perceptions people rely heavily on others. They showed, moreover, that when individuals with different assessments are thrown together, their interactions give rise to norms that serve as frames of reference for all subsequent assessments.[10]

New light was shed on the process of social influence by Solomon Asch in a study initiated in the 1940s. The finding that the urge to conform is very powerful, Asch suspected, might be an artifact of the experiments themselves; in conceptually or perceptually difficult situations, people's reliance on one another might reflect no more than an effort to escape the limitations of their own senses. Asch then hypothesized that in an experiment that presents a perceptually trivial problem, individual judgments would be immune to group pressures. The experiment he went on to conduct became instantly famous, partly for its elegance, but partly because it stunned the intellectual community by disproving his hypothesis.

The experiment involves a group of individuals who are instructed to match the length of a given line with one of three other lines.[11] One of the comparison lines is equal to the standard; the other two are appreciably different. All but one member of the group are confederates of the experimenter and are under instruction to provide unanimously wrong judgments. The remaining member is unaware of this prearrangement. From time to time he hears the other subjects respond unanimously with answers that contradict the evidence of his senses. Yet, in fully 32 percent of the trials, he goes along with the wrong view of the majority. By comparison, the rate of wrong answers falls to less than 1 percent when subjects are asked to judge individually. Very simply, the experiment thus demonstrates the considerable power of group pressure on individual choice.

The Asch experiment has generated thousands of variants. Some establish that the individual conforms to the group norm even when he knows that incorrect responses will be costly to the group at large, to himself personally, or to both.[12] Others demonstrate that conformism falls markedly when subjects are led to believe that dissenters will endure no criticism.[13] Still others show that preferences expressed in the presence of others are substantially more conformist than those expressed in writing.[14]

In Asch's own variant, the confederates of the experimenter make no effort to exert pressure on the uninformed participant. They do not intimidate, belittle, mock, or threaten him. Jerry Harvey infers that the observed conformism is due to "fear of separation," rather than to "conformity pressures."[15] I would point out that these two factors are not mutually exclusive. A subject who *perceives* that he is being pressured will sensibly think that to differ from the group consensus would be to risk being treated as separate. But why would he consider himself under pressure when the confederates do nothing to discourage differences of opinion? In daily life, deviants are routinely made to feel uncomfortable, so among strangers people tend to consider dissent imprudent. Justified or not, they feel pressured to fit in, lest they be pushed out. Such an interpretation is supported by those variants of the Asch experiment in which the experimenter or the confederates try to assuage the subject's possible fears. The rate of conformist responses is dramatically lower in these variants than in the original experiment.

Next to the Asch experiment, the most famous experiment in social psychology was conducted by Stanley Milgram. In the early 1960s Milgram set out to determine the conditions under which individuals would refuse to obey a legitimate authority's orders to perform cruelty.[16] To this end, he recruited volunteer subjects, telling them that they were to administer or receive electric shocks to provide information on how punishment affects learning. Each subject was assigned the role of "teacher," and he entered the laboratory in the company of another volunteer, assigned the role of "student." The latter was actually a trained confederate of the experimenter. The "student" was wired to an electric chair, and the "teacher" was placed in front of a shock generator with 30 switches running from 15 to 450 volts. The generator's panel contained verbal designations for eight ranges of voltage, from "slight shock" at the low end, to "very strong shock" in the middle, to "XXX" at the high end. Given this setup, the experimenter would instruct the "teacher" to ask the helpless "student" certain questions and to administer increasingly intense shocks for each wrong answer. Because Milgram's objective was to see how far his subjects would go, the "student" continued to make mistakes even as the shocks intensified.

How did Milgram's subjects behave? Did they ask to be released from the experiment as the shocks became severe and the "student" started to show signs of feeling great pain? In trials where "student" and "teacher" were placed in separate rooms, as many as 65 percent of the subjects obeyed the experimenter's orders to the very end, going so far as to administer shocks in the "XXX" range. Although the obedience rate was lower in sets of trials where "student" and "teacher" were in close proximity, it was still at least 30 percent. The rate dropped to 21 percent in trials where the experimenter gave his orders over the phone, suggesting that a physically remote person's potential disapproval is less serious a threat than that of someone close by.[17] But even this rate is much higher than one might have predicted. The whole experiment testifies most vividly to our fear of social criticism.

Much other evidence is consistent with the experimental findings. Psychologists report that most people, including experienced orators and entertainers, are intimidated by speaking before a group, lest they provoke a controversy that leads to rejection.[18] And biologists have discovered that the anticipation of interpersonal conflict produces a series of physiological reactions, known in everyday language as stress.[19]

The punishments that people endure for their conveyed preferences vary widely in both form and severity. Some public preferences elicit disapproving gestures, such as raised eyebrows and derisive stares. Others also generate negative remarks, which may range from guarded criticism to unmerciful vilification. Another form of punishment is the denial of opportunities. A person considered on the wrong side of an issue may be denied a job or turned down by a social club. Still another form is physical. The individual may suffer harassment, incarceration, torture, even death. On the positive side, a person may receive various benefits for an expressed preference. The possible rewards include smiles, cheers, compliments, popularity, honors, privileges, gifts, promotions, and protection.

A preference acceptable to one group might be unacceptable to another. A house cleaner who reveals her opposition to the welfare system might annoy her neighbors on the dole while simultaneously pleasing her employers who consider their taxes too high. The net payoff a person receives from the various responses to a public preference is his *reputational utility*—utility from the reputation of harboring that particular preference. The reputational utility conferred by the revelation of a preference can vary with time and place. This variability will receive attention beginning in Chapter 3.

Earlier I defined a given individual's net payoff from an option's implementation as his intrinsic utility. The distinction between intrinsic and reputational utility is crucial to what follows. Intrinsic utility flows from substantive outcomes, reputational utility from reactions to one's public preferences. With respect to veiling, for example, the intrinsic utility comes from the benefits and costs of veiling itself, the reputational utility from the rewards and punishments associated with one's public attitudes toward the practice.

Expressive Utility

Now suppose, for a moment, that the decision-making group containing the individual whose choice has been under consideration numbers one million. Further, imagine that the group reaches a decision by averaging the public preferences of its membership. Our individual's impact on the group decision will obviously be negligible. By switching his public preference from 0 to 100, or vice versa, he would alter the decision by only 0.000001 units. For all practical purposes, therefore, he may treat the group decision as beyond his control and, hence, his intrinsic utility as given.[20] Will he then base his public preference solely on reputational considerations? Will he automatically choose the public preference that yields the most favorable reputational payoff? To put the question concretely, let his private preference, x, equal 20 and the public preference offering him the most favorable reputational payoff, y, equal 100. Will he convey a preference for 100? Not necessarily. As individuals we resist some of the demands placed on us, occasionally at substantial personal risk and when protest is unlikely to be effective.

In the reported experiments, not all subjects submit to social pressures. Moreover, in certain variants resistance is very common. In one variant of the Asch experiment, where a confederate of the experimenter provides the correct answer before the subject can speak, with all the other confederates continuing to give incorrect answers, the proportion of promajority errors falls to 5.5 percent.[21] There is a similar variant of the Milgram experiment: the naive "teacher" is accompanied by two peers, who are confederates instructed to defy the experimenter's orders at prearranged times. The example set by the peers lowers the obedience rate to 10 percent.[22]

Experimental social psychology thus suggests that social pressures, though very powerful, are not necessarily decisive. As individuals, we are evidently prepared to endure some social conflict to say or do what we really want. Our choices must be satisfying a need other than social approval and respect. This other need, I submit, is a need for individuality, autonomy, dignity, and integrity. I am proposing that we value the freedom to choose; that we derive self-esteem from resisting social pressures and establishing ourselves as people to be reckoned with; and that we find satisfaction in speaking our minds, opening up our hearts, acting ourselves. In short, I am suggesting that there is an ever-present voice in each of us that says: "To thine own self be true." By following this dictate we achieve a sense of satisfaction, if not exhilaration, though possibly at the cost of inviting reprisals. Conversely, when we opt to suppress a thought, misrepresent a want, or assume a phony demeanor, we feel discomfort at having compromised our personhood.

Within the framework introduced earlier, the need for self-assertion means the following. The individual cultivates his individuality maximally by supporting publicly whatever option between 0 and 100 he likes best in private. I will call the ensuing satisfaction his *expressive utility*. In terms of the notation introduced above, the maximization of expressive utility entails setting y equal to x. The individual would sacrifice such utility by supporting an option other than his most preferred point, in other words, by setting y at a point other than x. It is reasonable to suppose that the greater the degree of preference falsification, the larger the loss of expressive utility. If the individual has a private preference of $x = 20$, he will forgo less expressive utility by selecting a public preference of $y = 40$ than by setting $y = 70$.

It is worth remembering that Asch designed his experiment to demonstrate the powers of individuality, not those of society. Contrary to common thinking, he wanted to discredit superficial ways of thinking about conformity, particularly the idea, rendered fashionable by the rise of Nazism and Stalinism, that people are puppets governed only by social demands.[23] Asch recognized that individual actions are driven by conflicting demands, those of personhood and those of society. His experiment confirmed this view, though the urge to conform turned out to be more powerful than he had hypothesized. The essential contribution of the Asch experiment lies in the support it furnishes to the existence of a tradeoff between outer security and inner peace, between social approval and personal autonomy.

The individual's quest for autonomy should not be confused with anticonformism, which is a desire to go against the crowd. The quest is akin, rather, to nonconformism.[24] Where the conformist derives comfort from pleasing powerful groups, the anticonformist would rather provoke their wrath. He takes pleasure in disappointing social expectations and withdrawing from social relationships. In effect, he has a perverse reputational utility function. But such perversity is not incompatible with the desire for self-assertion. As with the conformist, the anticonformist's reputational needs are in contest with his needs for cultivating his individuality. Let us say he privately wants 20, whereas an overwhelming majority of the community favors 30. If he supports 10 just to be contrary, his public preference is still contrived; he has given up a measure of autonomy.

Nor should the need for self-assertion be viewed as a strictly selfish motive, as a narcissistic desire for uninhibited expression, regardless of the consequences for others. To be sure, it can take such a form. Think of the "let it all hang out" philosophy of the hippies of the late 1960s, which glorified freedom from all social restraints—except the norms of the hippy counterculture. The need for self-assertion may also be driven by other-regarding motives. The sentiment that one craves to express may be a revulsion at bombing civilians. Expressive needs are not necessarily, therefore, a sign of social irresponsibility. This is not a trivial point, for no one will sympathize with, or consider morally defensible, every odd expressive impulse. In any case, all that matters here is the existence of an expressive need. The argument applies to all of its manifestations, irrespective of how we judge them.

By suppressing the complexity of the real world, laboratory experiments enable one to isolate a phenomenon of interest. Yet precisely because of their simplicity, they leave open whether the phenomenon plays a significant role in everyday situations. Thus the experiments of Asch and Milgram suggest that the need for autonomy is significant in the rarefied atmosphere of the laboratory. They do not establish its significance in the types of choice situations one encounters in ordinary life. Fortunately, an array of clinical studies offer supportive clues. In combination with the experimental evidence, these point to the generality and universality of the individual's need for self-assertion.

The clinical psychologists who have identified the need include such figures as Sigmund Freud, Gordon Allport, Erich Fromm, and Abraham Maslow.[25] Their observations suggest that from an early age people derive satisfaction from making up their own minds, expressing their ideas freely, and directing their own destinies. The process of individual maturation, they show, is marked by a struggle to discover and establish an independent identity, to break society's control over one's decisions. Although differing on theoretical specifics, these clinicians agree that the need for independence stems from a deeply rooted impulse. They agree, moreover, that social demands routinely force the individual to suppress this need.

Researchers have devoted much energy to understanding the personal costs of such self-suppression. In *Civilization and Its Discontents,* Freud argues that, while individual renunciation makes possible what we know as civilization, it also gives rise to diverse psychological problems.[26] Following in Freud's footsteps, other researchers have traced feelings of insult, anger, and rage, and diverse anxieties, obsessions, and phobias to the "tyranny of the should"—the suppression of individuality under the burden of getting along with others.[27] Still others have identified an association between self-suppression and physical illness.[28] Although these researchers' methodologies and conclusions remain controversial, they essentially claim that preference falsification contributes to physical disorders like stomach ulcers and hypertension.

The drive for truthful self-assertion appears to differ greatly across individuals. Some people adhere to their positions no matter how severe the costs. Consider Socrates, Mansur al-Hallaj, and Giordano Bruno, each of whom refused to abjure his ostensibly corrupt views, even in the face of death. Throughout history, countless lesser-known figures have held to their causes under torture, many because they preferred to die for freedom rather than live without it. Alongside such strong-willed and insistently independent people are masses obsessed with meeting social expectations and pleasing authority.

Every culture exalts historical figures who have suffered for holding to their beliefs, resisting subordination, or opposing authority. A recurring theme in the epics of the Turkish novelist Yaşar Kemal is that of an outlaw whom peasants revere as a dauntless fighter against oppressive conditions they themselves cannot resist.[29] Likewise, the hero of a Hollywood Western is typically a free-willed man who stands apart from the crowd and refuses to accept injustice. A basic reason we consider uncompromising independence a heroic trait is that it is the exception in human history, not the rule. Another is that we all identify, at some level, with personal independence.

Self-evident as differences of character may seem, some students of human behavior doubt that the need for self-assertion differs significantly across individuals. The prime determinant of all human action, they maintain, is social incentives. People are impelled to make different choices because they face different reward and punishment schedules; fix these schedules, and they will behave identically.[30] By this logic, heroes act heroically because they enjoy opportunities unavailable to others. They take great risks because, for instance, they have uncommonly high chances of attaining fame.

Social rewards and punishments are certainly a good part of the story. But it hardly follows that the need for self-assertion cannot constitute an additional motivation. Nor does it follow that the need, assuming it exists, must be the same across all people. If attributes like intelligence and trustworthiness can vary across individuals, so can the need for self-assertion. It is revealing that in the experiments of Asch and Milgram subjects facing identical social pressures differed in their readiness to conform to the majority. Disparities may exist also in any one individual across contexts. A nun who would sooner die than forswear her religion might falsify, in the name of courtesy, her dislike of some painting. Evidently certain expressive compromises constitute grave threats to a person's individuality and self-esteem whereas others are just irritants.

There is no easy explanation for variations in the human need for establishing autonomy and displaying sincerity. Genetics must play a role, for children raised in the same social environment can develop very different personalities. Yet the role of upbringing is hardly insignificant. In growing up children learn to view certain adaptations as undignified. Many learn, for instance, never to compromise the honor of their family and to be loyal at all cost to their country. If the human personality were immutable, parents and teachers would probably not devote enormous time to imbuing the young with honor and loyalty. Nor would societies try to instill in their members norms helpful in withstanding external demands.[31] As an example of such a norm, consider the Confucian ideal of sincerity, which is to be able to say: "If upon looking into my heart I find that I am right, I will go forward though those that oppose me number thousands and tens of thousands." To those faithful to this norm, Confucius promised a priceless reward: peace of mind.[32]

Much more could be written on the determinants of the need for decisional autonomy. For our purposes, however, it is sufficient to recognize that in any given context each person has *some* need for self-assertion. Social pressures might make it prudent for one to misrepresent certain sentiments. I turn now to the underlying calculations.

Choosing a Public Preference

The gist of the argument thus far is that the choice of a public preference gives rise to three distinct returns: intrinsic utility, reputational utility, and expressive utility. These returns generate tradeoffs of the kind Woody Allen's comedies capture brilliantly. Allen's characteristic protagonist feels superior because he is self-consciously trying to play himself, yet inferior because others appear better adjusted socially.

Our task now is to give specificity to the tradeoffs. For simplicity, let the sources of utility be additive. This is to say that an individual's *total utility* from a particular public preference equals his intrinsic utility from society's decision *plus* his reputational utility from the engendered social reactions *plus* the expressive utility he derives from the displayed self-assertiveness.[33]

By definition, the individual's private preference, x, is the option between 0 and 100 that maximizes his intrinsic utility. Because his expressive utility is maximized when he is perfectly honest about his wants, the public preference that maximizes his expressive utility is identical to x. This can be seen in Figure 2.2, where both utilities reach their maximum at 20. Note that the intrinsic utility function shown here looks different than the one in Figure 2.1. This is because society's decision will remain within a narrow range regardless of the preference our individual chooses to convey. Intrinsic utility still peaks at 20, however, which means that he can bring society's decision *closest* to his private preference by setting $y = x$.

The public preference at which reputational utility reaches its maximum is 80. It is hardly surprising that the figure differs from 20, for the sources of reputational utility differ from those that determine the individual's private ordering of society's options.[34]

Figure 2.2 shows that the individual's optimal public preference, that which yields him the highest total utility, is $y^* = 70$. It entails a misrepresentation of 50 units. By pretending to favor 70 he achieves more reputational utility than if he were to be totally truthful and support 20. But the added reputational utility exacts a cost: both intrinsic utility and expressive utility remain below their respective maxima.

As already noted, in a decision-making group with many members, one member's influence over the outcome is generally negligible. But

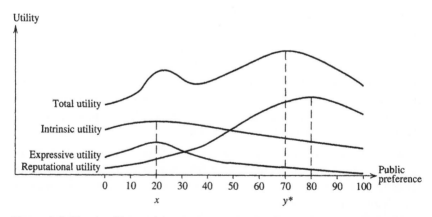

Figure 2.2 Total utility and its components. The horizontal axis displays the individual's expressive options. He would maximize the sum of the three forms of utility by choosing a public preference of 70.

the word of a well-placed member may carry substantial influence. For example, a prime minister can sway millions through a pronouncement, and the weight of her own public preference could be significant. For the typical member, however, society's decision is essentially fixed. As shown in Figure 2.3, a fixed decision renders the intrinsic utility function nearly flat. With the same reputational and expressive utility functions as in the previous figure, the optimal public preference has moved to 75, implying a misrepresentation of 55 units. Observe that even when the individual has no hope of influencing society's decision, his private preference might affect his public preference.

The outlined framework posits that people are capable of ranking the consequences of their public preference options along several dimensions. They can form estimates of future possibilities and judge how "near" a given option is to their ideal option. A possible objection is that people lack the cognitive resources to make the fine distinctions depicted in the figures. This is certainly a valid point. Yet the purpose of a model is to highlight a facet of reality, not to reproduce it. The essence of the framework is that people choose their public preferences on the basis of expected rewards and punishments. We are all capable of distinguishing between an angry stare and social ostracism, and

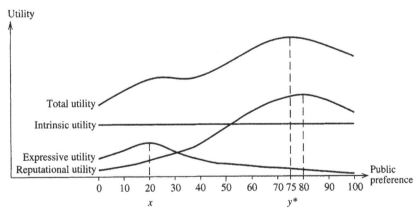

Figure 2.3 A case where society's decision is effectively beyond the individual's control. His intrinsic utility being fixed, he selects a public preference on the basis of a two-way tradeoff between his reputational and expressive utilities.

between freedom of attire and an order to veil. The framework just presented captures the key elements of the process by which we weigh such distinctions to arrive at some expressive choice. This framework forms one of the building blocks of the dual preference model that I shall use to explore the social effects of preference falsification.

The Possibility of Preference Falsification

It is time to address the issue of how we control our public preferences. Is the act of preference falsification as simple in practice as picking a point on a number line? And is it truly in our power to project *whatever* preferences we want?

Managing one's public preferences is an art that some perform better than others. A citizen trying to convey the impression that he supports a particular candidate may have to say so in an appropriate tone of voice and carry out actions consistent with this declaration, such as objecting when a rival candidate is praised. Yet involuntary gestures and body movements may rob such efforts of credibility.[35] Eye blinks, head movements, and facial expressions can give away his insincerity. Observers may detect in his body language subtle hints that he feels uncomfortable with his declaration. They may be able to tell that he is hiding something, even if they cannot determine what it is. His intention to convey a particular political orientation may also suffer from speech errors. Through stammering, stuttering, grammatical slips, and incomplete sentences, he may betray hesitation, confusion, or equivocation. Goffman's famous essay, *The Presentation of Self in Everyday Life,* shows that impression management is a skill distributed unevenly across a population. People differ in their control over body language.[36]

Successful politicians, like successful actors and entertainers, are invariably people with great talent at impression management. But their skills are not always in use; when they think they are out of public view, they relax and lower their guard. Occasionally, therefore, they convey impressions they then come to regret. In June 1990, during a speech by Mikhail Gorbachev, Robert Dole, Minority Leader in the U.S. Senate, sat in the audience unaware that the Soviet government had asked a television station to broadcast the speech live. At one point, Gorbachev started lambasting Israel for resettling Soviet Jews in the occupied territories. A camera caught Dole nodding his head in assent. Dole reportedly regretted having nodded, fearing that he had damaged his already strained relations with Jewish-American groups.[37]

Blushing is an involuntary expression that exposes feelings one is trying to hide. It is triggered by an awareness that one's image or self-image is being depreciated. Either we realize that we have given away feelings that we would rather have kept suppressed—we are ashamed; or we wish we had mustered the courage to convey our true feelings— we feel guilty. In either case, we experience uncontrolled discomfort, which reddening of the face turns into common knowledge. The propensity to blush sets in after infancy, and it peaks in adolescence, a time of adjustment to the world of adults; thereafter, it declines with age, suggesting that emotional control improves with social experience.[38] Within our framework, blushing may be interpreted as a sign of failure to mediate satisfactorily between one's expressive and reputational concerns.

A person adept at impression management may have several public preferences on a given issue, each tailored to a different audience. In 1989, a Soviet citizen admitted to having worn "six faces" under communist repression: "one for my wife; one, less candid, for my children, just in case they blurted out things heard at home; one for close friends; one for acquaintances; one for colleagues at work; and one for public display."[39] These faces stood in decreasing order of openness and truthfulness. He could open up more safely to his close friends than to strangers. In addition, people with whom he interacted regularly were relatively harder to fool. Attuned to the quirks of his body language, they could pick up signs of prevarication that strangers would not even notice, much less know how to interpret.

In practice, then, the "publicness" of a preference may vary along a continuous spectrum. At one extreme lies its private form, known literally to a single person. At the other is its most public form, that projected in the presence of strangers. Throughout this book, when mention is made of a person's public preference without qualification, it is the latter polar variant that will be implied.

Although an attempt at preference falsification does not always produce the intended effect, the point remains that it is an act performed adroitly and widely in a panoply of socially significant con-

texts. And it has always been an indispensable tool for personal success. A sixteenth-century maxim puts it succinctly: *Nescit vivere qui
nescit dissimulare*—He who does not know how to dissimulate does
not know how to live.[40]

Personal versus Collective Choice

As the argument unfolds, we will encounter various implications of a
feature that has played no key role thus far: the constraints on the
individual's ability to receive, store, retrieve, and process information.[41] A pertinent implication here is that nobody can formulate an
educated opinion on every human issue. Of biological necessity, we
must all concentrate on matters of immediate relevance to our well-
being and within our power to control, deferring on other issues to
the judgments and choices of others.

With each of us devoting attention to a small subset of the prevailing
issues, most issues receive very few people's attention. A good many
issues are decided by a single person, with other people neither taking
a position nor sanctioning the person who does. As a case in point, I
generally decide on my own what to have for breakfast. No one chas-
tises me if I opt for cereal or congratulates me for having a glass of
juice. My selections are essentially free of reputational consequences.

We have just identified the defining characteristic of *strictly personal*
choice. One appears in Figure 2.4, where the individual's total utility
lacks a reputational component. Note that in this special case his optimal public preference coincides with his private preference.

Starting with the assumption that any issue may attract widespread
interest, we have thus found that many issues do not. Unable, despite
the meddlesome tendencies of its members, to regulate everything, society effectively allows each of us a domain of personal decision
making—a domain in which we are free to do as we please. A formal
embodiment of this transference of power is the right to privacy.
Within our own homes, we are generally free to make our own decisions, guided by our own knowledge, expectations, and priorities.
Outside the home, our freedoms are more limited.

Earlier I considered an issue in which a single individual's impact
on a group's decision is negligible. Such an issue offers the individual
a two-way tradeoff between reputation and self-assertion, as in Figure

2.3. The corresponding choice may be characterized as *strictly collective*.

Strictly personal and strictly collective choices represent extremes. In the former, reputational utility is absent; in the latter, intrinsic utility is essentially fixed. Many issues fall between these extremes. If my neighbors scoff at my desire to erect a high wall around my yard and their revealed hostility makes me reconsider my plan, my choice effectively involves a weighing of several preferences, meriting the designation of "collective." My choice is not strictly collective, however, because my own public preference is decisive to the outcome. Whether the wall gets built depends entirely on my own action. On certain decisions that are collective in the sense just given, reputational utility far outweighs the other sources of utility. An example would be one's choice over what to wear to a ball.

Many in the field of economics, the discipline that has developed the most rigorous theory of individual choice, hold that reputational utility is never significant and loss of self-respect never a serious possibility. They postulate that intrinsic utility equals total utility. Accordingly, many leading textbooks in economics teach us to conceptualize the decision maker as "sovereign"—free of the need to

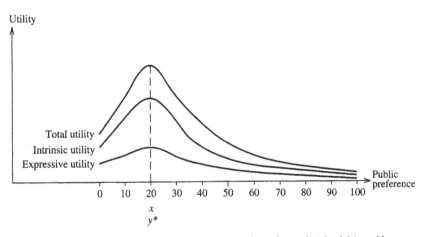

Figure 2.4 A strictly personal choice. No one but the individual himself cares about the outcome, so his total utility has no reputational component, and his optimal public preference equals his private preference.

accommodate the wishes of others.[42] For reasons already stated, in some contexts the sovereignty assumption provides a reasonable approximation to reality. Yet many choices of central concern to economists are more reasonably viewed as personal choices with social involvement, or simply, *semipersonal.* Part of the satisfaction from buying a car or house comes in the form of social status.[43]

So it is a mistake to treat all market choices as strictly personal. But it is a particularly serious error to carry the sovereignty assumption into spheres of activity in which reputational considerations are almost always highly significant. Such spheres include politics, where people have an abiding interest in one another's preferences. Issues of political importance present individuals with tradeoffs between outer and inner peace. Frequently, therefore, these matters force people to choose between their reputations and their individualities.

There are contexts, of course, in which such tradeoffs are dealt with by remaining silent—as when an American refrains from taking a position on allowing homosexuals to serve in the military. Silence has two possible advantages and two disadvantages. On the positive side, it spares one the penalty of taking a position offensive to others, and it may lessen the inner cost of preference falsification. On the negative side, one gives up available rewards, and one's private preference remains hidden. On some controversial issues, the sum of these various payoffs may exceed the net payoff to expressing some preference.

Certain contexts present yet another option: abandoning the decision-making group that is presenting one with difficult choices. This option, "exit," is sometimes exercised by group members unhappy with the way things are going, yet powerless to effect change.[44] A homeowner alarmed by her neighborhood's rising crime rate may pack up and leave. But in a huge array of contexts exit is prohibitively costly. A Tanzanian shopkeeper may not be able to escape local conditions that he finds oppressive. His skills would be worth little elsewhere, and there might not exist another country willing to take him. Likewise, an American taxpayer who considers most government spending wasteful cannot exempt himself from the duty to pay taxes, except at the risk of jail time. For all practical purposes, exit is not always a viable option. Often our choices are limited to expressing some preference or remaining silent.

The Divided Self

The foregoing model depicts the individual as having multiple sources of happiness: economic, social, and psychological. These three sources have tended to be studied within separate disciplines that differ in their conceptions of the individual. *Homo economicus* is a self-controlled, calculating utility machine, who is immune to social pressure and a stranger to inner turmoil. *Homo sociologicus,* his very identity the product of social stimuli, is ruled by social demands. And a common conception of *homo psychologicus* is as an impulsive and tormented soul, struggling, seldom successfully, to escape the dictates of his conscience.

However simplistic, these constructs provide valuable insights into human behavior. Yet they obscure as much as they enlighten. A more composite construct allows glimpses, we shall see, into phenomena that its unidisciplinary rivals oblige us to ignore.

The notion of a "divided self"—a self with multiple, possibly competing, inner needs—is not novel in and of itself. It goes back at least to Plato's "three parts of the soul," whose objectives are wisdom, social distinction, and gratification of appetite.[45] Adam Smith's early writings distinguished between the individual's private interest and his interest as a member of society.[46] Kant's "categorical imperative" relies on a division between actor and judge of actions.[47] A highly controversial variant is Freud's trinity of the id, the ego, and the superego.[48] Finally, Jon Elster and Thomas Schelling have promoted a variant featuring successive selves that represent the individual's interests at different times.[49] That the concept of a divided self has many variants is not problematic. Many serve a purpose, just as we benefit from partitioning society by age in some studies, by occupation in others.

The tridivisional construct presented here does not invalidate methodologies that assume a unidivisional self. But it does limit their useful domains. Where reputational considerations are insignificant, our tridivisional individual behaves, as noted, like the unidivisional individual of a standard economics textbook: homo economicus. This said, I ought to point out that, being emotionless, homo economicus would have no reason to go to confession or to seek help from a psychiatrist. Our tridivisional individual might, for his choices can give him a troubled conscience. An inner voice may keep castigating him for having caved in to social pressure or for having sacrificed a cherished principle in the interest of material comfort. Even if the passage of time were to convince him that he made the best choice, he could endure persistent guilt and bitterness.

Imagine that a tyrannical regime asks our individual to implicate his best friend in some fabricated crime. If he complies, he will be allowed to live in peace. If not, he will be killed. He decides to implicate his friend, who then suffers a painful death. It is not hard to imagine that the decision will torment him for the rest of his days. The illustration is admittedly out of the ordinary. Yet our daily lives are replete with choices that generate lasting inner tensions.[50] We see such tensions as a sign of normality, provided they remain within bounds.

Selecting a public preference is an act that may offer a choice between inner and outer peace. The insight was captured beautifully by Rumi, the thirteenth-century Anatolian mystic. Each soul must decide, he said, to stay on the safe land of routine predictabilities, custom, and religious law, or to answer the call of its inner voice and launch into the deep.[51]

The task of the next three chapters is to put the dilemma posed by Rumi into a social context. When *many* souls have to choose between inner and outer peace, how do their decisions influence one another?

3

Private Opinion, Public Opinion

An activity forms a *political issue* if it is a matter of social concern, a *nonissue* if it is widely considered a matter of personal choice. Scientific experimentation on animals is currently a political issue, one that pits scientists against the animal rights lobby. It would turn into a nonissue if public interest in regulating the laboratory were to disappear.

Implicit in this distinction is a view of politics that highlights people's meddlesomeness. To say that experiments on rats constitute a political issue is to take note that one group is trying to control the decisions of another. In this simple illustration, the animal rights lobby is on the offensive, scientists on the defensive; the former wish to restrict customary scientific liberties, the latter to protect them. There are also issues where disagreement involves only the details. A community in agreement on building a railway station may split on the matter of location, with competing factions trying to control the communal decision.

Such control may be accomplished through persuasion or through social pressure. Those who want *B* may convince others that *B* would serve them best; or they may punish the supporters of other sites and reward those of *B*. Of these two political instruments, persuasion shapes public preferences indirectly, through private preferences; social pressure accomplishes the same task directly.

Here we begin to explore the determinants and effects of social pressure. In Chapter 11, I will show that persuasion and social pressure are not neatly separable instruments: the former may emerge as a by-product of the latter. But my immediate objective is to elaborate on the conception of politics that is implicit in my example of the railway station.

Issues and Nonissues

An infinite number of human concerns are candidates for becoming political issues. A small minority actually do. Political discourse focuses on a few concerns at a time, treating the rest as nonissues. Society's political agenda evidently has a limited "carrying capacity."[1]

The root cause is a factor I have introduced but not yet discussed: the limitations of the human mind. Although a person may mitigate these limitations by handling issues sequentially, the problem is ultimately insoluble, for the hours in a day are fixed. In any case, politics interferes with directly productive activity, which is one reason why most people devote little time to it. Highly politicized societies, observes Giovanni Sartori, fall behind economically; "political hypertrophy" brings "economic atrophy." The democratic cities of ancient Greece required their citizens to give so much of themselves to politics that little time was left for the production of wealth.[2]

To enter a society's political agenda a concern must be shared by more than one person. A few of the concerns that make it into the agenda will enjoy very widespread attention. As major issues, they will get regular attention from the media, preoccupy the government, dominate social conversation, and become foci of academic research. During the half-century following World War II, the superpower rivalry was just such an issue.

Given the limits on the carrying capacity of society's agenda, the emergence of new issues is bound to generate turnover. Edward Carmines and James Stimson observe in this connection that "a complex governmental environment superimposed on a disparate social order can be counted on to raise new issues in abundance," just as natural genetic variation produces "a plenitude of variations in species."[3] Indeed, the complexity of the social order produces a steady stream of new aspirations, sensitivities, and grievances. In his theory of the "civilizing process," Norbert Elias documents how, over time, the growing complexity of human interactions transformed the boundaries of proper human behavior. Social pressures and individual fears changed character, creating new codes of conduct. As each change got under way, a new issue entered the social agenda, generally displacing another.[4]

Coincidences may play a role in determining which concerns become general political issues. Suppose ten thousand Cairenes come to feel, through separate experiences, that the municipal building code needs tightening. Being scattered around the city, they do not learn how numerous they are. Consequently they fail to produce a lobby, and the code remains a nonissue. Then an earthquake draws attention to construction standards. The idea of reform enters ordinary discourse, allowing the proponents of a stricter code to identify one another and coordinate their efforts. Through the ensuing campaign, construction standards dart up the political agenda, siphoning attention from older issues.

If one consequence of the limitations of reason is the boundedness of society's political agenda, another is that an individual's positions on issues may be mutually inconsistent. A person may consider both government spending too high and all proposed cuts unwise, or believe simultaneously that women are the full equals of men and that they need special protections.[5] Such inconsistencies are common because cognitive limitations keep us from incorporating the multitudes of variables and relationships that impinge on our happiness into a single, comprehensive model. Unavoidably we ignore many interconnections among political issues, treating closely related phenomena as unrelated.

The Paradox of Political Participation

Before going any further, we must face up to the paradox that people incur the costs of politics even when their expected personal gains are very small. It is not unusual to find people devoting time and donating money to causes—like the tightening of a building code—whose benefits will fall primarily on others and only in small part on themselves. Even in groups as large as a modern nation, individuals pursue causes intended to serve the group at large, often at sacrifice to themselves.

Mancur Olson argues that political participation in large groups is generally attributable to the presence of "selective incentives"—rewards and punishments that operate not indiscriminately on the community as a whole but, rather, selectively in favor of the participants.[6] Another explanation, by George Stigler, stresses the heterogeneity of the potential participants in a movement. People with individualized needs join the movement to gain a voice in shaping its demands. For example, a producer of pajamas contributes to a movement pursuing an import tariff on clothing to ensure that pajamas get included among the protected items.[7]

Each of these explanations, like several others, presupposes the existence of political participation—precisely what needs elucidation.[8] There can be no Olsonian incentives until someone is already active. Likewise, a Stiglerian concern with a movement's agenda makes sense only if the movement already exists.

The risk of personal loss is greater for the first person to take up a cause or enforce a selective incentive than it is for the contributor to a cause already on the road to success. So it is doubly difficult to explain the genesis of a political movement. But there is a mitigating factor in the analyses of Olson and Stigler: a presupposition that the potential beneficiaries of a movement can easily, if not costlessly, communicate. Producers pursuing a tariff may confer with one another on how to get organized, apportion duties, and settle conflicts. Under such favorable conditions, potential participants need not commit themselves to the cause until they are certain of broad participation. They might waste time on discussions aimed at forging an initial agreement, but no further resources need be committed by anyone acting alone. In sum, while open communication does not guarantee political participation, at least it alleviates the difficulties of getting it started.

A separate attempt at resolving the paradox lies in recognizing that people are not entirely selfish. In various laboratory experiments subjects demonstrate a willingness to incur personal costs for the wider benefit of the community. Evidently "free riding," the act of refraining from participation in activities whose benefit falls heavily on others, is sometimes eschewed. Some analysts have inferred that the origins of certain pressure groups lie in altruism.[9] But the finding establishes neither that free riding is uncommon nor that altruism is a sufficiently powerful motive to activate *all* potentially viable pressure groups. In any case, other research indicates that altruists tend to become less altruistic as they gain awareness of free riding on the part of others. Equally significant, it appears that altruism is dampened when potential contributors to a collective effort cannot communicate with one another.[10]

A closely related attempt at resolving the paradox invokes the notion of ethical commitment. People feel compelled, say some observers, to do their fair share for the attainment of jointly desired outcomes.[11] Such observers fail to explain, however, why a person would take major personal risks when it is clear that few others are doing *their own* fair shares.[12]

Still another explanation rests on a cognitive illusion. It suggests that movements are initiated by people who overestimate their personal political powers.[13] This explanation falters in the face of evidence that political leaders are often amazed to see their efforts bear fruit. Serious consideration of the evidence must await a later chapter, but a brief portion will be presented shortly.

All these explanations, except the one based on ethical commitment, run into difficulty in contexts that contain obstacles to open communication among potential participants. Just such an obstacle lies in the costs associated with revealing an unpopular preference. If these costs make sympathizers of a cause refrain from publicizing their wishes, the potential for success will seem less than it actually is—not more, as the cognitive illusion explanation asserts; preference falsification will make political action seem futile, if not foolish. Obstacles to open communication also limit the relevance of Olson's and Stigler's explanations. If you do not know who shares your objectives, you cannot even begin to negotiate joint participation or to fine-tune your collective demands.

Consider the anticommunist cause in Czechoslovakia prior to the revolution of 1989. Czechoslovaks voicing support for a change in regime risked harassment, ostracism, and imprisonment. Consequently, very few opposed the communist regime publicly. Moreover, members of the public opposition found it difficult to communicate with one another and to recruit additional supporters. Under the circumstances, the odds of toppling the regime appeared slim. It requires explanation, therefore, that there were any dissidents at all. Why did Václav Havel shoulder the enormous burden of starting an opposition movement? Why did he opt for hardship when as a gifted writer he could have achieved comfort and respect as an apologist for communism?

Havel's choice could not have reflected the influence of Olsonian selective incentives. Until the revolution, such incentives militated against dissidence, not for it. Nor is the choice explicable by a Stiglerian desire to shape the consequences of opposition, for it was not clear that there would be any successes within Havel's own lifetime. The altruism explanation raises the question of why anyone would have wanted to incur the risk of punishment when such a sacrifice was unlikely to bring social benefits. Prior to 1989, trying to crush communism through open internal opposition must have seemed like trying to level the Carpathian Mountains with a hammer. If cognitive illusion was a factor, its role was not necessarily to enhance the attractiveness of dissidence. As documented in Chapter 16, right up to the revolution Havel remained pessimistic about the chances of meaningful political change. Finally, the ethical commitment explanation begs the question of why Havel continued doing his "fair share" when few others would do theirs.

The outlined explanations are not without merit. They all shed light on political participation, which may be driven by multiple factors. Even collectively, however, they leave the paradox of political participation unresolved.

Expressive Needs and Political Activism

A complete theory of collective action requires recognition that some people have unusually intense wants on particular matters, coupled with extraordinarily great expressive needs. Relative to most people, such individuals are insensitive to the prevailing reputational incentives, because they obtain unusually high satisfaction from truthful self-expression. They are inclined to speak their minds even at the risk of severe punishment, and regardless of whether truthful speech can make a difference. Their goals may be selfish or altruistic, good or evil, conservative or revolutionary. The characteristics of the goals matter less than the fact that they are held intensely and expressed sincerely.

Such exceptional individuals who will undertake to activate a movement may be characterized as *activists*. It is they who, depending on the context, form cells, distribute leaflets, articulate new demands, concoct slogans, establish command structures, and most important,

try to woo others into the movement through promises of moral, social, and material support. The generally far more numerous *nonactivists* are too sensitive to reputational incentives to take part in the
activation process. They are followers who will participate only if
others have already lowered the cost or raised the benefit of participation. Thus, where the support of the activists is unconditional, that
of the nonactivists is conditional on the prevailing political conditions.

Of the hundreds of thousands of Czechoslovaks who participated
in the demonstrations that ended a half-century of communism, the
preponderance had no previous record of anticommunist dissent.
Many were card-carrying members of the Communist Party. With
respect to the country's political regime, they formed the masses of
nonactivists. A small minority, including Havel, had dissented on earlier occasions. They were the activists who, having formed an anti-
regime vanguard, would not submit to the regime's demands even
under severe pressure. There were also activists within the establishment: officials, like the Party leader Gustav Husák, who would not
turn against communist dictatorship even if a crushing majority were
to switch sides.

Russell Neuman observes correctly that an activist on one issue may
be a nonactivist on another.[14] But his distinction between activists and
nonactivists differs from mine. Neuman's rests on differences in
knowledge, rather than in expressive need. In his perspective, people
specialize in matters that impinge directly and substantially on their
happiness. Turkish-Americans follow American policy toward
Turkey, and accountants track developments pertaining to tax legislation, with each group serving as the activist core on its own pet
concern. Activists are indeed generally better informed than nonactivists with respect to their issues of specialization. Not all well-informed
people become activists, however, because if they act on their superior
information the benefits will accrue mostly to others. Many Czechoslovaks, although they required no education on the failings of their
regime, refrained for years from lending the opposition public support.
Knowledge alone does not explain why they remained docile while
Havel was defiant.

We may never understand *exactly* why Havel demanded so much
of himself while most of his compatriots played it safe. This does not
make expressive need any less critical to resolving the paradox of po-

litical participation. Nor does it make the notion of expressive need any less compatible with scientific analysis. While we do not understand fully why tastes in automobiles vary, we do not leave the variations out of our explanations of basic consumption patterns. In any case, many controlled experiments, including some surveyed in Chapter 2, lend support to the variability of self-assertiveness in any given context.

Pressure Groups

To influence a society's actual decisions, activists must do more than satisfy their expressive urges. Working in common with like-minded activists, they must somehow win the support of sufficient numbers of nonactivists. The resulting collectivity, composed of activists and nonactivists professing support for a particular cause, is called a *pressure group*.

The term pressure group encompasses, but is not limited to, the notion of a "special-interest group" or "faction." James Madison, one of the founders of the United States, defined a faction as "a number of citizens, whether amounting to a majority or minority of the whole, who are united and actuated by some common impulse of passion, or of interest, adverse to the rights of other citizens, or to the permanent and aggregate interests of the community."[15] By comparison, a pressure group's efforts do not necessarily conflict, in either intended or actual effect, with the general interest. Another critical distinction concerns the motives of individual members. Whereas the members of a faction share a common interest, those of a pressure group need not. Some, even all, of the nonactivists within a pressure group may privately abhor the goals they are supporting publicly, their presence in the group being driven solely by the rewards of preference falsification.

Even a unidimensional issue might generate many distinct pressure groups. The spectrum from 0 to 100 could feature, say, eleven groups, each at a different point. Typically, however, fewer options enjoy the endorsement of a pressure group, often just a couple. There is a tendency for issues to turn into dichotomous choices that mask complexity, subtlety, and ambiguity. One is either a believer or an unbeliever, for or against equality, a committed revolutionary or an apologist for the status quo.

Take the struggle over abortion, which has been characterized as a "clash of absolutes."[16] Neither side of the debate shows much willingness to compromise. The prolife side equates *almost all* abortion with murder; the prochoice side insists that *any* restriction would infringe on a woman's basic rights. Most people recognize that the issue admits more than two responses. And many feel that it can, and perhaps eventually will, be resolved by splitting the difference—allowing some abortions and prohibiting others. Nevertheless, absolutist groups have dominated the debate to the near-exclusion of voices for moderation.

As a practical matter, then, political competition limits the degree of political pluralism. One reason is that group size is a determinant of political success. Another is that the image of a divided or confused pressure group can be a recipe for political ineffectiveness. Still another is that our cognitive limitations make it unfeasible to debate all possibilities down to the finest details.[17] For all these reasons, activists with similar concerns will often suppress their differences and focus on their common goals. Once a set of pressure groups has formed, activists may either join one of these or develop some new group. The latter course is fraught with uncertainty, if only because the new group's potentially most enthusiastic members might refrain from committing themselves until it proves itself viable. Reticence to join new pressure groups gives existing groups an advantage over new entrants, often blocking the formation of potentially powerful new groups.

My argument is not that, on any established issue, the set of pressure groups is immutable. Precisely because of the heterogeneity of its membership, a pressure group is vulnerable to internal strife. The ranks of a national resistance movement may include rich industrialists and poor farmers, free-traders and protectionists, intellectuals and illiterates. Such diversity can fuel attempts to shift or broaden the movement's objectives, and the consequent disunity can result in defections, even precipitate the group's collapse. Nevertheless, the set of pressure groups often shows durability. Part of the reason is that perceptions of a group's demands are resistant to change. And in many contexts another is that group leaders take measures to punish their deviant members.

I will capture the forces against the proliferation and reorientation of groups by postulating the existence of just two pressure groups with fixed positions at 0 and 100. That the groups lie at the extremities of the spectrum of options is not crucial to the argument, but it simplifies the exposition. What *is* significant is that the pressure groups cover only some of the positions that members of society may favor privately. On sensitive issues featuring diverse private preferences, this makes widespread preference falsification very likely.

A pressure group is not necessarily organized, if by this one means having an address, a set of bylaws, and a formal chain of command. The term subsumes associations ranging from spontaneous protest mobs to entrenched industrial lobbies steered by paid professionals.[18] The opposition that toppled Czechoslovak communism had no formal headquarters. And Civic Forum, the association that represented it in the negotiations that led to a transfer of power, had no elected or appointed officers. Civic Forum's leader, Havel, derived his authority simply from years of articulate dissidence.

All our political actors are now on the scene. There are two competing pressure groups. Each group features an inner core of activists, and insofar as it is successful, an outer ring of nonactivists. The activists have fixed public preferences that are more or less consistent with their private preferences; the nonactivists' public preferences depend on the prevailing reputational incentives. Our next task is to explore why a pressure group must add to its core of activists a ring of nonactivists.

Private and Public Opinion

In *The Prince*, Machiavelli instructs Lorenzo de' Medici that he must "never let himself be hated by the people," lest they reject his government.[19] Two centuries later, Hume reiterated the point: "It is . . . on opinion only that government is founded; and this maxim extends to the most despotic and most military governments, as well as to the most free and most popular."[20] Later writers have coined terms such as public opinion, mass sentiment, and climate of opinion to describe what Machiavelli and Hume identified as the ultimate source of political power.

For our purposes none of these terms is sufficiently specific. Take the most commonly used term, public opinion. The word "public" may mean either "open" or "collective." Since I have been using it exclusively in the former sense, it would be confusing to start using it also in the latter. As for "opinion," in both lay and academic discourse it may connote either "preference" or "belief." Let me define, then, *public opinion* as the distribution of public preferences and *private opinion* as the corresponding distribution of private preferences.[21]

The distinction between the two types of opinion is elementary and of obvious relevance. So it is startling that neither scientific terminology nor lay discourse has accommodated it. Elisabeth Noelle-Neumann offers a possible reason. Modern social thinkers tend to avoid the distinction, she says, for fear of coming in touch with facts contrary to the "self-image of modern man."[22] In particular, they are afraid to acknowledge the great significance of individual fear as a shaper of democratic decisions. Indeed, to acknowledge the universality of preference falsification would call into serious question some of the alleged virtues of democracy, possibly to the detriment of groups that benefit from existing social arrangements.

The flaws of democracy will receive attention in Chapter 5. Here let me suggest another reason for the persistence of terminological confusion: the failings of the crowd psychology literature of the late nineteenth century. This literature, which includes the works of Gustave Le Bon,[23] promoted the notion that collectivities are irrational, infantile, uncivilized, and reckless. When thrown together in a crowd, the literature claimed, cultured and educated people shed their critical senses and lose their moral restraints; afraid to stand alone, they participate in violent outbursts, panics, and surges of enthusiasm.[24] In focusing on wild collective behavior, crowd psychology neglected to make clear that frenzy is uncommon. And in emphasizing the sensational, it neglected to explore why and how collectivities change character. Especially in times of political calm, such omissions allowed crowd psychology to be dismissed as fanciful.

A basic flaw of crowd psychology was its tendency to oversimplify the human personality. It failed to bring out the tensions people endure in mediating between their needs for personal assertion and those for social approval. Had these tensions been appreciated, crowd psychology might have generated a more plausible theory that accommodates a broader class of social states. And in the process, it might have developed the distinction between private and public opinion.

The Source of Political Power: Public Opinion

Let us return to our stylized political arena. Recall that it features two pressure groups, one promoting 0 and the other 100, and a sea of nonactivists with private preferences spread between 0 and 100. If the issue in question is sufficiently sensitive, the reputational advantages of joining one pressure group or the other will outweigh, for all nonactivists, the psychic cost of any preference falsification involved.[25] This is because, first, the pressure groups will impose substantial penalties on anyone challenging their positions, and second, by definition, a nonactivist with respect to any given issue is someone whose pertinent expressive needs are relatively weak. To keep matters simple, I assume that all nonactivists find it personally advantageous to join one pressure group or the other.

In a polarized political environment, individuals may not be able to position themselves on neutral ground even if they try. Each side may perceive a declaration of neutrality or moderation as collaboration with the enemy, leaving moderates exposed to attacks from two directions at once. Once again, the issue of abortion is apposite. Both the prochoice and prolife lobbies pigeon-hole compromisers as foes. In terms of the model being developed, they both treat people with intermediate public preferences ($0 < y < 100$) as though they are in the rival camp. Pigeon-holing thus helps sustain polarization. It helps keep public opinion bimodal, with public preferences concentrated at 0 and 100.

Some public preferences that enter the distribution may have more impact on society's collective decision than others. If a colonel and a peasant both join a movement aimed at toppling the government, the former's switch will catch greater notice and be taken more seriously. Hence it will carry greater weight in public opinion. But to simplify the presentation of key ideas, I will generally suppress differences in personal influence.[26]

Two more definitions are necessary. Let Y be the arithmetic mean of all public preferences and X the corresponding mean of all private preferences. Like the distributions from which they are drawn, X and Y will ordinarily differ. Imagine that people's private preferences are spread evenly across the decimal positions between 0 and 100, as shown in Figure 3.1. X is obviously 50. Y might be lower or higher, however, because the pressures on behalf of 0 could be relatively stronger or weaker than those on behalf of 100. In the figure, $Y = (0.7 \times 0) + (0.3 \times 100) = 30$.

As already noted, it is public opinion, rather than private opinion, that undergirds political power. Private opinion may be highly unfavorable to a regime, policy, or institution without generating a public outcry for change. The communist regimes of Eastern Europe survived for decades even though they were widely despised. They remained in power as long as public opinion remained overwhelmingly in their favor, collapsing instantly when street crowds mustered the courage to rise against them. For another example, since about 1970 the U.S. government has promoted, against the consistently strong opposition of private opinion, race-based employment and admission quotas. As will be explained in Chapter 9, quotas have spread and survived because of highly favorable public opinion. The point is not that private opinion is irrelevant to politics. On the contrary, it is an important determinant of political stability. My present claim is simply that a

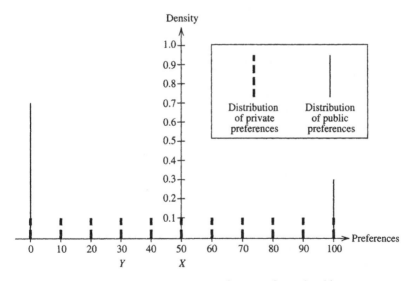

Figure 3.1 Reputational pressures may result in a polarized public opinion even if private opinion is not polarized. Here, the polarization favors 0 over 100 by a margin of 7 to 3.

favorable private opinion is neither necessary nor sufficient for the success of a political cause.

To capture the relationship between public opinion and political power, we can postulate that the substantive outcome of political competition is related directly to Y. Accordingly, a low Y implies a decision favoring the position 0, and a high Y implies one closer to 100. We do not need to be concerned with the relationship's exact nature. It can take various forms, including majority-take-all and strictly proportional compromise. A government under pressure to legalize a new drug may go ahead with full legalization simply because the public supporters outnumber the opponents. Then, on a budgetary controversy, it may opt for a roughly proportional compromise. The important point is that a group may enjoy a plurality of support without being able to impose its total will on the wider community. Also relevant to its power may be the *size* of its plurality. The smaller a group's plurality, the weaker its mandate, and so the less effectively it is able to implement its expressed will. That is the practical meaning of the insights of Machiavelli and Hume.

An implication is that pressure groups have an incentive to extend their support as much as possible. This may seem to contradict the "size principle," which asserts that distributional coalitions (like industrial cartels and legislative alliances) prefer to become exclusive after they reach a certain size.[27] In fact, there is no conflict. A pressure group might represent the interests of a cartel seeking the retention of the regulations essential to its survival. While the cartel remained exclusive, the pressure group would remain open to all segments of society, including those harmed by barriers to competition. If barriers benefit only a small minority, the group's ultimate success will depend on the stands of nonbeneficiaries.

It bears repetition that the promoters of a policy cannot even count on the support of the policy's potential beneficiaries. Negative social pressures might make a group's natural constituents join the opposition.

Political power, it might be said, is rooted in social institutions and in ideology. To take the latter factor first, I am not suggesting that ideology is politically insignificant. I will argue later that it exerts enormous control over beliefs and perceptions. I will also show, however, that ideological success is not a precondition for political success. As for institutions, I will argue that they are sustained by public opinion. And I will recognize that some institutions complicate the correspondence between public opinion and policy outcomes. But the complications are best postponed until Chapter 17. For the time being, let us treat the correspondence as perfect. The next logical step is to explore the formation of public opinion.

4

The Dynamics of Public Opinion

Absent preference falsification, public opinion would always mirror private opinion. In reality, as we have seen, any number of distinct public opinions are compatible with a given private opinion. This chapter investigates how one particular alternative gets established. Because the variability of public opinion is linked to the variability of social pressures, I start with preliminary points about the dependence of pressures on numbers.

From the standpoint of the individual bearer, some forms of pressure are independent of the delivering group's numerical size. To the person who is beaten for an act of dissent, it hardly matters whether his injuries were caused by one assailant or five. Likewise, if an organization pays tribute to his courage through a monetary prize, he may not care whether the organization acted on behalf of five people or five thousand. Other rewards and penalties do depend critically on the size of the delivering group. If our dissenter becomes the butt of an insulting joke, it matters how widely the joke is told and heard. And if he receives a medal, the benefits will depend on how many consider the medal an honor.

Like the effects of social pressure on the receiving individual, the costs to the delivering group can depend on numbers. The cost of rewarding members monetarily grows with the size of the membership, just as that of punishing nonmembers physically rises with the number of nonmembers. It might be prohibitively expensive, therefore, for a small group to harass everyone who refrains from joining it and, likewise, for a large group to buy off every recruit.[1] So a group whose incentives were limited to monetary rewards and physical punishments might not be viable at any size. Yet the number-dependent incentives on which pressure groups rely for their growth do not all require monetary outlays or the use of physical force. The pressures that flow from public opinion often pay for themselves, in the sense of being self-reproducing. A critical implication is that, to achieve the public opinion that will serve their substantive goals, pressure groups frequently rely on incentives created by public opinion itself.

The Link between Public Opinion and Social Pressures

One reason why public opinion is a source of social pressure is that individuals trying to enhance the credibility of their chosen public preferences show approval of people who have made the same choice and disapproval of people who have made other choices. On abortion, for instance, individuals representing themselves as prochoice will greet the prochoice statements of others with nods of approval and prolife ones with frowns.

People feel compelled to back up their declarations of support with concrete actions precisely because preference falsification is common and understood to be so. Anyone can express a particular political view, so by itself a verbal declaration of being prochoice carries little weight. To be perceived as sincere, whether or not one actually is, one's words must be coupled with concrete actions. Nodding and frowning are two credibility-building actions, albeit ones of minor consequence. More effective ones include heckling a politician, praising an op-ed piece, participating in a demonstration, and donating to a political cause. Taken by individuals for their own reputational needs, all such actions help shape the social pressures that influence the public preference choices of others.

These points may be reinforced through variations on the old maxim, "When in Rome, do as the Romans do." The maxim proposes that to achieve social approval one must behave in accordance with the prevailing norms. Like all maxims, it has its limitations. A Venetian passing through Rome might want to act his Venetian self, yet realize that if he fails to observe Roman customs, he will be ridiculed. So a more precise form of the maxim might be: "When in Rome, *appear* as the Romans do." In some contexts, appearing Roman will come naturally. Like the Romans, the Venetian will want to walk erect; he will have no desire to crawl on all fours. In other contexts, however, appearing Roman will require efforts at impression management, with all the consequent inner tensions. Such efforts will include shows of respect to people appearing Roman and of condescension toward those appearing foreign. In effect, the Venetian will follow the maxim: "When in Rome, *reward* those appearing Roman and *punish* those appearing un-Roman."[2] By rewarding the seemingly Roman and punishing the seemingly un-Roman one achieves more credibility than one would through a mere declaration of Romanness. In the process, one makes it all the more prudent to do the things that Romans do and also all the more imprudent to act as a Venetian.

At the time of the Spanish Inquisition, the Marranos tended to distance themselves from unconverted Jews. They felt that to befriend practicing, nondissimulating Jews could cast doubt on their own ostensible conversions to Christianity. Going further, many converts participated in the persecution of practicing Jews. Significantly, both the first inquisitor general and his immediate successor were of Jewish descent.[3] When a convert persecutes nonconverts, the reason could be that he is acting out of animosity. But he could also, or alternatively, be motivated by a wish to make his chosen public preference appear genuine—to signal, that is, his sincerity.

Granted that such signaling may achieve its purpose, does it follow that it is a requirement for appearing sincere? Suppose that individuals *a, b,* and *c* all profess to support abortion rights. Will *a* come across as insincere if he neglects to chastise the opponents of these rights? Will *b* then become suspect herself if she refrains from attacking *a?* And will *c* lose all credibility if, in turn, he fails to criticize *a* and *b?* "Not necessarily" is the answer to all these questions. For one thing, turning on others is not the only way to establish credibility. For another, it is often impractical for every member of a group to participate in punishing every suspected opponent. Ordinarily, members can signal their sincerity by responding to some fraction of the offenses they can reasonably be expected to notice.

To generalize, it is neither practical nor logically necessary for every member of a pressure group to contribute to each of its various rewards and punishments. A group will ordinarily exhibit some division of labor, and its members will not discredit themselves for choosing to specialize in a subset of the group's functions. An abortion opponent who demonstrates in front of abortion clinics and articulates prolife slogans at every opportunity need not lose her credibility merely for neglecting to chastise a man who appears unenthusiastic during a prolife speech. As long as her behavior generally conforms to the prolife agenda, she will be given the benefit of the doubt when she remains passive. Her passivity in the face of another's lack of enthusiasm may be taken to mean that the offense escaped her notice or that she was unusually tired.

There are contexts where individual political stands are easily monitored. When a legislature votes by a show of hands in front of television cameras, for example, it is easy to identify each legislator's position. In other contexts, however, identification presents problems. Following a riot, the government may not be able to generate a reliable list of the participants. It may know only that most rioters came from a certain neighborhood or that most belonged to a certain clan. Acting on such information, it may punish an entire group, understanding full well that some rioters will go unpunished and that the punished will include some nonrioters. For all its inequities, such collective sanctioning may serve as a powerful deterrent to future dissent. The knowledge that the government will punish a trouble-making community creates incentives for individual citizens to control each other's rebellious tendencies.[4]

Equilibrium

A pressure group thus confers benefits on its members and imposes costs on nonmembers. It does so partly through its members' efforts to signal their loyalty and sincerity. Together, these observations mean that as a pressure group expands the incentives to join it will grow.

A further implication is that, when two groups do battle over public opinion, the winner will not necessarily be the one with the richer, stronger, and better organized core of activists. The advantage a group enjoys on account of its superior core may be overtaken by the disadvantage of a smaller membership; and conversely, a group can compensate for a weaker core of activists with a relatively large membership.[5]

Recall that in a large community the individual's ability to influence a collective decision is negligible. His intrinsic utility is practically fixed, therefore, and he chooses a public preference on the basis of a tradeoff between expressive utility and reputational utility. The latter form of utility depends on public opinion. For example, the reputational utility of a person who chooses to support the position 0 over 100 will rise as public opinion becomes increasingly favorable to 0. To keep things simple, let me treat reputational utility as a function of the mean of all public preferences, rather than as a function of the entire distribution. I shall refer to this mean, the Y of Chapter 3, as *mean public opinion* or, where it is obvious that I am talking about the average and not the distribution, simply as public opinion. From Chapter 2 we know that the individual's expressive utility is highest when his public preference coincides with his private preference and that it declines as the two preferences move apart. Remember also that if an issue is sufficiently sensitive, the prevailing social pressures will make everyone want to be in one of the two groups.

Against this background, consider our individual's public-preference declaration decision on an issue of great sensitivity. His private preference happens to be $x = 20$, so, given a choice between 0 and 100, he would rather support the former. If the pressures from the two groups are equal, he will obviously choose 0 as his public preference. Start, then, at a position of equality, and tilt the balance of pressures increasingly in favor of 100. The advantage to supporting 0 will progressively weaken, and there may come a point where he is indifferent between supporting 0 and supporting 100. If we now go a bit further, he will be better off supporting 100. The switchover point, t, is our individual's *political threshold* on the issue in question. In precise terms, it is the public opinion that makes him indifferent between his two options. If $Y < t$, he supports 0; and if $Y > t$, he sup-

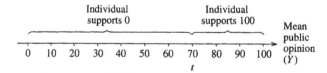

Figure 4.1 The individual's political threshold. If public opinion is sufficiently favorable to 100, he will publicly support 100.

ports 100. If $Y = t$, he might as well toss a coin. It will simplify the presentation, without any substantive consequences, to posit that in cases of indifference everyone always chooses 100.

Figure 4.1 shows our individual's threshold to be 70. Various factors could make this threshold move. If we hold all else fixed, a rise in his private preference would reduce the expressive disadvantage to supporting 100, thus lowering the threshold. Likewise, the threshold would fall if the group promoting 100 were to become more efficient at converting its numerical support into social pressure. By contrast, if the individual's expressive needs were to increase, his threshold would rise, because it would then take greater pressures to offset the expressive advantage of supporting 0.

Individuals differ in their psychological constitutions, and on any given issue their private preferences may vary. So, too, therefore, may their political thresholds. One possible distribution of thresholds is shown in Figure 4.2. The depicted curve represents the *cumulative*

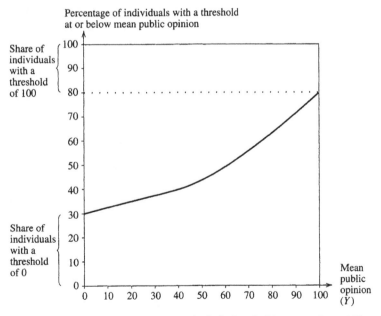

Figure 4.2 The propagation curve. Half of all thresholds are at 0 or 100, with the remaining half distributed between the extremes.

distribution of thresholds. It is found by plotting, for each Y between 0 and 100, the percentage of society with thresholds at or below that level. In the curve shown, 30 percent of all thresholds are at 0, 80 percent are below 100, and naturally, 100 percent are at or below 100. Because the cumulative distribution will determine the propagation of preference falsification, I shall refer to it as the *propagation curve.*[6]

At any particular time, each member of society will have some expectation of mean public opinion in the period just ahead. Let us assume that *expected public opinion,* Y^e, is the same for everyone. Given Y^e, the prevailing propagation curve will yield a realization of public opinion. This can be seen in panel A of Figure 4.3, which contains the same propagation curve as that in the previous figure. The lower horizontal axis represents expected public opinion; the left vertical axis records the realization.

Remaining focused on Figure 4.3, imagine that the expected public opinion somehow starts out at 20. The propagation curve indicates that 35 percent of the population has a threshold at or below 20. So this share of the population will give its public support to 100 and the remaining 65 percent will support 0. An expectation of 20 has thus generated a public opinion of 35. Having turned out to be an underestimate, the initial expectation will be revised upward.

According to the figure, *any* expectation below 40 will fall short of the corresponding realization and generate further revisions. To become self-fulfilling, and thus self-reproducing, the expected public opinion must rise to 40. The figure shows $Y^e = 40$ to lie at the only intersection between the propagation curve and the diagonal. So there is a single self-fulfilling expectation, a unique *equilibrium.*[7] Only when individuals base their public preferences on the expectation of a public opinion of 40 does actual public opinion match the expectation that generated it.

Panel B of Figure 4.3 uses a topographic metaphor to capture the movements of public opinion. It depicts a valley whose lowest point is at 40. If a ball is placed at 40, it will remain at rest indefinitely. Placed anywhere else, it will roll toward 40.

The equilibrium in Figure 4.3 is an *interior equilibrium*—one that lies inside the spectrum of possible expectations. As such, it features open dissension: 40 percent are publicly supporting 100, with the remaining 60 percent supporting 0. An equilibrium situated at an extremity, like the one shown in Figure 4.4, is a *corner equilibrium*. Here the threshold curve intersects the diagonal at 100, so the only self-sustaining expectation is unanimous support for 100. Remember that an activist is someone whose public preference is effectively independent of public opinion. Strictly speaking, then, the establishment of a corner equilibrium entails the demise of one core of activists. If some hardy activists were to remain in opposition, the equilibrium would be very near, but not quite at, an extremity. It would be a *near-corner equilibrium*.

Corner and near-corner equilibria are not uncommon. The Inquisition turned Spain into a country where virtually everyone professed Christianity, controversy being limited to disputes over the specifics of Catholic orthodoxy. In pre-1989 Czechoslovakia, a near-corner

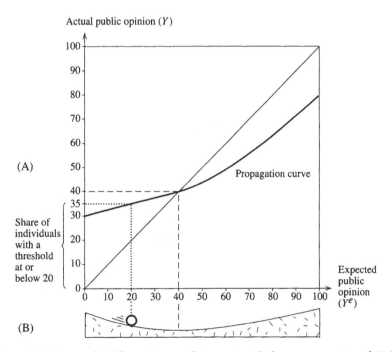

Figure 4.3 Expected public opinion and its motion. Only an expectation of 40 is self-fulfilling and self-reproducing. Any other expectation will result in adjustments toward 40.

equilibrium existed on the legitimacy of the prevailing regime. Very few were openly defiant of the communist monopoly on power. Taking a preference of 0 to represent support for the monopoly and one of 100 opposition to it, we could say that public opinion stood in equilibrium near 0.

Tocqueville, one of the most astute observers of nineteenth-century America, was intrigued by the commonness of corner equilibria in the United States. "At the present time," he wrote, "the most absolute monarchs in Europe cannot prevent certain opinions hostile to their authority from circulating in secret through their dominions and even in their courts. It is not so in America; as long as the majority is still undecided, discussion is carried on; but as soon as its decision is irrevocably pronounced, everyone is silent, and *the friends as well as the opponents unite in assenting to its propriety.*"[8] What makes this

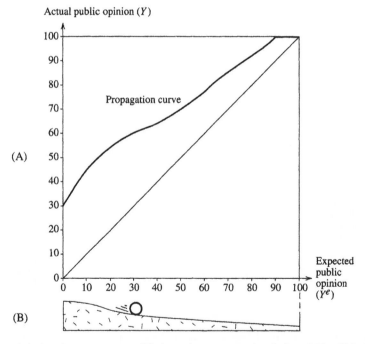

Figure 4.4 A unique corner equilibrium. Any expectation below 100 will induce upward self-corrections.

passage relevant is not just its description of corner equilibria. It captures the role of preference falsification in sustaining an appearance of unity.

Multiple Equilibria

There is no reason why public opinion must feature a single equilibrium. The propagation curve could cross the diagonal more than once, in which case there would exist *multiple* equilibria. A case with three equilibria appears in Figure 4.5. Of the three, those at 20 and 100 are *stable,* in that expectations in their vicinity generate revisions toward them. The stability of these equilibria is most easily seen in panel B, where 20 and 100 correspond to the lowermost points of two local valleys. The middle equilibrium at 60 is *unstable,* in that nearby expectations generate revisions away from it. If expected public opinion happens to be 60, it will be confirmed. But a slightly different expectation will produce adjustments toward one of the stable equilibria. Our unstable equilibrium appears as a hilltop. It is theoretically possible but practically impossible for a ball to remain perched at the peak of a hill; a whiff of air will push it over.[9] Likewise, it is theoretically possible but practically impossible for public opinion to remain in unstable equilibrium.

A quick inspection of Figures 4.3 through 4.5 will show that an equilibrium is stable if the propagation curve crosses the diagonal from above, unstable if it crosses the diagonal from below. When the propagation curve intersects the diagonal more than once, stable and unstable equilibria must alternate. This is analogous to saying that if there are two hilltops, a valley must lie in between; and if there are two valleys, they must be separated by a hill.

Among the social sciences, economics has made the greatest contribution to the analysis of social equilibria. Yet only recently has it begun to treat multiple equilibria as worthy of study. And still much economic theorizing begins with a search for assumptions that will guarantee a unique equilibrium. In reality, there is no empirical basis for ruling out multiple equilibria. Even in domains falling within the narrowest conception of economics, like production and exchange, only the most unrealistic assumptions will guarantee uniqueness. The multiplicity of equilibria, therefore, far from being a rarity or pa-

thology that can safely be ignored in the interest of relevance or usefulness, is a common phenomenon that merits serious attention.[10] Beyond the central concerns of economics, like the determination of
public opinion, there is even less justification for insisting on uniqueness.

Why have many economists, including some of the giants of our
century, been committed to the notion of uniqueness? The answer lies
only partly in the discipline's emphasis on theoretical "elegance." A
more fundamental reason is the vulnerability of the core propositions
of neoclassical economics, and of its basic analytical techniques, to
the complexities engendered by multiplicity. As Chapter 17 will show,
in the presence of multiple equilibria persistent social outcomes are
not necessarily optimal. Contrary to what a long line of economists

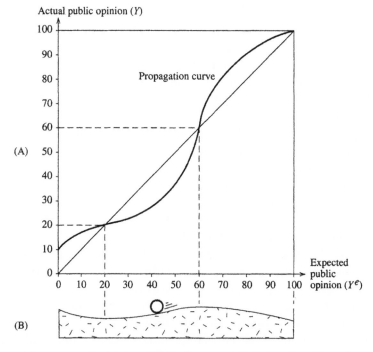

Figure 4.5 A case with three equilibria. Expectations below 60 will result in cor-
rections in the direction of 20; and ones above 60 will generate adjustments toward 100.

have held, "what exists" need not be "what is best." Nor are outcomes predictable from the characteristics of the decision-making population. Figure 4.5 demonstrates that a single set of population characteristics might produce very different outcomes.[11]

In the discussion so far, the term equilibrium applies specifically to public opinion, not to the entire social order. Later chapters will show that a public opinion at rest unleashes long-term forces that act upon the underlying private preferences. The ensuing changes may ultimately strengthen the reigning equilibrium; alternatively, they may move or destroy it. The equilibria with which we are presently concerned may be characterized as *temporary,* as opposed to permanent.

Expectations and Bandwagons

No matter how many equilibria exist, only one can be in place at any given time. The expectation of public opinion determines which gets selected. Turn back to Figure 4.5, which contains two stable equilibria, 20 and 100. Public opinion will go to one or the other, depending on whether the initial expectation of public opinion is below or above 60. The initial expectation is critical because, by establishing people's initial perceptions of their reputational incentives, it determines how these perceptions will evolve. With an initial expectation of 61, reputational incentives are sufficiently favorable to supporting 100 that more than 61 percent of the population actually do so. The choices make the incentives even more favorable to supporting 100, and the percentage of actual supporters goes even higher. Each new person on this upward *bandwagon* induces additional people to climb on, until the entire population is on board.[12] A slightly lower initial expectation, 59 instead of 61, would produce a dramatically different outcome. Fewer than 59 percent would actually choose 100, activating a downward bandwagon toward 20.

For a bandwagon to form and start moving, it is necessary though not sufficient for individual choices to be interdependent. The people making choices must also be heterogeneous, at least in the sense that it takes different amounts of pressure to elicit a particular response. If the same amount were required, they would make their switches en masse.[13] The heterogeneity condition is obviously satisfied in the present context, because members of society differ in their private preferences, expressive needs, and fears of disapproval. Such variations imply a distribution of political thresholds. With heterogeneous decision makers, a bandwagon can keep rolling as long as the changes in social pressure induced by new riders impel at least one additional person to jump on. There is no reason, of course, why the bandwagon should keep rolling until everyone is aboard. At some point, the additional social pressure created by the latest rider might fail to activate the next in line. In Figure 4.5, the downward bandwagon comes to a halt before 0.

A bandwagon can complete its course at great speed. In 1975, right before Indira Gandhi declared an Emergency throughout India, her government seemed vulnerable. The streets were teeming with antigovernment agitators confidently vowing never to give up. In this atmosphere, the opposition leader J. P. Narayan asked an animated audience of students whether they would go to class or to prison. "Prison!" they shouted in unison. Then came the Emergency and the round-up of opposition leaders. With hopes of revolution fading, millions quietly returned to their classes within a matter of weeks.[14] Evidently the Emergency altered the dynamics of public opinion by making it seem that Gandhi's government would manage, after all, to hold on to power and regain public support. Some protesting students responded by withdrawing from the streets, which then induced further withdrawals. In the process, the protests fizzled out.

The critical role of expectations has been verified through systematic experiments. One experiment, conducted in England by Catherine Marsh, explored this role with regard to public opinion on abortion.[15] In one set of conversations, she gave two groups of subjects, all unaware that an experiment was under way, information about the trend in public opinion. She told the first group that public opinion was becoming increasingly permissive toward abortion, the second that it was becoming increasingly restrictive. When she then inquired about the preferences of her subjects, she found that 12 percent more of the first group than of the second expressed opposition to tightening restrictions on abortion. Coming into the interview, most of Marsh's subjects knew that the permissive position was more popular than the restrictive, doubtless because of extensive press coverage. Yet few possessed reliable information about the trend of public opinion, perhaps because the media give little coverage to trend information. The subjects, proposes Marsh, being both ignorant about the trend and eager to learn about it, were responsive to the interviewer's impressions. Her argument suggests that when people sense that public opinion is moving, their shifting expectations may make them adjust their public preferences. At the same time, given an expectation that they themselves will be in the minority, they may opt to remain there indefinitely.

This interpretation is in line with the argument offered here. The mere fact that people expect a position to be in the minority will not necessarily make them rush away from it. In Figure 4.5 an expected public opinion of 20 makes one in five side with the minority, with no subsequent switches; members of the minority do not join the majority upon seeing their minority status confirmed, for such a confirmation offers no new information. By contrast, if the expected public opinion were 30, the subsequent realization would be smaller, which *does* imply new information. As in Marsh's experiment, some switches would follow.

The Power of Small Events

If even minor differences in expectations can affect the realization of public opinion, it is of interest to know the determinants of expectations. When an issue presents itself, what establishes the starting expectation?

Ordinarily, multitudes of events come into play, including many that would seem unimportant. An activist who champions the position 0 catches the flu, which forces her to withdraw from a televised debate. Another activist, a promoter of 100, wins a promotion right before a talk-show appearance; his self-confidence boosted, he makes an unusually good impression. Coincidentally, a long-scheduled conference brings together hundreds of professionals who tend to support 100; reporters covering the conference unwittingly give views favorable to 100 disproportionately greater exposure. The joint effect of these fortuitous events is to bias initial perceptions of public opinion, and thus expectations, in favor of 100.

None of these events would catch the attention of social scientists trying retrospectively to explain why public opinion darted up and not down. The circumstances that fixed the timing of a conference and a debater's mood or health are factors that even a trained investigator would overlook. They are *small events,* happenings which, for all practical purposes, leave no retrievable records.[16] Depending on the context, analysts focus on easily observable phenomena such as demographic trends, the economic costs and benefits of the available options, and the demonstrated strengths of the concerned pressure groups. Such phenomena are obviously relevant and important. Yet they are not always decisive. In the presence of multiple equilibria, an occurrence of no intrinsic significance may have a dramatic impact on the course of public opinion. Specifically, it may determine which of two or more bandwagons get pushed into motion.

In the social sciences, it is seldom appreciated that small events can have large effects. The most obvious reason is that most small events have no long-term consequences. The timing of a promotion or of a person's illness ordinarily has no political impact. A less obvious reason lies in the common tendency to think that the possible outcomes of human interactions are unique. Where there is only one equilibrium, slight variations in expectations may alter the speed at which the system comes to rest, but not the eventual outcome. Since all paths go to the same place, small events might lengthen or shorten the trip but not affect the ultimate destination. Matters are different in the presence of multiple equilibria. With two or more destinations, small events can influence both the speed of adjustment *and* the ultimate destination. Still another reason why small events are underrated is that the concept conflicts with the "representativeness heuristic," a mental shortcut we all use in trying to cope with our cognitive limitations. The representativeness heuristic makes us expect causes to resemble their effects, as when the cause of a devastating war is taken to be an economic depression.[17] By the logic of representativeness, a small event is unrepresentative of a great outcome, so the two cannot be linked causally. The assassination of an American president cannot be the work of a deranged gunman acting alone; there must have been a sinister plot orchestrated by some powerful enemy, for only a great event is representative of a great outcome. By definition, a great force is visible; a small event is not.[18]

The Expectations Game

If the importance of small events is commonly underestimated, it hardly follows that political actors always behave as though small events are politically insignificant. Knowing that expectations can feed on themselves and have real consequences, politicians, statesmen, and lobbyists undertake campaigns to shape perceptions of where public opinion stands and where it is headed.

An American fundamentalist group long called itself the "Moral Majority." Feminists opposed to its objectives countered by setting up a "Fund for the Feminist Majority." Each of these group names makes a claim about the preferences of Americans. The former asserts that Americans support the moral objectives of the fundamentalists, at least in private; the latter asserts that Americans tend to support the goals of organized feminists. To be sure, the two claims could be valid simultaneously. The limitations of human cognition allow the peaceful coexistence of contradictory beliefs, so a person may favor both traditional "family values" as understood by the fundamentalists and "women's liberation" as understood by organized feminists. In fact, neither group's far-reaching agenda commands anything near majority support. Whatever the extent of cognitive inconsistency, each claim of support represents an overstatement. Nevertheless, they are both advanced repeatedly, because their promoters know that on issues apt to generate rampant preference falsification, even an extreme claim can become self-fulfilling. Indeed, activists on both sides understand that they can compensate for their small numbers and organizational weaknesses simply by turning expectations in their favor.

Efforts to distort perceptions of public opinion take various additional forms. Lobbies dwell on polls showing their positions to be popular and attempt to discredit unfavorable polls. They manipulate surveys through the selection and wording of questions. They inflate the participation rates in their rallies, phone-ins, strikes, and boycotts. And through such instruments as textbooks, opinion articles, and mass demonstrations, they endeavor to get their stands accepted as "normal," as positions that respectable people consider reasonable, beneficial, and efficacious.[19] Such efforts also help, we shall see, to mold private beliefs and preferences. But the immediate goal is usually to control perceptions of the prevailing public opinion.

Apparently, political activists have a basic understanding of preference falsification, the bandwagon process, the possibility of multiple bandwagons, and ways of influencing which bandwagon gets under way. This is not to say that they could articulate a coherent theory of the political process. If asked to explain why an exaggerated claim might make a big difference, their answers would probably not live up to scholarly standards. But one can have the right intuition without being able to offer a comprehensive and logically tight explanation. After all, builders without exposure to formal physics take account of gravity.

Through their explanations and predictions, scholars contribute to the manipulation of expectations, often unintentionally. A book on Japanese economic growth may affect perceptions of public opinion with regard to free trade. A treatise on street crime may distort the perceived popularity of the death penalty. The potential power of academic research is supported by the fact that lobbies threatened by particular findings commission counterstudies. Part of the reason is to control private opinion; a more pressing reason is often the control of public opinion.

Pluralistic Ignorance: Public Opinion

When a group's agenda is contested, its efforts to shape expectations of public opinion will usually encounter challenges. The efforts may be offset by the efforts of rival groups. Feminist overstatements neutralize some fundamentalist overstatements, and vice versa. Not every effort to influence expectations is frustrated, however, by some counterbalancing effort. Fortuitous circumstances, or differences in the resources of rival groups, leave some efforts uncountered.

How effective can such uncountered efforts be? Are expectations of public opinion sufficiently malleable to make attempts at shaping them worthwhile?

For an answer, one must explore the formation of individual expectations. Consider someone who wants to get a feel for public opinion concerning abortion. He draws some information from the public statements of his face-to-face contacts. But the people with whom he exchanges political views tend to have backgrounds and concerns similar to his own, so their views are unrepresentative of the broader public opinion. Sensing the biases involved, he looks for information of a more representative nature. A poll catches his eye; listening to a radio discussion on women's rights, he hears that "only reactionaries reject a woman's right to choose"; and in a movie that he watches an abortion opponent is portrayed as a villain. Aggregating these bits of information, he concludes that public opinion is sympathetic to abortion rights.

This person is unlikely to use the information at his disposal in a manner that would satisfy a statistician. Psychological research shows that people routinely weight information inappropriately, thus producing systematic errors when they characterize populations on the basis of fragmentary information. Even individuals who have studied formal statistics violate basic statistical principles in everyday contexts. However well they know that small samples are not as reliable as larger ones, they sometimes ascribe undue significance to information derived from tiny samples. And however well they understand the concept of sample bias, they often fail to appreciate the biases caused by particular sampling procedures. In one pertinent experiment, a group of students were given mean course evaluations that summarized the opinions of dozens of previous students. A second group then heard a few former students evaluate the same courses on a similar scale and offer comments consistent with their evaluations. The concrete, personal evaluations heard by the second group had a substantially greater effect on their subsequent course selections than the abstract, large-sample means had on the selections of the first group.[20]

Other experiments indicate that in attempting to gauge public opinion people tend to attach inordinate weight to the concrete, personal, and vivid data embodied in their face-to-face contacts.[21] Insofar as this bias is significant, the activities of rival pressure groups will fail to homogenize individual expectations of public opinion. Variations will be particularly pronounced when the groups are similar in size, for then competing claims about public opinion, or about its trend, may be advanced without straining credibility. Expectational variations enhance both the urgency and the potential effectiveness of propaganda concerning the state of public opinion. Where expectations show appreciable differences, there are many people to surprise; and a message that surprises the right people at the right time can activate a bandwagon that changes public opinion dramatically.

Once a bandwagon gets under way, people cannot but notice that public opinion is changing. In self-interest, they become more alert to signals emanating from the wider community, and their reactions may cause the bandwagon to speed up. Thus a bandwagon that develops following a period of confusion over public opinion may run its course very quickly. Think of Iran in the winter of 1978–79. As the anti-shah opposition mushroomed, the shift in public opinion became increasingly obvious. In the process, the shah's claim that the demonstrators represented a small fringe became patently unconvincing. Even members of the shah's entourage, who interacted primarily with other loyalists, came to realize what was happening. In the initial stages of the uprising, the trend had not been so clear.

Social psychologists use the term *pluralistic ignorance* to describe misconceptions of preference distributions.[22] In our context, to raise the possibility of pluralistic ignorance is to recognize that in assessing public opinion people use mental shortcuts that violate basic statistical principles. The commonness of erroneous judgments does not imply, of course, that individual assessments are *independent* of actual trends. Large shifts in public opinion tend to be widely noticed, and dramatic events make people more receptive to broad indicators of public opinion.

Pluralistic Ignorance: Private Opinion

The term pluralistic ignorance is usually applied to private opinion rather than to public opinion. There is a voluminous literature that explores individual perceptions of private opinion. It finds that people often misjudge private opinion substantially—a finding with implications for an issue raised in Chapter 2, the *possibility* of preference falsification. Let us first turn to the evidence.

A set of studies uncovered a marked tendency in the 1960s and 1970s for white Americans to overestimate private white support for forced racial segregation. According to one study, 18 percent of the whites favored segregation, but as many as 47 percent believed that most did so.[23] The misperception afflicted all status groups, age categories, and regions. A related result concerned views on whether "white people have the right to keep Negroes out of their neighborhoods if they want to." The perception of a segregationist white majority had little effect on the answers of whites favoring either enforced segregation or enforced desegregation. Among those favoring neither, however, the perception fostered a willingness to endorse racial segregation in housing.

To interpret these results, let 0 represent a preference for segregation, 100 one for desegregation, and values around 50 one for neither. The belief that segregationists constitute a majority will create segregationist social pressure and, hence, a reputational incentive to support 0. For people with private preferences above 0, there is also a counterincentive, however: a loss in expressive utility. This loss is smaller for a person with a private preference of 50 than for one who privately prefers 100. Hence segregationist pressure that makes the former support segregation may fail to bring on board the latter.

The key finding was that, although few whites favored enforced racial segregation, many were willing to endorse it in the mistaken belief that most whites were segregationists. The finding would not have surprised Gunnar Myrdal, author of major works on American race relations. He commented on the willingness of whites to hire blacks: "In my contacts with businessmen in many fields—bankers, insurance people, industrialists, and directors of department stores—I have been told time and time again that they have nothing against employing Negroes, and I believe they are telling the truth. What holds them back are the considerations they have to take about the attitudes of customers and co-workers."[24] The passage harbors two important points. First, racism on the part of employers is less a matter of private sentiment than of public behavior. And second, employers who are not racists themselves discriminate against blacks under perceived pressures from their customers. Discrimination by employers is thus often a manifestation of preference falsification. Yet the ostensibly racist customers might themselves be engaged in preference falsification. It could be that their racist demands reflect not their own private prejudices but simply their strivings to accommodate the apparent prejudices of others.

The foregoing interpretation suggests that at least some of the observed racism entailed preference falsification in response to preference falsification on the part of others. This brings us back to the question of whether preference falsification can be credible. Take a white employer and a white customer, both free of racist feelings. If they behave as racists, will each know that the other is merely role playing? Remember that involuntary body movements may give away feelings that one is trying to hide.

If such movements were effortlessly observed, and if they revealed exactly the feelings being concealed, then it would be impossible to feign racism. Just as Pinocchio saw his nose grow when he lied, so too a person free of racist feelings would emit involuntary signs of his nonracist disposition at every insincere act of racism. Moreover, like the Blue Fairy who knows exactly why Pinocchio's nose is lengthening, the audience of the phony racist would easily identify the nonracist private feelings that he was trying to hide. But Pinocchio and the Blue Fairy are figments of a talented storyteller's imagination. The signs of insincerity are rarely as obvious as an overgrown nose. Nor, when noticed, do they always lend themselves to easy interpretation.

In Nazi Germany, officials trying to ascertain an individual's loyalty relied partly on his public statements and partly on such indicators as his greeting style, his willingness to make donations to the Party, and the behavior of his children. Sensing that the regime was feared, officials considered public opinion an unreliable indicator of private opinion.[25] Yet they probably were not very successful at identifying their insincere supporters. Many cases of preference falsification must have gone undetected. By the same token, the citizens accused of secret hostility to the Nazis must have included some true believers. Scientific evaluations of people's success at detecting deception show that accuracy is significantly better than chance, yet modest in absolute terms.[26] Preference falsification is not always self-revealing.

No one would argue that insincerity is never transparent. We all understand that the person who presents his wallet to armed muggers is acting out of fear rather than generosity. We cannot be so sure, however, about the genuineness of a preference that might have been motivated by self-interest. When a Muslim university student wears a headscarf, is she responding to social pressure, exercising an inner urge for feminine modesty, or a bit of both? None of these possibilities can be ruled out a priori. Even if presented with extensive information about her personality, her religious convictions, and political conditions in her community, we may not be able to determine her motivations with certainty. It is one thing to recognize that social pressures are at work, another to identify their exact influence on a particular person's choices.

Nevertheless, we routinely draw inferences in cases of this sort. Do any systematic biases creep into our inferences? Specifically, are our errors of interpretation biased in favor or against the situational factors that generate preference falsification? The evidence is that we tend to underestimate the impact of social pressures on public preferences. Discounting the power of pressure, we often mistake public preferences for the underlying private preferences.

In a revealing experiment, a group of subjects were told about the Milgram experiment, including the fact that 65 percent of the "teachers" obeyed orders to deliver shocks in the "XXX" range. The subjects were then offered descriptions of two "teachers" who delivered the maximum possible shock and asked to rate them in terms of traits such as warmth, likableness, and conformism. The ratings tended to be highly uncomplimentary to the "teachers." The knowledge that delivering the shock was the modal response did not keep the respondents from attributing the behavior of the "teachers" to personality flaws.[27] In a similar experiment, subjects were exposed to a reenactment of the Milgram experiment, witnessing one "teacher" obey instructions to the point of delivering the maximum shock. When subsequently asked to predict how other "teachers" would behave, they severely underestimated the effectiveness of the pressures they had witnessed. They even erred after an opportunity to play the role of "teacher" themselves. The experience did not keep them from attributing the actions of subsequent "teachers" to character defects.[28]

The human tendency to underemphasize the external determinants of human choices and overemphasize the internal determinants is known as the *fundamental attribution error*.[29] The normatively correct principle of attribution calls for caution in ascribing an act to the actor's personal disposition insofar as that act is typical.[30] For instance, if a committee votes unanimously for reelecting the current chair, one should infer little from this fact alone about the dispositions of individual committee members. Such inferences are justified only if the pressures in operation during the vote are well understood. If it is known that the incumbent chair had some challengers and that the vote was by secret ballot, it is reasonable to infer that she was considered the best person for the job. If the vote was by a show of hands and there were signs that opponents of her reelection would be ostracized, however, nothing should be inferred about any particular voter's private feelings. Yet research shows that people tend not to distinguish properly between such situations. The tendency to misconstrue the forces at work in the Milgram experiment offers an exceptionally clear demonstration.

Earlier we saw that pluralistic ignorance may exist with respect to public opinion. Now we see that it may also exist with respect to private opinion. Laboratory experiments show that we commonly infer personality traits from actions driven by situational factors. In other words, we regularly mistake public preferences for private preferences. There is no denying that we sometimes recognize the existence, and generally understand the prevalence, of preference falsification. The point is that our means of identifying *specific* occurrences of preference falsification are far from perfect. One does not become a good fisher just by knowing that the ocean is teeming with fish. Likewise, one does not become an expert detector of preference falsification just by knowing that people commonly misrepresent their wants.

An important consequence of our tendency to mistake public preferences for private preferences is to compound the power of small events and thus the potential impact of political activities that shape individual expectations. Insofar as we overrate the genuineness of public opinion, we will overestimate its permanence and adapt more readily to its apparent shifts. Therefore public opinion may be very sensitive to signs that it is in flux. A minor demonstration, or a conference that would normally get little attention, may generate a large shift in people's perceptions, thus activating a bandwagon that will culminate in a dramatically different public opinion.

We have seen that pluralistic ignorance is possible with respect to both public and private opinion. Moreover, each type of pluralistic ignorance may have significant effects. The expectations that shape our public preferences need not be accurate, and our misjudgments may be decisive to the course of public opinion. In addition, we may greatly underestimate the contribution of preference falsification to the persistence of public opinion. These conclusions have implications for the efficiency of governance in general, and democracy in particular. To identify these is among the next chapter's objectives.

5

Institutional Sources of Preference Falsification

Up to this point, the argument has accorded no formal role to the institutional framework within which personal and collective choices are made. In exploring the process of individual expressive choice, I did not pay attention to variations in the definitions political regimes give to individual rights. Nor, in analyzing the formation of public opinion, did I distinguish among regimes in terms of the controls they impose on the process of collective choice. This inattention to political institutions may seem odd, for there are palpable dissimilarities between, on the one hand, democratic polities like Canada, Finland, and post-Independence India and, on the other, authoritarian polities like Nazi Germany, pre- and postrevolutionary Iran, and North Korea. Only in the former group do the ruled get periodic opportunities to replace their rulers through peaceful means and to express their preferences freely.[1]

Distinctions between democratic and authoritarian polities have a sound basis in fact. Yet they do not necessitate multiple frameworks of analysis. They simply require recognition that regimes can constrain the basic process through which public opinion is formed and exercised. By way of analogy, the demand and supply model of economics is applied fruitfully to both free and regulated markets.

Just as there are basic commonalities between the operation of the New York Stock Exchange and that of the market for illegal drugs, so there are basic commonalities between the collective choice process in a constitutional democracy and that in a ruthless autocracy. In all political systems, the power to govern, make laws, and interpret decisions rests on public opinion. Equally critical, none precludes the distortion of public opinion through preference falsification. This is not to propose that democratic societies are no better off than authoritarian ones. It is to suggest, rather, that democracies are not always responsive to private opinion and that the choices they give citizens do not always get exercised.

Expressive Constraints

The penalties people incur on account of their public preferences may be physical, economic, or social. Nondemocratic regimes usually have recourse to all three forms. The political prisons of Iran, the reeducation camps of China, and the Gulag Archipelago all bear testimony to the severe penalties that authoritarian regimes impose on dissidents. Democracies worthy of the name prohibit physical sanctions and restrict the scope of economic sanctions. In a proper democracy no one is jailed merely for expressing radical ideas.

Even democratic regimes, however, discriminate against individuals who refuse to pay homage to popular symbols and ideals. Lobbyists for the legalization of heroin are less welcome in the halls of American government than are lobbyists for farm subsidies. And there is little to prevent the proponents of free trade in drugs—or cultural absolutists, or communists, or racial segregationists—from being stigmatized, ridiculed, and ostracized.

What makes a regime democratic is not, then, that it keeps people from being penalized for their public preferences. Democracy merely restricts the menu of possible penalties. The formal embodiment of this restriction is the "free speech" clause of a democratic constitution. Where the clause serves as more than window dressing, not only is the government barred from physically penalizing people for their political views, but it is held responsible for ensuring the expressibility of all views, including the misguided, the shocking, the hurtful, and the irreverent. Under the watchful eye of the American Civil Liberties Union, the U.S. government allows the American Nazi Party to publish brazenly racist literature. It even defends Nazi marchers against attacks from outraged citizens. Nevertheless, avowed Nazis suffer stiff penalties. Treated with contempt by most segments of society, they are burdened with an overwhelmingly hostile public opinion.

Through much of history power holders have enjoyed the legal authority to persecute unyielding political minorities. In principle, democracy fuses majority rule with a tolerance for the expressive rights of political minorities. These rights, enshrined in the law, are upheld through the norms of political pluralism. But no human law is immutable, and in unusually threatening times pluralism might appear luxurious. In any case, even the most liberal legal system allows exceptions to freedom of speech. In the United States, the courts recognize the principle of "clear and present danger," whereby speech may be proscribed if it poses a grave and imminent risk. This principle was crafted by Justice Oliver Wendell Holmes in a 1919 opinion upholding the conviction of a socialist charged with promoting draft evasion during World War I. Holmes argued that speech or conduct permitted in peacetime need not be protected in wartime. He thus held that expressive rights are not absolute but relative to the prevailing circumstances.[2] Defenders of the principle may disagree, of course, on its practical implications. Even constitutional scholars differ on what qualifies as a serious and immediate threat.

In the aftermath of World War II, the principle of "clear and present danger" was used to justify McCarthyism, the drive to suppress communism through sensational investigations. Opinion surveys of the period show that McCarthyism enjoyed great acceptance. In 1954 only 27 percent of Americans were prepared to allow a communist to speak in their community. About three-fourths would remove books written by communists from public libraries, and half would put communists in jail.[3]

Intolerance for leftists in general, and communists in particular, has fallen since the 1950s, along with the perceived danger of a communist takeover. Between 1954 and 1973, the percentage of Americans willing to let a communist speak in their community rose from 27 to 53.[4] But as a practical matter intellectual freedom continues to be rejected. As of the late 1970s, only 4 percent of the population believed that a professor "suspected of spreading false ideas" in his classes should not be interfered with; as many as 77 percent would "send someone into his classes to check on him." Four-fifths would permit a newspaper to publish its opinions "only if it doesn't twist the facts and tell lies."[5] These figures are consistent with dozens of other scientific surveys conducted over many decades.

Yet the rights to speak, write, assemble, and worship freely and to be safe from arbitrary restraints are all deeply ingrained in the American political ethos. Americans cherish the ideal of tolerance, and most view it as the sine qua non of democracy. Accordingly, support for freedom of speech *in the abstract* is overwhelming. Nearly nine out of ten "believe in free speech for all, no matter what their views might be." And almost as many hold that "people who hate our way of life should still have a chance to be heard."[6]

These findings concerning freedom of speech in the abstract give special significance to the preceding figures about popular attitudes on specific issues. In its embrace and glorification of free speech, the United States leads the family of nations. Expressive freedoms hold a less prominent place in the West European hierarchy of values, and in many other nations they are not even endorsed in the abstract. Surveys conducted in Soviet Russia, Argentina, and Libya, among other places, have uncovered widespread intolerance, with majorities repudiating even the principle of expressive freedom.[7] If in practice even Americans demand restrictions on the scope and content of dissent, one may safely conclude that absolute tolerance is nowhere the norm.

So social pressures aimed at regulating expression are apt to enjoy, even in societies that cherish the idea of individual liberty, the willing support and active participation of the masses. The democracies of our time offer examples in abundance. Significantly, many of the ongoing campaigns to regulate public speech are spearheaded by groups that define themselves as socially liberal.[8] Such groups are actively promoting, invariably in the name of some higher purpose, encroachments on the freedoms of others, even as they protest efforts to limit their own freedoms. The defenders of the freedom to exhibit scatological art of the kind made famous by Robert Mapplethorpe include feminists who want the law to define pornography as violence against women.[9] And the campaign to enforce "politically correct" speech codes on American campuses is spearheaded by groups that consider themselves oppressed by traditional expressive norms. The latter case receives detailed attention in chapters ahead.

The fact that contemporary democracies repress individual expression would not have surprised the great social philosophers of the eighteenth and nineteenth centuries. Tocqueville observed that in protecting individual citizens from government despotism American democracy had subjected them to a worse form of tyranny, the burden of conformism. So great is the force of American public opinion, he thought, that Americans conform to it readily, even as they glorify freedom, autonomy, and nonconformism.[10] In a similar vein, John Stuart Mill held that government oppression is generally less burdensome than the tyranny of friends, neighbors, and fellow citizens.[11]

Like other luminaries of their time, these thinkers were also critical of the democracies of antiquity. They understood well, as romantic idealizers of the ancient world do not, that in the Hellenic democracies popular power often produced individual repression.

In the fifth-century city-states of the Aegean basin, ordinary citizens routinely participated in decisions of general interest, thus wielding enormous collective power. Sometimes they used this power to restrict individual liberties. From time to time, for instance, they voted to banish the promoters of unpopular views. The practice was known as ostracism. Another punitive practice was *graphe paranomon,* a procedure used to prosecute people deemed to have made "illegal proposals."[12] The democracies of antiquity were thus not havens of unfettered speech. They imposed costs on citizens expressing doubts about conventional wisdom or challenging popular positions. Under the circumstances, public opinion was doubtless an important factor in individual political expression, and preference falsification must have been common.

The great virtue of democracy is that it restricts the government's means of controlling individual expression. Yet no democracy can guarantee the exercise of expressive freedoms. Just as the right to invest does not ensure an investment boom, so the right to speak does not make citizens uniformly open or fully truthful. In its applications, democracy has always fallen short of the ideal. The basic reason is that no one exhibits an absolute commitment to free speech. In practice, even people who consider themselves tolerant are prepared to regulate public expression, and thus public opinion, when it suits their own political goals. They often achieve their objectives through acts that make it personally advantageous to express some views and disadvantageous to express others.

Official Responsiveness to Public Opinion

If no political regime can prevent the distortion of public opinion, might a critical difference between democratic and authoritarian regimes lie in their responsiveness to public opinion? Lay thinking holds that elected governments are responsive to public opinion whereas dictators are not. Such thinking confuses public opinion with private opinion. Democratic and authoritarian regimes differ in their responsiveness to private, rather than public, opinion. All governments, including the authoritarian, are sensitive to public opinion.

To stay in power, democratically elected governments try to avoid treading on public opinion. Ones that ignore public opinion inevitably draw fire from powerful pressure groups, damaging their reelection chances. On occasion, of course, miscalculation will make a government take steps that produce an uproar. Typically, it will back down quickly. In 1986, for instance, the French premier Jacques Chirac proposed to raise university tuition to about $125, introduce a diploma that reflected performance, and allow universities to admit students on the basis of merit. When students marched in dozens of cities, he promptly withdrew his key proposals.[13] Six years earlier in the United States, when Ronald Reagan became president, his appointees promoted an environmental policy that would expand drilling and mining on national parklands. When the conservationist lobby kicked up a storm, Reagan left key provisions of his agenda unimplemented.[14] Both Reagan and Chirac could have held firm. In compromising, they opted to limit the damage to their popularity.

Relative to their democratic counterparts, authoritarian governments command greater opportunities to stifle dissent. History is replete with examples of dictatorships that have silenced their constituents through brute force. Does it follow that authoritarian governments are immune to social pressure? Are their policy choices independent of public opinion? Inasmuch as an autocratic government's heavy-handed measures succeed, its opposition is silenced. It governs, therefore, with the assent of public opinion, and it is able to implement its agenda because objections stay private. Yet opposition to a nondemocratic government need not remain concealed forever. Through processes to be described later, public opinion may turn against the government or against its policies. In the former case, the outcome is a revolution. When angry crowds in Prague turned against communist rule, Czechoslovakia's communist regime collapsed in a matter of days. Similarly, when huge antigovernment protests broke out throughout Iran, the shah's power vanished. Adverse public opinion plays an equally limiting role with respect to specific policies. In Poland under the communists and in Egypt under Sadat and Mubarak nominally powerful governments were forced by popular unrest to rescind increases in food prices. Even "dictatorial" regimes must retain the public allegiance of potentially powerful groups.[15]

In all types of regimes, public opinion influences policies officially under government control. It signals how lightly the government must tread to stay in office. A democratic government that goes against public opinion on a sufficiently important set of issues will create the impression that it has lost its mandate to govern, prompting calls for its resignation. For a nondemocratic government, the consequence of unfavorable public opinion may be an insurrection, or a coup aimed at forestalling one.

Official Responsiveness to Private Opinion

In what sense do democracies and nondemocracies differ in their responsiveness to private opinion? Insofar as the former have fewer means of restricting expression, the incentives they create for preference falsification will be weaker. Two conclusions follow. First, democracies will tend to display less preference falsification than dictatorships. And second, if a democratic government and a dictatorship both abide by public opinion meticulously, the policies implemented by the former will tend to adhere more closely to private opinion. The differences, to be sure, are ones of degree. Even in a democracy committed to personal liberties, social pressures beyond the government's control may drive a huge wedge between public and private opinion.

Because preference falsification plays a crucial role in all political systems, the framework outlined in previous chapters may be applied meaningfully to the collective choice process in both democracies and autocracies. Remember that public opinion may attain either an interior equilibrium, which entails open dissension, or a corner equilibrium, which features public unanimity. No political system excludes the possibility of a corner equilibrium on any particular issue. Nor can any system guarantee a corner equilibrium. But in dictatorships corner equilibria are more likely than in democracies, at least on issues the government deems sensitive.

The fact that the model under consideration can accommodate a variety of political regimes offers two advantages. First, it provides a basis for comparing regimes in terms of the genuineness of their respective public opinions, and for explaining any observed differences. In later chapters the model will be used to explain why public opinion in communist Eastern Europe differed markedly from that in the democratically governed societies of the West. The second advantage of a common framework is that it can incorporate regime changes. Further on, Eastern Europe's sudden transition to pluralist democracy will be portrayed as a massive realignment of public opinion.

The Secret Ballot

The case that democracies and authoritarian regimes differ in degree rather than in kind rests on the observation that preference falsification is a universal phenomenon that produces, in every type of regime, political choices at odds with private opinion. A skeptic might point out that every well-functioning democracy harbors a mechanism for according private opinion a direct say in the selection of high public officials: periodic elections by secret ballot. Indeed, in a democracy disliked officials can be voted out of office at the first election. An ouster might occur even if public opinion favors the political status quo. If voters are somehow afraid to criticize the incumbent government openly, they can give it their public approval, only to turn against it in the privacy of the voting booth. Such a possibility makes democratically elected governments sensitive to confidential opinion surveys and other indicators of private opinion.

The notion that secret balloting gives private opinion a political role is consistent with the fact that in democracies government turnovers tend to be less momentous events than the social explosions that end autocracies. In the aftermath of a democratic election that brings to power a new leadership, the outgoing government is generally not as despised as was the Czechoslovak government of Husák. Nor are the subsequent changes in direction as significant as those that might follow a revolution. A British election won by the opposition is ordinarily followed by changes in economic policy; but these are minor compared with the massive transformation initiated by the first post-communist government of Czechoslovakia.

It would be a mistake, however, to conclude that whenever public and private opinion differ a democratically elected government is more responsive to the latter. Elections decide not specific issues but the deciders. In the words of Robert Dahl, "all an election reveals is the first preferences of some citizens among the candidates standing for office," for a majority of first preferences among candidates does not imply a majority of first preferences on any particular issue.[16] Consequently, a party in power can work against private opinion on numerous issues and still cruise to victory in the next election. Imagine a society concerned with four issues. Even if the government's policies go against private opinion on the first three, it might win reelection on account of its stand on the fourth.

Political parties that offend private opinion on large numbers of issues are all the more likely to retain or extend their electoral strength insofar as the political system limits voter choice. Electoral battles are generally fought on narrow ranges of issues, with differences on details blown up to look like major differences in philosophy. On most issues that matter to citizens, rivals take the same positions, often by tacitly agreeing to focus on trivialities. By implication, voters offended by the incumbent party's stand on certain issues might find the platforms of the challengers equally unattractive. Their realistic choices might be limited to candidates committed to publicly popular positions.

Candidate similarity is ensured by the control that powerful pressure groups exert on the process of party nomination. Potential candidates who challenge major pressure groups quickly draw fire, hurting their chances of winning. For this reason, serious candidates tend to have committed themselves to positions that conform to public opinion on many key issues, especially on ones engendering little public controversy. In the United States, no credible candidate for high national office dares to oppose government transfers to the retired; the farthest a serious candidate will go is to suggest slowing their growth or limiting subsidies to the very rich.[17] It merits repetition that a pressure group enjoys political clout to the extent that it dominates public opinion. The supporters of keeping retirement benefits at current levels constitute a formidable lobby because their cause enjoys strong public support. On issues where public opinion is divided more or less evenly, no lobby is powerful enough to stamp out differences among candidates. Thus on the hotly contested issue of abortion, one finds many prochoice candidates and many others who are prolife.

A prominent theme of Tocqueville's acclaimed book on the French Revolution is that the elected assemblies of postrevolutionary France failed to voice private opinion, much less implement its dictates. "The much vaunted 'free vote' in matters of taxation," Tocqueville says, "came to signify no more than the meaningless assent of assemblies tamed to servility and silence."[18] To make sense of his observation, one needs to recognize that French citizens did not vote directly on taxation or, for that matter, on any other issue. They went to the polls to choose representatives authorized to vote on the issues of the day. Elected representatives cast their votes openly, however, so pressure groups came to control their decisions.

Tocqueville's observation illustrates an additional problem with the claim that democratic elections accord private opinion an important role in social decision making. Legislatures elected through votes cast under cover rarely resort to secret balloting themselves. In democratic legislatures voting tends to be by acclamation, roll call, or show of hands. Each such procedure forces individual legislators to declare their positions in full public view, making them vulnerable to reprisals. Indeed, legislators who vote against a bill supported by powerful lobbies know that they will pay a high price for their displays of independence. The same pattern applies to the boards, commissions, and committees that run or oversee enterprises, agencies, schools, associations, foundations, and other organizations. Even if elected by secret ballot—many are elected by open ballot or simply appointed—such bodies reach most of their decisions through open voting. Consequently their actions reflect not just the private preferences of their members but also the prevailing social pressures.

The Rarity of Secret Balloting

The rarity of secret balloting presents a puzzle. By the very fact that electoral voting tends to be secret, we know that preference falsification is understood to be significant. Why, then, is voting generally open in legislatures and other assemblies? Given that the ostensible purpose of voting is to find out what voters want, why do the members of assemblies not insist on secrecy as a matter of course?

Most obviously, open balloting is sometimes cheaper and quicker. A committee that takes frequent votes can save itself time by relying on shows of hands. But the matter of relative cost hardly explains why open balloting is the norm in national legislatures. Many issues on which parliaments take votes are sufficiently important to justify any added expenses of secret balloting. And it is precisely on such weighty issues that preference falsification is apt to distort the vote count. In any case, in the present age of electronics secret balloting is not necessarily more expensive than open balloting. It may even be *cheaper* to have legislators cast anonymous votes by the push of a button.

A possible explanation for the rarity of secret balloting is that powerful pressure groups prefer open balloting. As the beneficiaries of the consequent preference falsification, they have much to lose from procedural changes that would allow individuals to vote without fear of retribution.

By the same logic, though, groups whose causes suffer from preference falsification should insist on secret balloting, at least on their own pet issues. Struggles over voting procedure are not unknown. A blue-ribbon panel formed by the U.S. Congress after the 1988 elections to propose budget cuts decided to meet behind closed doors, ostensibly to keep its deliberations from creating chaos in financial markets, but actually to insulate itself from political pressures. Several news organizations and a consumer advocacy group challenged the decision, and to the delight of many lobbies, a judge ordered the commission to deliberate openly.[19] Congress is empowered to exempt a commission from the open meetings requirement of federal law. Significantly, however, no member of Congress moved to grant the panel an exemption, even though some had previously acknowledged that open meetings would jeopardize support for significant budget cuts. The panel proceeded to hold open sessions, reaching no memorable decisions.

There exist sound justifications for keeping policy meetings open. Openness serves to educate the citizenry.[20] In seeking to close its meetings the panel suggested, in effect, that the educational objective could be self-defeating. Positions that would be defended in closed session might be withheld in open session. A related rationale for openness is that it allows citizens to monitor their representatives. But in the presence of social pressures that make the articulation of some positions imprudent, a representative voting openly might have a harder time serving his constituents than if he could vote by secret ballot.

In any case, there is no necessary connection between open deliberation and open voting. A panel can debate an issue openly and then vote by secret ballot. Yet if the issue is sensitive, members might refrain from proposing a secret vote. Suppose, for the sake of argument, that someone has taken the necessary first step. Obtaining the endorsement of a majority could prove impossible, because the vote on balloting procedure would be open.[21] Individuals who favor secret balloting might hide their inclinations for fear of revealing their readiness to dissent on the issue itself. In brief, the very pressures that generate misrepresentations on the substance of an issue will generate them also on the matter of voting procedure. So it is that sensitive issues—the very ones on which the form of balloting might make a huge difference—are rarely decided by secret ballot.

A telling image of the "people's republics" formed in the twentieth century is of a legislature passing a bill by a unanimous show of hands. Many individual legislators in the Soviet Union, China, and elsewhere must have entertained the thought that on critical issues secret balloting would transform voting patterns. Yet very few ever challenged the established voting procedure, doubtless because the likelihood of success was minuscule and the personal risk of demanding change enormous. In the assemblies of modern democracies, the risk is not nearly as great. No American senator who demanded a secret vote on social security would be sentenced to hard labor. One should not infer, however, that the potential cost would be negligible. The senator would invite intense attacks from the senior-citizen lobby. Hence the mere possibility of secret balloting does not guarantee its use.

On issues where public opinion happens to be divided, struggles over voting procedure are relatively more common, even in nondemocratic regimes. The reason is that people already identified with the minority have little to lose, and possibly much to gain, from proposing a secret vote.

In 1986 the Iranian Parliament was the scene of an intense debate on a bill to legalize postrevolutionary land seizures. The vocal opponents of the bill sensed that deputies were reluctant to be identified as defenders of the rich. To make it easier to vote negatively, they demanded a secret ballot. The speaker, a supporter of the bill, refused the request, insisting that deputies indicate their preferences orally. His tactic worked, in that many deputies who had expressed serious reservations in private refused to be counted as opponents. The bill passed on a close vote.[22]

In many democracies, unionization struggles often involve disagreements over voting procedure. In the United States, for instance, unions seeking recognition generally hold that authorization cards—the cards that employees sign as a show of support—provide reliable indications of employee sentiment. Employers tend to favor secret representation elections, on the grounds that employees asked to sign cards are influenced by peer pressure. Unions frequently lose representation elections in units where they enjoy a card majority.[23]

In each of the two foregoing illustrations, there are people already identified with the position likely to lose under open voting. In demanding a secret ballot, they reveal no new information about their private preferences. When public opinion is highly concentrated, however, there exist few such individuals. It is also obvious that a change in voting procedure would only serve the opposition. People who request a secret ballot are therefore suspected of holding dissenting views. Their demands *do* reveal new information about their private preferences, thus exposing them to retaliation.

John Stuart Mill supported the secret ballot in contexts where voters felt enslaved by "the mischievous power of the Few over the Many."[24] Given that he classified social pressures as an awesome source of tyranny,[25] one might expect him to have championed wider use of the secret ballot. In reality he maintained that open voting has some overriding virtues, at least in representative democracies. Openness promotes altruism, he suggested, keeping in check votes cast out of "malice," "pique," "personal rivalry," and the "prejudices of class or sect." It also fosters seriousness, because people who might have to account for their votes think carefully about what they are doing. Finally, it contributes to intellectual growth: individuals try to speak responsibly, so public discourse gains in sophistication and the citizenry becomes more knowledgeable.[26]

In advancing these propositions, Mill vastly underestimates the voting distortions that occur under open balloting.[27] The experience of the panel on the American budget shows that the fear of alienating powerful lobbies can easily overshadow the fear of substantive failure. Confirming evidence lies in the Milgram experiment, which vividly demonstrates that having the eyes of others upon oneself will not necessarily keep one from performing acts of cruelty; it is revealing that Milgram's "teachers" delivered punishments *more* readily when an authority figure was close by. As for the claim that open voting makes people consider their alternatives carefully, such a benefit could be outweighed by the induced deterioration of knowledge. The pressures that distort public opinion also distort public discourse, which is an important source of personal information. The last point will be developed later, beginning in Chapter 10.

The Principle of Tolerance and Its Frequent Violation

Secret balloting would serve no purpose if everyone were willing to put up with every offensive idea. Under such conditions of exemplary tolerance, no one would ever seek punitive actions against others for their political views. By this account, to show tolerance is to object to an idea without objecting to its expression. It is to be prepared, moreover, to live with the consequent inner tensions. Perfectly tolerant individuals would not even frown at a speaker promoting the most repulsive ideas. They might, of course, express reservations and offer alternatives. Tolerance is not apathy, indifference, or diffidence. What it requires is acceptance of the principle that no political end, however noble, justifies the suppression of an idea.[28]

No one is perfectly tolerant. Most people exhibit a readiness to censor views that are unexceptional even within their own communities. This should not come as a surprise, because, as the framers of the American Constitution recognized, tolerance is not a natural disposition. In our own century, Ortega y Gasset has characterized tolerance as a cultivated value, one that is neither inherent nor instinctive in the human personality. It is the cornerstone of a liberal worldview that proclaims a "determination to live with an enemy, and even more, with a weak enemy."[29]

Expounding on Ortega y Gasset's insight, two authors of a study on tolerance observe that "people who believe they know the 'truth' on a particular issue . . . may find it difficult to understand why they have an obligation to permit someone with a contrary (and hence obviously false) view to enjoy an equal opportunity for freedom of expression."[30] If one knows that "racists," or "killers of unborn babies," or "heathens" will say things that are erroneous, offensive, and immoral, why should one allow them to spread their views? Moreover, why should one provide a platform to dangerous groups who, if they got the chance, would deny others the right of free expression? When faced with such questions with respect to groups that *they themselves* consider a threat, even the citizens of countries with long democratic traditions betray a willingness to limit expressive liberties.

In view of the intolerant streak in the human personality, it is hardly puzzling that acts of intolerance have been common throughout history. What *is* puzzling is that tolerance has become a widely endorsed political ideal, at least in the abstract. It is puzzling, too, that democratic institutions have been adopted and preserved.

In Chapter 3, I noted that there is no reason in principle why people should refrain from turning every human concern, no matter how trivial or personal, into a political issue. The reason very few concerns actually become politicized is that the limits of cognition drastically constrain the number of matters to which one can pay attention. Herein lies, I now submit, the key to why the past few centuries have seen the emergence of tolerance as a supreme, if frequently compromised, ideal. Societies have become increasingly complex and individual fortunes increasingly interdependent. Hence we have more reason today to control one another's expressions than our ancestors did thousands of years ago. We can expect, moreover, to be affected by the expressions of many more strangers. But this rise in social interdependence has not been matched by a commensurate improvement in our cognitive faculties. We are not substantially more intelligent than our hunter-gatherer ancestors, and we find ourselves able to observe and influence just a minute fraction of the behaviors pertinent to our own happiness. Whether we like it or not, we have to limit our authority, nosiness, and activism to few of the matters of potential concern to ourselves.

The principle of tolerance amounts, then, to a recognition that it has become prohibitively costly to control public opinion in every possible context. This interpretation is consistent with the common observation that cities, whose residents remain unknown to most other residents, exhibit greater tolerance than small towns, where everyone knows everyone else.

We have not lost the urge, I repeat, to make our ends the ends of others. Equally important, our cognitive powers are not so restrictive as to make us abandon all political activity. These observations explain why many matters that could be treated as personal end up in the political realm, and also why there is never a shortage of political issues. On politicized matters tolerance is *not* the norm: people commonly impose costs on public dissenters.

The foregoing explanation reconciles the great support that freedom of speech enjoys in the abstract with poll results that find large majorities prepared to restrict, if necessary with government help, the expressive freedoms of anyone who threatens their cherished values, objectives, or institutions. People are receptive to the principle of tolerance because it rationalizes and legitimizes unavoidable patterns of behavior. At the same time, where they feel a need to control the expressions of others, they readily display intolerance.

Precisely because tolerance is not a natural human trait, democracy requires legal safeguards for expressive freedoms. At the very least, it requires a ban on physical reprisals against political minorities. But why should a *general* prohibition gain acceptance? If it is instinctive to silence the holders of "dangerous" views, why would one grant them freedom of expression? Expressive liberties might gain recognition when large numbers see that an ideological war would cause great devastation without any guarantee of eliminating the troublesome differences. A stalemate among equally matched rivals could thus generate expressive protections as an alternative to potentially disastrous conflict.[31]

Such an interpretation is consistent with the history of the American colonies. The most divisive issue in the colonies was religion. Each colony promoted one particular orthodoxy and fought other orthodoxies. Describing seventeenth-century New England, a historian writes:

> Those who did not hold with the ideals entertained by the righteous ... had every liberty ... to stay away from New England. If they did come, they were expected to keep their opinions to themselves; if they discussed them in public or attempted to act upon them they were exiled; if they came back, they were cast out again; if they still

came back, as did four Quakers, they were hanged on Boston Common. And from a Puritan point of view, it was good riddance.[32]

Colonial intolerance was driven by the view that religious diversity is menacing and that one person's "bad religion" will impair the "good religion" of another. Most individual colonists were unwilling, of course, to compromise their own religious beliefs merely in the interest of religious unity. An equilibrium came into being where communities clung to their own canons of orthodoxy. Observing the established balance, eminent colonists realized that their own communities could lose a struggle over the correct orthodoxy and that the only war they might win would be inordinately costly. In self-interest, they decided to accept the status quo, effectively endorsing the right to disagree on the relative merits of the competing orthodoxies. And to stabilize their "live and let live" arrangement, they agreed to a separation of church and state. Such separation, they hoped, would keep government officials from turning their powers against particular orthodoxies.[33]

In terms of the diagrams in Chapter 4, a political stalemate is an interior equilibrium, and religious homogeneity characterizes a corner equilibrium. The colonists sensed the existence of multiple equilibria and also that one or more equilibria would bring damage to their own religions. They agreed to constitutional safeguards as a way of blocking paths to the disagreeable equilibria. And in return for such insurance, they conceded to the blockage of paths leading to their favored equilibria.

The Fragility of Democracy

There are two ways to perpetuate established democratic rights. One can devise institutions that protect the right to speak, or one can indoctrinate individuals with respect for expressive diversity. The U.S. Constitution pursues the former strategy. Treating intolerance as ineradicable, it grants the individual a broad array of expressive freedoms. At the same time, it lowers the likelihood of government despotism through a separation of powers among the legislative, judicial, and executive branches of government. The framers expected the latter provision to make leaders check one another's intolerance. "The great security against a gradual concentration of the several powers in the same department," wrote Madison, "consists in giving to those who administer each department, the necessary constitutional means, and personal motives, to resist encroachments of the others. . . . Ambition must be made to counteract ambition."[34]

The institutional strategy of the framers has succeeded in protecting religious liberties. It has also protected the expressive rights of minorities in nonreligious contexts. To be sure, the original Constitution did not extend protections to all minorities. Most tragically, in legitimizing slavery it denied basic freedoms to blacks. But the expressive rights of diverse minorities have enjoyed protection, with the government upholding even the rights of widely despised nonconformists. Official protections extended to flag burners and to Nazi marchers are two examples from recent times.

There is a distinction between a right and the exercise of that right, however. The pressure of public opinion may make minorities refrain from exercising their constitutional rights to dissent. As a practical matter, institutional checks and balances do not even guarantee that *majorities* will exercise their expressive rights. Even without government coercion, majorities might submit to the wishes of vociferous minorities. Protections against government tyranny do not prevent societies from tyrannizing themselves through the force of public opinion.

In any case, democratic protections against government tyranny are never fixed in stone. As noted earlier, in exceptionally threatening circumstances they are apt to be restricted, even removed. It follows that a measure of agreement on fundamentals will facilitate the emergence and preservation of democratic rights. Giovanni Sartori finds, in this connection, "overwhelming evidence that unless a democracy succeeds in creating, over time, a basic consensus, it performs as a difficult and fragile democracy."[35] Where such a consensus is lacking, democracy is liable to be partial and susceptible to breakdown. If one of the religions prevalent in the American colonies had been Wahhabi Islam, the militant sect of modern Arabia, the framers of the Constitution would probably not have been as eager to extend religious freedom to *all* Americans. Although counterfactuals can never be proven, Wahhabi Americans would probably have been treated differently from, say, Presbyterians. Nor would Americans have had much trouble rationalizing the double standard. Recall how, two centuries later, McCarthyism received broad support under the pretext of an imminent danger to basic liberties.

Turkey adopted a democratic form of government in 1946, partly to join the Western military alliance for protection against Soviet expansionism. Turkish democracy has been a restricted form of democracy, in that "extremist" political causes, notably communism, Islamic fundamentalism, and Kurdish separatism, have faced government suppression. Most Turks, including many Westernizers, have rationalized these limits on the grounds that they are not obligated to facilitate the revocation of their own liberties. In Algeria, analogous reasoning led the army to cancel, in January 1992, the country's first democratic elections. The Islamic Salvation Front, which had promised an Islamic state within a year, was expected to win handily.[36] Although part of the Front had promoted freedom of speech, a militant faction was promoting the suppression of "un-Islamic" expression. Apprehensions about the militant faction made many promoters of democracy welcome the army's plainly undemocratic intervention.

A stable democracy requires general agreement on fundamentals because such a consensus gives people the security to grant others expressive freedoms. Yet even with broad agreement on fundamentals, as when a vast majority rejects communism categorically, issues of lesser importance might become the focus of widespread intolerance. Some evidence from the United States has already been given. Much more lies ahead.

Thus far, I have developed a framework for investigating the impact of preference falsification. Starting with an inquiry into preference falsification itself, I went on to examine the social process whereby members of society jointly create the pressures that shape public opinion. I showed that there may exist several self-sustaining public opinions, and that the one adopted need not be that which is closest to the underlying private opinion. This chapter has shown that disparities between private and public opinion are not limited to nondemocratic regimes. The book now turns to the long-term effects of preference falsification. Chapters ahead examine its effects on the pace and direction of social change, and on the creation and destruction of knowledge.

II

Inhibiting Change

6

Collective Conservatism

Societies routinely adopt laws, regulations, and policies that they then retain indefinitely. At any particular time, therefore, a social order incorporates multitudes of decisions inherited from the past. This characterization applies both to societies perceived as inert and to ones considered exceptionally dynamic. It applies even to those that promote the notion of "permanent revolution." No community keeps all of its social arrangements constantly open to change.[1]

Some observed social continuities reflect the fact that a measure of social stability is indispensable. If the social order were highly fluid, in the sense that any decision or agreement could be changed instantaneously, people would live in great uncertainty regarding the future, and their incentives to learn, invent, save, and invest would be impaired. Certain continuities help protect critical expectations, and for this they are tolerated, if not actively sought. Consider the law that affords an American president four years in office. Even though this law makes it difficult to oust a president who proves incompetent, it is valued for the protection it gives expectations concerning American government.

Other continuities arise from obstacles to implementing change. One impediment, explored in Albert Hirschman's *Exit, Voice, and Loyalty,* consists of individual decisions to "exit": menacing elements of the status quo survive as people capable of making a difference opt to abandon the relevant decision-making group.[2] Another such mechanism lies at the heart of Mancur Olson's book on patterns of economic growth, *The Rise and Decline of Nations:* unpopular choices persist because the many who support change are less well organized than the few who are opposed.[3]

Here I argue that preference falsification is a complementary, yet more elementary, reason for the persistence of unwanted social choices. Hirschman's exit is a form of public identification with change, as is his "voice," which he defines as vocal protest. Preference falsification is often cheaper than escape, and it avoids the risks inherent in public protest. Frequently, therefore, it is the initial response of people who become disenchanted with the status quo. As for Olson's theory, it posits an identifiable potential opposition to the status quo. Yet preference falsification may cause everyone, including those privately supportive of change, to underestimate the extent of popular dissatisfaction. Such misinformation is a more basic obstacle to change than the organizational weaknesses of readily recognizable reformers. It obscures, even conceals, both the desirability and the possibility of reform.

Like the mechanisms examined by Olson and Hirschman, the one described ahead constitutes a vehicle of *collective conservatism,* as opposed to *personal conservatism.* Collective conservatism entails resistance to change on the part of a community; personal conservatism is an attitude against reform on the part of individuals. The latter is not a necessary condition of the former. A community might display a collective attachment to the status quo even if none of its members has any affinity for the status quo as such.

This chapter focuses on exploring a general mechanism, building on insights presented in Chapter 4. Concrete examples are kept to a minimum, because the next three chapters offer detailed case studies.

The Role of History in the Persistence of Public Opinion

Let us return to the political arena depicted in the top panel of Figure 4.5, reproduced here as panel A of Figure 6.1. Recall that we have two pressure groups trying to pull public opinion toward 0 and 100. The S-shaped propagation curve records, for each possible expectation of mean public opinion, the percentage of society that will actually support the position 100. It crosses the diagonal from above at two values of public opinion, which represent stable equilibria. Expectations below 60 drive mean public opinion to 20, and those above 60 drive it to 100.

At any particular equilibrium, public opinion is self-reproducing because, period after period, everyone makes the same choice. This is not a sign of personal conservatism. Individual behavior shows persistence because past expectations and realizations of public opinion govern present reputational incentives, not because some person or group attaches special significance to the status quo. In equilibrium, the expected public opinion is identical to the most recent realization. The individual reasons as follows: "Yesterday I expected 20 percent of society to express a preference for 100 and the rest for 0. My expectations were confirmed. Chances are that the shares will be the same today, so I should not alter my public preference." Such reasoning leaves individual public preferences, and thus public opinion, unchanged.

In short, public opinion shows persistence because its realization in the immediate past shapes present expectations. Had the recent past been different, individuals would have formed other expectations, and their choices might have differed. This is not to say that the *magnetism of recent history* is the sole factor in the persistence of public opinion. Another relevant factor is the *magnetism of the prevailing equilibrium*—the incumbent equilibrium's capacity to reshape expectations of public opinion in its own image. Even if history were forgotten, the same equilibrium could form and then persist indefinitely.

To distinguish and weight the two factors, it will help to conduct a quick thought experiment in which individuals make expressive choices *without* guidance from history. By comparing this experimental outcome with the outcome when individuals do use historical information, we will be able to identify, and even quantify, the impact of past public opinion on present public opinion. The experiment will bring precision to the role of preference falsification as an obstacle to change. It will also lay the groundwork for my later argument that preference falsification produces politically stabilizing shifts in private opinion.

Imagine that, with public opinion settled at 20, every member of society suddenly forgets all past expectations and realizations of public opinion. Before the memory loss, people's expectations were self-fulfilling and thus self-reproducing. Now that their memories are

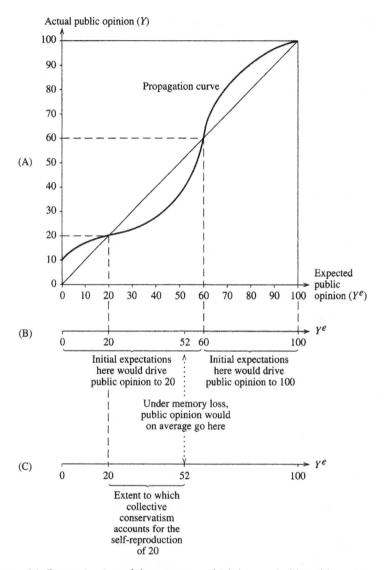

Figure 6.1 Determination of the extent to which history holds public opinion at 20. Panel B provides an experiment to abstract from the role of history. Using the outcome of that experiment, panel C then measures collective conservatism.

empty, they have no reason to hold any particular expectation. If they thus treat all realizations of public opinion as equally likely,[4] there is a 60 percent probability that they will form an expectation below 60, in which case public opinion will settle at 20, as indicated in panel B of Figure 6.1. And there is a 40 percent probability that they will form an expectation above 60, in which case public opinion will go to 100. If this experiment is repeated many times, where *on average* will public opinion be located? The answer requires weighting the two possible outcomes by their respective probabilities: (60 percent × 20) + (40 percent × 100) = 52.

Turn now to panel C, where this calculation is used to quantify the role of history in holding public opinion at 20. If the propagation curve stays fixed after the equilibrium gets established, public opinion will remain at 20 indefinitely. In any subsequent period, people will remember that their previous expectation was self-fulfilling, and their consequent decisions will keep public opinion undisturbed. Period after period, that is, public opinion will be 20. As panel C indicates, the equilibrium of 20 differs by 32 units from the average realization of public opinion under the hypothetical condition of memory loss. Because public opinion can take on values between 0 and 100, this distance corresponds to 32 percent of the full range of public opinion.

The figure of 32 percent provides a measure of collective conservatism—a measure, that is, of the grip of history.[5] It indicates that the prevailing public opinion owes 32 percent of its persistence to the magnetism of recent history, and the remaining 68 percent to that of the prevailing equilibrium. The source of the latter magnetism is that initial expectations below 60 produce, whatever the content of people's memories, adjustments in the direction of 20.

The measure of collective conservatism that I have just presented runs from 0 to 100 percent. For any established public opinion, the higher the degree of collective conservatism, the more it owes its persistence to history.

To complete the exercise, I shall now quantify the collective conservatism inherent in the other stable equilibrium of Figure 6.1. Without memory loss, public opinion remains indefinitely at 100. But with the memory loss, public opinion goes, for reasons already developed, on average to 52. The difference between the two figures is 100 − 52 = 48. By the logic developed earlier, the degree of collective conservatism inherent in the persistence of public opinion is 48 percent. There are two reasons why the degree of collective conservatism turns out greater in this case than in the previous one. First, 100 is farther away from 52 than is 20. This implies that people's memories of public opinion exert a greater influence on their choices of a public preference. And second, 100 attracts a narrower range of expectations than does 20, which implies that in the absence of history its chances of being selected would be relatively lower.

Chapter 4 showed that in the presence of multiple equilibria small events may determine which equilibrium gets selected. A new insight is that the small events responsible for the establishment of a particular equilibrium are not averaged away over time. Precisely because history *does* contribute to the persistence of a public opinion, once an event has tipped public opinion toward one equilibrium or the other, its impact need not be undone by subsequent events. Suppose that after public opinion settles at 20, something creates the impression that public opinion has jumped to 30. According to Figure 6.1, such an expectational shift would galvanize reverse adjustments toward 20. The disturbance would thus be self-correcting, and so the events responsible for establishing the equilibrium would retain their influence indefinitely.[6]

Stable Public Opinion in the Face of Changing Private Opinion

Thus far nothing has been said about changes in private preferences. The determinants of such changes will be explored further on. What needs recognition here is a point introduced in Chapter 4: shifts in private preferences alter individual thresholds and, hence, society's propagation curve.

With public opinion at rest at 100, let private opinion shift dramatically toward 0. The propagation curve thus moves down, as shown in panel A of Figure 6.2. There are still two stable equilibria. But the lower one has fallen from 20 to 0, and its magnetism has grown. In this situation, panel B indicates, any expectation up to 90 would drive mean public opinion to 0. Yet public opinion itself will not necessarily move, for the established public opinion of 100 remains an equilibrium.

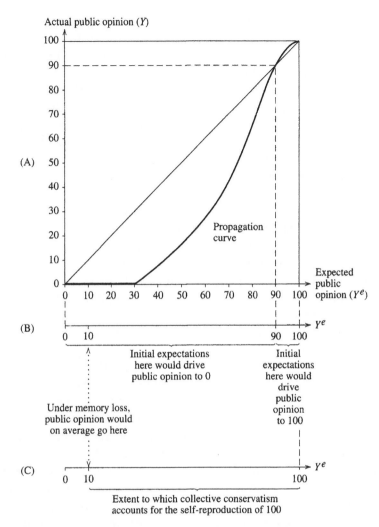

Figure 6.2 With public opinion at 100, private opinion shifts toward 0, pushing the propagation curve downward. Public opinion remains at 100, largely under the influence of history.

If the expected public opinion happens to change, there may be some defections. But the defectors will quickly return to the fold as long as the expected public opinion remains above 90. Only if the belief develops that more than 10 percent have already defected will enough people actually switch to activate a downward bandwagon toward the new equilibrium. But the formation of such a belief can be blocked indefinitely, because individuals would rather not be the first to challenge the status quo. Under the prevailing reputational incentives, people will not switch for fear that others will not, and others will not for fear that *they* will not.

Public opinion may thus outlive the circumstances that created it. When new conditions make a once-popular decision appear to have been a mistake, or when a once-functional structure becomes patently dysfunctional, public opinion will not necessarily adjust. Such frozen conformity in the face of increasing private opposition implies rising collective conservatism, as can be seen through the experiment devised above. Under the memory-loss scenario, public opinion goes on average to (90 percent $\times$ 0) + (10 percent $\times$ 100) = 10. Without memory loss, public opinion stays at 100. The difference between the two figures, in relation to the range of public opinion, is 90 percent. This exceeds the figure of 48 percent we found for the higher equilibrium in Figure 6.1. There are two reasons why the degree of collective conservatism is now higher. First, the alternative to the status quo is relatively lower: 0, as opposed to 20. And second, a relatively wider range of expectations would drive public opinion away from 100.

These exercises have demonstrated that the contribution of history to the persistence of public opinion may vary. But in every case that history matters, the reason is the same. Individuals preserve an established public opinion in trying to be prudent—in endeavoring, that is, to select their public preferences at least partly on the basis of reputational incentives inferred from the history of public opinion.

The Spiral of Prudence

In a light-hearted commentary on academia, Francis Cornford once suggested that "nothing is ever done until every one is convinced that it ought to be done, and has been convinced so long that it is now time to do something else."[7] The just-discussed mechanism offers a possible reason why widely desired changes might fail to materialize. When large numbers of people conceal their misgivings about the status quo, individuals may consider their own disenchantments exceptional. They may think that they are in conflict with the rest of society and hence that by being truthful they would only invite trouble. Through preference falsification, they may thus hold in place structures that they could, if only they acted together, easily change.

The perceived conflict would be phony conflict, of course, not real conflict based on genuine disagreement. Jerry Harvey notes in this connection that organizations suffer less from inability to manage their internal disagreements than from failure to manage their agreements.[8] His observation also applies to much larger collectivities. Entire nations can torment themselves by failing to recognize and act upon their broad agreements on reform.

The process whereby reformists capable of instituting change jointly sustain the status quo has been characterized as the "spiral of silence."[9] This concept captures the critical role of the interdependencies among individual decisions. Still, it is inadequate, if not misleading. In actual contexts people reluctant to publicize their disenchantments do not just slip into silence. Were they all to stop talking, they would end up revealing their private preferences. To make their efforts at preference falsification convincing, they tend to take steps to affirm their support for the status quo—as when an anticommunist Soviet citizen signs a letter condemning a dissident whom she admires. Such personally prudent acts of affirmation may result in massive pluralistic ignorance with regard to private opinion. The term *spiral of prudence* is a superior alternative, therefore, to the spiral of silence. It accommodates the notion that in trying to escape the costs of truthfulness individuals can go beyond self-censorship.

Collective Conservatism across Generations

In the illustrations above the population was fixed. Yet in practice communities renew themselves through births and deaths. And new cohorts may differ from earlier cohorts in terms of their private preferences. To see the implications for conservatism, let us reconsider the two figures of this chapter, thinking of the depicted shift in the propagation curve as resulting from the replacement of an old generation by a new generation with generally lower private preferences. According to Figure 6.2, if the new generation were to start the collective choice process from scratch, mean public opinion would go to 0 with a probability of 90 percent and to 100 with a probability of only 10 percent.

In practice, however, no generation enjoys the luxury of restarting the political process. Its members enter the political arena at different times, all facing a set of issues on which a public opinion has already formed. Imagine, then, that members of the new generation all arrive after public opinion has settled at 100. The propagation curve that they form is that of Figure 6.2. Each will find it personally optimal to support 100, even though many would rather support 0. In the process, they will reproduce the public opinion established by their forebears.

There are two additional lessons here. First, a generation may continue to influence public opinion long after its days are over. Second, an established public opinion may get carried into the future by generations that bear no responsibility for its inception.

Conservatism, Traditionalism, Persistence, Rigidity

Like change, the absence of change is so common that a plethora of terms exist to convey its meaning. These terms tend to be used imprecisely, however, and often in more than one sense. Such terminological looseness is at once a cause and an effect of the lack of sophistication in our thinking on social evolution. Semantic confusion hinders intellectual progress. A few definitions will prepare us for later refinements.

I have been using the term *conservatism* to connote a decision's causal dependence on the status quo. In everyday usage the term is commonly associated with the principle of laissez-faire and the agenda of the political "right." Here, no such association is assumed. A conservative society is one that conserves, and what it conserves depends on the particulars of its social legacy. When a society overthrows its long-standing communist dictatorship, it becomes less conservative, not more. An analogous point was once made by Friedrich Hayek at a time when he was under attack as a conservative for his advocacy of basic liberties. In a tract entitled "Why I Am Not a Conservative," he observed that state interventionism, the butt of his critical works, is the hallmark of modern government. It follows, he went on, that the epithet conservative best suited his critics.[10]

Like conservatism, *traditionalism* connotes a causal relationship. But there is a difference: conservatism conveys an attachment to the status quo, traditionalism to *any* social structure believed to have existed. Traditionalism does not imply conservatism, because the object of attachment could be a structure that has ceased to exist. In fact, it may be a structure only imagined to have existed. When Pakistan bans interest in an effort to reinstitute economic relations thought to have existed among the first Muslims in seventh-century Arabia, it displays traditionalism but not conservatism. It is trying not to conserve an existing institution but, rather, to revive one presumed to have existed in the distant past.

I have been using the terms *continuity* and *persistence* in an entirely descriptive sense to convey uninterrupted existence. Accordingly, the statement "elections have been a persistent feature of British politics" represents nothing more than an observation. Other terms describe breaks with the past. They include *change, shift, adjustment, transformation, reform,* and *revolution.* The last two convey information about the size and speed of change.

A term that I have not yet had occasion to use, *rigidity,* carries comparative significance: it conveys slowness or incompleteness of change, relative to some standard. To characterize a society as rigid is to claim that under ideal or normal conditions it would have changed more, or that it changes more slowly than others. The term *flexibility* captures the opposite concept.

To see how the foregoing terms complement one another, consider the following illustration. Countries *A* and *B* institute import controls to protect their local industries. The consequent weakening of competitive pressures makes their industries increasingly inefficient. *A* responds by lifting its controls, but *B* stays the course for a while longer. By definition, *B* displays rigidity relative to *A.* Without further information, however, we cannot say anything about causation. It could be that *B*'s controls enjoy the full support of private opinion and that their retention reflects no attachment to the status quo itself. In this case the persistence of *B*'s controls would not be a manifestation of conservatism.

It bears recognition that the present notion of conservatism relies only on the preferences and choices of the relevant decision maker. The preferences of outsiders do not enter the picture. If *B* were displaying conservatism, this would have nothing to do with the preferences of people belonging to other societies.

Persistent Inefficiency

In certain segments of the social sciences, the persistence of a social structure is regarded as prima facie evidence of its "efficiency." Used in the sense of Pareto, the term *efficiency* refers to the absence of opportunities to benefit a subset of society without harming another.[11] Analysts who equate persistence with efficiency rest their case on two claims. When a structure is inefficient, they say, this rarely remains a secret. And evidence of an inefficiency induces quick changes in the individual choices that sustain it.[12] In other words, every decision worth making is made without delay; no opportunity for social improvement remains unexploited for long.

Such optimism is neither new nor limited to scholarship. In lay discourse it finds expression in such maxims as "right will prevail" and "the triumph of evil is short-lived." Medieval Muslims captured the idea through a saying attributed to the Prophet Muhammad: "My people shall never agree on error."[13] For their part, the Europeans paid homage to the proverb *"Vox populi vox Dei"*—the voice of the people is the voice of God.[14] Yet the efficiency claim that is implicit in such aphorisms has never enjoyed unanimous acceptance. Some old proverbs convey pessimism about the wisdom of collective decisions. They include *"Vox populi vox diaboli"*—the voice of the people is the voice of the devil—and *"Vox populi vox stultorum"*—the voice of the people is the voice of stupidity.[15]

The model under consideration does not suggest that public opinion—the voice of the people—necessarily breeds inefficiency. In the presence of multiple feasible outcomes the chosen equilibrium may well be one without a socially preferable alternative. Yet nothing precludes the selection of a suboptimal equilibrium, and an established inefficiency may endure indefinitely. Of the two stable equilibria in Figure 6.2, the one at 0 may yield an outcome that is socially preferable to its alternative. Indeed, it may be the case that individuals who prefer 0 could compensate everyone else and still come out ahead.

Even under this condition, however, 100 can remain an equilibrium indefinitely.

In principle, a socially inefficient choice can endure because of people's *deficiency* in pursuing their personal interests—a deficiency caused, for instance, by institutional constraints. This chapter has shown, however, that the cause of lasting inefficiency may also be people's *proficiency* in pursuing their interests. When an inefficiency is sustained by preference falsification, the source of the problem is not some incapacity to maximize personal utility. Rather, it is the capacity to pursue one's needs. The catch is that when multitudes of self-regarding individual efforts get aggregated into a public opinion, the resulting individual utilities may fall short of their potential. This theme will be developed further in Chapter 17.

If one objective of scholarship is to find causal relationships among variables that might otherwise appear unrelated, another is to establish that identified links show up in diverse temporal, geographical, and functional contexts. In this spirit, I will now demonstrate, through three case studies taken up in separate chapters, the outlined theory's generality.

7

The Obstinacy of Communism

Communist parties came to power in Russia, and then in Eastern Europe and elsewhere, vowing that "scientific socialism" would pioneer new dimensions of freedom, eliminate exploitation, vest political power in the masses, and raise living standards to unprecedented heights—all while the state was withering away. They did not deliver on these promises. Under their stewardship, communism came to symbolize repression, censorship, militarism, red tape, and economic backwardness.

The failures of communism prompted a few Soviet and East European citizens to criticize official policies and institutions. Such dissidents, as they became known in the West, expressed their frustrations through clandestine self-publications *(samizdat)* and writings published abroad *(tamizdat)*.[1] Given the chasm between the rhetoric of communism and its achievements, the existence of an opposition is easily understood. Harder to comprehend is the rarity of public dissent prior to the collapse of the communist political monopoly in 1989. The crushed uprisings of earlier years—notably, East Berlin in 1953, Hungary in 1956, and Czechoslovakia in 1968—are exceptions that prove the rule. For most of several decades, most members of communist-ruled societies displayed a remarkable tolerance for tyranny and inefficiency. They remained docile, submissive, and even outwardly supportive of the status quo.

This subservience is attributable partly to punishments meted out by the communist establishment. In the heyday of communism, a person speaking out against the political leadership or in favor of some reform could expect to suffer harassment, demotion, and imprisonment. Even worse horrors befell millions of suspected opponents. Think of the forced-labor camps of the Gulag Archipelago, the show trials of Stalin, and the liquidations carried out by intolerant leaders under the pretext of historical necessity. "We can only be right with and by the Party," proclaimed a theoretician of communism, "for history has provided no other way of being in the right."[2] Such thinking served to rationalize horrible crimes against nonconformists.

The Wellspring of the Communist System's Stability

Yet brute terror is only one factor in the obstinacy of communism. The system and its instruments of violence were supported by a pervasive culture of mendacity. Individuals routinely applauded speakers they disliked, joined organizations whose mission they opposed, ostracized dissidents they admired, and followed orders they considered nonsensical, unjust, or inhuman, among other manifestations of consent and accommodation. "The lie," wrote Alexander Solzhenitsyn in the early 1970s, "has been incorporated into the state system as the vital link holding everything together, with billions of tiny fasteners, several dozen to each man."[3] He then asked rhetorically, "What does it mean, *not to lie?*" It means "*not saying what you don't think,* and that includes not whispering, not opening your mouth, not raising your hand, not casting your vote, not feigning a smile, not lending your presence, not standing up, and not cheering."[4]

In an essay entitled "The Power of the Powerless," published clandestinely in 1979, Václav Havel speaks of a greengrocer who places in his window, among the onions and carrots, the slogan "Workers of the World, Unite!" What, wonders Havel, is the greengrocer's motive?

> Is he genuinely enthusiastic about the idea of unity among the workers of the world? Is his enthusiasm so great that he feels an irrepressible impulse to acquaint the public with his ideals? Has he really given more than a moment's thought to how such a unification might occur and what it would mean?

Havel's answer is worth quoting at length:

The overwhelming majority of shopkeepers never think about the slogans they put in their windows, nor do they use them to express their real opinions. That poster was delivered to our greengrocer from the enterprise headquarters along with the onions and carrots. He put them all into the window simply because it has been done that way for years, because everyone does it, and because that is the way it has to be. If he were to refuse, there could be trouble. He could be reproached for not having the proper "decoration" in his window; someone might even accuse him of disloyalty. He does it because these things must be done if one is to get along in life.[5]

Our greengrocer displays the assigned slogan not to communicate a social ideal but to signal his preparedness to conform to the political status quo. By removing it—or worse, replacing it with the slogan, "Workers of the World, Eat Onions and Carrots!"—he would expose himself to charges of subversion.

The greengrocer's prudence has an unintended consequence: reinforcement of the perception that society is at least publicly behind the Party. In effect, his conformism becomes a factor in the willingness of other greengrocers to promote the unity of the world's workers. Moreover, it pressures farmers, miners, artists, writers, and bureaucrats to continue doing and saying the things expected of *them*.

Efforts to prove one's loyalty to the political status quo often took more tragic forms than the display of a well-worn Marxist slogan. Consider the case of Anna Akhmatova, who, throughout the 1920s and 1930s, composed moving poems on love and religion. For her free-spiritedness she was denounced as "bourgeois and aristocratic," banned from publishing, and subjected to material hardship. When she remained defiant, her son was arrested, tortured, and forced to confess that his mother had instructed him to assassinate a certain official. Her resolve broken, she recanted in verse:

> Where Stalin is, there too are freedom
> Peace and earth's grandeur.[6]

Countless other Soviet and East European intellectuals endured punishments for refusing to build their careers on communist apologetics. Most of the survivors went on to accommodate the demands imposed on them. The poet Aleksander Wat recalls how he responded to persecution: "I acted like a coward. I lied. I knew that they would arrest me, that [my family] would go under. I was trembling in my boots. I pretended that, yes, I had regained my faith in communism."[7]

One must not infer that the pressures on intellectuals came solely from the Party. They came also from other intellectuals who, to stay on good terms with the regime, refrained from defending their officially condemned colleagues and even participated in their vilification. Scores of renowned writers joined the campaign against Boris Pasternak, blacklisted for producing *Doctor Zhivago,* a novel they would have been proud to have written themselves. When the Writers' Union moved to denounce Pasternak as an enemy of the Soviet Union, the vote was unanimous—although a few writers found it convenient to be in the washroom during the open balloting. We now know that many Soviet intellectuals suffered silently for participating, actively or passively, in a campaign they found disgraceful. Their participation testifies to the strength of the pressures they all helped to create and sustain.[8]

In 1977, a group of Czechoslovak intellectuals established a loose association, Charter 77, dedicated to the basic rights that Czechoslovakia agreed to respect by signing the Helsinki accords of 1975. The government launched a campaign against the association and detained its leaders.[9] In the course of the campaign millions denounced Charter 77 by issuing statements of condemnation, sending hate letters to newspapers, and ostracizing its signatories. Many citizens participated in betrayal of their inner selves, simply to convince the regime of their loyalty.

Some participants in this campaign may have seen Charter 77 as a menacing organization bent on tarnishing Czechoslovakia's image. Likewise, some of Pasternak's critics may have considered it irresponsible for a novelist to dwell on the blemishes of early Soviet history; and some others may have had motives other than a desire to please the communist establishment, for instance, jealousy or professional competition. Members of communist-ruled societies turned on each other even in the absence of personal motives, however.

Citizens of communist societies understood that, when under attack from authorities, they could not count on friends, not even on close friends with similar private views. In Poland's relatively relaxed decade of the 1980s, a schoolteacher who criticized her headmistress in a faculty meeting received no support from her colleagues. Yet later she learned that they were "very glad that the headmistress had heard the truth." Had she vocalized her criticisms at an earlier date, the schoolteacher suggests, she would have been fired from the school under a barrage of public criticism from her own colleagues. They might still have supported her in private, but in front of the headmistress they would have insisted that she be "tamed."[10]

Describing the Soviet Union under Stalin, Leszek Kołakowski observes that a common requirement for survival was talebearing. People earned the right to be left alone and to join the privileged ruling class by spying on, and destroying, their neighbors, friends, and co-workers. Multitudes thus "became accessories to crime for the sake of personal advancement."[11] At a later date, about 20,000 secret police officers and 150,000 informers were on the payroll of the Czechoslovak Ministry of the Interior. Additionally, several hundred thousand people spied regularly on their acquaintances without pay. In total, up to 5 percent of the population served the regime as paid or unpaid informants.[12] In East Germany, about 300,000 people informed for the secret police; at any one time, as many as one East German in fifty was spying for pay.[13] But such figures do not begin to capture the extent of collaboration with the regime. In one way or another, almost everyone took part in the punishment of targeted citizens.

Let us return to the story of the greengrocer. Havel asks us to "imagine that one day something in our greengrocer snaps and he stops putting up the slogans." The greengrocer also "stops voting in elections he knows are a farce"; he "begins to say what he really thinks at political meetings"; and he "even finds the strength in himself to express solidarity with those whom his conscience commands him to support." In short, he makes "an attempt to *live within the truth*."[14] Here are the likely consequences:

> [The greengrocer] will be relieved of his post as manager of the shop and transferred to the warehouse. His pay will be reduced. His hopes for a holiday in Bulgaria will evaporate. His children's access to higher education will be threatened. His superiors will harass him and his fellow workers will wonder about him. Most of those who apply these sanctions, however, will not do so from any authentic inner conviction but simply under pressure from conditions, the same conditions that once pressured the greengrocer to display the official slogans. They will persecute the greengrocer either because it

is expected of them, or to demonstrate their loyalty, or simply as part of the general panorama, to which belongs an awareness that this is how situations of this sort are dealt with, that this, in fact, is how things are always done, particularly if one is not to become suspect oneself.[15]

The brilliance of this parable lies in its insights into the pressures that kept individuals loyal to their inefficient, tyrannical regimes. Official repression met with the approval of ordinary citizens. Indeed, it was predicated on their complicity. By falsifying their preferences and helping to discipline dissenters, citizens jointly sustained a system that many found abominable. In Havel's own words, the crucial "line of conflict" thus ran not between the Party and the people but "through each person," for everyone was "both a victim and a supporter of the system."[16]

Havel's observation found vivid expression in a banner hung, after the fall of the Berlin Wall, above the altar in an East German church: "I am Cain *and* Abel."[17] The implied intrapersonal conflict is rooted, of course, in the clash between the need for self-assertion and that for social acceptance. Under communism, East European and Soviet citizens tended to resolve the clash in favor of social acceptance. In avoiding open battles with their oppressive regimes, they acquiesced to battle silently with themselves. Most achieved a measure of outer security, though at the expense of inner peace.

Thus for decades mendacity formed the wellspring of the communist system's stability. But for widespread preference falsification, the communist regimes of the Soviet bloc would have faced persistently significant opposition, and they would have lacked the power to resist political and social reforms.

Fear, Pluralistic Ignorance, and Powerlessness

Soviet and East European citizens sought refuge in preference falsification partly for material benefits and partly for fear of punishment. Until the 1960s common forms of punishment included execution, torture, imprisonment, and harm to one's relatives.[18] Moreover, one could be penalized for a trifling offense such as failure to show up at a Party-sponsored event. A Polish sociologist speaks of a manager who kept a record of people who skipped Party events and then stripped them of their bonuses.[19] Even one's gestures, tone of voice, or choice of a necktie could be taken as a sign of disloyalty. One could get in trouble, observes Czesław Miłosz, for "a smile that appears at the wrong moment" or "a glance that is not all it should be."[20] A 1949 issue of the Soviet publication *Oktyabr* featured the following instruction:

> One must not content oneself with merely paying attention to *what* is being said for that may well be in complete harmony with the Party programme. One must pay attention also to the *manner*—to the sincerity, for example, with which a schoolmistress recites a poem the authorities regard as doubtful, or the pleasure revealed by a critic who goes into detail about a play he professes to condemn.[21]

Not that people were entirely defenseless against unfortunate slips in demeanor. They could compensate for inadvertent infractions through ceaseless displays of loyalty. For example, they could refer at every opportunity to the Soviet Union's achievements, carry Marxist classics under their arm, hum revolutionary songs, and speak of the failures of capitalism.[22]

Beginning in the 1960s, the degree of repression declined. Fewer people were executed or tortured, and it became increasingly uncommon to be punished merely for objectionable demeanor. Havel's disobedient greengrocer gets demoted, harassed, and subjected to financial hardship; he does not find himself in a dungeon. But even such lesser penalties sufficed to discourage most citizens from open dissent.[23]

The communist regimes of Eastern Europe called themselves "people's democracies." And at least in form, they all met the most basic requirement of representative democracy, the selection of legislators through secret-ballot elections. Typically, only one candidate appeared on the ballot. But voters had the option of striking out the printed name, so at least in principle a majority of voters could force a new election. In practice, negative votes were rare, because voters tried to avoid arousing suspicion. Most did not even exercise their legal right to vote behind a curtain, lest the election monitors interpret secrecy as a sign of dissent.[24] Out of fear, they tended to vote within public view, which made it doubly difficult for other disenchanted citizens to vote secretly.

A by-product of this fear-induced reticence to register opposition was pluralistic ignorance with respect to private opinion. The multitudes who objected to communism did not know how widely their resentments were shared. They could sense the repressed discontent of their conformist relatives and close friends; they could observe the hardships in the lives of their fellow citizens; and they could intuit that the mass uprisings of the past would not have occurred in the absence of widespread discontent. Still, they lacked reliable information on how many of their fellow citizens favored radical political change—to say nothing of knowing others' readiness to react. The government-controlled press exploited the ignorance of the citizenry by stressing the "unity of socialist society" and its "solidarity in supporting the Party." Insofar as such propaganda led potential opponents to underestimate the prevalence of discontent, it weakened their incentive to challenge the status quo.

Pluralistic ignorance thus fueled a pervasive sense of powerlessness. It made individuals believe that they could do nothing to change their government or its policies, that attempts at reform were futile, and that the only prudent course of action was cooperation with the Party. Systematic investigations have confirmed this perception of helplessness. In 1985 a survey conducted in Hungary, by then one of the two most relaxed Soviet satellites, found that only 10 percent of the population felt capable of doing something against a decision inimical to their interests. The figure compares with 46 percent for the Netherlands and 75 percent for the United States.[25]

The Ethos of Dissidence

Commenting on the common feeling of powerlessness, Miłosz observes that the resulting mendacity produced painful inner tensions: "If Hell should guarantee its lodgers magnificent quarters, beautiful clothes, the tastiest food, and all possible amusements, but condemn them to breathe in this aura forever, that would be punishment enough."[26]

This impression of silent suffering is supported by the euphoria that

marked the uprisings of 1989. The excitement reflected the relief felt
by millions who, after decades of conformism, could finally vent their
accumulated frustrations. The same interpretation may be given to the
excitement of earlier uprisings. During the Prague Spring of 1968, the
poet Jaroslav Seifert extolled the ongoing (but soon to be crushed)
democratization experiment for delivering his nation from the stress
of lying. The reforms had instilled in him the hope that his nation
would throw off its mask of contentment and start living in truth:

> . . . so I want to believe the time has come at last
> to call murder by its proper name of
> Murder![27]

From the fact that the postcommunist governments of Eastern
Europe and the former Soviet Union lost little time in committing
themselves to economic liberalization, one might infer that the dissidents who challenged the old order were disciples of Friedrich Hayek
and Milton Friedman. In reality few were sympathetic to capitalism,
and even for them economic issues were secondary. Objecting first
and foremost to restrictions on individual expression, the dissidents
insisted on the right to speak one's mind, differ from the consensus of
the moment, and criticize official structures. Accordingly, their associations were deliberately nonideological: they remained open to citizens subscribing to diverse political views. In 1986 Havel characterized Charter 77 as "the embryo of a genuine social tolerance." It was
a phenomenon, he said, that would be impossible to expunge from
the national memory no matter what the subsequent course of events:
"It would remain in that memory as a challenge that, at any time and
in any new situation, could be responded to and drawn on."[28]

The significance of Charter 77, like that of similar associations
elsewhere, lay not in its size, nor in the novelty or specificity of its
program. It lay in its threat to the uniformity of public opinion.[29] By
articulating their opposition to the status quo, dissidents upset the
apparent harmony and unity of communist society. They brought
the existence of social discontent into the open. They signaled that
the political stability of communism derived partly from collective
conservatism. Through the example of their own behavior and
through persistent calls for truthfulness and tolerance, they inculcated citizens with the will to think aloud and protest earnestly, thus

subverting incentives essential to the continuation of widespread preference falsification. Finally, they exposed the vulnerability of the status quo. They showed that the disaffected were *not* powerless to do something about their condition, that collectively they held the power to achieve freedom and dignity.

There was a fundamental difference between the efforts of dissident groups and those of reformists operating *within* official communist bodies. Official reformists took issue with particular policies, but they did not challenge the system itself. Nor did they explore, much less articulate, why problems had arisen and persevered. Take Nikita Khrushchev, whose 1956 speech to the Twentieth Congress of the Communist Party of the Soviet Union contained an unprecedented denunciation of Stalin's campaign of terror. Khrushchev did not probe into the factors that allowed Stalin to stay at the helm of the communist world until his death. He did not ask why Stalin's crimes generated little public opposition or why millions acquiesced in their own victimization. In sharp contrast, the dissidents of later years focused on the most critical flaw of the communist system, its culture of mendacity.

Scores of dissident writers, including Havel and Solzhenitsyn, maintained for years that communism would collapse instantly if ever their fellow citizens stopped falsifying their political preferences. The Prague Spring had proved the point. When the citizens of Czechoslovakia threw off their masks and called for change, it took an armed intervention of the Warsaw Pact to reinstate hard-line communism. Another confirmation would come in 1989, when, in the absence of Soviet intervention, all of Eastern Europe's communist regimes fell apart under pressure from the streets. Significantly, this regionwide revolution came just a few years after the Soviet Union entered the era of *glasnost* (public openness). Widely considered unshakable, the entire system suddenly collapsed as millions of long subservient citizens stood up for their own beliefs.

But I must interrupt the story here. The uprisings that brought down communism will be interpreted in Chapter 16. Sticking to the role of preference falsification in promoting collective conservatism, I turn now to a different part of the world: India.

8

The Ominous Perseverance of the Caste System

On March 27, 1991, a sixteen-year-old girl and her twenty-year-old lover were hanged from a banyan tree in Mehrana, a village near New Delhi. The girl was a high-caste Hindu, her lover an "untouchable." Their crime was to have defied a key injunction of India's caste system, the prohibition of cross-caste liaisons. Almost all of the three thousand residents of Mehrana watched the executions, which were implemented in compliance with a unanimous decision of the village council.[1]

The caste system is widely perceived as the quintessential example of cultural petrification. It divides Indian society into ranked occupational units, or castes, with membership determined primarily by descent. It has persisted for more than two millennia, surviving anti-Hindu movements, foreign invasions, and the penetration of relatively egalitarian religions, including Islam and Christianity. In modern times the caste system has drawn fire from various groups, and discrimination against the traditionally subservient castes is now illegal. Moreover, some caste norms have weakened under the impact of urbanization and industrialization. Yet as a practical matter caste alliances remain a powerful force in Indian social and political life,[2] as evidenced by the lynchings in Mehrana.

My concern here is with the system's extraordinary endurance, which tends to be attributed either to the economic advantages of the caste norms or to the rapaciousness of the privileged castes. Identifying the deficiencies of these explanations, I shall propose that members of

128

all castes have contributed to the system's perpetuation, often through preference falsification.

The Caste System

There are several thousand castes in India, known locally as *jatis*. They range in size from a few hundred members to several million. Most castes have a single occupation, and many are divided into specialist subcastes. By tradition, the castes fall into five groupings, four of which are known as *varnas*. In order of superiority, the varnas are the *brahmans* (scholar-priests), the *kshatriyas* (warrior-rulers), the *vaishyas* (farmers and merchants), and the *shudras* (artisans and servants). Considered "beyond the pale of decent society," the final grouping incorporates the so-called untouchables. In the early twentieth century, at least a fifth of all Indians were untouchables.[3]

By tradition, caste affiliation determines much more than one's occupation. It establishes one's rights and duties in a huge range of domains, including hygiene, dress, social etiquette, worship, politics, possession, and burial. Because most castes, and often their subcastes as well, are endogamous, lineage governs one's choice of a marriage partner. And typically a person cannot eat food prepared by someone belonging to a lower caste.[4]

The heaviest burden of this system of differences falls on the untouchables. Because they perform highly undesirable tasks, like sweeping and latrine cleaning, the untouchables are considered "polluted" and are barred from contact with the "purer" castes. Accordingly, they often live in segregated quarters and are denied admission to hotels, tea shops, and temples. Until recently, they even had to keep their shadows from falling on high-caste Indians, to protect the latter from defilement.[5] In some regions, their right of way on the road was so restricted that upon noticing an approaching brahman they had to leave the road and walk in the fields, even if this meant getting into water.[6]

The stigma of untouchability does not necessarily vanish when a caste changes its occupation or renounces Hinduism. During World War II, Hindu soldiers from the four varnas often dined together and with adherents of other religions, but they would not sit with untouch-

able soldiers. Courts have had to adjudicate on the rights of Christian
parishioners who wanted to retain a wall erected to insulate untouchable worshipers from the rest of the congregation.[7] Some upper-caste
Muslims still refuse to dine with untouchable Muslims.[8]

Causes of the Caste System's Resilience

Volumes could be written on the hardships and indignities suffered by
the untouchables. My interest here is in explaining the caste system's
remarkably long life and its extraordinary resistance to outside influences.

A popular explanation is that the system was economically functional, in that it afforded a high standard of living and guaranteed
everyone a job. It is certainly true that by the standards of the time
India was a prosperous place during the first millennium and a half of
the caste system's existence.[9] It is not obvious, however, that the caste-
based division of labor contributed to this economic success. Although
certain divisions may have promoted economic efficiency at least for
a while, there is no empirical basis for believing that all, or even most,
were economically advantageous. Nor were the hardships imposed on
the lower castes helpful to India's economic advancement. What economic benefits could have flowed from rules of the road that made
untouchable boys take hours to walk a short distance to school, because of the brahmans that had to be avoided along the way?[10]

In any case, if we credit the caste-based division of labor with India's
economic ascent, we cannot absolve it of responsibility for the nation's
subsequent descent. As numerous writers have noted, India's ongoing
poverty is attributable partly, if not largely, to caste rigidities that
impeded the rise of individualistic capitalism and hampered the adoption of new technologies. In the words of Max Weber, "a ritual law
in which every change of occupation, every change in work technique,
may result in ritual degradation is certainly not capable of giving birth
to economic and technical revolutions from within itself, or even of
facilitating the first germination of capitalism in its midst."[11]

Many leaders of modern India have shared Weber's view. Nehru
attributed India's economic backwardness to "the growing rigidity
and exclusiveness of the Indian social structure as represented chiefly
by the caste system." He even saw India's fall to the British and its

earlier fall to Muslims as inevitable consequences of the caste system.[12] If Nehru was even partially correct, one has to reject as inadequate the functionalist argument that the caste system persevered because of its social benefits. After all, if its favorable effects were the only relevant factor, it should have collapsed, or at least undergone drastic reforms, as soon as unfavorable effects overtook the favorable ones.

There is a more fundamental objection to the functionalist explanation. Granted that during the first phase of the caste system India prospered, it is not self-evident why the lower castes would have considered this a reason for upholding the status quo. Why would untouchables have supported an institution that condemned them to poverty, subjugation, and humiliation? Many untouchables tried, in fact, to escape their fate by converting to Islam or Christianity. Significantly, these religions drew their adherents disproportionately from the low end of the social ladder. As already indicated, however, neither Islam nor Christianity succeeded in abolishing the significance of caste. Each retained caste as a point of social reference and accommodated most caste distinctions.[13]

Nonetheless, some students of the caste system are impressed not by its rigidity but by its flexibility in the face of changing conditions. A major change in a caste's economic fortunes, they observe, will eventually alter its social status. Also, new castes will emerge from time to time through the fission and fusion of existing castes. But such observations do not negate the resilience of the caste system as a whole. As an institution, the system has exhibited great stability. "The pattern alters," says a student of caste, "but the principles that govern it, the frames that hold the pattern so to speak, are exceptionally constant for a human institution."[14]

The Role of Preference Falsification in the Caste System's Stability

The genesis of the caste system is a matter of rich speculation, although we know that its establishment was anything but a peaceful affair.[15] The central puzzle is that, once in place, it persisted with remarkably little use of force. My own explanation for this persistence accords a key role to preference falsification.

The castes formed in any given locality were economically interdependent. The latrine cleaners were dependent for food on the cultivators, who worked on land belonging to landowners, who used the services of various servants and artisans, and so on. Such interdependencies meant that if a caste broke away from society, it would both jeopardize its own survival and harm the interests of other castes. The interdependencies generated pressures to keep individuals loyal to the system, lest one withdrawal provoke others.

A potent source of pressure was the threat of ostracism. A person trying to escape his hereditary predicament would typically be cut off from the life of the community, at least temporarily losing the rights and privileges of his caste. He would become, literally, an *outcaste*. Untouchables and outcastes are often lumped together in commentaries on the caste system, but there is a crucial difference: whereas untouchability is hereditary, one becomes an outcaste by being ejected from one's caste of birth.[16] Outcastes generally came from the untouchables, vaishyas, and shudras, who tended to have the strongest motives to renounce the system, but they also included some brahmans and kshatriyas.[17]

An outcaste would generally receive no help from his caste of origin. V. S. Naipaul speaks of a foreign businessman who, recognizing the brilliance of his young untouchable servant, decided to give him an education and place him in a better job. Years later, when the businessman returned to India, he found that his former servant had reverted to cleaning latrines. "He had been boycotted by his clan for breaking away from them; he was barred from the evening smoking group. There was no other group he could join, no woman he could marry. His solitariness was insupportable, and he had returned to his duty."[18]

Why would latrine cleaners participate in the ostracism of a fellow latrine cleaner seeking a better life? Given that successful defections would undermine the caste system, one might think that they would encourage anticaste behavior. But punishing violators is an effective way to reaffirm one's loyalty to the established order. By ostracizing a peer who has taken a better job, the latrine cleaners can protect *their own* personal and collective reputations. They can signal to the entire community, including groups higher up in the social hierarchy, their willingness to live by the prevailing social rules.

The transgressions for which caste members will punish each other go beyond switches in employment. Individuals who break the rules of intercaste etiquette can expect to be reprimanded both by outsiders and by their own fellows. If their violations continue, they may be ostracized.[19] Such ostracism will be carried out, as with cases involving employment violations, partly by low-caste individuals seeking to prove their loyalty to the status quo.

Why, in the first place, is such proof considered necessary? What is it that makes Indians, especially those socially disadvantaged, seek personal security through actions aimed at hurting the interests of their ambitious peers? Until recent times, Indians were born into a society where public opinion greatly favored the caste system, and where, moreover, they were expected to participate in actions supportive of the status quo. Under the circumstances, the individual Indian's choice was often to meet the system's demands or become an outcaste. Most Indians opted to go along with the system, even if privately they found it offensive.

This explanation sheds light on how the caste sanctions have been self-reproducing, not on how the sanctions arose. At some stage, the upper castes must have used massive force to put the system in place. But once formed, the system would have continued to reproduce itself, generation after generation, with the upper castes joining, though not always leading, the campaigns against rule breakers. By helping to punish challengers, the lower castes would have played a major role in upholding the system.

The Social Determinants of Individual Passivity

Sanctions that castes impose on their own recalcitrant members, together with those imposed by other castes, repress the individual Indian's temptations to break away from the existing order. Sanctions breed resignation. A discontented Indian thus defers to people he loathes, sticks to his ancestral occupation when he considers himself qualified for better employment, follows dietary codes whose purpose he does not understand, and even penalizes people with the courage to challenge in public what he himself rejects only in private. In short, he abides by an inherited system in opposition to his genuine desires. A by-product of this preference falsification is a reinforcement of social obstacles to resistance. Like the greengrocer in Havel's parable, the individual Indian becomes an architect of a public opinion that inhibits overt opposition, a perpetrator of the pressures responsible for his own civil disabilities. He contributes to the conditions that sustain collective conservatism with regard to the social status quo.

Violations of the system's occupational restrictions carry potential benefits not only for people who step out of their customary occupations but also for the utilizers of their illicit services. Suppose that a landowner replaces an unproductive shudra employee with a latrine cleaner who will work harder for less. The change benefits both the hired untouchable, who obtains a better job, and the landowner, who boosts his farm's profitability. This illustration points to the existence of economically viable coalitions that could break away from the system to establish self-sufficient colonies that would be both more productive and more egalitarian. But their formation would require collective action within and across castes, each of which might be frustrated by free riding. Because society will generally ostracize anyone who abandons the caste system, the potential member of an anticaste colony is likely to withhold his participation until it appears likely to succeed. With other potential members reasoning likewise, the colony will remain unformed.[20]

A more fundamental obstacle to the formation of anticaste colonies is that the caste system sanctions even the expression of discontent and resentment. Because of the costs of sincerity, people conceal their willingness to subvert the system, except perhaps from family members and trusted friends. The landowner hides his preparedness to hire an untouchable, and the untouchable refrains from publicizing his readiness to work the land. Such preference falsification suppresses knowledge about the existence of economically viable anticaste coalitions. As a consequence, the disenchanted perceive the system as inescapable, unaware of their collective power to institute reforms.

Some Indian villages have councils that coordinate punishments against code breakers and arbitrate disputes within and among the local castes. Although these councils vary in size and organization, they generally deter inquiries into the rationale for caste regulations. In their meetings protests and assertions of difference are discouraged, apparently to foster an image of harmony. Conflicts are generally settled by caste leaders through deals made behind the scenes. Voting, when it occurs, is by a show of hands, and the verdict is generally unanimous.[21] Mehrana's council heard no protests during its night-long meeting that condemned a couple to hang. The village councils thus contribute to the difficulties of identifying viable anticaste coalitions. They reinforce the perception that attempts to break away are doomed to failure.

"Classes, once they have come into being, harden in their mold and perpetuate themselves, even when the social conditions that created them have disappeared." So wrote Joseph Schumpeter, in dismissing ahistorical explanations of observed class structures.[22] The foregoing explanation for the extraordinary durability of India's caste system accords a central role to the past. It suggests that expectations rooted in history have played a key role in keeping Indians loyal to the system. If Indian history had been different, so would subsequent Indian perceptions and expectations and, hence, subsequent Indian choices concerning employment, marriage, and social association. The caste system's extraordinary durability has stemmed, therefore, at least partly from collective conservatism.

India's current anticaste movement promotes a conspiratorial thesis: the system's genesis and persistence have stemmed simply from the power and prestige of the brahmans. In this view, the brahmans introduced castes forcibly into a previously classless society, as a means of exploiting the conquered natives. They then solidified their privileges by establishing laws in their favor and by poisoning the Indian mind with justifications for hereditary differences.[23] My own explanation does not deny the brahmans' role in imposing and preserving inequality. It insists, however, that the subjugated castes contributed to the system's persistence through their willingness to uphold caste regulations and to sanction their nonconformist peers.

There is much truth to the view that the minds of Indians, including those of the lower castes, have been shackled by an ideology that exalts hereditary differences. As we shall see when we revisit the caste system in Chapter 12, Hinduism has reinforced India's social stability by weakening individual Indians' inner resistance to discrimination. Many brahmans have been among the beneficiaries of various Hindu tenets. In and of itself, however, this observation sheds no light on the diffusion or endurance of the caste system. Why would people at the foot of the caste ladder accept beliefs that justify their own subordination? The answer, whose details must be left until later, is that preference falsification distorts not only public opinion on the caste system but also the evolution of beliefs regarding caste.

From India's past, I will now jump across the globe and forward in time, to American politics in the present. My final case will demonstrate that the theory under construction speaks to all societies, not simply to "backward" societies lacking democratic mores or to "traditional" societies that extol conformity.

9

The Unwanted Spread of Affirmative Action

In 1990 the *New York Times* published a series on why American politics "is failing to produce the ideas and leadership needed to guide the United States in a rapidly changing world." The essays began with quotations suggesting that America has lost its capability to debate and resolve critical issues. Neither administrators nor legislators, observed various commentators, are putting forth bold proposals concerning chronic poverty, falling educational standards, or the budget deficit, mainly for fear of alienating vocal constituencies. "Social Security is the third rail of American politics," went a joke in Congress. "Touch it and you die." A retiring senator complained about "wet-finger politicians"—officials who spend more time testing the political winds than solving social problems.[1] The essays stopped short of claiming that politicians lack creativity. Rather, they argued, officials are not disclosing their ideas, except to trusted friends.

The *Times* is not the first publication to remark on the fraudulence of American politics. Moreover, politicians of every persuasion have complained about the risks in addressing important problems in an honest way.[2] Responding to such complaints, the Kennedy Library in Boston decided to bestow its first Profile in Courage Award upon a public official who follows his conscience. "Think about that," implored a lead editorial. "Has conscience become so rare in Washington that the exercise thereof merits a reward of courage?"[3]

This picture of frozen conformity may seem overblown. American newspapers make a point of featuring a spectrum of opinions, and almost any reformist view can find a forum. But such observations establish only the *existence* of overt opposition to the status quo. Public opinion can be divided yet heavily favor the status quo, with the few public dissenters being treated as deviants, opportunists, or villains. If millions have misgivings about a policy but only hundreds will speak up, one can sensibly infer that discussion on the policy is not free.

Preference Falsification on Race Relations

A political realm in which preference falsification is especially common is race relations. The source of preference falsification on the issue is the fear of being stigmatized as a racist or, in the case of black Americans, as an abettor of racism. Racism evokes such dreadful images that individuals to whom the charge sticks can expect to suffer social indignities, attacks from the press, and even the destruction of their careers. And the possibility of being accused of sinister racial motives is present in a vast array of contexts. On matters as diverse as rape, broadcasting standards, and deficit reduction, one may be accused of racism for taking a position perceived as unfair to minorities, especially to blacks. Race thus makes for a huge "gap between the public and private selves," observes Shelby Steele. "Publicly, we usually adhere to the received wisdom that gives us the most advantageous 'racial face'; privately we are harassed by the uncensored thoughts and feelings that occur to us spontaneously."[4]

Although the United States has had a long history of institutionalized discrimination against blacks, few whites remain wedded to the goal of white supremacy. Polls that provide anonymity consistently show that almost all Americans now accept the principle of equal rights for blacks. By 1972, 96 percent of all whites endorsed equality of opportunity in employment, up from 42 percent in 1944. Attitudes on interracial marriage, interracial socializing, integrated schooling, and open housing have all followed similar trends.[5]

Nor is the revolutionary change limited to attitudes. Between 1970 and 1990, black-white marriages tripled.[6] In the early 1990s, several black-hosted television shows were receiving sky-high ratings in largely white communities. And in the past two decades black mayoral candidates have defeated white opponents with majority white support in various predominantly white cities, including Seattle, Los Angeles, Kansas City, and Charlotte.[7] The significance of the latter two observations lies in the fact that they reflect choices made *in private*. Whatever the pressures against public expressions of racism, in choosing a television program in the privacy of one's own home or in voting behind the protective curtain of an election booth one can vent any prejudice without fear of retribution. If majorities of whites are prepared to support a black candidate over a white, and if they will watch a black-hosted show when they could be watching something else, it is obvious that racism is no longer the force it once was. While white racism may not have been eradicated, it evidently has ceased to be an insurmountable obstacle to black advancement. The statistics suggest that huge numbers of whites are now willing to honor the principle of equal treatment in both word and deed.

Equal treatment for individuals does not imply equality of results for racial groups. Most Americans reject the racial quotas, timetables, and guidelines instituted under the rubric of "affirmative action" as a means of moving blacks toward parity with whites in education, employment, and ultimately wealth and status. In 1976 only 10 percent of the whites in a national sample, but 37 percent of the blacks, thought that a medical school should lower its standards to enroll a black "who may not have the right qualifications but shows real promise."[8] In 1984, 9 percent of a sample of whites, but 49 percent of a black sample, supported "giving blacks preference in getting jobs over equally qualified whites because of past discrimination against blacks."[9] And in 1992, merely 16 percent of a national sample were more likely to vote for candidates who espoused "giving blacks preference over equally qualified whites for jobs and college admissions because of past discrimination"; as many as 70 percent were less likely to vote for such candidates.[10] As with any issue, answers are sensitive to how the questions are framed. The approval rate rises markedly when affirmative action is presented as a method that avoids "rigid quotas." The rate is consistently very low, however, when it is characterized as a compensatory remedy for past racial injustices or as a method for achieving racial balance in results.

In safe settings, many whites will argue that they themselves bear neither responsibility nor blame for past injustices or present disparities. "We have not owned slaves," they will say, "and we have done nothing to hold anyone down. Besides, for at least a generation blacks

have enjoyed great opportunities to get ahead. So the practice of reserving places for blacks amounts to reverse racial discrimination."[11]
Although such reasoning keeps private opinion clearly opposed to affirmative action, few Americans express misgivings in public. College
students who hold rallies against homelessness do not organize
marches to protest the race-conscious practices that many see as
threats to their own advancement.[12] Factory workers who strike for
better pay do nothing to overturn the racial quotas they detest.[13] And
as of late 1994 politicians who read polls religiously have taken no
concrete steps to end the racial policies that they know to be highly
unpopular. The Republican "Contract with America," whose bold
promises contributed to the Republican victory in the midterm elections of 1994, contained no provisions regarding affirmative action.

Paul Sniderman and Thomas Piazza have undertaken a sophisticated examination of American attitudes on racial matters. They find,
first, that, while prejudice against blacks has not disappeared, it no
longer makes large numbers of whites oppose public policies to assist
blacks; and second, that whites are overwhelmingly opposed to policies that make blackness a source of advantage.[14] Two of their experiments are particularly instructive.

In one experiment, a random sample of white respondents are asked
whether a person who lost his or her job is entitled to government
assistance in finding another one. In the process, respondents learn
about the laid-off worker's race, sex, marital status, and dependabil-
ity. The results show more, not less, support for government assistance
to a black laid-off worker than for a white one. Even more significant,
in the case of a black worker support for help rises dramatically when
he or she is characterized as dependable.[15]

In the other experiment, half of a sample of whites are asked their
view of affirmative action, then their image of blacks; the other half
are asked the same questions in the opposite order. It turns out that
the mere mention of affirmative action encourages dislike of its beneficiaries. Of those who have just been asked about affirmative action, 46 percent describe blacks as "irresponsible," as against 23
percent of those who have not heard the issue mentioned. Similarly,
31 percent of the former group describe blacks as "lazy," as against
20 percent of the latter.[16] The results of the second experiment are
particularly striking in view of the rarity of public opposition to af-

firmative action. They reveal that affirmative action is a source of widespread white resentment.

Evidence from Elections

Further evidence for the prevalence of preference falsification comes from electoral politics. Between 1968 and 1988, the American electorate moved steadily "leftward" on various social issues, including abortion, homosexual rights, and the environment.[17] Yet the Democratic Party, which championed leftist positions on these issues, lost five of the six presidential elections held in this period, some by landslides. Seeking an explanation, Thomas and Mary Edsall observe that the Republicans capitalized on the undercurrent of resentment over racial double standards, including affirmative action. Republican campaign slogans about welfare queens, crime, urban decay, and quotas all drew on hidden racism, but also—and more significantly—on concerns about efforts to exempt blacks from standards applied to the rest of society. Ingeniously, the slogans enabled Republicans to speak to these concerns without having to challenge double standards openly.[18]

The most celebrated television advertisement of the 1988 Bush campaign featured Willie Horton, a black murderer who raped a white woman and stabbed her male companion while on furlough from prison. The spot gave expression to worries on the minds of large blocs of voters and, most important, to the fear rooted in the high incidence of criminal behavior among young black males. Suggesting that the problems of blacks are their own fault, the ad recast whites in the role of victim rather than victimizer. Implicitly, therefore, it berated the attribution of racial disparities to white racism and questioned the fairness of established black privileges. The spot allowed Bush to portray himself as responsive to the electorate's submerged concerns about racial policies, but without embroiling himself in explicit public controversy. As such, the ad was at once an opportunistic response to preference falsification and a prominent manifestation of it.

Easily elected president, Bush took no bold steps in the following four years. Having branded proposed civil rights legislation a "quota bill," he ultimately signed it into law after it was amended to outlaw formal quotas while leaving intact its provisions that would encourage informal ones.[19] Earlier in his term, he exhibited the same caution when an assistant secretary of the Education Department, Michael Williams, pronounced almost all scholarships designated exclusively for minority students to be illegal. The 1964 Civil Rights Act prohibits recipients of federal funds from tying financial aid to race, and the Civil Rights Restoration Act of 1987 extends the prohibition to private higher education. Bush thus possessed a legal basis for standing by Williams, who is black. Instead, when civil rights groups set off a firestorm, he quickly caved in.[20]

While Bush waffled, compromised, and played safe, local elections were providing evidence of widespread preference falsification on racial matters. In the 1990 U.S. Senate election in Louisiana, the incumbent candidate was predicted to score an overwhelming victory over David Duke, a former grand wizard of the Ku Klux Klan whose platform rested explicitly on opposition to affirmative action. Polls projected that Duke would garner no more than 25 percent of the vote. Yet he won 44 percent, including 60 percent of the white vote,[21] suggesting that many voters would not even admit their support of Duke to a nameless pollster. Duke's covert supporters undoubtedly included some genuine racists. But it is hard to believe that all were bigots. Many must have been nonracist citizens attracted to his anti–affirmative action message.

This interpretation is bolstered by another election in which polls were dramatically off. On the eve of the 1989 mayoral election in New York, polls gave David Dinkins, a black candidate, leads between 14 and 18 points over Rudolph Giuliani, who is white. Exit polls showed Dinkins winning by 6 to 10 points. His actual margin of victory was only 2 points.[22] Neither candidate had taken controversial positions on racial matters or used racist symbolism, although it was understood that Dinkins would promote affirmative action more vigorously. The two candidates had other differences, of course, so Giuliani's supporters could have given any number of socially respectable reasons for their choice. But racism is the *most obvious* reason why a white voter would oppose a black candidate. Giuliani's supporters might have deceived pollsters simply to avoid giving the impression of being prejudiced.

To sum up thus far, white Americans are overwhelmingly opposed to special privileges for blacks. But they show extreme caution in expressing themselves publicly, for fear of being labeled as racists. In the process, they drive a wedge between public and private opinion on an array of issues that touch on race, including affirmative action.

The Origins and Impact of Affirmative Action

Although affirmative action grew out of the civil rights movement, it was not among the movement's original goals. In the 1960s, millions of Americans—black and white—joined hands simply to bring an end to practices that made white skin a source of advantage. "I have a dream," exclaimed Martin Luther King, Jr., in his most memorable speech, "that my four little children will one day live in a nation where they will not be judged by the color of their skin but by the content of their character."[23] In accordance with King's dream, the Civil Rights Act of 1964 destroyed the legal foundations of white racism, committing the United States to the principle of "equal opportunity." Within just a few years, however, the civil rights agenda metamorphosed into a campaign to achieve "equal results" in short order through affirmative action. Whatever its intent, the new approach promoted blatant color consciousness: a firm that must have a racially balanced work force cannot judge applicants solely by the "content of their character."

What has been the impact of racial affirmative action? Educated and already well-off blacks have most certainly benefited handsomely.[24] By the mid-1970s the percentage of black high school graduates entering college matched, and in some years exceeded, the percentage among whites.[25] Black employment expanded enormously in government and in companies monitored by the Equal Employment Opportunity Commission.[26] Gains in employment have continued or at least held steady even under administrations known to have reservations about color-conscious hiring practices. And these practices have been accompanied by improvements in compensation. The return on black education has risen relative to that for whites, and in some fields blacks now earn more. As early as 1973, twenty-five- to twenty-nine-year-old black men with college degrees earned 9 percent more than their white peers.[27] In the same year, accomplished black professors got paid more than white professors with similar records.[28]

Bidding wars among universities seeking to meet affirmative action targets have continued to benefit black faculty.

The extent to which the recorded gains are attributable to the guidelines and timetables of affirmative action is a matter of controversy. Some of the gains would probably have occurred even under color-blind procedures. Significantly, black representation in prestigious schools, high government offices, the most lucrative professions, and the military command were already rising rapidly by 1970, when affirmative action programs began to be widely enforced.[29] Still, there is no question that affirmative action has helped the black middle class to expand and prosper.

Equally clear is that the living standards of poor blacks have deteriorated relative to poor whites, relative to wealthy blacks, and even in absolute terms. Between 1973 and 1987, families in the top quintile of the black income distribution became 33 percent richer in constant dollars, as against a 25 percent gain for families in the top white quintile. During the same period families in the bottom black quintile suffered a loss of 18 percent, as against a smaller loss of 7 percent for the poorest white families. For the overall white distribution, the ratio of the bottom quintile to the top quintile fell from 14 percent to 11 percent; the corresponding black ratio fell even more, 10 percent to 6 percent.[30]

The primary reason for the adoption of affirmative action programs was black poverty. As an answer to poverty, these figures suggest, the programs have been a failure. Although blacks least in need of special help have reaped visible gains, those with the greatest need have suffered unmistakable losses.

The losses show up in statistics on poverty, unemployment, family conditions, and crime. Two decades after the spread of racial affirmative action, about a third of all blacks, as against a tenth of the whites, were living below the official poverty line. The unemployment rate of blacks was more than twice that of whites. A black child was about three times as likely to be born into poverty. More than half of all black children were living in single-parent families, as opposed to only a sixth of white children. A black man was six times as likely as a white man to be murdered, and his murderer was likely to be black. Most significant, since the 1970s these racial discrepancies had either widened or held steady.[31]

Such grim statistics suggest that affirmative action may not be the most effective response to black poverty. Indeed, a number of eminent scholars, including some who are black, maintain that affirmative action is a remedy better suited to past maladies than to those of the present. Their ranks include Stephen Carter, Richard Epstein, Nathan Glazer, Glenn Loury, Thomas Sowell, Shelby Steele, and William Julius Wilson.[32] These dissenters do not deny that many individual blacks have benefited from the instituted racial quotas. They recognize, however, that the gains have gone disproportionately to blacks already well-off. And they emphasize that the benefits have been accompanied by high social, psychological, and economic costs. Double standards put *all* blacks under a cloud of suspicion, including those advancing on their own merits. The knowledge that certain places are reserved for minorities discourages black effort. Decisions made to satisfy affirmative action targets create inefficiencies that reduce the competitiveness of the American economy, with adverse consequences for all groups. Nonblacks whose careers have been thwarted to make room for less qualified blacks, and many others who suspect that they may have suffered, see themselves as victims of "reverse discrimination"; their resentments fuel racial disharmony. Finally, by making it hazardous to fire, demote, or even fail to promote blacks, lest one be sued for job discrimination, affirmative action breeds credentialism— a tendency to put great weight on qualifications that third parties can readily understand, such as educational degrees and formal experience. Credentialism favors the ablest and best educated blacks; it hurts the unskilled, the poorly educated, and the young, especially since affirmative action has been extended to other groups with generally superior credentials, like white women.

Vilification of Dissenters

On any social policy, open-minded analysts may differ over the magnitude of various costs and benefits, and there is certainly room for disagreement on affirmative action. Often cited justifications include the endurance of white racism, the benefits of black role models, the right to compensation for injustices against one's ancestors, and the advantages of ethnic diversity in schools and in the workplace.[33] The crucial point here is that some serious thinkers consider such advantages to be outweighed by the costs of affirmative action.

From its inception, however, affirmative action has been treated as beyond criticism. People expressing misgivings have routinely been vilified as self-serving foes of racial equality. Black critics have tended to be labeled as traitors to their race, whites as promoters of white supremacy.

The pattern of intimidation took shape in 1965 when Daniel Patrick Moynihan, then assistant secretary of labor, endured fierce criticism for a policy paper, *The Negro Family: The Case for National Action*.[34] Now known as the "Moynihan Report," the paper argued that if black poverty is to be eradicated blacks will have to gain not only the same opportunities as whites but also the same resources for taking advantage of opportunities. Yet, the report went on, the breakdown of the black family through divorce, separation, and desertion is depriving black children of the self-confidence, discipline, and habits that are among the prime determinants of achievement. Moynihan attributed the high incidence of family breakdown to generations of slavery and discrimination: by sapping the black man's economic strength, oppression had undermined his standing within the family. As of the mid-1960s, Moynihan pointed out, almost a quarter of black families were headed by females, and about the same share of black births were illegitimate. Children born into these circumstances were doing poorly in school, then failing to get jobs, and ultimately producing new generations of socially deprived children. "The present tangle of pathology," he concluded, "is capable of perpetuating itself without assistance from the white world." Programs to wipe out black poverty will fail unless they are "designed to have the effect, directly or indirectly, of enhancing the stability and resources of the Negro American family."[35]

In attributing the black family's dissolution to slavery Moynihan was echoing a thesis developed by Franklin Frazier.[36] Subsequent research has discredited Frazier's thesis. We now know that most slaves grew up in two-parent households and that slaves denied families typically formed strong marriages as soon as they were freed.[37] But whatever his misconceptions, Moynihan was not pointing to a nonexistent problem. At the time he wrote, the female-headed family was already a salient feature of the black community. Accordingly, many black leaders reacted favorably to the report.

Other black leaders felt, however, that demanding changes in black behavior would slacken the nation's commitment to racial equality. They responded angrily, branding Moynihan a "subtle racist." One critic characterized the report as "a massive academic cop out for the white conscience," adding that it would provide "the fuel for a new racism."[38] To demand modifications in black behavior was a ploy, insisted another, to avoid changing "the capitalistic system" responsible for black poverty.[39] As the controversy heated up, most of the black leaders who had endorsed the report's thesis repositioned themselves. One stated that America "can no longer discuss the pathology of Negro society without discussing also the pathology of the white society that permits that pathology to develop." Disagreeing that the black family was falling apart, this observer contended that white society had never allowed it to flourish.[40]

Fearful of being tainted with the charge of racism, "progressive" whites joined the attacks. A white psychologist denounced Moynihan for depicting blacks as savages: "The implicit point is that Negroes tolerate promiscuity, illegitimacy, one-parent families, welfare dependency, and everything else that is supposed to follow. . . . The all-time favorite 'savage' is the promiscuous mother who produces a litter of illegitimate brats."[41] With pressures mounting, the administration sought to dissociate itself from the Moynihan thesis. The secretary of labor argued that the report may have reflected an overemphasis on the breakdown in black family life. He even denied that the report was an official document of his department.[42] "There was a massive failure of nerve among whites," Moynihan writes in a retrospective account of his ordeal, "a spare number of academics excepted. There was seemingly no untruth to which some would not subscribe if there appeared to be the least risk of disapproval from the groupthink of the moment."[43]

The Moynihan Report was thus brushed aside, even as the problems it identified deepened. Where a quarter of all black households were headed by women in 1960, well over half were in 1990.[44] Many more children were being born to teenagers unable or unwilling to give them proper care. In line with Moynihan's thesis, these children were gen-

erally failing to develop the skills necessary for success in life.[45] They
were turning to crime in large numbers. Businesses were leaving their
neighborhoods. Families with the means to get out, including black
families, were fleeing to the suburbs. The "young black male" was
becoming a growing source of fear, with terrible consequences for the
law-abiding black majority. The consequences are epitomized by the
taxi driver who will not stop for a black man for fear of getting
robbed—or even a black woman, lest she ask to be driven to a gang-
infested area.

The observed patterns of avoidance indicate that the pathologies of
the black community are widely understood. Indeed, these pathologies
have generated enormous resentment among whites and blacks alike.
When in 1984 Bernhard Goetz shot four black teenagers who hassled
him for money in a New York subway, New Yorkers of all ethnic
backgrounds supported his action—although black sympathy fell
markedly when it became apparent that Goetz fired an additional shot
after his muggers were down.[46] Even the mother of one of the wounded
youths said he deserved it; her own husband, the father of her son,
had been murdered trying to stop a thug from stealing his taxi.[47] When
a jury acquitted Goetz for the shootings, the verdict met with the
approval of 90 percent of the city's whites, 83 percent of the His-
panics, and 52 percent of the blacks.[48]

Shortly after the Goetz incident, a commentator wrote that Goetz's
shots released "long-buried" feelings of anger and despair.[49] She meant
only that New Yorkers had exploded with condemnations of street
crime, not that they were suddenly prepared to speak their minds on
all racial matters. Several years later, in fact, during the Senate confirmation hearings of Clarence Thomas, a black judge nominated to
the Supreme Court, the same commentator would observe that candor
is rare on matters related to race. She had just spoken about the hearings to a college class. Her openness made the students visibly nervous.
"The truth is," they told her later, "they hadn't felt free to offer an
opinion in public and did not really expect to hear one."[50]

Few of these students knew of the Moynihan incident, which occurred before they were born. But their reticence was a conditioned
response to social pressures and expectations that the incident helped
to shape.

The years since the Moynihan Report have not been devoid of challenges to the established agenda for improving black living standards. A small number of intellectuals, including those named earlier, have challenged the agenda publicly, pointing to the costs of specific policies and suggesting a shift in emphasis, if not an entirely new approach. Many have been attacked as enemies of racial justice, and each episode of condemnation has served to remind other potential opponents of the high price of open dissent.

In the mid-1970s, when the sociologist James Coleman and two of his colleagues found that busing programs designed to achieve racial balance in urban schools were causing white flight and thus harming the long-run interests of poor blacks, the president of the American Sociological Association attempted to have him censured. And the association organized a plenary session at its 1976 convention, ostensibly to discuss Coleman's research, but apparently also to raise questions about his motives. The wall behind the podium where Coleman and the other participants spoke was plastered with posters linking Coleman's name with Nazi swastikas and ugly epithets.[51]

Another of many such vilifications occurred a decade and a half later, when the *Philadelphia Inquirer* ran an editorial advocating incentives for poor black women to use long-term contraceptive implants: "The main reason more black children are living in poverty is that the people having the most children are the ones least capable of supporting them. . . . There are many ways to fight back. . . . Why not make a major effort to reduce the number of children, of any race, born into such circumstances." There was an uproar. A columnist for another Philadelphia paper wrote: "Hitler could have written the same editorial without pausing to breathe between sentences." The *Inquirer*'s editors quickly accepted blame, admitting that they had been "insensitive and counterproductive."[52]

Black critics of affirmative action programs have suffered similar abuses.[53] Sowell, an opponent of racial double standards from the time they were introduced, has been treated as a deranged man bent on destroying his own race. Loury has seen his views characterized as "treasonous" by the head of the National Association for the Advancement of Colored People.[54] Wilson, who has sought to bring the pathologies identified by Moynihan back into poverty research, and who supports color-blind policies to combat poverty, has been denounced by the Association of Black Sociologists.[55]

There are many blacks who agree with the black dissenters and admire their courage, but under the prevailing circumstances few are prepared to come to their defense. Stephen Carter, a critic of affirmative action, observes:

> Many black professionals, although expressing privately the same views that prominent dissenters express publicly, mute their public votes. These private dissenters are understandably reluctant to "offend the sensibilities and aspirations" of other black people, sometimes because they agree that public disagreement would be harmful, but just as often, I suspect, because of their unwillingness to face the personal attacks, the slurs on their loyalty, that an open break frequently sparks.[56]

Nor are whites generally prepared to defend black critics of the orthodox racial agenda. In effect, many give the black establishment license to determine, on behalf of all Americans, who is a respectable black and who is a menacing deviant to be defamed and silenced.

The same license extends to whites stigmatized as evil racists. In a book on the politics of race in New York, Jim Sleeper notes that the city's "liberal" white activists have tended to lend unqualified support to black leaders and militants in their disputes with white managers, teachers, and welfare workers. When black militants turned on the white managers of the city's public housing projects, for example, white activists assumed that the managers had to be guilty of racism. The most common source of friction at the projects was the practice of screening applicants and monitoring tenants for proper civic behavior. Because disproportionate shares of black and Hispanic families had members with criminal records, the practice was more likely to deny residency to a minority family than to a white one. On this basis, minority leaders launched a campaign against the project managers. Before long, the managers were driven out of office with the support of white activists, and the behavioral selection criteria gave way to ethnic quotas. Living conditions in the projects then deteriorated rapidly, producing an exodus of socially responsible families—to the great detriment of families unable to move.[57]

The Tenacity of the Civil Rights Agenda

The militants who fought against the behavioral standards of New York's housing projects claimed to speak for all minorities. Yet many black residents of the projects had favored the enforcement of behavioral standards. This is not an isolated case of division between black leaders and the black rank and file. On various issues, confidential opinion polls reveal sharp differences between, on the one hand, the perceptions and attitudes of elected black officials and the officers of civil rights organizations and, on the other, the views of ordinary black citizens.

In a 1985 poll, for instance, 74 percent of the leaders reported that they themselves had suffered job discrimination, as against 40 percent of a random sample of blacks. On affirmative action, the gap was even wider. Whereas 78 percent of the leaders supported giving blacks preferential treatment, the same percentage of the random sample *opposed* this position. Another issue that produced remarkable differences involves the rights of nonblacks to own stores in black neighborhoods. Of the leaders, 44 percent held that these stores should be owned by blacks, with the remaining 56 percent saying that ethnicity should make no difference; for the national black sample, the corresponding figures were 9 percent and 90 percent.[58]

Yet black public opinion remains highly supportive of the national black leadership. Part of the explanation is that individual blacks refrain from publicizing their differences with their leaders, especially on key issues like affirmative action. Afraid of being accused of treason, they keep quiet and even endorse the established objectives. Their fears are reinforced every time a black dissenter endures attacks.

Fear-induced preference falsification explains the paucity of public black opposition. However, it leaves unexplained why orthodox black leaders repeatedly win elections decided by secret ballot. My resolution of the latter puzzle comes in four parts.

First, voters in agreement with the official black agenda constitute a majority in some black organizations and some predominantly black voting districts. Second, candidates represent bundles of positions, and voters can differ on some specifics from the candidate of their choice. A citizen opposed to a candidate's stand on affirmative action may support him on account of his positions on other issues. Third, blacks in positions of influence are admired even by voters who disagree with them on important issues. This gives an advantage to incumbent black politicians, who tend to be supportive of affirmative action. Finally, and perhaps most significant, because almost all candidates for high office in major civil rights organizations and in heavily black districts support the conventional black agenda, voters rarely get much of a choice on affirmative action.[59]

Like black politicians, white politicians take positions on multitudes of issues. They can go against private opinion on some of the issues and still win elections. Affirmative action offers a case in point. The fact that most Americans reject it in private has not kept white politicians from making conspicuous efforts to preserve and strengthen affirmative action programs. Ordinarily their challengers have been equally supportive of affirmative action, so elections have tended to be decided on other criteria.

But why, in the first place, has it been so exceptional for politicians to take clear stands against affirmative action? If Duke could win three out of five white votes by lambasting racial quotas, other candidates could probably do the same. True, Louisiana had a troubled economy at the time Duke ran for the Senate, but recessions hit other places, too. Besides, Duke's white supremacist past tarnished his credibility as a champion of racial evenhandedness. A candidate with a less offensive background could conceivably do *even better* running against affirmative action.

The reason so few politicians have opposed affirmative action openly and unequivocally is that they have been afraid of opening themselves to the charge of racism. However unfounded, the charge could have several negative consequences. Constituents anxious to maintain an antiracist reputation would withdraw their support. The accused politician would run into difficulty raising money. And her efforts to fend off the charge would detract heavily from activities essential to her electability.

I began this chapter by noting that American politicians seldom speak frankly on major social problems. This reticence is both symptom and cause of a more general failure: a pattern of spinelessness within the wider American citizenry. There is a fundamental difference between opposing a misguided policy in a poll, knowing that one's response will become an anonymous statistic, and opposing it forcefully at social occasions, in the classroom, at work, or in one's writings. In settings with strong social pressures, decisive majorities might embrace policies rejected in polls. Politicians are especially vulnerable to social pressures, which is one reason why bold and innovative leadership is so rare.

Blaming the Victim?

In each of the foregoing illustrations of collective conservatism—communism, the caste system, and affirmative action—a society perpetuates a structure that is widely disliked and resented. Although privately unpopular, the structure persists because reform-oriented individuals refrain from publicizing their views, thus reinforcing the social incentives for such preference falsification. Insofar as affirmative action hurts blacks as a group, individual blacks who have supported the official agenda bear some responsibility. And insofar as American society suffers, every American who has engaged in preference falsification carries a share of the blame.

Does my explanation amount to "blaming the victim"? If by this one means that victims contribute to their own victimization, the answer is an emphatic yes. The victims of oppressive, misguided, and counterproductive policies invite the perpetuation of their misery whenever they hide, shade, or distort their convictions. That they face very strong pressures to conform does not deny them free will. They are not passive objects caught in the toils of a machine made and preserved entirely by others. The abusive machine may have been built at an earlier time, possibly before they were born; but at some point they themselves began, or will begin, taking part in its maintenance. The pressures that weigh on victims of a policy are sustained at least partly by their own choices.

However, if "blaming the victim" is taken to mean that the victim is unequivocally wrong to engage in preference falsification, the answer is no. It is not immoral to avoid social isolation, material deprivation, and physical injury—although people who willingly bear such penalties do deserve special recognition. Nor is it a sign of mental deficiency to perceive that the penalties for speaking out outweigh the probable gains. The victim's conformism is ordinarily based on a keen appreciation of his powerlessness as a person and of the advantages of social approval. He is as much a prisoner of an oppressive situation as he is a perpetrator, for he cannot correct it unilaterally.

The antithesis of "blaming the victim" is the conspiracy theory, an explanation that puts the blame on some group that benefits from the victim's sufferings. In many contexts, of course, one finds groups organized to block changes inimical to their own narrow interests. In my general model this role is played by the activist leadership of the dominant pressure group, and in my three illustrations it has been filled by the Communist Party, the village council, and the civil rights lobby. Yet the undertakings of activists explain patterns of stability only up to a point. Were all believers in reform to stand up for their beliefs, their incentives to support the status quo would weaken appreciably, and some change would certainly follow.

Conspiracy theories posit a sharp line between victims and victimizers, the powerless and the very powerful. In the interpretations developed here these categories are overlapping. The untouchable who turns on a fellow untouchable seeking a better life, the disaffected Czech who hurls abuses at a dissident, and the New Yorker who remains silent while her representatives demonize an opponent of group rights have in common something significant. Each is both a victim and a victimizer.

With respect to the examples considered, it might be noted that the undesirable structures have not survived forever: communism has fallen, the caste system is now illegal, and in the United States there is a growing willingness to question old presumptions regarding racial disparities. None of this negates the fact that collective conservatism extends sufferings and exacerbates failures. The share of black children born into single-parent households has doubled in the quarter-century since the Moynihan Report was dismissed as the work of a wicked racist. Even if the emphasis were now to shift from black privileges to policies for strengthening the family, we would still be a quarter-century behind where we might have been in developing answers to mass poverty. There will still have been, as Moynihan puts it, a "moment lost."

Upcoming chapters will explore, within the same framework, the social process by which the loss of moments is arrested. But first we must turn to the inner world of the individual, the world of personal values, perceptions, and beliefs. So far we have treated this world as static and, hence, private preferences as given. The next task is to examine the dynamics of the individual's inner world.

III

Distorting Knowledge

III

Historical Knowledge

10

Public Discourse and Private Knowledge

The seventeenth-century thinker Leibniz depicted the human being as a "windowless monad"—a creature whose personality is closed and fixed.[1] The Leibnizian metaphor sees little use nowadays, but the analytical construct that it represents has proved highly resilient. A modern school of thought that promotes the construct is neoclassical economics. Within the mainstream of this school, preferences are considered impervious to social pressures, trends, and outcomes.[2]

Up to now nothing in this book has challenged the monadic tradition. In principle, preference falsification can alter the appearance of one's personality without modifying its essence. Yet in practice preference falsification does affect private preferences. It distorts *public discourse*—the corpus of assertions, arguments, and opinions in the public domain. In turn, the distortion of public discourse transforms *private knowledge*—the understandings that individuals carry in their own heads. The transformation of private knowledge ends up reshaping private preferences.

To explicate this chain of effects is the book's next challenge. This chapter offers an inquiry into the sources of private knowledge. It is a preparatory chapter, in that it provides no role for preference falsification, except at the end. The processes identified here will be used in the next chapter to explore how preference falsification affects the dynamics of knowledge construction, use, and reinforcement.

I ought to acknowledge immediately that every individual has an essentially immutable core. We are all born with drives to breathe and to eat. It is equally true, however, that the actions through which we

157

satisfy our biological drives are often based at least partly on acquired knowledge. We seek lean meat because saturated fat is said to cause heart disease. And we place faith in the market because experts consider it the best mechanism for making meat available. One can distinguish between two components of private knowledge, an *innate* component that is fixed and an *acquired* component that is variable.[3] To understand the latter component, one must peer into the silent microcosm we call the mind.

Heuristics and Models

The human mind is capable of perceptual and conceptual feats unmatched by even the most powerful computers. Yet its competence pales in comparison to the complexities of the physical and social environment. The mind can receive, store, retrieve, and process only a fragment of the potentially useful information.[4]

Severe as they are, the mind's limitations are not paralyzing. As individuals, we overcome them through various means that help conserve cognitive resources.

First, we take shortcuts in inferring causal relationships and in estimating magnitudes, frequencies, and probabilities. For example, in evaluating the possible explanations for a global economic recession we typically discount those, like the failure of a local bank, that appear unrepresentative of a major event. The underlying simplifying principle is one of several mental shortcuts, or *judgmental heuristics,* that we bring to bear on our estimations and inferences. These heuristics serve us well in many contexts, though in others they lead to costly errors.[5]

In coping with our cognitive limitations we rely, second, on *models* that order and simplify our observations. A model treats some pieces of information and some dimensions of causation as privileged, suppressing the rest. It provides not the whole truth but a truncated version that obscures subtlety, variety, and complexity. Models have been studied under such labels as frames, schemas, patterns, theories, paradigms, worldviews, ideologies, and mentalities.[6] Some of these concepts are broader than the others; a mentality, for instance, is a cluster of interconnected submodels. Moreover, some models are subconscious, which is to say that they are inaccessible to introspection. We cannot always identify why we like someone.[7]

The models that an individual applies to an issue need not be mutually consistent. A person may subscribe to conflicting models, for instance, a "big government" model that justifies lower taxes together with an "educational crisis" model that calls for more government services. Our use of multiple models explains why opinion researchers find that seemingly trivial changes in question form affect the expression of individual attitudes.[8] Question form can make a difference by triggering one model instead of the other. Cognitive psychologists use the term *framing effect* to describe the consequent attitudinal inconsistencies.[9] Even the *same* version of a question may elicit different responses when asked at different times, because the considerations at the top of a respondent's head are variable.

To ensure consistency among their models, people would have to unite them in a coherent supermodel. The task would overwhelm their cognitive capacities, of course, defeating the very purpose of using multitudes of models. The down side of using many unintegrated models is that the inevitable inconsistencies exact costs. Yet ordinarily these are minor. People will not even become aware of the costs, provided their models yield reasonably satisfactory choices and generate fairly accurate predictions.

What is the origin of the models that individuals carry in their heads? One source is personal experimentation. Trial-and-error learning can be slow, however, and potentially very costly. The first fertilizer that a farmer tries could destroy his crops, leaving him bankrupt. In any case, making sense of even a narrow segment of reality can overwhelm a lone individual's cognitive capabilities. "If man were forced to demonstrate for himself all the truths of which he makes daily use," wrote Tocqueville, "his task would never end. He would exhaust his strength in preparatory demonstrations without ever advancing beyond them."[10] In practice, therefore, we derive only a minute fraction of our models from personal effort alone.[11]

The Politics of Persuasion: Appeals to Reason

Most of our models are based at least partly on knowledge provided by others. In a vast array of contexts, we rely heavily on public discourse to decide what is fair, right, good, natural, safe, and economical. Conscious of our acute need for ready knowledge, groups pursuing particular agendas fill public discourse with observations and arguments advantageous to their own causes. They end up regulating our private knowledge, and thus also our private preferences.

Groups clamoring to control our dispositions rarely admit that they are motivated by self-interest. They do not say forthrightly: "The virtue of our program is that it gives us privileges." Typically, they claim to be promoting some conception of the *common* good. "Although we ourselves might benefit," they say, "larger gains will accrue to the wider community." And where it is obvious that they themselves would be the main beneficiary, they rest their demands on prevalent notions of equity.

Such attempts at persuasion are often coupled with efforts to discredit rival positions. Groups expose the distortions in opposing arguments and discount whatever is valid. They also attribute selfish motives to the promoters of rival arguments, as when bureaucrats clamoring for more regulation are accused of wanting to line their own pockets. "We seek the common good, but our rivals are motivated by greed," groups frequently suggest, and "We educate, whereas others engage in propaganda."

Messages aimed at persuasion often entail deliberate distortions.[12] Aerospace companies habitually overrate the capabilities of their planes and exaggerate the danger of war. Agricultural interests argue that farm subsidies are necessary to protect the "endangered family farm," even though the gains go mostly to corporations owned largely by urbanites. Such deceptive claims are common because they are effective. And they are effective precisely because of the limitations of human reason.

The link between intentional deception and cognitive limitations was made five centuries ago by Machiavelli. "Men are so simple and so ready to follow the needs of the moment," he wrote, "that the deceiver will always find someone to deceive." Having observed that people can be made to believe in causes inimical to their interests, he then went on to advise prospective rulers: "It is good to appear clement, trustworthy, humane, religious, and honest, and also to be so, but always with the mind so disposed that, when the occasion arises not to be so, you can become the opposite."[13] Machiavelli thus understood that it is easier to rally people behind a socially useful cause than behind a socially harmful one. He also recognized, however, that people can be drawn into causes contrary to their personal interests.[14]

To Machiavelli's insights one might add that the prevailing stock of private knowledge makes certain ideas easier to disseminate than others. If I know that there have been several abortive attempts at reform, a suggestion that the newest attempt is destined to fail will probably strike me as reasonable. Insofar as the suggestion is supported by myths, folk wisdom, proverbs, and other forms of generalization, its credibility is enhanced. The old French expression *Plus ça change plus c'est la même chose*[15] gives generic support to any claim regarding the futility of reform.[16]

The point remains that we are easily fooled. A witticism may serve to strengthen a falsehood, as when it breeds cynicism about a truly workable plan for reform. Also, since our preconceptions could be flawed, an easily accepted claim might be totally false.

The exponents of a false claim need not be aware of its falsity. Their own cognitive inadequacies guarantee that their understandings will harbor many distortions. Even if they earnestly try to speak only the truth, they cannot always avoid misleading their listeners. Moreover, they may intentionally disseminate falsehoods even in the absence of a desire to swindle. Consider a lobbyist who sincerely believes in the benefits of some subsidy. Conscious of the mental limitations of her listeners, she reasons that certain facts would turn them against the subsidy. By disregarding or discrediting these, she shields her listeners from information they might misuse. Political philosophy has long harbored a paternalistic tradition that endorses "noble lies"—falsehoods concocted in the audience's own interest.[17]

Another instrument of paternalism is censorship. Egged on by pressure groups, many governments censor publications, often to protect the masses from harmful information or to keep public discourse "balanced." Whatever the rationalization, the ultimate objective of censorship is to suppress information inimical to some agenda dear to the censor.[18]

Commercial advertising molds our consumptive preferences as surely as political persuasion molds our political preferences. There is an important difference, however. The buyer of a slickly advertised car is in a position to appraise its performance. Moreover, if something goes wrong, he has a great incentive to identify the cause. By contrast, he cannot easily determine the effects of, say, a tariff on textiles. In any case, since any benefits of a change in the trade regime would accrue primarily to others, and since his own impact on the regime's determination is minuscule, he has little incentive to undertake a costly investigation. As a result, the individual is more dependent on society in political contexts than in the realm of ordinary consumption. This greater dependence implies a greater vulnerability to deception.[19]

The logic of this argument is supported by indications that people are generally very ignorant on political issues. In the words of Russell Neuman, the evidence is overwhelming that "even the basic facts of political history, the fundamental structure of political institutions, and current political figures and events escape the cognizance of the great majority of the electorate."[20] This is now one of the most widely accepted discoveries of social science, yet even seasoned observers show surprise at concrete findings. Only a third of adult Americans recognize the term "welfare state." At the height of the Soviet-American rivalry, little more than half could explain the Cold War.[21] One survey asked a sample of Americans whether the U.S. Constitution contains the phrase "from each according to his ability, to each according to his need." No fewer than 45 percent answered in the affirmative.[22]

Widespread ignorance on a given issue does not preclude the existence of some knowledgeable individuals. The activists within pressure groups are often highly informed about their pet issues. These are the people who take it upon themselves to feed information to the uninformed. But a person who is very knowledgeable in one particular context is apt to depend on society in various other contexts. No one can be a knowledgeable activist with respect to more than a fraction of the issues on society's political agenda.[23]

The Heuristic of Social Proof

What gives the informed potentially immense power over the minds of the uninformed is that free riding on the knowledge of others is an essential vehicle for overcoming one's cognitive limitations. If others have investigated an issue in depth and their judgment can be trusted, one can dispense with the trouble of reflection by appropriating their apparent understandings.[24] So it is that we consult travel agents in planning a vacation and draw on the views of pundits in assessing the merits of competing political programs. In seeking guidance from experts we effectively transfer to them control over our thoughts.[25]

What makes us trust someone as an expert? When a television speaker claims that the stock market will rise we pay attention largely because *others* seem to consider the person an authority. After all, we reason, if the commentator did not know something he would not have been invited to speak on television. To trust an expert, then, is to let ourselves be guided by society's collective attribution of expertness. It is also common to draw on society's collective judgment concerning the substance of an issue, as opposed to its judgment regarding the relevant experts. We often put faith in a political agenda on account of its apparent popularity.

In either case we rely on a special heuristic, the *heuristic of social proof*.[26] If a great many people think in a particular way, they must know something we ourselves do not—as in the maxim "two heads are better than one." The basis of our own judgment becomes that "everyone knows" what is best or right. In effect, we believe an explanation, assertion, prediction, or evaluation because most others do.

The uses of social proof are not limited to matters on which we do not experiment or think for ourselves. Even where we possess independent knowledge, the fact that our perceptions are shared assures us of their correctness. This was recognized by James Madison, who wrote: "The strength of opinion in each individual, and its practical influence on his conduct, depend much on the number which he supposes to have entertained the same opinion. The reason of man, like man himself, is timid and cautious, when left alone; and acquires firmness and confidence, in proportion to the number with which it is associated."[27] Significantly, Madison attributed conformism to both "man" and the "reason of man." The conformism of man manifests itself in preference falsification; that of reason, in a pervasive reliance on social proof.

Like other heuristics, the heuristic of social proof serves us admirably in diverse contexts. A very common view usually carries a great deal of truth. As a rule, therefore, we make fewer mistakes by accepting a dominant belief than by rejecting it. Through social proof we can settle complex decisions without having to think deeply. Yet social proof is not a riskless device for economizing on mental effort. If an erroneous belief gains a foothold in people's minds, the use of social proof may cause it to spread and strengthen.

The Politics of Persuasion: Appeals to Social Proof

Conscious of the possibility of turning private knowledge, and thus private opinion, in favor of their agendas merely through social proof, groups do whatever they can to make their positions appear popular. A phrase like "the American way," when uttered on behalf of a particular agenda, signals that most Americans, or at least most "respectable" Americans, agree on what is appropriate. Of course the claim embodied in such a phrase may harbor much exaggeration. Other methods of exaggeration include dwelling on biased polls and overstating the size of a demonstration. All such methods constitute direct appeals to social proof.

Groups also make indirect appeals to social proof by seeking to ground their positions in the wisdom of widely respected figures, including ones no longer living. Dead authorities are particularly convenient to invoke, for their teachings can be revised or reinterpreted without challenges from the authorities themselves.[28] Centuries after the Prophet Muhammad, Muslim leaders attributed to him words and deeds concerning problems that had arisen long after his time.[29] But the rewriting of history does not always involve outright fabrication. Often it takes the form of identifying a new cast of heroes and villains and refocusing attention on a new array of events.

Whereas substantive arguments are intended to influence how people think about the issues of the day, direct or indirect appeals to social proof are intended to make people accept particular positions uncritically. Their effectiveness rests, as I have argued, on the degree to which people rely on social proof. Insofar as there are people trying to free ride on the thoughts of others, one can enhance the popularity of a position by offering convenient rides to it. Generally, in fact, making such rides available is essential to political success. If a group seeks to persuade solely through appeals to reason, the free riders in its audience will accept rides from others.

So appeals to reason and to social proof are not mutually exclusive categories of persuasion. Indeed, as a rule they are undertaken together. A lobbyist arguing that his constituents deserve a subsidy will in the same breath claim that most members of society feel the same way. Even in scholarship, where the authentication of ideas is supposed to be based solely on logic and evidence, appeals to social proof are common. Academic writers routinely cite great scholars to bolster the credibility of their assumptions and inferences. The sixteenth-century essayist Montaigne was once asked why his writings contained so many quotations from ancient luminaries. "It is really for the sake of public opinion," he replied, "that I appear with this borrowed finery."[30] Scholars also draw support from the presumed agreements within their disciplines. Many academic writings are peppered with phrases like "the standard assumption" and "as is well known."[31]

The effects of appeals to reason and to social proof are mutually reinforcing. The knowledge that an opinion is common justifies the effort one may devote to understanding its rationale. Conversely, convincing justifications for an opinion bolster the credibility of claims that it is widely shared.

Repetition as Social Proof

Anyone familiar with political campaigns knows that they are highly repetitive. Campaigners reiterate the same points at every opportunity, partly to reach new people, but also to get the campaign's messages accepted as demonstrated truth. Like politicians, advertisers of consumer goods use repetition as an instrument of mass persuasion. They expose us to the same slogans, gimmicks, and selling points over and over again. In surveys about attitudes toward advertising, such repetition is a standard source of complaint. Yet repetitive advertising is commonplace, evidently because familiarity fosters attraction and liking. A shopper who intends to buy a detergent will reflexively reach for a familiar brand—and her familiarity is likely to come from advertisements.[32] Scholars, too, use repetition as a means of raising their credibility. By advancing the same point in several different forms, often within the same body of work, a writer will try to give it validity by force of repetition. Many falsehoods have attained the status of unquestioned truth through reiteration. The error is known as the "fallacy of argument ad nauseam."[33]

From a logical standpoint, mere repetition should not enhance the attractiveness of a choice. If you already know that I consider defense spending too high, reiterations of this point give you no new information; hence, they should not affect your own judgment. In reality, we routinely accord informational value to such repetition. We equate multiple exposures to a single belief with the consensus of a group, effectively substituting reiteration for social proof. This is why repetition is a common instrument of persuasion.

The informational value of repetition is rooted in one of the heuristics we use to overcome our cognitive limitations: the *availability heuristic*. A person employs this heuristic "whenever he estimates frequency or probability by the ease with which instances or associations come to mind."[34] For instance, he might estimate the proportion of philatelists in the general population by recalling the philatelists among his acquaintances. For us, the heuristic's significance lies in the link it forges between repetition and perceived validity. The more a person has been exposed to a particular view, the easier its retrieval from memory and, hence, the higher its perceived validity.

Some evidence for the power of repetition lies in studies that find a clear connection between what issues the mass media cover extensively and what people consider important.[35] Additional evidence comes from psychological experiments. In one experiment, a group of subjects were exposed to sixty plausible statements, each either true or false.[36] Here are two examples: "In the U.S., divorced people outnumber those who are widowed" (which at the time of the experiment was false), and "In Malaya, if a man goes to jail for being drunk, his wife goes too" (which was true). After hearing the statements, the subjects were asked to rate the validity of each on a seven-point scale. Two weeks later, and again two weeks after that, the subjects were exposed to additional sets of sixty statements, each of which included twenty from the original list. As with the first session, the subjects were asked to rate each statement for its validity. A comparison of the ratings from the three sessions shows that the subjects treated exposure as a criterion of validity. For the repeated statements, whether actually true or false, the mean rating was significantly higher in the second and third sessions than in the first. Moreover, the repeated statements received appreciably higher ratings than the new ones.

Variants of this experiment have extended the generality of its main finding. Repetition apparently bolsters perceived validity even when subjects familiarize themselves with all statements before the experiment begins and even in sessions featuring no new statements.[37] The experiment thus confirms that if people hear a view often enough they may believe it. The likelihood of persuasion through repetition is all the greater, of course, with respect to matters not analyzed in depth.

Hard and Soft Knowledge

Our knowledge about the world thus rests only partly on personal observation, inference, and analysis. To conserve cognitive resources we rely also on social proof. The beliefs we adopt through social proof can be substantially biased, however, if only because we do not differentiate adequately between genuine consensus and repeated exposures to a single source of information.

To convey how social proof contributes to private knowledge one might distinguish between hard and soft private knowledge, or simply *hard knowledge* and *soft knowledge*. Hard knowledge is grounded in substantive facts and systematic reasoning. By contrast, soft knowledge is grounded in one or more forms of social proof. Either type of knowledge may be erroneous, of course. Just as the causes of a social phenomenon may be misperceived, perceptions of public opinion may be substantially off. In practice, moreover, "hardness" and "softness" form a continuum. Beliefs concerning social phenomena are ordinarily based both on personal observation and on perceptions of what others think. Still, the dichotomy will prove helpful.

For an illustration of the difference between hard and soft knowledge, suppose we ask three individuals to give us their thoughts on a free-trade treaty under negotiation with another country.[38] The first person happens to be an economic theorist. Drawing on years of reflection, she reasons that an elimination of trade barriers will produce a mutually beneficial reallocation of resources. Our second individual works in a textile factory. He lacks a coherent theory of international trade. Yet, knowing that wages are low in the other country, he believes that the elimination of import restrictions will harm the local textile industry. Afraid of losing his job, he thinks the treaty would harm the national interest. The final member of our sample is a physician. Having avoided economics in college, he has no coherent view on what the treaty might bring. Nor can he identify ways in which trade would impinge on his own happiness. But the treaty is a source of open controversy, so he senses that it will have *some* impact. To assess the nature of the impact, he searches his memory for the preferences to which he has been exposed. Most of those he retrieves are favorable, so he infers that "free trade would be a good thing."

The thoughts of our trio differ greatly in substantive content. If the scholar were asked to justify her faith in the treaty, she could speak for hours on the merits of free trade. The textile worker possesses no comparable theory. But he could say, based on his own thinking, that towns with textile plants will decline. As for the physician, if he were asked to justify his belief he would first draw a blank, because the reason he supports the treaty is simply its apparent popularity. If pressed for an explanation, he would say something like "Trade makes a country rich. Everyone knows that."

The scholar and the physician both consider the agreement beneficial, the former on the basis of hard knowledge, the latter on the basis of soft knowledge. The scholar's belief is supported by an elaborate model and scientific evidence. For his part, the physician is simply trusting his community's apparent collective judgment. He feels compelled, however, to have a view of his own, so when asked to justify his support, he makes up a shallow explanation. Subsequently, he may reckon that his opinion of the treaty stems from his own reasoning and that his thinking preceded this opinion. In fact, his opinion came first, the justification being an *afterthought*. He could not possibly have become protreaty through mental endeavor, since he knows almost nothing about trade.

Our physician's illusion might be likened to that of the occasional museum visitor who arrives in front of a Cubist painting signed "Picasso." Cognizant of Picasso's fame, the visitor reckons that he is looking at a masterpiece. "Phenomenal!" he exclaims. His companion then asks what it is that he likes about the painting. "It's creative, and the colors are subtle," he responds. In reality, he is impressed because most discriminating critics consider Picasso a genius. He first notices that the painting is by a famous artist, then he decides to like the painting, and finally, when asked to justify his taste, he concocts an explanation suitable to almost any painting in the museum. Suppose we had replaced the signature on the painting with "R. Barney" and placed it among works by unknown local artists. Our visitor might well have dismissed the otherwise identical painting as unimaginative.

Readers accustomed to thinking that we always act for reasons we understand and can articulate may find it difficult to swallow the notion that private preferences may precede the reasons for having them. For the benefit of such skeptics, here is another illustration.

The Eiffel Tower now symbolizes Paris, much as the Colosseum symbolizes Rome. People of all types admire its metallic elegance and imposing height. Yet the tower was not always considered beautiful. When its construction began in 1887, the leading artists and intellectuals of France were offended by its uselessness and by the specter of its inescapable presence throughout Paris. After struggling to stop its construction, they continued to heap scorn on it. Among the tower's critics was the writer Guy de Maupassant, who would tell people that he frequently lunched at its restaurant even though the food was tasteless. "It is the only place in Paris," he would explain, "where I can be certain not to see it."[39] Now, a century after the tower's construction, we cannot even think of reasons for considering it an eyesore. If it boasts universal admiration, part of the reason is that we all learn at an early age that it is among the wonders of the world.

To return to politics, we all have views on social issues about which we are ignorant. Those of us who know little about the international economy have opinions on trade legislation; and those of us without military expertise have opinions concerning aircraft procurement. Many of us may even have opinions on fictitious issues. In 1984 researchers at the University of Cincinnati conducted a survey containing, among many questions on real issues, questions on the Agricultural Trade Act of 1984, the Monetary Control Bill of 1984, and the 1975 Public Affairs Act—all fictitious. Amazingly, more than half the subjects offered opinions on the first and second fictitious measures, and more than 40 percent on the third.[40] One can easily imagine the criteria on which the participants with opinions based their answers: "Monetary control lowers inflation, so it must be good"; or, "Monetary control will freeze wages—the less the better."

The Cincinnati survey confirms the ease with which people form opinions on unfamiliar issues. Psychologists have conducted complementary experiments on people's ability to rationalize opinions formed under ignorance. In one such experiment, subjects were given the purportedly correct solution to a tricky problem and asked to justify it. They were also asked to rate their confidence in the validity of their explanations. The recipients of incorrect solutions had no more difficulty in supplying an explanation than those of the actually correct solution. Nor were their confidence ratings significantly lower.[41]

The critical implication is that the flimsiest suggestion as to the merits of a political option may serve as grounds for embracing it with confidence. If the opinions of others are known, so much the better. On the assumption that others have reasons for taking the positions they do, we will internalize whatever opinion seems dominant. Should the need arise for justifying a borrowed opinion, we will do so easily. Our justifications often come from slogans, generalizations, and assertions offered by the mass media. The media help shape not only our positions on issues of the day but also the shallow explanations with which we meet challenges to our views.[42]

The finding that we are prepared to develop opinions on issues that we scarcely understand reinforces my point that persuasion campaigns need not be limited to substantive argumentation. Polls, statements by ostensible authorities, repetitive propaganda, and other means of social proof may be effective even in the absence of sound logic and evidence. This is because to accept something as optimal we do not need to understand *why* it is optimal. We might not even want to know, for our cognitive limitations require us to think selectively. And ordinarily we need just a few simple points to justify ourselves whenever put on the spot. However unsophisticated, our justifications may sound erudite, at least to people as uninformed as ourselves.

The softness or hardness of a belief must not be confused with its *power,* which is its potential influence over behavior. A belief based solely on social proof—one that is extremely soft—may generate wild passions, as when a student participates fervently in a revolutionary movement whose program she has never read. By the same token, a belief formed through extensive personal experience—one that is very hard—might elicit little action. An educator convinced that schools are in decline will not necessarily act on this information; fearing objections, he might opt to keep quiet.

The variability of the power of beliefs will assume significance in the next chapter. For the time being, I will continue to explore the implications of variability in relative hardness.

Belief Perseverance

Writing in the 1950s, Daniel Lerner defined modernization as a process whereby people become efficient adapters to change.[43] Where a medieval peasant saw the social future as ordained, the modern urbanite sees it as manipulable. The former would reject innovation by saying "We have always done it the old way"; the latter is more likely to ask "Will it work?" and try the new way without inhibition. A modernized person, suggested Lerner, is open to new ways of thinking and willing to shed habits that have become dysfunctional.

Lerner's proposition may be contrasted with a theory of adaptation developed by Ronald Heiner.[44] Noting that human behavior is "rule governed," Heiner observes that the individual will modify a routine only when he is sufficiently certain that the environment has changed. Naturally, the complexity of the relevant environment varies from one context to another. The more complex the environment, the less adequate is the individual's relevant knowledge and, hence, the less he can trust signs that his routine is obsolete. This argument has a far-reaching implication: the more complex the environment, the *less* sensitive individual behavior is to actual environmental shocks.

If we were capable of processing infinite amounts of information, we would respond reliably to the slightest environmental perturbation. In ever-changing environments our behaviors would thus always be in flux. Heiner's insight is that we do *not* respond to every perturbation, because our cognitive limitations frequently keep us from identifying the best response. Moreover, while greater knowledge enhances our flexibility in the face of environmental change, increasing complexity has the opposite effect.

In the light of Heiner's theory, let me return to Lerner's proposition. Insofar as modernization is fueled by greater knowledge, we should be becoming increasingly open to innovation. But the rising complexity of modern civilization should be having the reverse effect. In principle, then, modernization's effect on mental flexibility could be positive in some contexts and negative in others. In the realm of ordinary consumption, it appears that we exhibit more flexibility than our ancestors. Casual observation also suggests, however, that in the political realm we are not nearly as flexible. We all have acquaintances whose political beliefs seem impervious to the failures of their favored platforms.

Substantive facts and arguments that conflict with existing convictions are relevant, of course, only to the extent that the convictions are hard. The failure of a program will not affect what I think if my relevant knowledge is based entirely on social proof. Suppose I consider a program optimal because this is the conventional wisdom. My mind is not going to change simply because of a contrary scholarly finding. Since I ignore the pertinent scholarly literature, the finding will not even catch my attention. What *would be* relevant is a perceived change in the nature of social proof.

The process of assessing social proof can vary in complexity. If my estimates come from opinion surveys, a single poll may suffice to convince me that the character of social proof is changing. This is consistent with the common volatility of individual political positions.[45] But polls are not the only source of information on public opinion. When estimates come predominantly from social interactions, signs of a shift in public opinion may be discounted or overlooked. For the same reason that environmental complexity imparts inflexibility to hard knowledge, the complexities of social proof may make soft knowledge inflexible.

Let me return to the treaty illustration. Imagine that after trade barriers are eliminated the country slips into recession. The economist remains wedded to her model of competition, convinced as ever that trade is socially beneficial. After all, she reasons, economic activity is also affected by factors excluded from the model of competitive markets. As for the physician's support, it had been based on social proof. After trade barriers are lifted he remains alert to indicators of collective judgment. It so happens that he does not follow formal polls; his estimates come from the passing comments of his acquaintances. These appear to be turning against free trade, but he is not quite sure. For a while, therefore, he remains wedded to the idea that free trade is beneficial. Only as the signs of a shift in social proof multiply does he change his mind.

Both individuals display what psychologists call "belief perseverance."[46] Data that might have had an impact before their beliefs took shape have no immediate influence when they arrive afterward. A more basic source of belief perseverance is that our beliefs govern what we notice in the first place. We perceive selectively, noticing facts consistent with our beliefs relatively more readily. This bias imparts resistance to our beliefs by shielding them from counterevidence.

Scientific confirmation for belief perseverance comes from a broad array of experiments. In one experiment, the figure of a penguin was made to change gradually into that of a man through a succession of images, or vice versa.[47] People who saw the sequence in the penguin-to-man direction generally labeled most images as "penguin"; those who saw it in the reverse direction tended to label most as "man." The middle images were taken to represent whatever the sequence started with. If a viewer first saw a penguin, he kept seeing a penguin until the human features became highly dominant.

Another experiment presented two studies on capital punishment to university students who strongly believed either that capital punishment deters crime or that it does not.[48] One study supported the affirmative position, the other the negative. When subsequently questioned, students rated as more convincing the results and procedures that confirmed their own prior beliefs. In addition, the students' views became more polarized than before. The proponents of capital punishment became even more convinced that such punishment deters crime; the opponents became more convinced that it does not.

The latter experiment shows vividly that people treat information asymmetrically. If the subjects had been equally open and responsive to all information, they would all have become less confident of their prior beliefs, not more so. A virtue of this experiment is that it confirms the significance of selective perception. If insensitivity to unreliable signals were the only source of mental resistance, the subjects might have remained wedded to their beliefs, but without becoming more confident. That confidence levels rose suggests that subjects noticed more of the evidence favorable to their beliefs than of the counterevidence.

Students of the same phenomena often subscribe to radically different interpretations. Where some economists see harmonious growth and efficient markets, for example, others observe deepening poverty and crises of accumulation. Such conflicts might be driven by incompatible political agendas. But they might emerge even in the absence of motivational variation because, as the above experiments suggest, our preconceptions regulate what we see. The same trends may seem fundamentally different to a scholar trained in neoclassical economics than to one trained in Marxian economics. One will recognize as crucial what the other's education makes her overlook. One will detect a pattern even where it is absent; the other will miss the pattern even where it is strongest.[49]

The opening of this chapter dismissed the Leibnizian metaphor of a windowless monad as seriously flawed. Having seen that the human personality does have windows, we must now recognize that only some of these can be open at any one time. The closed ones narrow the individual's field of vision, thus keeping certain events, patterns, and phenomena out of his view. Consequently, his beliefs enjoy some protection from counterevidence.

The Illusion of Individual Autonomy

As mentioned earlier, acts of preference falsification do not necessarily make a person lose sight of his own personal interest. His private knowledge, and thus his private preferences, may well remain intact. It would be a mistake, however, to infer that the individual is, in essence, an autonomous entity. In a vast array of contexts, a person's perceived self-interest will rest on information drawn from public discourse. Therefore, what he considers his self-interest may actually be the interest of others.

Insofar as private knowledge rests on public discourse, it can show sensitivity to anything affecting the substance or constitution of public discourse. Faulty models or flawed accounts of public opinion may warp an individual's private knowledge. So can preference falsification on the part of other individuals trying themselves to avoid social penalties. Some forms of preference falsification alter public discourse, and all affect public opinion. Therefore, preference falsification can distort any private knowledge, hard or soft. To specify the processes by which the distortions occur is the challenge of the next chapter.

Lest this seem a trivial exercise, I should repeat that contemporary social thought houses traditions that deny society's influence over individual dispositions. Neoclassical economics tends to consider preferences autonomous. Political theories in the neoclassical tradition thus posit that parties compete by tailoring their agendas to fixed voter preferences. In reality, of course, parties also try to shape what voters want. They would not do so were voters windowless monads.

A related claim of neoclassical economics is that people's ostensibly autonomous preferences reflect their "objective" economic interests. Yet studies show that measures of self-interest are poor predictors of policy preferences.[50] They find, for instance, that young and old Americans are almost equally supportive of subsidies to retirees.[51] Related research finds ideology to be an irreducible factor in policy choices.[52] Building on the conclusions of this chapter, the argument in the next will demonstrate why ideology can swamp any "objective" measure of self-interest.

Another tradition that treats personal conceptions of self-interest as immutable is a Marxian-inspired literature that seeks to disprove the possibility of oppressed groups becoming mentally enslaved by their oppressors. James Scott, a contributor to this literature, observes that the oppressed act out their assigned roles without losing sight of their overriding interest, the overthrow of the oppressive order. "There is little chance," he writes, "that acting a mask will appreciably affect the face of the actor. And, if it does, there is a better chance that the face behind the mask will, in reaction, grow to look *less* like the mask rather than more like it."[53] Scott's argument rests on reactance theory, which holds that under strong physical threats overt agreement will coexist with covert reactance—an unexpressed desire to rebel.[54] In applying reactance theory to politics, Scott confuses resistance to an oppressor with cognitive autonomy from the oppressor's ideology. One can despise an oppressor, and still, precisely because of the social conditions created by the oppressor, fail to develop a worldview that is essentially one's own. To show that the oppressed do not accept every element of the oppressor's worldview is not to prove that they remain mentally uninfluenced.

In any case, the forces that regulate an oppressed group's beliefs are never just physical. As the next chapter will show, they often take the form of social pressures that violate the stringent conditions of reactance theory.

11

The Unthinkable and the Unthought

The Islamic scholar Mohammed Arkoun makes two distinctions in characterizing public discourse in the Islamic world. One is between the *thinkable* and the *unthinkable*, the other between the *thought* and the *unthought*. Noting that past generations of Muslims treated key tenets of the European Enlightenment as unthinkable, he argues that present generations cannot even conceive of applying the methods of historical criticism to sacred texts and cherished traditions. "The resurgence of Islam," he goes on to assert, "is taking place on the basis of an immense unthought accumulated over centuries." Herein lies "one of the deep but secret reasons for so many current problems."[1] Many others have pointed to the impoverished character of contemporary Islamic thought, tracing it to the suffocation of Muslim intellectual activity from about the tenth century onward.[2]

An unthinkable belief is a thought that one cannot admit having, or even characterize as worth entertaining, without raising doubts about one's civility, morality, loyalty, practicality, or sanity. An unthought belief is an idea that is not even entertained. Underlying Arkoun's interpretation of Islamic history is the notion that a belief treated as unthinkable eventually disappears from human consciousness, that it moves from the realm of the thought to that of the unthought.

I wish neither to challenge nor to promote Arkoun's thesis on Islam. The objective of this chapter is to explore the *process* that is implicit in his sweeping historical claim. Specifically, I want to suggest, drawing on the previous chapter, and operating within the earlier developed framework of public opinion formation, how the unthinkable can become the unthought. The relevance of the process to be outlined transcends, of course, the world of Islam. The preceding chapters on caste, communism, and affirmative action highlighted certain expressive taboos of other societies. Chapters ahead will revisit these three cases to show that the identified taboos have all upset, perverted, and constrained individual understandings.

Arkoun's terminology affords a succinct statement of this chapter's argument. By transferring beliefs from the realm of the thinkable to that of the unthinkable, social pressures induce the withdrawal of those beliefs from public discourse. The consequent reconstitution of public discourse distorts private knowledge. In particular, it makes people progressively less conscious of the disadvantages of what is publicly favored and increasingly more conscious of the advantages. As a result, private opinion moves against the publicly unfavored alternatives. Having lessened their public popularity, preference falsification thus ends up also lessening their private popularity.

Public Discourse and Knowledge Falsification

In developing the notion of preference falsification, I posited that, whether private or public, preferences take the form of numbers representing identifiable social options. I will continue to exploit this convenient fiction, but it should be recognized that selecting a public preference generally involves the communication of some form of knowledge. The communication may entail the articulation of a philosophy, the interpretation of an event, the rejection of a claim, or the choice of a word, among other possibilities. Without stating how she feels about tariffs, a professor speaks of the virtues of free trade. Her audience infers that she is for free trade and against tariffs.

Insofar as *public discourse* carries information on public preferences, pressure groups have an incentive to regulate it. They do, in fact, reward the articulation of certain thoughts and penalize that of others. They establish what facts may be stated, what words used, and what arguments advanced with impunity. Just as pressures against the vocalization of particular preferences breed preference falsification, those against the expression of particular thoughts generate *knowledge falsification*. Undertaken as a means of preference falsification,

knowledge falsification has an unintended effect: it alters the composition of public discourse, making favored messages more common
and unfavored ones less so. An immediate consequence is the distortion of public opinion, and a longer-run consequence is the distortion
of private knowledge and private opinion.

To explore the latter consequences, imagine a society that is in
agreement on some goal. Two ways, A and B, have been identified as
means of achieving the goal. There is disagreement on the merits of
these alternatives, however, and for a while the rival camps carry on
a vigorous public debate. One day, it becomes socially unacceptable
to advocate B, and people still partial to B begin feigning support for
A. With public opinion thus becoming increasingly more favorable to
A, individuals genuinely sympathetic to A continue to speak their
minds freely. But people only pretending to favor A cease being honest
about their thoughts, lest they be suspected of harboring sympathies
for B. They do not publicize their misgivings about A. Nor do they
state the justifications for B, except to ridicule or discredit them.

Let me now examine the consequences for soft private knowledge.
An examination of the effects on hard knowledge will follow.

How the Distortion of Public Discourse Reshapes Soft Knowledge

Regulated as it is by social proof, soft knowledge does not depend on
the substance of public discourse. If most people are defending A and
opposing B, then public opinion appears to favor A, and this is all
that matters. Never mind whether the pro-A arguments are cogent or
accurate. What is relevant to social proof is only that A appears to
have broader support. As public discourse shifts in favor of A, then,
so does social proof. And in the process, soft knowledge becomes more
favorable to A, causing the gap between private and public opinion
to shrink.

It is possible, of course, for belief perseverance to slow down the
adjustments. A person accustomed to seeing public opinion divided
equally between A and B may take a while to perceive the tilt toward
A. This form of perseverance needs to be distinguished, however, from
that driven by substantive preconceptions. The mind of a person who
has avoided giving serious thought to an issue harbors no relevant

knowledge except some sense of public opinion. Being unencumbered by substantive preconceptions, his understandings can evolve with changes in public opinion, provided the changes are noticed.

In any case, belief perseverance affects only the speed of adjustment. As long as public opinion remains heavily favorable to *A*, all soft knowledge will eventually complete the transition. From then on, moreover, preference falsification will cease to be a factor in the expressive choices of individuals dependent on social proof. They will all support *A* out of conviction rather than compulsion.

Their support may well be based on flawed information. Yet such a situation can endure indefinitely. Even if the thinkers on the issue—those possessing hard knowledge—recognize the flaws of *A*, public opinion will not necessarily move. Preference falsification may keep the potential switchers publicly loyal to *A*.

The Impact on Hard Knowledge

Turning to hard knowledge, we must remember that the substantive ideas on which it rests do not just vanish when social pressures induce widespread knowledge falsification. An agnostic Iranian does not forget the virtues of secularism when conditions force her to pay lip service to theocratic rule. Belief perseverance might keep her wedded to beliefs at odds with her adopted public preference. By no means, however, does belief perseverance insulate hard knowledge from the biases of public discourse. There are two countervailing factors.

First, no system of beliefs explains every fact that it may be called on to clarify or interpret. Every model provides only a partial grasp of reality, so it will prove inadequate in the face of certain facts. As philosophers of science point out, even "laws of nature" violate some aspects of reality. When it comes to social models, anomalies—observations they leave unexplained—are even more abundant. Yet the anomalies need not catch attention. The holder of a publicly unquestioned belief faces no reminders of its weaknesses. He finds public discourse to be loaded with facts and arguments consistent with his belief. By contrast, the holder of a belief at odds with public discourse is routinely reminded of the flaws in his thinking. He feels pressured, therefore, to revise his beliefs. If nothing else, he finds himself gripped by doubt and confusion.

The second countervailing factor is the fundamental attribution error, introduced in Chapter 4. Remember that this fallacy produces a tendency for people to underestimate the extent to which social pressures determine individual choices and to overestimate the significance of individual dispositions. The fallacy is rooted in two judgmental heuristics already discussed, representativeness and availability. Actors are more *representative* causes of their choices than are social pressures, because they themselves do the acting. And data about the sources of social pressure are often unsalient and, hence, *unavailable*.

Insofar as the fundamental attribution error is driven by the availability heuristic, actors should succumb to it less readily than their observers. After all, actors do not see themselves, and their attention focuses on their own opportunities and constraints. The experimental evidence confirms this reasoning. Actors are more inclined than observers to attribute their choices to situational factors.[3] Yet even actors accord inordinate weight to dispositional factors. In interpreting their own actions, they routinely overlook the importance of subtle pressures contrived by experimenters.[4]

This finding has a crucial implication. In subsequently interpreting a public preference, a preference falsifier might underestimate the degree to which it differed from his private preference. This is because his beliefs might adapt subconsciously to those he has had to express publicly. In the process, moreover, the falsifier might come to underrate the disharmony between public discourse and his original thoughts. It is as though a chameleon understood that it turned green to blend into the surrounding foliage, yet misperceived how greatly its color had to change.

The speed at which hard knowledge gets transformed will vary from one context to another. Where ongoing personal experience or accumulated reflection is an important source of information, hard knowledge will be especially resistant to the conflicting messages contained in public discourse. Even then, however, there will be some effect. One may sense that central planning is unviable and retain this perception in the face of decades of antimarket propaganda, yet lose the ability to learn more about the limitations of planning. Moreover, a hard belief may be held in varying degrees of confidence. To the extent that it conflicts with public discourse, it is likely to fuel doubt.

The distortion of public discourse thus affects both hard and soft knowledge, but through different mechanisms. Soft knowledge changes readily because its mobility is constrained only by difficulties in ascertaining the course of public opinion. And in any case, perceptual obstacles lose significance where public opinion shifts massively. In contrast to soft knowledge, hard knowledge does not necessarily move with perceived shifts in public opinion. Someone with information favorable to a certain program will not lose faith in it merely because public opinion now favors an alternative. His faith in the program may be shaken, however, and he may be unable to discover new justifications for rejecting the alternative.[5]

Recognizing that hardness and softness are matters of degree allows the foregoing conclusions to be refined. Social pressures against free expression can affect any particular belief, although the impact and speed of adjustment will depend inversely on the belief's hardness. Very soft private knowledge will change fastest and most comprehensively; very hard private knowledge will exhibit the greatest perseverance. Yet the net effect of expressive constraints is to shift private knowledge *against* ideas perilous to express. It is, in other words, to lessen the influence of the unthinkable.

Mitigating Cognitive Dissonance?

In the above argument changes in private knowledge are unrelated to personal motivation. Beliefs get abandoned in response to transformations of the corpus of public information, not because individuals decide to change their own minds. This unmotivated adjustment mechanism may be contrasted with the motivated mechanism Leon Festinger offers in his classic work on "cognitive dissonance."[6] Festinger's key assumption is that people strive toward cognitive consistency. Someone who harbors mutually inconsistent attitudes is in a state of cognitive dissonance. Dissonance being uncomfortable, the person tries to lessen it, and also to avoid situations that may raise it. In effect, he adjusts his beliefs deliberately in an effort to minimize the tensions they create.

Preference falsification is a form of personal inconsistency, and Festinger devotes much attention to the efforts people make to overcome the resulting dissonance. His experiments show that when a person accommodates a social pressure to obtain a big reward or avoid a stiff punishment, his private preference changes little, if at all. But when the incentive is barely enough to elicit his compliance, his private preference undergoes a major transformation. Here is Festinger's own interpretation. The magnitude of the dissonance created by a conflict between one's inner and outer selves varies inversely with one's incentives for accommodating external demands.[7] If an Iranian defends Islamic rule under the threat of imprisonment, she can easily justify her compliance as a small price for avoiding great hardship. If instead her motive was to win the approval of her peers, she may be hard-pressed to find a satisfying justification. What if she had been candid, and her peers went no further than to frown? Her dissonance will be greater, therefore, than in the former situation. And so, by Festinger's logic, she will try harder to adapt her private preference to her chosen public preference.

Let me reinterpret the illustration in the light of my own theory. If it takes a harsh threat to make an Iranian support Islamic rule, a possible reason is that she is convinced that secular government would be better. One might expect, then, belief perseverance to shield her convictions from public arguments supportive of Islamic rule and, hence, the disharmony between her private and public preferences to persist. If instead she will yield to mild pressure, the reason could be that her reservations are minor or, if major, that they rest on superficial understandings. In either case, her resistance to new ideas is likely to be low. The crucial point is that differences in attitudinal change will tend to reflect differences in cognitive resistance, not differences in motivation.

Another of Festinger's findings is that people seek dissonance-lowering information and avoid information likely to raise dissonance.[8] His interpretation is that the consequent reduction in dissonance is deliberate. In this view, an Iranian feigning approval of Islamic rule will pay special attention to official propaganda and will avoid listening to critical foreign broadcasts. Through such selective exposure to information, she will brainwash herself, thereby bringing her private preference in line with her public preference.

Again, there is an alternative explanation. Someone who wants people to think she supports Islamic rule knows that to be convincing she must bolster her chosen position with appropriate reasoning. Official propaganda carries suitable arguments and slogans in abundance; foreign broadcasts do not. So she might consciously expose herself to the former in order to gain better control over her public image. A complementary benefit of selective exposure is that it sends a prudent signal as to her disposition. An ostensibly pro-Islamic Iranian caught listening to Voice of America, when she could be tuned in to Radio Tehran, risks being branded a hypocrite. By listening to Radio Tehran when others are in earshot, she makes her chosen public preference more credible.

In my own explanation, then, selective exposure reflects a quest for outer peace as opposed to inner peace. It is undertaken to justify one's public position to *others* rather than to *oneself*. It is itself a form of preference falsification.

When a phenomenon admits two explanations, it is not necessary that one be false. Festinger's explanation and my own are not mutually incompatible. An Iranian may listen to progovernment broadcasts both to obtain comforting knowledge and to signal a socially acceptable stand. But if my argument is correct, the person who listens to Radio Tehran in the presence of others will, whenever an opportunity arises, listen secretly to Voice of America. If Festinger is right, this will not happen, because it would defeat the purpose of listening to Radio Tehran.

I might add that the theory of cognitive dissonance conflicts with the plain fact that contradictory beliefs may coexist in a person's mind indefinitely. As already discussed, we are simply unable to incorporate into a comprehensive model the multitudes of variables and relationships that bear on our happiness. We all have to partition reality into many distinct models. Within Festinger's framework this observation presents a puzzle. If we feel uncomfortable maintaining contradictory ideas, what explains why we manage to reduce only *some* of our inconsistencies?

Here is a possible answer. When a person's beliefs change this happens not through his own personal efforts but, rather, through a *social process* in which he is just one of many participants. If public discourse treats two issues as unrelated, he is apt to do the same, because he cannot explore all possible connections. He may well remain unaware of important connections without feeling any discomfort.

In a vast array of contexts the linkages individuals make among events, outcomes, and phenomena are governed largely by public discourse. Where public discourse is itself inconsistent—as when it promotes the literal accuracy of the Bible while also celebrating the explanatory power of modern biology—people may not even notice the contradiction. Many will do so, however, if the inconsistency begins to receive public attention.

From Unthinkable to Unthought

In the argument thus far, social pressures can block the articulation of ideas and fuel doubts about their validity but, provided some people hold them for substantive reasons, not drive them into extinction. It follows that if the composition of society were fixed, ideas would never die. In reality, of course, the composition changes through births and deaths. The next step is to explore how the distortion of public discourse affects the prevalence of ideas over periods long enough for full population renewal. The step entails outlining an *intergenerational mechanism of ideological transformation* to complement the already presented *intragenerational mechanism of individual conversion*.

When people die they take with them their private knowledge, including their ideas at odds with public discourse. Like their genes, their expressed ideas live on in their descendants; their unexpressed beliefs may not. Their offspring will form worldviews through experience, experimentation, study, and various forms of social proof. Wherever social proof comes into play, the worldviews of the offspring will bear the influence of taboos that reigned during the life span of the parent generation. The insight that each generation helps shape the knowledge of the next is not new, of course. The significance of the following argument lies in its emphasis on socially induced expressive constraints as a major determinant of the content of knowledge transmission across generations.

It will help to distinguish between issues where public opinion is divided and ones where it is not. Where public opinion is divided, public discourse features genuine debate. So the young cannot but notice the existence of an unsettled issue. Some will devote attention to it out of a sense that it bears on their happiness, others out of curiosity. Whatever their impetus for giving the issue some thought, these members of the young generation will put what they hear to the test of their own personal experiences. A fraction of them might have experiences that steer their thoughts away from the dominant strand in public discourse—as when a laid-off American worker discovers virtues in socialism. Others who think about the controversial issue will have experiences supportive of the dominant viewpoint.

A cohort exposed to a full spectrum of viewpoints is likely, therefore, to display considerable diversity in its own thoughts. Yet a divided public discourse is not neutral in its effect on young minds. The ideas that the young inculcate influence how they interpret their subsequent experiences, and these ideas are likely to be those commanding the greatest social acceptance. So whereas public discourse is not the only determinant of what the young think, its role is important. To the extent that public discourse favors a particular social option, the thoughts of the young will reflect the bias. Their life experiences could produce, of course, a counteracting bias. But unless it is strong their thoughts will tend to conform to the dominant ideas of their parents' generation. In any case, not all members of a young cohort will reflect on any given controversial issue. Some will pay it little heed, opting to free ride on social proof. These nonthinkers will tend to internalize the viewpoint that dominates public discourse.

Even when divided, then, the public discourse of one generation leaves its mark on the private knowledge—and thus the private preferences—of the next. Whether the young rely on social proof or on the substance of prevailing arguments, they are influenced by public discourse, although some end up absorbing views in the minority. The discourse that shapes a young generation's worldview need not, of course, reflect the old generation's true convictions.

I turn now to the extreme case where public opinion is undivided. Suppose that in public, though not in private, the old generation has achieved agreement on the advantages of a particular social option. Public discourse thus consists of unchallenged justifications for a publicly unopposed option. The young are no better equipped than any other generation to think seriously about every possible matter. Because of their cognitive limitations, they must think selectively, relying extensively on social proof. They will thus treat as settled most matters on which they have inherited no public disagreement, reserving their mental powers primarily for ones that appear controversial. In the process, they will come to treat many of yesterday's issues as nonissues. Where their parents saw problems demanding discussion, they will see only fully justified solutions.

Such an outcome is all the more likely on matters where personal experience offers little help in discriminating among possible options. An unchallenged ban on a medical procedure will not arouse the interest of nonscientists. Even medical researchers might refrain from exploring the ban's practicality and turn their attention to other problems. By contrast, on matters where personal experience does provide reliable signals, the young might easily rediscover options that their predecessors had discarded. Individuals born into a society committed to living outdoors would quickly rediscover the benefits of shelter.

The unthinkable of one generation thus does not automatically enter the unthought of its successor. People are certainly capable of rediscovering social options and of finding fault with widely accepted arguments. Yet the limitations of human cognition steer one's attention away from undiscussed matters. Therefore, unexpressed ideas are less likely than ones expressed openly to enter the worldviews of later generations.

The outlined intergenerational process through which the unthinkable enters the realm of the unthought can be a formidable source of social persistence. Making people progressively less conscious of justifications for change, the process can dampen private support for reform. The transformation can take place without any planning, although deliberate indoctrination might well be a complementary factor. Simply by withholding its reservations about the status quo, a community can keep its descendants unaware of ideas for reform. Once sustained because people were afraid to challenge it, the status quo might come to persist because its alternatives are no longer known.

"The transmission of knowledge from one generation to the other must be predominantly tacit," says Michael Polanyi, writing about the social power of ideas that serve as tacit presuppositions.[9] No generation, Polanyi explains, let alone each member of it, can test all the knowledge to which it gets exposed. It must take much as given. The *significance* of tacit thought is independent of preference falsification. People whose ancestors were perfectly candid would still accept much without examination. The *boundaries* of tacit thought, however, do depend on preference falsification. When social structures with known flaws cease to be challenged, their alleged benefits come to be accepted as self-evident.

Attitudinal research shows that society exerts more influence on *what the young think about* than on *what they think*. Through the family, the workplace, and the mass media, society apparently plays a central role in determining where the young draw the boundaries between the thought and the unthought. Society exerts less control over the perceptions the young develop on problems to which they devote serious attention.[10] Related cognitive research shows that on problems they choose to reflect upon young generations often generate novel perspectives, partly because they combine existing ideas in new ways and partly because these ideas interact with their personal experiences.[11] The point is not that the young are able to think independently, only that they can break away from *some* of the thought patterns that they have inherited.

It might be said that ideas of great consequence are never lost completely to public discourse, that people of unusual courage and imagination always find listeners unlikely to bring them harm. Indeed, ideas concealed from the general public might live on indefinitely within small groups. Yet this hardly negates the general argument. It is difficult to achieve deep understandings in secrecy. Ideas gain clarity and precision when they are expressed publicly and debated widely.

Another possible objection is that unthinkable ideas might live on in books and other permanent records and eventually be rediscovered. For example, a long-unexpressed idea might be noticed and then reintroduced into public discourse by some historian of social thought. True enough, but such a fortuitous discovery is less probable than is the spotting of an idea found routinely in contemporary publications and expressed openly in daily conversation. The point remains that ideas purged from public discourse are less likely to remain in human consciousness than ones still expressed freely.

The Ideological Generation Gap

If one common intergenerational theme is that the old influence the thoughts of the young, another is that the old and the young see things very differently. Where the young look toward the bright days ahead, the old reminisce about the "good old days." Where the young em-

brace innovations enthusiastically, the old resist novelty and shun experimentation. Generations are divided, in effect, by an *ideological
generation gap.*

Within the framework here, such a gap admits the following interpretation. On an issue where public opinion is somewhat divided, new
entrants to society take to thinking on their own, and some of them
produce novel ideas. The rest of the young find these ideas reasonable,
whereas the old, because of their preconceptions, tend to remain skeptical. The two generations thus drift mentally apart.

Any particular generation gap will wither away as population renewal shrinks the share of society tied to old beliefs. In the process,
private opinion will shift, possibly precipitating a change in public
opinion. As shown further on, the latter shift may involve sudden
jumps. Suffice it to observe here that, once the new ideas gain wide
acceptance, they themselves may gain resistance. Where one generation found them hard to accept, later generations may find them hard
to reject. The argument applies, of course, only to issues where private
preferences are grounded in hard knowledge. On issues where most
people rely on social proof, huge transformations in both private and
public opinion can take place over short periods of time. Major dispositional transformations depend on population renewal insofar as
private knowledge is hard.

By this logic, population renewal should be the primary vehicle for
revolutions in science. After all, science is more thought-intensive than
any other human endeavor. The historian of science Thomas Kuhn
argues, in fact, that scientific revolutions are made by new generations
of scientists who are less tied to the old paradigms of their disciplines.[12]
A scientific paradigm is the corpus of observations, concepts, techniques, and solved problems that in the course of normal research the
members of a scientific community treat as given. Individual scientists
inculcate a paradigm through training, and their commitment hardens
as they become increasingly competent at applying it to novel questions. Along the way they lose the ability to see their paradigm's limitations. Equally important, they lose the capacity to appreciate the
power of some new paradigm. Their successors are exposed to the
new paradigm before their minds get molded by the old, so they have
less trouble appreciating its superiority. As they assume positions of

influence, the scientific community effectively abandons the old paradigm for the new.

The Copernican theory of the universe now makes sense even to a child. It seemed contrived, however, to astronomers trained to see planets orbiting the earth rather than the sun. It thus took four decades for the heliocentric theory of Copernicus to gain a secure foothold in astronomy. It eventually triumphed, but not because of the discovery of incontrovertible empirical evidence. Rather, young astronomers who learned about it at the start of their careers found it believable, and astronomy underwent a revolution as they rose to key positions.[13]

Ideological Transformation and the Dissipation of Collective Conservatism

I now return to the process whereby the unthinkable becomes the unthought. As already discussed, an immediate consequence of the extinction of some idea is a shift in the relevant distribution of private preferences. What effect does the shift have on the collective conservatism that society exhibits? And what does it imply for political stability?

To answer these questions, we must reconsider the formal framework last presented in Chapter 6. Because people derive utility from candor, changes in their private preferences alter the tradeoffs they face in choosing their public preferences. Remember that the expected public opinion at which an individual is indifferent between supporting 0 and supporting 100 is that individual's threshold. The threshold varies inversely with the underlying private preference.[14] Figure 11.1 reproduces part of Figure 6.1, except that the propagation curve is now time-specific, to accommodate changes in individual thresholds. If the fading of ideas favorable to 0 lowers individual thresholds, the propagation curve will move upward, possibly changing the set of equilibria.

This observation leaves us in a quandary. If an equilibrium is vulnerable to human adaptation, is the concept still meaningful and useful? The answer is a definite yes. First of all, private preferences are not necessarily in perpetual motion. On any given issue, there may be long intervals during which they stay fixed, possibly because people are focused on other issues. Second, even where private preferences are moving, public preferences, and thus public opinion, may remain unchanged. Finally, at any given moment private preferences are set, so one may speak of equilibria that are conditional on the prevailing private preferences.

According to Figure 11.1, in period 15 there are two stable equilibria. To take the simpler case first, imagine that public opinion has settled at 100—in public everyone supports 100 and rejects 0. With public discourse providing many justifications for the option 100 and none for 0, private opinion moves over time in favor of 100, partly through individual conversions and partly through natural replacement. In the process, the propagation curve shifts upward. By period 25, it has assumed, say, the form shown in Figure 11.2.

Public opinion has remained at 100 between periods 15 and 25. And the set of equilibria now contains only 100. By virtue of this uniqueness, the persistence of public opinion no longer owes anything to the magnetism of recent history. If people were to forget where

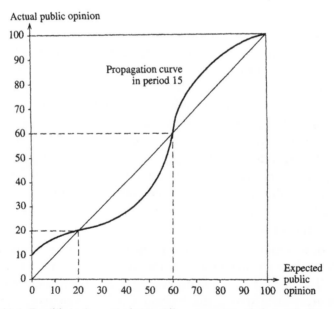

Figure 11.1 Equilibria in period 15. All expectations below 60 drive public opinion to 20, and all those above 60 drive public opinion to 100.

public opinion was, their subsequent choices would inevitably restore the preexisting equilibrium. Iperiod 15, by contrast, history did play a role in the persistence of public opinion. If no one knew what public opinion had been a period earlier, any expectation below 60 would have driven public opinion to 20.

Chapter 6 presented a measure of collective conservatism to quantify the role of history in the status quo's preservation. It also showed that in the diagram reproduced here as Figure 11.1 the degree of collective conservatism inherent in the persistence of 100 is positive. The shift recorded in Figure 11.2 lowers the degree of collective conservatism to 0.[15] This decline reflects the fact that when the incumbent equilibrium is unrivaled, it is necessarily the ultimate destination of all expectational adjustments. History cannot matter to public opinion if there exists only a single equilibrium.

On the surface, nothing has changed between periods 15 and 25. They feature the same public consensus. Below the surface, however,

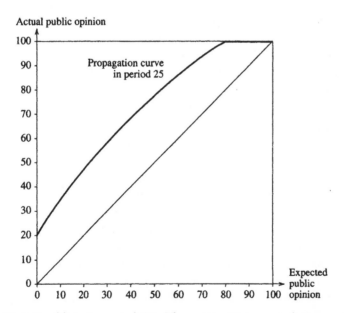

Figure 11.2 Equilibria in period 25. The propagation curve has moved up, leaving 100 as the only equilibrium. History is no longer a factor in the persistence of 100, because there remains no alternative to it.

the consensus enjoys greater private support in period 25 than in period 15. Private opinion has moved closer to public opinion, so the status quo now harbors less inner tension. Once an alternative to the established public consensus, the unselected stable equilibrium of Figure 11.1 has vanished, and the status quo has thus gained immunity to expectational shocks.

Walter Bagehot once remarked that what is used strengthens and what is unused weakens.[16] His maxim applies well to the case at hand. Of the two stable equilibria in period 15, that which is used, namely 100, becomes increasingly less vulnerable to displacement, and the unused one eventually disappears. Yet Bagehot's maxim should not be construed as a general principle. If in period 15 the incumbent equilibrium were not 100 but 20, *all* the equilibria could eventually vanish.

Such an outcome would obtain if the equilibrium at 20 were to push private preferences sufficiently strongly toward 0. Then the propagation curve would be drawn downward, as in Figure 11.3. We see here that the interior equilibrium of 20 has given way to a corner equilibrium of 0, and the other preexisting equilibria have vanished. As in the previous case, the new equilibrium is immune to an expectational perturbation. And thus the history of public opinion is no longer essential to its persistence.

But why would private preferences be drawn toward 0, as opposed to 20? When public opinion stands at 20, the option 0 has four times as many promoters as the option 100. Consequently, people hear justifications for 0 four times as often. To the extent that they rely on social proof, their private preferences are drawn toward 0.

On issues where knowledge is hard, however, a divided public opinion may be self-reproducing. This is because selective perception can keep people's attention focused on arguments that reinforce their prevailing inclinations. People already leaning toward 0 will become more convinced as to the superiority of 0; those leaning toward 100, less so. In the process, private preferences will become increasingly polarized, possibly keeping intact the interior equilibrium of 20. Under certain conditions, then, Bagehot's maxim will also apply to the case of an interior equilibrium.

The generic name for adjustments that reinforce a tendency, orientation, or outcome is *positive feedback*.[17] In the present context, the instrument of positive feedback is adjustments in private preferences. These adjustments either strengthen the incumbent equilibrium or replace it with a more extreme alternative. Either way, they have a far-reaching implication for social efficiency: an inefficient decision will become efficient if enough people support it publicly for a sufficiently long time.

Imagine a regulation that is highly inefficient at the time of its adoption, in that it brings more harm to people privately opposed than benefit to people privately supportive. If the regulation is nonetheless retained, even its private opponents might come to discover its advantages. As observers, therefore, we may look at the whole dynamic process, from the regulation's entry into the public agenda, through the achievement of public consensus and the regulation's adoption, to the attainment of private consensus, and conclude that it has produced

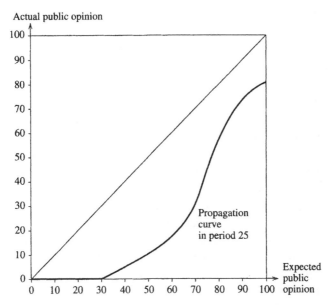

Figure 11.3 Equilibria in period 25. The propagation curve has moved down, destroying all preexisting equilibria. There is now a unique equilibrium at 0, so history will no longer be a factor in the stability of public opinion.

an efficient outcome. Yet the positive feedback that enhanced the regulation's efficiency took many years, and as it ran its course the regulation's perceived net benefit was not always positive.

In view of the common tendency to equate "what exists" with "what is best," this is a significant finding. Also significant is that efficiency, inasmuch as it is attained, need not result from a careful balancing of preexisting private interests. Efficiency may be the outcome of adjustments driving private opinion into conformity with an originally inefficient choice.

The Unthought and Social Stability

Earlier I showed that preference falsification may cause the persistence of an inefficient choice. This chapter has shown that preference falsification may also account for cognitive adjustments that will make the inefficiency disappear. Each of these two processes contributes to social stability, the former by blocking the attainment of reformist objectives, the latter by pushing such objectives into the unthought. As an inhibitor of change, preference falsification gets the status quo accepted publicly through the stick of punishment and the carrot of social acceptance. As a distorter of knowledge, it gets the status quo accepted privately.

Theories exist that attribute bandwagons to individual needs to rely on one another for information. For example, Sushil Bikchandani, David Hirshleifer, and Ivo Welsh explain fads, fashions, and customs through "informational cascades" that arise as people imitate others to avoid the trouble of studying their options.[18] Other theories attribute bandwagons to sanctions on deviants. Thus George Akerlof attributes social customs to reputational losses imposed on the violators of emerging behavioral regularities.[19] The theory in progress here integrates the two approaches. Specifically, it allows for interdependent bandwagons at two levels, private and public. The integration provides many new insights into social dynamics, some to be developed in theoretical chapters ahead.

But first I will test the argument of this chapter with respect to the illustrative cases introduced in Chapters 7 through 9: caste, communism, and affirmative action. In each of these cases we found preference falsification to be a factor in the persistence of privately disliked social arrangements. Left out of the picture was the evolution of private variables. Is there evidence that the identified manifestations of preference falsification have distorted private knowledge and private opinion? And what does the argument just offered explain that other pertinent arguments leave unexplained?

12

The Caste Ethic of Submission

A key tenet of Hindu thought is the doctrine of karma. According to this doctrine, an individual's actions influence his future lives, or reincarnations. If a person accepts his present position in the social hierarchy and patiently fulfills his duties, he will move into a higher caste in his next life. Conversely, if he fails to perform, he will move down in rank. By implication, the untouchable's degradation is the result of sins he committed in his former lives. To achieve a higher status in his next life, he must conform to the dictates of the cosmic order. Karma thus eschews the concept of "accident of birth," the notion that people's social privileges and handicaps have something to do with factors beyond their control. The doctrine explains and justifies both low and high status as the merited consequence of past conduct.[1]

In Chapter 8, I showed that the persistence of the caste system owes much to preference falsification on the part of the underprivileged segments of Indian society. My discussion paid no attention, however, to the ideological consequences of this preference falsification. Here I explore how preference falsification has influenced the dispersion and remarkable durability of the ideas that support the caste system. The chapter will thus offer a first application of the theory of Chapter 11.

My objective is not, of course, to account for every detail of the caste system. Rather, I seek to provide a parsimonious and internally coherent account of the system's fundamental and most intriguing characteristics.

196

Knowledge Falsification and the Worldview of the Untouchables

It has been asserted that no one subscribes in earnest to the doctrine of karma—nor, for that matter, to the other props of Hindu ideology. In this view, Indians simply pretend to accept Hindu ideology, the dominant to sustain their privileges and the dominated to fend off trouble. Ravindra Khare argues that most untouchables appear "ignorant, crude, and passive" *by choice.* He quotes an untouchable as saying: "I may talk with you but not inform, and may inform but not really share my mind. I may inform as well as misinform you until I am sure that you are honest in your intentions." To people they trust, says Khare, the untouchables convey many misgivings about the Indian social order.[2] In a similar vein, Joan Mencher observes that many untouchables subscribe to nonreligious explanations for their lowly status, although they consider it dangerous to express these outside their own communities.[3] At least in safe settings, Mark Juergensmeyer reports, untouchables attribute their social disabilities to misfortune; some go so far as to claim that they never took a true plunge in status, that they are really brahmans in disguise.[4] And M. N. Srinivas shows that certain codes enjoy strict observance in public yet are routinely broken in the privacy of the household. Chicken bones are found in the garbage of households belonging to vegetarian castes.[5]

Having held that preference falsification is a key factor in the caste system's endurance, I would be the last to take these observations lightly. But to identify incongruities between public Indian behavior and private Indian thought is not to prove that Hindu ideology is simply a sham. One can reject a part of Hindu ideology without rejecting the rest. The untouchable who considers himself a covert brahman might still believe in reincarnation, hereditary impurity, and the caste hierarchy. Indeed, it is one thing to think that one should be situated higher in the social hierarchy, quite another to reject hierarchy itself. In any case, the skepticism of some Indians does not preclude the genuine commitment of others.

Of the writers who consider Indian public discourse unrepresentative of actual Indian thought on caste, few, in fact, go so far as to assert that Hindu ideology exerts no influence on the beliefs and perceptions of the low-ranked castes. Khare recognizes that the untouchables do not reject the caste-based worldview unequivocally. Noting that many accept caste as the key principle of social organization, he attributes this fact to the dominance of Hindu ideology in Indian public discourse.[6] Juergensmeyer finds that almost a third of all lower castes accept that a person's social status is the result of his behavior in previous lives.[7]

Other ethnographies and some autobiographies suggest that the influence of Hindu ideology is even more widespread. They show that *most* untouchables accept, in some form, the notion of individual mobility through reincarnation. They also reveal that the untouchables accept the notion of ritual impurity, the defining element of their own inferiority. The untouchables rank themselves on a continuum of impurity, thereby turning the foot of the Hindu hierarchy into a microcosm of the extended hierarchy.[8] A nineteenth-century observer writes of two untouchable castes: "If a Pooleah by accident touches a Pariar, he must perform a variety of ceremonies and go through many ablutions before he can be cleansed from the impurity."[9] Listen also to Hazari, untouchable author of an informative autobiography: "We consider the untouchables of the Punjab lower than ourselves in the United Provinces; we would not marry with them, or even drink from the same vessel."[10]

There is evidence, then, that Hindu ideology has contributed to the untouchables' acceptance of their deprivations as fair, that it has made many treat their wretched existence as natural, and that it has facilitated their complicity in an order that degrades them. Max Weber was right to observe that Hindu ideology has served as an ethic of submission, a moral code keeping the subjugated complacent.[11] Here again is Hazari: "Our philosophy of life was that God had created us and that He would provide for our needs according to His will. Our fortunes, good or bad, were the will of God, and we were always taught to think that our lot was better than that of most people."[12]

How are we to make sense of the fact that untouchables have inculcated key elements of an ideology that sanctifies their degradation? For many centuries, Indian public discourse treated anticaste ideas as unthinkable. This induced people with egalitarian views to engage in knowledge falsification, which concealed from others their doubts about Hindu tenets. Low-status individuals born into these conditions must have had difficulty becoming acquainted with social ideas and ideals not based on caste. The unthinkable would easily have remained within their unthought—outside, that is, their comprehension and imagination. Their repertoire of social conceptions would have centered on the notion of caste. Accustomed to view society as divided into ranked castes, they would have found it natural to subdivide their own communities into ranked units.

The Spread of the Caste Ethic

The foregoing argument explains how low-status Indians inculcated the dominant ideology of their society but not how that ideology achieved dominance in the first place. No one knows exactly when and how the Hindu system of beliefs emerged. What is known is that the beliefs took shape a remarkably long time ago. The caste-based conception of Indian society is found in ancient texts, beginning with the *Rig Veda,* composed about 1000 B.C.E. Historians living much later, between the tenth and thirteenth centuries C.E., wrote about groups who were "not reckoned among any caste or guild," and whose touch was avoided by others.[13] And in the sixteenth century, Portuguese traders noted that Indians grouped themselves in *castas.*[14] However, we have no records on what distant generations of Indians actually thought. There exists some indirect evidence, in the form of ethnographies conducted in the early years of British rule. These suggest that Indians of all walks of life subscribed to concepts identified with Hinduism.[15]

Given the available data, theorizing about the evolution of Indian thought is bound to be speculative. We will never know when Hindu precepts gained widespread acceptance, nor what they meant to generations long gone. What follows is a plausible account of how Hindu ideology might have spread and strengthened.

Let us jump back a couple of millennia, to a time when the caste system was still in formation. As has been noted, various groups fought the restrictions placed on them. Evidently more egalitarian social systems initially enjoyed substantial public support. Under different expectations concerning public opinion, then, Indian society might have followed an evolutionary path radically different from the one it actually did. Specifically, if an alternative social order was perceived to be gaining popularity, the nascent caste system might have been discarded. Yet because of events lost in history, expectations caused the caste system to gain strength. Because private opposition would not have disappeared overnight, we can infer that, for a while, collective conservatism was a major factor in the system's persistence.

Moving forward in time, we observe the castigation of the system's vocal opponents, even individuals simply questioning its wisdom or fairness. The threat of punishment makes most opponents keep their private preferences and beliefs to themselves. Public opinion is thus distorted and public discourse truncated. New generations of Indians grow up hearing much in favor of the system and almost nothing against it. Along the way, the rationale for the system becomes increasingly elaborate, partly through the efforts of high-caste Indians seeking to justify their privileges. Through incessant repetition the new arguments become part of conventional Indian wisdom.

Like other religious convictions, certain key elements of Hindu ideology constitute soft knowledge: they cannot be put to the test of one's senses. No one has observed a reincarnation, and ritual impurity does not lend itself to empirical verification. Over the years, Indians have inculcated these notions through social proof, taking their validity for granted on account of their ubiquity in public discourse.

Past generations of Indians undoubtedly included some independent-minded people. Some of them must have entertained doubts about the validity of the Hindu view of the cosmic order. For instance, there must have been people who could not accept the doctrine of karma. Sensing that they might get in trouble for speaking their minds, these skeptics would generally have avoided pursuing the implications of their heresies. The more inquisitive might have come to see greater social equality as both possible and desirable. To escape opprobrium, however, they would have tended to withhold their reasonings from others. All such acts of individual prudence would have contributed to keeping public discourse uncontaminated by ideas inimical to the caste system. And as an unintended by-product, most Indians would have continued to see the desirability of the inherited order as self-evident.

The concept of untouchability appears to have emerged after the caste system was already in place. The *Rig Veda* does not mention it. The earliest reference to untouchability is found in the *Laws of Manu*, developed sometime between the second century B.C.E. and the third century C.E. Yet the concept got incorporated into Hindu ideology, and its delayed emergence was eventually forgotten.[16] The suppression of critical discourse probably played a key role in this collective loss of memory.

Let us resume our journey through time. Reaching the onset of the colonial era, we find that the system enjoys much genuine support. Some untouchables abide by the caste norms out of fear, many others out of conviction. The latter stay out of temples and use separate wells simply because they consider such behavior natural. They have no way of knowing why they subscribe to the caste ethic. Nor can they appreciate that it rationalizes inequalities to which their distant ancestors refused to grant legitimacy.

Such ignorance, I am suggesting, is a consequence of the distortion of public discourse that accompanies preference falsification. Low-ranked Indians have played a key role in this distortion and, hence, in their own indoctrination. By refraining from publicizing their objections to Hindu ideology, they have strengthened the status quo; and in the process, they have deprived one another of facts and arguments essential to defining their lot in life as unacceptable.

Received Theories of the Caste System

To put this thesis in perspective, it is instructive to review the most popular alternatives in the scholarly literature. Within neoclassical economics, racial discrimination is commonly attributed to innate tastes for discrimination. Thus in an influential essay on discrimination in the United States, Gary Becker attributes regional differences in overt racism to differences in taste.[17] Tastes are exogenous to Becker's framework, which begs the question of why the desire to discriminate differs systematically across regions. Why, to repeat the question in the context of the caste system, have leatherworkers been treated as subsocial in India, yet accorded a relatively decent status in, say, Egypt? And why have the leatherworkers of India exhibited a "taste" for being exploited? Is it by coincidence that leatherworkers exhibit this taste in a society segmented into castes? A theory that treats tastes as exogenous is unequipped to answer such fundamental questions.

Louis Dumont offers a theory whose methodological basis is collectivism, as opposed to individualism. Where Becker treats the individual as a monad, Dumont treats him as a helpless prisoner of his culture. Curiously enough, the two theories share the same limitation: they both take dispositions as given. According to Dumont, Indian culture subordinates the individual's identity to the interests of the wider community, thus turning him into a "collective man."[18] But he neglects to explain why Indians are more socialized than non-Indians. This lack of interest in *explaining* cultural differences is shared by most other modern anthropologists, who seem content with *describing* them in exhaustive detail.[19]

Writers in the Marxist mold generally maintain that the caste system rests on the economic power and ideological influence of the brahmans. They argue that a low-ranked Indian abides by the caste norms because the brahmans have left him economically vulnerable, created a "myth" about their own holiness and infallibility, and finally, brainwashed him into believing in the doctrine of karma.[20] Unlike Becker, Marxist writers accept the variability of preferences; and unlike Dumont, they try to explain observed preference patterns. But their thesis is fundamentally deficient, for compulsion itself does not make people accept a system that oppresses them. Compulsion merely facilitates conviction by silencing doubt and disagreement. Another critical flaw of the Marxist thesis is that it portrays disadvantaged Indians as the naive, helpless, and passive recipients of an ideology that serves only their masters. In reality, I have argued, the disadvantaged have had considerable responsibility in shaping and spreading the beliefs that oppress them.

The Marxist thesis happens to conflict with Marx's views concerning the origin of ideologies serving the economically dominant. Although Marx never developed a coherent theory, scattered passages in his writings suggest that he ascribed to the oppressed both the motivation and the ability to *invent* such ideologies. The motivation reflects a desire for peace of mind. By concocting theories pointing to the inevitability and fairness of their fate, the exploited equate possibility with reality, thus absolving themselves of the duty to improve their lot. In modern parlance, they reduce their cognitive dissonance. As for the ability to form beliefs beneficial to the privileged, it rests on a cognitive illusion: the tendency to believe that what is true for oneself is also true for one's group. The exploited individual generalizes his own powerlessness vis-à-vis the social order to his class as a whole.[21] According to Marx, the untouchables grow the "opium" that puts them to sleep. According to his followers in Indian studies, this opium is forced on the untouchables by the brahmans.

My own theory shares with Marx's thesis the view that the downtrodden play an active role in their own indoctrination. But I view the indoctrination as a collective process, not as a collection of isolated cognitive adaptations. The account presented here thus explains why millions of untouchables developed essentially the *same* justification for their misery. The chances are infinitesimal, of course, that millions of untouchables, each thinking independently, would all invent the doctrine of karma. Insofar as they formed a common understanding of their predicament, the reason is that they shaped each other's worldviews through interdependent acts of knowledge falsification, acts undertaken in response to jointly produced incentives to engage in preference falsification supportive of the social status quo.

Since the nineteenth century a campaign has been in progress to purge the notion of caste from the minds of Indians, and in the middle of this century discrimination against people of low rank became illegal. The campaign has tended to draw its leaders from the higher castes and the most highly educated untouchables. From the standpoint of the theory developed here, this is not surprising. Having had the earliest exposure to foreign values, members of these groups would be the first to acquire ideas antithetical to Hindu ideology. Nor is it difficult to understand why the "caste question" entered India's political agenda in the nineteenth century. India's fall to the British, which coincided with a massive decline in the costs of communication and transportation, brought increasing numbers of Indians into contact with the egalitarian doctrines of Europe. As a consequence, new ideas entered Indian public discourse. Notions such as karma and impurity came to be debated more openly than before, throwing into question some of the old certainties of Hinduism.[22]

The reform movement, having originated as an attempt to weaken the role of caste affiliation in Indian life, has spawned an official system of quotas designed to uplift the most disadvantaged sectors of Indian society. Hundreds of subcastes have been classified as "scheduled" and accorded preferential treatment in schooling and employment. The instituted quotas have given many segments of the disadvantaged subcastes a vested interest in the continuation of their "backward" status, thus promoting a new form of caste-consciousness. I will not be analyzing this transformation of the role of caste in any detail. But I will give it brief attention further on, following an account of an analogous transformation in the American context. First, however, we return to the case of communism.

13

The Blind Spots of Communism

In comparison to the caste system, communism is a recent addition to our portfolio of social institutions. Its history is measured in decades as opposed to millennia. Nevertheless, it has had a profound influence on social patterns of thought. I argue here that this ideological influence was driven by preference falsification.

In Chapter 7 we saw how preference falsification played a critical role in sustaining Eastern Europe's communist dictatorships. Left out of the earlier discussion was the impact of preference falsification on East European patterns of thought. In what follows I offer evidence that preference falsification impoverished public discourse in communist-ruled countries. And I show that this impoverishment deformed, biased, and confused the thoughts of individual Soviet and East European citizens, rendering most, including many dissidents, incapable of recognizing communism's fundamental flaws.

The themes of this chapter appeared, decades before the collapse of communism, in some celebrated interpretations of the Soviet society, including Hannah Arendt's *Origins of Totalitarianism* and George Orwell's *1984*.[1] Alexander Solzhenitsyn reiterated them in the mid-1970s: "For decades, while we were silent, our thoughts . . . lost touch with each other, never learned to know each other, ceased to check and correct each other. While the stereotypes of required thought . . . made mental cripples of us and left very few minds undamaged."[2] When sincerity returned, Solzhenitsyn predicted, people who had endured decades of communism would not be able to move on with their lives as though they had never lived a lie. They would not be able to "wake up abruptly" and "shake off the cumulative effects of *all* those indoctrination sessions."[3] A decade and a half later, during the waning days of the Soviet Union, Solzhenitsyn remained as convinced that communism had infected the Soviet mind: "After seventy years of propaganda, our brains have been instilled with the notion that one must fear private property and avoid hired labor as though they were the work of the devil."[4]

Solzhenitsyn's thesis harbors two distinct claims. First, the distortion of public discourse paralyzed the critical faculties of individual citizens, making them accept lies as unquestionable truths and hollow slogans as profound wisdom. Second, citizens would remain intellectually diminished and confused even after the restoration of their expressive freedoms. I shall argue that Solzhenitsyn was correct on both counts.

Communist Propaganda

Although the communist parties of Russia and Eastern Europe attained power by force, their reliance on compulsion was to have been a transitional phenomenon. Theorists of the movement predicted that communism would eventually achieve unanimous acceptance, with everyone genuinely believing in its unsurpassed virtues. Private opinion would thus become as supportive as public opinion already was, rendering the continued use of force superfluous. Writing before the Bolshevik takeover, Lenin predicted that a socialist society would eventually be able to retire its police force.[5] This blissful state would be reached as people discovered the new system's fairness and efficiency through personal experience. Lenin's forecast drew strength from Marx's conception of history: "It is not the consciousness of men that determines their being, but, on the contrary, their social being that determines their consciousness."[6]

Yet ruling parties claiming fidelity to the teachings of Marx displayed little faith in this famous dictum. Having grabbed power in countries lacking, in the Marxian view, the "objective conditions" for socialism, they undertook to teach the masses their "objective interests." Denouncing thoughts at odds with socialism as "false consciousness," they established huge propaganda machines to disseminate "correct" positions on every conceivable social problem.

As goals changed and predictions failed, the ideologically correct positions shifted, often accompanied by rewritings of history. Accordingly, as communist heroes became villains and the Soviet Union formed new alliances, the *Great Soviet Encyclopedia* underwent repeated revisions. When Lavrenti Beria, Stalin's police chief, fell out of favor, owners of the encyclopedia were ordered to replace the long entry on him with exhaustive information on the Bering Strait. Toward the end of communist rule, a popular Russian anecdote had the host of a talk show being asked whether one can foretell the future. "It's easy," was the reply. "Marx told us what the future will be like. The problem is with the past. *That* keeps changing."[7]

Another instructive case comes from Czechoslovakia. In 1948 Party leader Klement Gottwald addressed a massive crowd in Prague, flanked by his comrade Vladimir Clementis. Pictures of the two men standing together soon graced posters and schoolbooks. Four years later Clementis was charged with treason and executed. Party officials immediately produced new "photographs" of Gottwald's speech, in which he was alone. Where Clementis once stood, there was now a bare wall.[8] With Clementis airbrushed out of history, the Communist Party absolved itself of having to explain how a "traitor" rose to its helm. It could continue to claim omniscience and infallibility.

The Distortion of Public Discourse

Propaganda went hand in hand with efforts to regulate public discourse. Under communism, observes a Hungarian sociologist, "traditional social networks, local, professional, cultural, religious, and—to some extent—even family networks, were destroyed by sword and fire."[9] The resulting atomization obstructed the spread of information about communism's failures. A complementary obstacle was censorship. Scholarship was tightly regulated, with punishments meted out to researchers who departed from official canons. Numerous economists, for example, were arrested for writing about the virtues of free markets. Journalists, too, were barred from commenting on official privileges, the shoddiness of local goods, and the domestic manifestations of "capitalist ills" such as debt, pollution, and crime. Nor were journalists and other writers permitted to discuss censorship itself. Out of fear, the vast majority stuck to safe subjects—like the failures of capitalism. Here is how, in the relatively relaxed atmosphere of 1986, a Soviet writer described the consequent distortion of public discourse:

> Imagine, comrades, that you have been sent on a reconnaissance mission. After carrying out your assignment you come back and report that you counted a hundred enemy tanks. "Ah," you are told, "that was too many. Report that there are no more than 20 tanks. It is more agreeable that way." That was roughly the situation in our literature until quite recently. Over the past year and a half, this evil . . . has been revealed on a scale which we did not imagine.[10]

Ordinary citizens, too, challenged the ruling orthodoxy at their peril. For straying outside the confines of accepted discourse, they could be sentenced to hard labor, placed in a psychiatric ward, even executed. It was hazardous to question the wisdom of a chosen policy or to profess ignorance as to its rationale, for any hint of unorthodoxy could be interpreted as sedition. Even a choice of words could render one suspect. To avoid trouble, people used euphemisms designed to disguise the failures of communism. Blatant discrimination became "the class approach to law"; religious freedom, "religious backwardness"; and freedom of association, "antistate activity." The official language, wrote a Czechoslovak dissident in 1979, "reaches into the most banal areas of everyday life: . . . an accident in a nuclear generating station is called a work stoppage, and when the district party secretary drinks himself to death, he is said to have laid down his life in the cause of socialism."[11]

Citizens were not even free to prove communist ideology wrong through toil and ingenuity. In 1969 a Soviet citizen named Ivan Khudenko obtained a plot in Kazakhstan to grow alfalfa using well-paid labor. The experiment was a huge economic success. Yet the farm was declared a capitalist failure and shut down, and Khudenko was arrested in 1973. Shortly after his trial, he died in prison.[12]

Not that communist rule did away with all forms of public protest. Newspapers received complaints about shabby housing, about the neglected graves of famous poets, and about the poor upkeep of neighborhood playgrounds. Yet protesters tended to stay within a Party-defined zone of acceptability. They generally refrained from probing too deeply into issues and avoided challenging communism itself. A schoolteacher writing furious letters about a defective appliance would stay clear of blaming the system that produces useless appliances. Nor would she sign a letter expressing solidarity with dissidents or join a demonstration for expressive freedoms.[13] As a rule, letters took shots at mid-level functionaries, sparing the top leadership.[14] The pattern reflected, of course, the Party's claim to be guided by a superior truth. Because the Party derived its legitimacy from this claim, anyone indicting top leaders was liable to be branded an enemy of world communism.[15] Under the circumstances, readers stuck to specific grievances, seldom venturing to draw generalizations or to implicate communism itself.

On those rare occasions when citizens challenged official positions directly, they bent over backwards to appear sympathetic to wider communist goals. Accordingly, they couched their arguments in official terminology and rooted them in Marxist philosophy. So it was with Nikolay Ivanovich Vavilov, a Soviet geneticist who in the 1930s got into trouble for challenging the Party-approved idea that plants can pass on the traits they acquire through care. When Vavilov refuted the claim through experiments, his opponents sought to discredit his results by questioning his Marxist credentials. They accused him of employing politically untrustworthy experimenters and of basing his arguments on Darwin rather than on the fathers of communism. Significantly, Vavilov did not question the Party's competence to pass judgment on biological research. Nor did he dispute the credentials of Marx and Engels on genetics, a science established after their deaths. Insisting that his deepest inspirations came from Marx, he made a point of sprinkling his articles with Marxist buzzwords. Still, he failed. At a time when his work was gaining international recognition, he perished in jail.[16]

The Internalization of Communist Ideology

The literature on the history of the Soviet bloc is replete with such examples of intellectual terror. We know that the terror did not keep the citizens of communist countries from becoming conscious of communism's shortcomings. People confronted daily with shoddy goods, shortages, and queues tended to recognize these as symptoms of failure. The popular reaction is clear in the ubiquitous jokes about communism's economic performance. One common joke has a talk-show host being asked whether socialism could make the Sahara Desert bloom. "Yes," he replies, "but after the first five-year plan sand would be in short supply." Another joke has an American asking a Romanian worker how it is to live under socialism. "Fine," is the answer, "we all live like on a ship." The American is puzzled: "What do you mean?" The worker explains: "Well, long-range perspectives and distant horizons are visible. Meanwhile, everyone is getting sick, though none can get off."[17]

Yet there is evidence that awareness of communism's endemic failures did not translate into clear recognition of the socialist system's unworkability. Even after 1985, when Gorbachev publicly acknowledged the need for serious reform, substantial segments of the citizenry remained devoted to communist objectives and showed ignorance about the free-market system. In a widely discussed 1988 article a Russian social scientist argued that seven decades of bureaucratic regimentation had suppressed individual creativity, reorienting the Soviet value system "away from revolutionary transformation to conservative immobility." Communism had quashed the very personal qualities on which the nascent reform movement had pinned its hopes.[18] In mid-1989 another Soviet observer confessed: "For three years I have tried to find out whether or not there is mass support for *perestroika,* and now I feel I can conclude that it does not exist." He blamed in part the Soviet ethic that equates social justice with economic equality.[19] Sharing his perception, many democratic reformers questioned the wisdom of promoting political liberalization ahead of economic liberalization. If given immediate political power, they reasoned, the citizenry would block structural reforms.[20]

Personal recollections on the part of knowledgeable observers support the view that the citizens of the Soviet bloc developed faith in communism even as they endured its painful consequences. Detlef Pollack, a sociologist who followed East Germany's harassed associations, recalls that the members of these associations tended not to be anticommunist. Apparently, most viewed themselves as foot soldiers for "true" communism.[21] Systematic evidence on the internalization of communist ideology falls into two categories: opinion surveys and the history of socialist revisionism.

Opinion Surveys

The leaders of the Soviet bloc were aware of the role of preference falsification in sustaining their regimes. Accordingly, they conducted periodic surveys to gain information regarding the private dispositions of various groups. As a rule, they kept the results secret—a sure sign that the results contradicted the rhetoric of socialist unity. Any information released for publication "was checked beforehand and given the appropriate interpretation," to keep it from emboldening potential dissenters.[22] Since the fall of communism, many previously secret surveys have been declassified. As one would expect, they confirm the existence of widespread discontent. But they also reveal broad support for the ideals of socialism.

From 1970 onward the Central Institute for Youth Development in Leipzig conducted surveys on behalf of the East German leadership. The subjects of these surveys registered their opinions anonymously, with no officials present in the rooms where they filled out multiple-choice forms. The surveys suggest that until the mid-1980s young East Germans were fairly supportive of official goals. In 1983, 46 percent of a sample of trade school students endorsed the statement "I am a devoted citizen of the German Democratic Republic," whereas 45 percent endorsed it with reservations and only 9 percent rejected it. And in 1984, 50 percent agreed that "socialism will triumph throughout the world," whereas 42 percent agreed with reservations and 8 percent disagreed. Between 1970 and 1985, the surveys showed little variation.[23] Although students are not representative of the wider population, it is significant that after 1985 the surveys registered sharp declines in both their attachment to the regime and their faith in socialism. The later figures will be presented further on, in the course of interpreting the collapse of East European communism.

Over the years, state-run opinion institutes in Hungary and Czechoslovakia ran surveys to determine, among other things, popular perceptions of the economic success of socialism in relation to Western capitalism. These suggest that East Europeans tended to consider socialism relatively more successful in economic terms.[24] In 1983, for example, the Hungarians who considered the socialist economic system generally unsuccessful outnumbered those who considered it successful by a margin of 18 percent. For the capitalist economy, by contrast, the unfavorable opinions outnumbered the favorable ones by a much wider margin, 75 percentage points.[25] In Czechoslovakia, meanwhile, 50 percent of a broad sample thought that in the future living standards would be better in socialist societies than in the capitalist West, with only 18 percent thinking the opposite.[26] As with the East German statistics, those from Hungary and Czechoslovakia reveal a plunge in the citizenry's attachment to socialism in the second half of the 1980s.

In the Soviet Union, a confidential poll was undertaken in the mid-1960s by *Pravda,* against the opposition of Yuri Zhukov, an editor known for his hard-line views. Confirming Zhukov's suspicions, the poll revealed the newspaper's readers to be divided in their beliefs and preferences. Much to his surprise, however, it also showed him to be a very popular writer—which strengthened his authority on *Pravda*'s board.[27] Although the results are open to competing interpretations,[28] they suggest that official policies commanded considerable private support. Another Soviet survey, conducted between 1967 and 1974, uncovered a widespread belief that living standards in Czechoslovakia were higher than in America, Sweden, and West Germany.[29]

The results of such official surveys are broadly consistent with polls of East European travelers conducted by Western organizations in the 1970s and early 1980s. With remarkable consistency and for each nation, these studies showed that in free elections offering a full spectrum of choices, including a Democratic Socialist Party and a Christian Democratic Party, the Communist Party would receive at most a tenth of the vote. Invariably, however, the socialists would be the winners.[30] These surveys disclose broad dissatisfaction with the incumbent communist establishment. They also show, however, that such dissatisfaction went hand in hand with broad acceptance of official ideals.

In Poland and Hungary, the two Soviet satellites where the 1980s brought a flowering of open dissent, independent scholars were able to conduct a number of unofficial surveys. These surveys confirm that socialist principles enjoyed general acceptance. According to a Polish survey from 1984, for example, only 16 percent of a sample of workers were satisfied with socialism in the form it took in Poland. But only 28 percent responded negatively to the question, "Do you think that the world should develop toward some other form of socialism?" And just 11 percent considered "private ownership of the means of production" a necessary feature of a good socioeconomic system, as against 60 percent who favored "social ownership of the means of production."[31] Similarly, a 1985 survey of Hungarians uncovered broad dissatisfaction with various specific policies. Sixty-three percent characterized housing as poor, and 61 percent were dissatisfied with the treatment of senior citizens. At the same time, when asked, "To what degree are you confident that the Hungarian government leads the country in the right direction?," 88 percent answered "fully" or "to a great degree." Moreover, the respondents tended to consider Hungary's economic achievements superior to those of its neighbors, especially in regard to employment.[32]

Since the mid-1980s, and especially in the 1990s, polling the nations of Eastern Europe has become a booming pursuit. Most scientific surveys have found attitudes to be in flux, yet there remains an unmistakable attachment to socialist ideals. A few months after the collapse of East German communism, the Allensbach Institute asked a sample of East Germans whether the country's ongoing crisis demonstrated the failure of socialism or the incompetence of politicians. Only 20 percent attributed the crisis to socialism itself, whereas 67 percent blamed individual incompetence. In contrast, a similar sample of West Germans gave answers divided more or less evenly between the two options.[33] For another such comparison, when given a choice between freedom and equality, 43 percent of the East Germans chose equality, as against 24 percent of the West Germans.[34]

With the collapse of communism, large majorities throughout the region came to accept the urgent necessity of structural reforms. Yet a dominant finding in many surveys is that the West is considered wealthy yet uncivilized and exploitative. In 1990 a private polling organization in Prague found only 10 percent of a Czechoslovak sample to favor an American-style free-market economy, although 36 percent favored a Swedish-style welfare state.[35] Similar results have been obtained in Hungary and Poland.[36]

The pivotal element of the ongoing transitions from socialism to capitalism is privatization, an objective endorsed by most postcommunist leaders. With privatization supported by an influential segment of public discourse, increasing numbers of citizens have come to consider it indispensable. Yet the majority do not quite know what privatization means. A private polling company in Budapest has found that most Hungarians consider privatization a good idea, although more than half lack even a basic understanding of the process.[37] Likewise, in Russia a formerly unthinkable concept such as market-clearing prices has gained substantial acceptance. But few Russians understand how prices relate to queues and shortages.[38]

To make sense of these results, we must reconsider the distinction between hard and soft knowledge. In a nutshell, the former rests on substantive information, the latter on social proof. Shortages, quality problems, and political repression all lie within the realm of individual experience. As such, they are all sources of hard knowledge. A Pole standing in a meat queue on a snowy day is apt to resent the hardship even if no one else seems bothered. In an economically unsuccessful repressive society, therefore, broad private discontent might develop even as public discourse remains supportive of the status quo. Insofar as citizens have access to information about better conditions abroad, as the peoples of the Soviet bloc increasingly did in the 1970s and 1980s, dissatisfaction will be all the stronger. It is, however, one thing to recognize the failures of one's own system, another to understand the underlying problems. The Russian who knows that Norwegians live better has neither the time nor the education to determine the reasons on his own. So he draws on social proof. Whatever the nature of social proof, his interpretation thus constitutes soft knowledge. Should public discourse shift, the interpretation may change rapidly.

Until the Gorbachev era public discourse in communist countries absolved socialism itself from responsibility for perceived problems. It attributed hardships to mistakes in implementation rather than to basic principles. Accordingly, most citizens of these countries retained faith in socialism. With the advent of *glasnost,* long-suppressed criticisms came to be openly expressed, pushing public discourse in the promarket direction. Concurrently, polls began to register a rise in promarket views. That they also revealed these views to rest on massive ignorance is consistent with the fact that matters of broad economic policy lie beyond the average person's realm of deep understanding.

Reform Communism

The surveys just reported are consistent with the hypothesis that the distortion of public discourse through efforts at preference falsification made it hard for East Europeans to grasp the root causes of communist failures. Further systematic evidence comes from the history of reform movements within the Soviet bloc.

When Khrushchev disclosed the enormity of Stalin's crimes, an opportunity emerged for debating ideas that until then had been unthinkable. Yet confused bureaucrats were unprepared to exploit it. However much they themselves had suffered, they could not identify measures to prevent the recurrence of tyranny. Distinguishing between Leninist and Stalinist communism, they reasoned that a return to uncorrupted Leninism would provide an antidote to despotism. They would struggle for years to salvage the system before recognizing its fatal flaws.[39]

Reformist movements within the satellites of the Soviet Union exhibited the same pattern. None sought to overthrow the prevailing structures of domination or to alter the social order fundamentally. Imre Nagy, the leader of Hungary's crushed revolution of 1956, denounced communist absolutism as undemocratic. But he remained wedded to "scientific socialism" as a doctrine of emancipation, without noticing that oppression was a logical consequence of the pretense of omniscience and infallibility characteristic of Marxian historical determinism.[40] Likewise, the Prague Spring of 1968 was rooted in illusions about the possibility of giving socialism a "human face" without dissolving the communist monopoly of power.[41] Not until the 1970s did movements emerge that sought to change the social order from outside the political establishment. One of the leading early dissidents, Adam Michnik of Poland, made clear, as did Havel in Czechoslovakia, that attempts to humanize socialism were doomed to failure and that meaningful change would have to come from outside the official structures of power.[42] For at least another decade, however, Michnik's views were widely treated as subversive. Most bureaucrats, scholars, journalists, and party officials remained committed to saving the existing social system. Even Gorbachev, whose actions unleashed the forces that killed communism, set out to make the old system work better.[43]

If there is any major issue on which leaders after Stalin were prepared to grant a modicum of expressive freedom, it was the economy. While continuing to preach the superiority of central planning and to forecast capitalism's imminent demise, they recognized certain economic problems and encouraged constructive suggestions for reform.

For many years, however, "revisionist" experiments remained wedded to key communist principles. Central planning continued to be regarded as indispensable, with only minor concessions made to the market mechanism. The harmful effects of monopolization, like waste and stagnation, were still seen as exclusive to capitalism. Privatization rarely became an issue, and when it did, the focus was on forms of cooperative ownership, as in the Yugoslav "labor-managed enterprise." Black markets came under constant attack, but rarely were their sources scrutinized.[44]

The starting point of all discussions was Marxism. Inspiration was drawn from "liberal Bolsheviks" like Lenin and Bukharin, rarely from Adam Smith or his followers. A critic of revisionist thought has characterized the reformists as "prisoners of their own discourse."[45] Other critics have identified four groups of revisionists: those who seek a "Third Way" between socialism and capitalism, fundamentalist Marxists who believe in the early writings of Marx, "technocratists" who want greater government action, and antibureaucrats who think corrupt bureaucrats should be given the boot and better people brought in.[46] Remarkably, none of these groups thought of replacing the visible hand of central planning with the invisible hand of the market.

Some revisionists found solace in the ongoing expansion of government in the industrialized West. They took this as proof of the inevitability of economic centralization. The most daring revisionists spoke of "market socialism," a system that would marry the strengths of capitalism and communism while avoiding their weaknesses. In a retrospective account of reform communism, János Kornai has characterized the reformers of the 1950s and 1960s, including his own past self, as "naïve." It was ridiculous, he confessed in 1986, to think that a bit of decentralization would bring the command system into harmony with the market process, ensuring efficiency, growth, and justice all at once.[47]

Many dissidents took little interest in economic matters. Havel, for example, stayed out of debates on decentralization, although he signaled that he did not see market capitalism as the solution. Dissidents who did comment on economics tended to betray an attachment to orthodox Marxism. In 1968 the Russian dissident Andrei Sakharov wrote that "it took socialism to raise the meaning of labor to the heights of a moral feat." And he asserted that "some absurdities [in the development of socialism] were not an inherent aspect of the socialist course of development, but a tragic accident."[48]

The point is not to belittle the achievements of reform communists: through the impact of their criticisms, and the disillusionments that followed their timid reforms, they set the stage for the transformations of the 1990s. Nor am I claiming that individual reformists *could* have seen the fatal flaws of communism. They, too, were handicapped by the biases of public discourse. As a Hungarian sociologist would recognize in the 1980s, there could not be a "second society" that was uncontaminated by the "first society" of official communism. With the possible exception of some exiled dissidents, the inhabitants of the "second" also inhabited the "first."[49] What they learned from official sources warped what they could see and understand.

Inner Contradictions of Popular Thought

Personal observations, opinion surveys, and revisionist writings thus all support the view that citizens of the Soviet bloc, however conscious they became of specific communist failures, tended to retain faith in communism itself. Evidently communist ideology blunted their ability to look at communism critically. Official indoctrination provides only part of the explanation. Another part lies in the distortions of public discourse generated by preference falsification on the part of the citizens themselves.

This thesis is consistent with the fact that throughout the Soviet bloc economic perceptions underwent massive changes in the late 1980s, when previously unthinkable observations, analyses, and proposals began to be articulated with increasing frequency. If official propaganda were the only factor in the formation of individual beliefs, perceptual shifts might have occurred in the Soviet Union, Poland, and Hungary, where leaders became openly sympathetic to reform, but not in East Germany, Czechoslovakia, Romania, or Bulgaria, where the official agenda remained essentially unchanged until the fall of 1989.

The evidence I have mustered could be challenged on the grounds that citizens of the Soviet bloc participated regularly, and at personal risk, in a complex underground economy operating according to capitalist principles. Indeed, workers obtained their blue jeans through the only free market to which they had access—the *black* market; and enterprise managers turned regularly to unauthorized suppliers for the spare parts they needed to meet their production quotas. From these observations, one might infer that the advantages of market liberties were widely understood. Touting the principle that "actions speak louder than words," one could argue that individual behavior betrayed understandings that public discourse concealed.

Yet the citizens of the Soviet bloc could participate in the underground economy without becoming proponents of economic liberalization. As Vladimir Shlapentokh observes, the workers and managers who traded in the black market did not automatically become believers in free enterprise.[50] This was so, he suggests, because the individual citizen's mind was divided into two layers, one "pragmatic" and the other "ideological." The former layer contained the practical information necessary to get things done, derived mostly from experience; it depicted market competition as convenient and lucrative. The latter consisted of abstract information, drawn primarily from public discourse; it portrayed competition as wasteful and evil. The two layers barely interacted, which is why their contradictions proved enduring.

The detachment of abstract Marxist thought from the problems of daily survival promoted mental inconsistencies by encouraging individuals to bifurcate incoming information. Slogans, official speeches, and Marxist forecasts went into the theoretical layer of people's consciousness; evidence of bureaucratic inefficiency and insights into the uses of markets went into the pragmatic layer. But why did Marxist thought *remain* partitioned from the concerns of everyday existence? The very factor that made citizens of the Soviet bloc conceal their opposition to communist rule made it hazardous to confront communist ideology with communism's practical failures. An observant worker could not point out, except at personal risk, that his "worker's state" offered him a lower standard of living than that enjoyed by workers in "bourgeois-ruled" states. Nor could he draw attention to the fact that shortages were far less common in market economies than in the planned economies. So he kept his thoughts to himself and even participated in the dissemination of official myths, misrepresentations, and sophistries. In the process, he refrained from giving his fellow citizens reasons to reconsider their theoretical convictions.

If my interpretation is correct, the official worldview's hold over the individual mind should have weakened as it became increasingly safe to express ideas contrary to official canons. With the contradictions between official canons and the facts of daily life receiving public exposure, skepticism about Marxist thought should have grown. People accustomed to separating Marxist predictions from their own experiences should have come to see the flaws of their long-held perceptions. Indeed, and as Chapter 16 will document, the acceptance of official ideology slipped after the mid-1980s.

If citizens of the Soviet bloc failed to make connections between their hardships and the official ideology, at least they defined their deprivations as potentially avoidable. It is not self-evident why they did, for we can convince ourselves of the inevitability, even the desirability, of a wide range of hardships. The untouchables of India offer a case in point: they learned to accept their lowly status as fair. Why, then, did the peoples of the Soviet bloc not learn to accept standing in food queues as an immutable requirement of modern existence? What makes the cases of caste and communism different?

One essential difference lies in the time spans of the two systems: millennia in the case of the caste system, less than a century in that of communism. If communism had lasted longer, individual Soviet and East European citizens might have found their queues less problematic. Another crucial difference involves openness to outside information. The transportation and information revolutions of the last century have made it difficult for societies to keep themselves uninformed about conditions and trends abroad. Impoverished or misgoverned nations can now readily compare their living standards with those of others. Not so when the caste ethic took root in the minds of deprived Indians. The early untouchables had little, if any, exposure to non-Indian theories of the cosmos; they did not realize, for instance, that the concept of ritual impurity was unknown to the monotheistic peoples of the Mediterranean basin. By contrast, every Pole standing in a meat queue enjoyed, thanks to modern media, some access to information about Western economic conditions. Such information served to keep Polish hopes alive that queues were avoidable. It might also have discredited communism as an economic system, but the distortion of public discourse, coupled with the propensity to separate ideological prescriptions from daily experience, kept most individuals in a state of confusion.

It might be said that information from abroad did not offer a consistently negative image of communism. Indeed, some Western voices were highly critical of the free-market economies of the West and laudatory toward the command economies of the Soviet bloc.[51] On the whole, however, foreign voices served as a corrective to the biases of local public discourse.

Alternative Explanations of the Stability of Communism

To put in perspective the argument begun in Chapter 7 and extended here, it will be instructive to contrast it with two common explanations for the communist system's stability.

The first, that communism survived through the threat and use of force, sheds light on why the oppressed peoples of the communist world remained generally subservient and quiescent for decades. But it provides no insight into the influence of Marxist ideology. Brute force can make individuals *act* against their own interests, but it cannot shape how they *think*. Another problem with this explanation is that military force played an insignificant role in the overthrow of the communist regimes of Eastern Europe. With the partial exception of the Romanian dictatorship, these regimes met their ends at the hands of militarily insignificant popular upheavals. If military force was indeed the sole source of the communist system's stability, it would have taken a superior military force to destroy it.

The second explanation for the endurance of communism invokes the privileges of officials. Fearful of losing their privileges, officials conspire to block reforms, even as they recognize the horrendous social costs of preserving the status quo. Jan Winiecki, a proponent of this perspective, observes that someone pursuing a reform was liable to be removed from office. In Winiecki's account, then, a strategically placed minority manages to block changes that would be popular, simply by virtue of its ability to punish any would-be reformer. One virtue of this explanation, he contends, is that it draws on identifiable economic incentives; another, that it avoids reliance on ideological factors.[52]

Kornai characterizes the sort of explanation advanced by Winiecki as overly simplistic. It is not true, he correctly observes, that there existed two mutually exclusive groups, one privileged and thus opposed to individual liberties, and the other unprivileged and thus sympathetic to freedom. The bureaucracy was neither homogeneous nor monolithic. Individual bureaucrats may have treasured their own power, but they had no stake in the power of other bureaucrats. As citizens, moreover, they wanted a wider selection of consumer goods, a say in their children's education, and the freedom to travel. The nonbureaucrats formed an even less homogeneous group. Many attached low value to individual liberties and had no fundamental disagreement with the command system. Here Kornai draws on a 1982 study that found a sample of Hungarians to attach much less value to individual freedoms than a comparable sample of Americans. Kornai goes on to propose a series of possible explanations. Years of centralized command might have left people afraid of freedom. Or people denied liberty might have learned to devalue freedom in an effort to adjust their aspirations to their possibilities. Or perhaps the biases of schools and the mass media left their imprint on individual minds.[53]

The first of Kornai's suggestions restates what requires explanation. The second and third are undoubtedly part of the story, though in Kornai's argument they are not logical implications of a general theory. This chapter has linked communism's ideological influence to preference falsification, the very phenomenon responsible for its endurance. The biases in education and the media were among the manifestations of preference falsification. And the possibilities to which individuals adjusted their aspirations resulted from millions of public preferences selected in response to jointly produced political incentives.

14

The Unfading Specter of White Racism

In Chapter 9 we saw that the racial disparities of the United States have generated a web of affirmative action programs. Billed as instruments to enhance the opportunities of disadvantaged but qualified individuals, these programs have spawned a privately unpopular system of racial quotas. They have faced slim public opposition, however, because to voice misgivings is to invite censure. Conscious of the risks, Americans have tended to hide their reservations behind a veneer of public consent.

Extending the earlier argument, this chapter proposes that, despite the strong opposition recorded by anonymous polls, preference falsification on affirmative action has produced widespread confusion and ignorance about its consequences. In particular, Americans scarcely recognize the costs of affirmative action. Many harbor misconceptions about its benefits and about its gainers and losers. Few realize how the emphasis on affirmative action has diverted attention from the root causes of the prevailing inequalities, to the detriment of truly disadvantaged Americans, black and nonblack. Only some appreciate how double standards are fueling tribalization and, ultimately, endangering the viability of the American nation. Preference falsification on matters of race has produced such effects by narrowing and perverting the relevant public discourse, including debates within Congress, the courts, universities, and the mass media.

The chapter focuses on one particular sector of American society: higher education. A perception of indelible white racism has become a persistent factor in university decision making, and this perception has spurred color-conscious policies with regard to admissions, faculty hiring, campus life, research, and the curriculum. I argue that the dominant responses of American intellectuals to the failures of affirmative action bear similarities to those of Soviet and East European intellectuals to the failures of communism. For example, the new "multiculturalism" arose as an attempt to rescue the incumbent racial agenda without confronting the illusions that undergird it.

The developments to be discussed are significant because, at least in principle, the university has been committed to open and frank debate, including the exploration of views that are unpopular or inconvenient. If debate gets truncated and distorted even within academia, it is unlikely to remain honest in other sectors of society. Academic debate feeds into general public discourse. The impoverishment of this debate thus has potentially serious consequences for the way ordinary Americans think and act. I begin with admissions.

Color-Conscious Admissions

Ever since university administrations committed themselves to affirmative action in admissions, they have prided themselves on enhancing the "diversity" of their student bodies. They have been essentially silent about affirmative action's educational costs. Keeping the focus on numerical representation, they have avoided discussion of the harm done to affirmative-action recruits lured to colleges they were unprepared to attend.

Yet data on graduation rates do not tell a story of success. At the University of California at Berkeley, for instance, only 38 percent of the blacks admitted as freshmen in 1983 had graduated by 1988, as compared with 72 percent of the whites.[1] The difference stems directly from Berkeley's multitrack admission system. Berkeley rates its applicants according to an academic index that incorporates grades, honors, and the Scholastic Aptitude Test (SAT), recently renamed the Scholastic Assessment Test. In 1986 whites needed at least 7,000 out of a possible 8,000 to have a 50 percent chance of admission, while blacks needed only 4,800.[2] Such sharp differences in admission qualifications are not unusual in college admissions, but few Americans realize how much standards have had to be altered to engineer appropriately "diverse" classes.[3]

Like undergraduate programs, graduate schools apply vastly different standards to different ethnic groups. One case that received publicity is that of Alan Bakke, a white applicant who had to go to the Supreme Court in order to be allowed to enter, five years after his initial application, the medical school of the University of California at Davis. Everyone familiar with the case knows that Bakke had credentials superior to those of specially admitted minorities. The extent of the contrast is not as widely understood. Bakke had a percentile score of 96 in the verbal section of the Medical College Admissions Test, 94 in the quantitative section, 97 in the science section, and 72 in the general information section. The corresponding *averages* for the "specially admitted" students were 46, 24, 35, and 33.[4]

Some educators assert that such painful discrepancies reflect the cultural biases of standardized tests. They say that the tests emphasize cultural experiences with which nonwhites have less familiarity than whites.[5] This claim collides with the fact that as a group Asian-Americans do even better than whites. Still, it has fueled efforts to eliminate the presumed cultural biases of the SAT. To date, all attempts to devise a culturally neutral version on which blacks do as well as whites have ended in failure.

An alternative explanation for the statistical gap between black and white scores is simply that black college applicants are in general less well prepared. This inference is consistent with conditions in the neighborhoods in which many black applicants live, the homes in which they grow up, and the schools they attend. Such a conclusion amounts, however, to an acknowledgment of the inadequacy of *contemporary* white racism as an explanation for racial disparities. Educators convinced of the all-encompassing power of racism have gravitated, instead, to the view that standardized tests measure only a subset of the aptitudes that determine success in life, specifically, those valued by whites.[6]

The focus of the debate has thus remained on rationalizing lower admission standards for the protected minorities. Scarce attention has been paid to the consequences of placing poorly prepared students in colleges too rigorous for them to succeed. Given the black graduation rate, this neglect is quite striking. One reason for the neglect is that college administrations have been notoriously reluctant to release information harmful to their affirmative action programs, lest they be accused of fueling doubts about the competence of low-performing minorities. A second reason is that some administrators have propagated falsehoods, as when Harvard's *Affirmative Action Newsletter* characterized as a "myth" the notion that "affirmative action means applying a double standard."[7] And a third is that administrations have taken, as I shall explain presently, various steps to discourage open debate in the wider university community.

Let us grant, for a moment, that good reasons exist for setting up admission quotas for low-performing groups. What are the appropriate criteria for determining the proper levels? On which overachieving groups should the burden fall? Further, if it is reasonable to alter standards for blacks because they underperform whites, is it also reasonable to change them for Christians and Muslims because they underperform Jews? Whatever one thinks of the legitimacy of ethnic quotas, the answers to such questions are not obvious. Yet they have not been debated openly and honestly, if for no other reason that many universities officially hold that affirmative action avoids multiple standards. A serious consequence is widespread ignorance about the ongoing practices.

In a recent year, white representation in the freshman class at Berkeley, the flagship campus of California's state university system, was 30 percent, even though whites represented 52 percent of the state's high school graduates. One reason for this low representation was the squeeze caused by special standards for "underrepresented" minorities. Another was that Asian-Americans, whose academic qualifications generally surpass those of whites and who tend to come from economically successful families, had avoided the squeeze through a new, "class-based" affirmative action program that heavily favors them over others—curiously, on the grounds that they are "socioeconomically disadvantaged." Asian-Americans, representing 14 percent of California's high school graduates, made up 35 percent of Berkeley's freshman class.[8]

Is it desirable for a state university to exempt Asian-American applicants from the burden of affirmative action, letting it fall entirely on whites? Questions of this sort are rarely discussed. Earlier I gave as a reason that whites tend not to complain publicly about the costs they privately resent, lest they be accused of racism. A contributing reason is that the rarity of honest discourse on affirmative action keeps them, like others, confused and ignorant about its effects.

Speech Codes

The justification for racial affirmative action in college admissions has always been the relatively poor credentials of most black applicants, a feature attributed to white racism, past and present. White racism is also held responsible for the generally poor performance of black college students. It is said to make the social atmosphere on campuses so inhospitable to minorities as to interfere with their learning.

Acting on this perception, hundreds of colleges have instituted speech codes that make it a potentially punishable offense to say or do things upsetting to designated "minorities"—women, homosexuals, and ethnic groups deemed oppressed. The University of Connecticut has gone so far as to prohibit "inappropriately directed laughter."[9] Colleges are also putting their students through "sensitivity" sessions where they learn, in addition to unobjectionable rules of politeness, what ideas to keep to themselves, what campus agendas not to challenge, what vocabulary to avoid, and what euphemisms to use often—in brief, to become "politically correct."[10] Harvard's sensitivity program includes a yearly AWARE week, AWARE standing for Actively Working Against Racism and Ethnocentrism. Its organizers designate "race relations tutors" for each Harvard House. The tutors "raise consciousness," "monitor the racial atmosphere," and "report violations."[11]

Ethnic harassment and name-calling had just about disappeared from the college scene long before the imposition of speech regulations. One can find contemporary examples of deliberate provocations against blacks, but they are not common. Why, then, have we seen the proliferation of measures against racist speech? Such measures shield specially admitted students not only from racial slurs but also from discomforting truths about their cultural backgrounds, the real causes of their academic failures, and the social costs of double standards. They suppress the communication of doubts about the efficacy of affirmative action programs. And their very existence implies that racism remains a paralyzing threat to blacks, thus justifying the color-coded campus agenda.

Whatever the purpose of speech regulations, one of their effects is to make students, not to mention faculty and administrators, ever more reluctant to speak freely on race-related issues, ever more afraid of using a word or uttering a thought that might be construed as a sign of bigotry. Ironically, this timidity is probably exacerbating racial tensions. Even before the codes came into place, nonblacks were accustomed to showing caution in their interactions with blacks, lest they find themselves embroiled in a "racial incident."[12]

Students admitted under affirmative action programs need not be lying or exaggerating when they claim to have been offended by statements critical of affirmative action. Precisely because they arrive on campus with relatively poor academic credentials, many have trouble keeping up with the coursework. Consequently they develop anxieties about their capabilities, becoming sensitive to reminders of their deficiencies. My point is not, then, that the defenders of speech regulations are motivated only by strategic reasons, with no real concern for disadvantaged students. I am suggesting, first, that the sensitivity of some minority students is a by-product of placing them in universities with inappropriately high standards and, second, that the main function of the speech codes is to silence campus dissent.[13]

The *Oxford Dictionary* defines racism as "the theory that distinctive human characteristics and abilities are determined by race." By this definition, racism need not be monochromatic. The campus speech codes rest on the view that threats to interracial harmony and black advancement come only from white racism. College campuses now feature, however, many signs of black racism: black dining tables, black theme houses, black study areas, black newspapers, and even black commencement exercises—all based on the notion that skin color is a legitimate cause for exclusion. Even entire buildings have been declared off-limits to nonblacks.[14] One possible interpretation for such separatist acts is that they are defensive responses to experiences of rejection and intimidation. In reality, more is involved than raw white racism. Colleges that have long been racially integrated now show signs of balkanization. And at universities across the country black students who socialize with whites routinely get ostracized by the wider black community.

For all the concern about racist speech, hardly any effort is made to regulate demeaning characterizations of whites. Under current conditions on American campuses, much can be said that offends whites, without fear of punishment. For example, black campus leaders can condemn *all* whites of racism without provoking administrative criticism. Double standards extend to theft, vandalism, and even violence. Where interference with an event sponsored by a black club would most certainly get its perpetrators in trouble, disrupters of campus events injurious to black sensitivities frequently get away with their infractions.[15] When a group of "Concerned Black and Latino Students" stole fourteen thousand copies of the *Daily Pennsylvanian* in objection to what they considered the paper's "blatant and covert racism," the response of the University of Pennsylvania administration was to fault the campus police for catching some of the offenders. Characterizing the theft as a "form of protest," the school refused to discipline the students.[16]

Like the double standards in college admissions, those in speech and behavior have been justified in the name of racial harmony and integration. On the whole, however, they are probably promoting discord and segregation. Whatever the benefits to individual black students, the establishment of a black dormitory reduces interracial contacts. It divides campus life into racially exclusive zones, making it harder for blacks and whites to form friendships and discover their shared interests as human beings. Similar effects arise from the practice of conferring upon black students expressive and behavioral privileges denied to their white peers.

It might be said that a small but vocal part of the black establishment has never been interested in color blindness in the first place. And it might be observed that some black leaders, including some academics, have a personal stake in heightening the social significance of race. There are grains of truth in each of these arguments. Yet anti-integrationists could not have gone so far without administrators willing to accede to most of their requests. Administrators have habitually given blacks things they would never give to white students. None would allow whites to hold a racially exclusive commencement.

Part of the reason for these double standards is that university administrators are afraid of angering black activists and their allies. Another is that many have become blind to certain realities of campus life. Having heard incessantly that the source of campus frictions is white racism, they can hardly imagine that a more serious problem now might be institutionalized black racism. Nor do they tend to recognize that affirmative action has stimulated black separatism and racial hostility. When a university admits large numbers of academically deficient students (whether athletes, alumni children, or ethnic minorities), they will form their own subculture. Tensions will follow. And insofar as the problems cannot be discussed openly and honestly, they are likely to persist, spread, and grow.

The New Multiculturalism

Ideological blinders have predisposed the promoters of affirmative action to believe that the college curriculum is so infused with racism as to constitute another huge impediment to black academic performance. There was a time when large segments of the humanities and social sciences denigrated non-European cultures. But this has hardly been the case in recent decades. Still, many academics have come to think that the traditional college curriculum promotes a "Eurocentric perspective" that distorts, marginalizes, and omits the cultures of the oppressed. This, they believe, lowers the self-esteem of minority students, destroying their already diminished capacity for academic success. *Brown v. Board of Education,* the 1954 Supreme Court decision that paved the way for racial integration in education, was based on the view that black students feel inferior if they do not receive the same education as whites. The wisdom now is that they feel inferior if they *do* receive the education that whites have traditionally received.[17]

So it is that massive efforts are under way to give the university curriculum a "multicultural" character. A 1993 directory of the American Council on Education lists more than two thousand curriculum projects, faculty-development programs, and student-recruitment plans aimed at bringing "diversity" to intellectual life on college campuses.[18] The prime targets of reform are the social sciences and humanities, but even mathematics and the natural sciences are under attack. Texts and manuals have appeared on "ethnomathematics."[19] As one might expect, the drive to restructure the curriculum goes hand in hand with efforts to make room for more minority faculty, especially ones who consider exploitation and oppression the prime movers of history.

If one stated objective of the new multiculturalism is intellectual balance and accuracy, another, not necessarily consistent with the first, is to make minority students feel good about themselves. Accordingly, efforts are being devoted to replacing course materials offensive to minorities with ones that will fill them with ethnic pride. Acceptable readings include ones that establish the African origins of achievements hitherto known as Eurasian and that ascribe the current problems of humanity, especially those of oppressed minorities, to Euro-American imperialism. In addition to repairing the wounded psyches of minorities, such readings are intended to cultivate a general awareness of the indelible differences among the cultures that make up the United States. Classic writers like Dante, Shakespeare, and Jefferson are no longer in favor. Stigmatized as "dead white males," they are accused of "cultural crimes," specifically, showing disrespect for cultural diversity.[20]

There are excellent justifications, of course, for teaching about other cultures and about the sources of intergroup conflict. If nothing else, the growing interdependence of societies is making it increasingly important to be informed about the values and sensitivities of groups other than one's own. But despite its name, the multiculturalism movement aims less at promoting cross-cultural understanding than at providing therapy for minorities and at reinforcing the perception that white racism, along with sexism and heterosexism, remains a terrible problem. As one commentator observes, the new multiculturalism does not expose students to the great achievements of non-European cultures, such as the *Prolegomena* of Ibn Khaldun or the *Analects* of Confucius. Nor is its focus on getting students to understand the great global phenomena of our time, such as the re-ascent of East Asia and the spread of religious fundamentalism. In practice, it teaches students to view world history and modern civilization from the perspective of discrimination, oppression, and imperialism, and it conditions them to overlook various other factors that are often more basic.[21]

The excitement of the movement has created an intolerant mind-set reminiscent of the McCarthyism of the 1950s. In an education manual distributed by the American Sociological Association, a Brandeis professor asserts that "it is not open to debate whether a white student is racist . . . He/she simply is."[22] To hold that an assertion is "not open to debate" is to say that dissenters who speak up deserve punishment and vilification. Faculty who have voiced misgivings about the reforms proposed in the name of multiculturalism know this through experience: many have been charged with racism, and some have even faced disciplinary action. At Santa Monica College, for instance, the social science faculty has censured the economist Eugene Buchholz for suggesting that ethnic- and gender-based studies "sidetrack students who could otherwise gain useful disciplines or skills."[23]

Professors have also been harassed for teaching courses or doing research at odds with the new priorities. Charges of "racial insensitivity" have forced Reynolds Farley of the University of Michigan and Stephan Thernstrom of Harvard to discontinue courses on American social history.[24] Christie Farnham Pope of Iowa State University, who has taught black history since 1978, has in recent years seen her classes repeatedly disrupted.[25] Linda Gottfredson of the University of Delaware, who brought attention to the prevalence of race norming, the practice whereby the government pads minority scores on employment tests reported to employers, saw the university cut off her outside funding and eliminate the credit one of her courses provided toward the sociology major. Some of her fellow faculty members denounced her as "racist," and her classes have been picketed. She was also denied tenure, although the decision was reversed on appeal.[26]

The examples could be multiplied, but even a comprehensive listing would not capture how seriously intellectual discourse has been perverted and truncated. For every discontinued course, there are many others never designed. There are also articles kept off syllabi, ideas excluded from lectures, and research questions never pursued. One cannot identify all such consequences. It is certain, however, that preference falsification on affirmative action has been accompanied by a squelching of critical discourse on elements of the incumbent racial agenda, like multiculturalism.

The university began in spirit, writes Allan Bloom, when Socrates committed himself to inquiry unfettered by public opinion or popular culture. In keeping with Socrates' mission, American universities have in the past endeavored to instill in faculty and students alike an openness to discussion, including a willingness to live with discomforting opinions. Staying in tune with public opinion has not been among universities' objectives, even if in practice they have sometimes failed to resist infringements on their intellectual liberties.[27] Nor have their objectives included making students "feel good about themselves." True, counselors have always been available to help students cope with their personal problems. But this is quite different from using the curriculum as an instrument of psychological therapy. It is also different from expecting professors to avoid subjects and self-censor ideas that some listeners may find upsetting.

The product of a confused mind-set, the new multiculturalism is itself a source of confusion. It handicaps both students and faculty by depriving them of exposure to facts and arguments relevant to pressing social problems and also by limiting what they may explore with impunity.

Color-Coded Scholarship

In addition to the regulation of intellectual discourse, the new multiculturalism seeks to give minorities greater representation among faculty. This latter objective, say its defenders, would promote fairness, give comfort to minority students, and ensure that minority issues get approached "correctly."

Such claims lie at the heart of an article in the *University of Pennsylvania Law Review* in which Richard Delgado proposes that the race-related scholarship of minorities be preferred over that of whites. The scholarship of whites tends to be unsatisfactory, suggests Delgado, for they themselves have not experienced racial oppression.[28] Is the ultimate objective to deny white scholars a voice? Delgado has no objection to "sensitive white scholars" contributing "occasional articles and useful proposals," but they must not make a career of race-related research. "The time has come for white liberal authors who write in the field of civil rights to redirect their efforts and to encourage their colleagues to do so as well." They should "stand aside" and let their positions "be filled by talented and innovative minority writers and commentators."[29]

This article has been followed by other publications in the same vein. Mari Matsuda of the University of Hawaii has argued that "apartheid in legal knowledge" can be eradicated "by making a deliberate effort to buy, order, read, cite, discuss, and teach" the scholarship of "women, people of color, poor people, gays and lesbians, indigenous Americans, and other oppressed people." What, precisely, is to be done? "When buying twenty books," one "should ascertain that some of them are written by white women, women of color, and men of color." Publishers and bookstores should help out by imposing diversity "quotas." And readers should read only works with appropriately diverse citation distributions.[30]

In the nineteenth century, W. S. Scarborough, an experienced black scholar of Greek and Latin, could not find an academic job. Not even predominantly black Howard University would hire him, for it held that "the chair in classical languages could be filled only by a Caucasian."[31] Implicit in the demands of Delgado, Matsuda, and their fellow travelers is an analogous presumption, namely, that each minority is inherently best qualified to address issues it considers its own. By this view, a black professor is better qualified to study black poverty than a white professor, even if the latter grew up destitute while the former was born into wealth. On the basis of such a race-based criterion, white specialists on race relations and African history have come under pressure to find themselves new pursuits. For example, the UCLA historian Gary Nash has been told by many self-professed Afrocentrists that only blacks should speak on black issues.[32]

The Grip of the Unthinkable

Some white scholars with creative insight into racial matters seem to have accepted the view that their ethnicity constitutes a professional handicap. A literary critic has declared that his whiteness disqualifies him from evaluating certain forms of "black writing." Arguing that blacks do not think or suffer in the same manner as whites, he has maintained that whites should read such literature but not question its assumptions or conclusions. And a distinguished student of race-relations law has responded to questions about the qualifications of whites in the field by noting that he has "no illusion of having crossed an uncrossable gap."[33]

The other side of this coin is that white scholars are endowing blacks with special authority on racial matters. Soon after Stephen Carter became a law professor, a white scholar whom he had never met sent him a draft of an article critical of his work on constitutional law.

Carter's work, the draft indicated, showed insensitivity to the experiences of blacks. When the white professor learned that Carter was black, rather than defend his claim, he simply dropped it from the article. "In his eyes," recalls Carter, "my blackness evidently provided an immunity from the charge; perhaps he thought I possessed a special perspective on racial matters that he did not, or maybe he decided that it was unfair or racist for him, a white professor, to make such an accusation against a black one."[34]

The new thinking on race posits a link between the merit of an idea and the identity of its holder. It treats whiteness as an insurmountable obstacle to producing dependable work on racial matters and blackness as a badge of intrinsic intellectual virtue. Notwithstanding the lip service the new thinking pays to Martin Luther King's vision, it thus perpetuates the very sort of race consciousness that he found so insidious. In point of fact, it is not unusual for outsiders to see things that insiders habitually miss. Outsiders' minds have not been conditioned by local sensitivities. They are also freer from the pressures that make insiders engage in preference falsification. Thus the most penetrating account of Soviet communism, 1984, was written by an Englishman who had never set foot in a communist country. More relevant to our present concerns, some of the key assumptions and arguments of contemporary research on race are traceable to *An American Dilemma*, by Gunnar Myrdal, a Swede.[35]

Specialists on race relations are not united, of course, behind the emergent race-conscious standards. Objections are heard. However, just as the dissenters against communism generally failed to identify the root causes of their system's failures, and just as Indians who turn against specific caste norms do not necessarily lose faith in Hinduism itself, intellectuals who object to race-conscious research do not always reject the political agenda that has spawned it. Nor do they recognize that efforts to impose a color line on scholarship is a logical response to the view that white racism permeates every facet of American society.

The work of the legal scholar Randall Kennedy offers an instructive example. Kennedy has written a powerful critique of Delgado and Matsuda's call for color-coded scholarship. Yet toward the end of a long argument that characterizes the Delgado/Matsuda agenda as thoroughly racist, he pleads for limited affirmative action, one where "race-conscious decisionmaking" enters some domains but without losing "its status as a deviant mode of judging people or the work they produce."[36]

Kennedy does not specify the boundaries of legitimate race consciousness or suggest how established boundaries can be preserved, however. Overlooking the social forces that prevent the containment of affirmative action, he remains convinced that one can keep it within bounds chosen by social planners. Even more revealing is his failure to recognize that the Delgado/Matsuda agenda is consistent with the spirit of affirmative action, as it is now understood. If it is acceptable to make a white medical-school applicant step aside in the interest of raising the number of black physicians, why should a law review not reject white-authored articles to make room for more articles written by blacks? It is not obvious why scholars should be exempt from the double standards they would impose on other professions. If the answer is that scholarship is too important to allow a relaxation of standards, there is the point that lowering standards for unqualified minority physicians could result in fatal misdiagnoses. Also unclear is why a university aiming for a "racially balanced" faculty should insist on color-blind selection procedures for scholarly publications. If it is necessary to expose students to an appropriately diverse faculty, there must be similar benefits to exposing readers to a diverse set of authors.

Racial affirmative action rests on the view that racial disparities stem largely, if not solely, from white racism and that the appropriate remedy is compensatory advantages for blacks. The proposals of Delgado and Matsuda do not flow inexorably from such thinking, but they are essentially consistent with the logic behind double standards in admissions, hiring, speech codes, and the new multiculturalism. By implication, there is a tension between Kennedy's opposition to these proposals and his continued commitment to the race consciousness from which they spring. In effect, Kennedy remains captive to the very ideology whose extreme applications he finds offensive and dangerous.

Reform communism was initiated by individuals aware of communism's shortcomings but too tied to old presumptions to generate viable responses. Many of the boldest and most insightful critics of the current racial agenda exhibit an analogous attachment to old ideas. Their thoughts stay clear of the unthinkable, that is, the riskiest connections, findings, and conclusions.

James Coleman has offered a personal example of how social pressures steer one's thoughts on race-related issues away from the unthinkable.[37] In the mid-1970s, he was directing a research project on inequalities of educational opportunity—the one that eventually led to his ugly experience mentioned in Chapter 9. One of his findings was that students' verbal achievements depend on their teachers' scores on vocabulary tests, another that as a group black teachers trained by segregated schools had relatively low verbal skills. Together, these findings raised the possibility that, whether black or white, students taught by black teachers would as a group be at a disadvantage relative to their peers taught by white teachers. But at the time, Coleman recalls, he did not make the connection. The reason was not that he was afraid of controversy. His oversight was rooted in two common assertions whose validity he had unthinkingly accepted: first, that black students need role models of their own race, and second, that they do better when taught by teachers who can fulfill this need.

In his retrospective account of this failure Coleman writes:

I believe that a dispassionate researcher concerned with finding facts relevant to the policy issues at hand (one of which was school staff desegregation) would have gone on to pose the question we did not ask. One could well argue that by not asking it, we aided in the sacrifice of educational opportunity for many children, most of whom were black, to protect the careers of black teachers. And one could argue that by not asking it, we encouraged the continued neglect of the kind of skill-specific retraining programs—not only for black teachers but for all teachers—that might have brought improvements in educational outcomes.[38]

In other words, Coleman and his colleagues did not even consider the possibility that black students might do better under white teachers, for its potential implications were simply unthinkable. This failure had the unintended effect of inhibiting measures to improve the skills of teachers.

Corrective Voices from Abroad

The adverse consequences of the impoverishment of academic discourse go way beyond the specific costs identified by Coleman. The impoverishment keeps alive a social agenda that has failed blacks most in need of help. By focusing attention on statistical disparities in school admissions and employment and by harping on racism as the all-encompassing explanation for everything discomforting, this agenda obscures the deeper causes of disparities. It fails to educate black and nonblack Americans victimized by violence, family breakdown, poor education, and unemployment about the connections among these problems. And by promoting the view that the entire socioeconomic system remains racist to the core, it facilitates the spread of conspiracy theories, like the theory that the AIDS virus was "deliberately created in a laboratory to infect black people"—a claim that 29 percent of a sample of black New Yorkers surveyed in 1990 considered true or possibly true.[39]

Nothing in this chapter contradicts the firmness of private opposition to affirmative action. As noted in Chapter 9, the justification for such opposition typically rests on a pair of moral convictions: first, that present generations of whites bear no responsibility for injustices committed by past generations of whites against past generations of blacks, and second, that living blacks are entitled to equal opportunity but not special privileges. A person can oppose affirmative action on these grounds yet have only the dimmest awareness of its implications for the country's future. Indeed, while most Americans recognize that race-conscious policies have bred resentment and squandered some of the interracial goodwill that developed in the 1960s, few realize that in fueling tribalization these policies are sowing the seeds of severe domestic conflict. Nor do Americans generally appreciate how the issue of race fosters political paralysis by subjecting reform proposals on issues like crime and government spending to the lethal charge of racial bias. Almost everyone can see that after a quarter-century of affirmative action a substantial share of the black minority lacks the skills to compete in a knowledge-based global economy. Few see that the emphasis on accommodating poorly qualified students, as opposed to giving such students a better education, has helped lower standards throughout the educational system, to the detriment of all ethnic groups. It is revealing that in spite of statistics showing the academic achievements of American secondary school students to lag behind those of their peers in every other major industrialized country,[40] most American parents remain satisfied with current educational standards.[41]

In discussing communism I argued that Western criticisms of communism undermined the power of communist ideology over individual minds, especially after it became safe to bring into domestic public discourse points damaging to official positions. The racial agenda of the United States has not been immune to foreign criticism. Many Japanese commentators, for example, have been saying for years that it is doomed to failure. Moreover, they have been suggesting that the agenda is damaging the American economy, even predicting that Japan's chief economic opponent in the twenty-first century will be China or Europe rather than America. The United States is failing miserably at mass education, many Japanese observers argue, especially when it comes to imparting marketable skills to its ethnic minorities. Even top Japanese statesmen have articulated such views, sometimes bluntly, crassly, and undiplomatically.[42]

Every gaffe has produced an uproar in the American media, with commentators using either clumsiness or the genuinely racist tendencies within Japanese society as an excuse for dismissing the underlying message, namely, that the United States has yet to come to terms with the demands of a knowledge-intensive and increasingly mobile global economy. Never have more than a few commentators defended the Japanese viewpoint, or even acknowledged that it is worthy of debate. Part of the explanation is that writers who display tolerance toward critics of the established racial agenda risk becoming stigmatized as racists. Another part, less obvious, is that the prevailing public discourse in the United States tends to separate racial matters from issues of national economic performance, thus keeping most Americans ignorant about the intricate connections. Discussions about racial justice typically proceed without regard to matters of international competitiveness.

Preference falsification has directly and indirectly kept critical Japanese opinion from correcting the distortions in American public discourse. There is an important lesson here. Dissent by people outside a society will fall mostly on deaf ears until it receives vocal support from a critical mass of insiders. In the Soviet Union Western views antithetical to communist doctrine became part of Soviet public discourse only after Soviet citizens came to feel that they could express similar views with impunity. The consequent broadening of Soviet public discourse was fueled by years of economic stagnation that made the top leadership acknowledge the need for fundamental change. The United States is a long way from such a crisis; for all its troubles, its economy remains quite strong in many respects. Consequently few Americans are sufficiently troubled to turn abroad for diagnoses and remedies.

The Shortcomings of Alternative Explanations

The whole thesis may be put in perspective by contrasting it with its alternatives. One popular explanation rests on "white guilt." In the 1960s, suggests Shelby Steele, guilt "changed the nature of the white man's burden from the administration of inferiors to the uplift of equals." In need of redemption, whites bent social policies "more toward reparation for black oppression than toward the much harder and more mundane work of black uplift and development." The source of white guilt, Steele goes on, was the "*knowledge* of ill-gotten advantage." The civil rights movement juxtaposed this knowledge with the gratitude whites feel for their whiteness, turning whiteness into a source of anguish. The ensuing quest for quick redemption gave blacks an ability to extract entitlements that go beyond fairness. In short, white guilt fueled "black power."[43]

By this account, affirmative action is the outcome of a simple exchange through which whites give blacks special privileges in return for redemption. The explanation has two shortcomings, the first of which concerns the size of the privileges. Can the guilt of a white Californian be so intense as to make her endure rejection from Berkeley for the sake of the admission of someone less well prepared? Probably not. If she continues to support affirmative action, the reason could be that she is afraid to vent her frustrations in public. It could also be that such preference falsification on the part of *others* has left her ignorant about the extent to which Berkeley has altered its standards in the interest of racial diversity. The other problem with the guilt-centered explanation is that it oversimplifies the involved exchange by relegating blacks and whites to opposite sides of the bargaining table. Blacks demand entitlements and supply redemption, whites the other way around. In reality, the demand for black privileges comes partly from whites, and some blacks view special entitlements as a badge of inferiority. The sources of black power are more complex than the "white guilt" thesis makes them seem.

A second popular explanation for the persistence of affirmative action puts the emphasis on vested interests. There are blacks, observes one writer, who have "developed a predictable stake in expanding the boundaries of racism in pursuit of moral and practical exemptions from social obligation."[44] These include bureaucrats, professors, businesspersons, and students whose positions and fortunes are tied to special programs for minorities. Such groups, the argument goes, extract large benefits for themselves, spreading the costs thinly over the rest of society. This argument explains why the manifest beneficiaries of affirmative action defend the status quo. But it fails to illuminate why affirmative action receives public support from many of the whites who shoulder its burden. Nor does it explain the pervasiveness of ignorance about the various costs and benefits.

A third explanation, related to the second, centers on intergroup differences in capacity for collective action.[45] Owing to their small numbers, black members of organizations that practice affirmative action are able to organize and press their case more easily than can their considerably more numerous white peers. There is much sense to this explanation. It leaves unexplained, however, why public opinion remains so favorable to affirmative action. It is one thing for the losers from affirmative action to remain unorganized, another for them to participate in a cause they privately oppose. The thesis is silent also on the deficiencies of private knowledge about the consequences of the incumbent racial agenda.

Finally, there is an explanation that stresses the exigencies of holding together the prevailing political coalition consisting of civil rights organizations, feminists, gay activists, socialists, and environmentalists. By this account, white feminists support race-conscious programs in return for black support on issues of special concern to feminists, like abortion. The generic name for such vote trading is logrolling.[46] This phenomenon is doubtless part of the explanation, but one must recognize that successful logrolling always involves preference falsification. The feminist who marches against racism does not wear a badge revealing her objections to color consciousness. On the contrary, she participates in the promotion of the color-conscious agenda. Her participation may reflect either opportunism or conviction. Either way, its effect is to tilt public discourse in favor of color consciousness. Because public discourse influences the worldviews of the grand coalition's members—not to mention those of nonmembers—preference falsification undertaken for the purpose of logrolling may turn people without a stake in racial affirmative action into genuine believers in its advantages. Universities contain individuals of various ethnicities who believe in the moral rectitude of the established racial agenda. In and of itself, the coalition-centered explanation does not account for this fact.

Are the Ideological Effects of Preference Falsification Necessarily Pernicious?

The common theme of the past few chapters has been that preference falsification promotes, fortifies, and preserves myths. Myths arise because the preconceptions that control our interpretations are based partly on social proof. Preference falsification distorts social proof by removing from public discourse facts and arguments that powerful groups deem unmentionable. As such, it has a profound effect on the evolution of private knowledge. It imparts credibility to myths by shielding them from corrective disclosures.

Like beauty, it might be said, truth is in the eye of the beholder—with or without expressive taboos. If all private knowledge were to become public, the mental models through which individuals interpret the world would still differ, if only because of variations in personal experience. As a practical matter, therefore, one cannot identify a set of beliefs that under unbridled freedom of expression everyone would recognize as true. By implication, an ideology shaped by the distortions of public discourse might lie closer to an observer's sense of reality than whatever beliefs he might have developed under perfect freedom of expression.

Nothing in my argument presupposes, however, that someone has an infinite capacity to distinguish fact from fiction, sound intuition from camouflaged prejudice, or right from wrong. Not even highly informed specialists can identify every relevant fact about current and future conditions or foresee every effect of a given policy. In addition, however much they aim for objectivity, their interpretations will inevitably bear the influence of their perceived interests. I bring this up as a way of acknowledging that future developments may refute some of my own views. For example, unforeseeable developments may yet prove race-conscious policies a boon to impoverished minorities. Someone may yet devise an economically viable form of socialism with a human face. And technological developments still unimaginable may yet turn India's caste system into a source of economic advantage. Human history is replete with policies that proved beneficial because of developments no one foresaw.

In any case, one can recognize the role of preference falsification in an ideology's dissemination without having to pass judgment on the ideology. Conversely, one can praise or criticize an ideology without losing sight of its dependence on preference falsification. Regardless of what we think of affirmative action, we can all recognize that Americans are terrified of being charged with racism and that the consequent distortions of public discourse have constrained American thought patterns on a host of issues.

To reiterate a point made earlier, public discourse is not the only determinant of human thought. If it were, private knowledge on complex social issues would become very stable. Once a belief emerged and spread, it would quickly gain unanimous acceptance and attain the status of unquestioned fact. Thereafter, private knowledge would be unmalleable. Direct experience is one element that interferes with this stabilizing process. Another is the impossibility of extinguishing individual curiosity and spontaneity. Even in highly regimented societies there are always people who, despite the hazards, let their minds wander. Some hit upon unconventional ways of looking at the world, and a smaller number show the courage to share their discoveries with others.

Commonly stigmatized as troublemakers or heretics, unconventional thinkers keep open options that conventional wisdom has discarded, giving them a chance to be tried or retried if public opinion somehow turns. Moreover, in discovering and publicizing the status quo's flaws, these thinkers slow down the internalization of its supporting beliefs. As we shall see next, they effectively keep the status quo vulnerable, holding social change within the realm of possibility. In Eastern Europe, these functions were served by the dissidents who prepared the ground for the explosion of 1989—an event to be interpreted in Chapter 16.

IV

Generating Surprise

15

Unforeseen Political Revolutions

Where the status quo owes its stability to preference falsification, there are people waiting for an opportunity, and perhaps others who can easily be induced, to stand up for change. Some eye-opening event or an apparent shift in social pressures may cause public opposition to swell. The public preferences of individuals are interdependent, so a jump in public opposition may be self-augmenting. Under the right conditions, every jump will galvanize further jumps.

The potential for change is not fully observable. We can never know exactly how a given event will be interpreted; whether a new technology will alter the balance of political power; or what it would take to turn public opinion against the status quo. Such predictive limitations imply that shifts in public opinion, especially large shifts, may catch everyone by surprise. Yet an unforeseen shift in public opinion may subsequently be *explained* with ease. The shift will bring into the open long-suppressed grievances and draw attention to factors that have made people cease supporting the status quo.

The case of Iran provides an example of an unanticipated revolution that now, after the fact, we have little trouble explaining. None of the major intelligence organizations of the Cold War—not even the CIA or the KGB—expected the Iranian monarchy to collapse in the winter of 1978–79. Right up to the revolution they all expected the shah to weather the gathering storm. Retrospective perceptions notwithstanding, the revolution came as a surprise even to the Ayatollah Khomeini, the fiery cleric who, from exile, masterminded the mass mobilization process that was to catapult him to Iran's helm. Nevertheless,

upheaval seems anything but surprising. It has
of explanations, including ones centered on disap-
nance failures, class conflicts, foreign exploitation,
nce. Plausible as some of the explanations seem,
why hindsight and foresight should diverge. Why
_____ ...at now appears as the inevitable outcome of powerful social forces surprise so many of its leaders, participants, victims,
and observers? The purpose of this chapter is to develop a general
framework for answering such a question.

Political Revolution

The dual preference model of this book posits a predefined issue on
which there is a political struggle between two pressure groups. For
this chapter and the next, the issue is the incumbent political regime's
legitimacy. The two pressure groups are the *government,* which recognizes its own right to govern, and the *opposition,* which does not.
Within this particular context, Y, our measure of public opinion, represents the size of the public opposition to the government. As usual,
it is expressed as a percentage of the population.

At the start of our story Y is near 0, indicating that the government
commands almost unanimous public support. A revolution would
take the form of a sudden and enormous jump in Y that makes it
impossible for the government to continue governing. By this definition, revolution entails a mass-supported shift in political power. It is
immaterial whether the transfer of power brings about meaningful
change in people's lives. All that matters is that the transfer be swift
and extensive.

For reasons that need no repetition, the individual's public preference depends on Y^e, the expected level of the public opposition, and
on x, his private preference. Given that his incentive to support the
opposition varies directly with Y^e and inversely with x, there is a critical value of Y^e at which he will abandon the government for the
opposition. This critical value is what may now be called his *revolutionary threshold.*

Individuals with different private preferences will tend to have different revolutionary thresholds. Associated with any given distribution of thresholds is a propagation curve, which gives, for each pos-

sible expectation of the size of the public opposition, the corresponding realization. For an illustration, consider the solid curve in Figure 15.1. This curve crosses the diagonal from above at 10 and 90, which are the self-sustaining levels of public opposition. The former represents our starting point. Initially, therefore, 10 percent of the population publicly supports the opposition and the remaining 90 percent supports the government.

The private preferences that influence the levels of individual thresholds need not stay fixed over time. If they rise, implying that individuals have privately become more sympathetic to the opposition, revolutionary thresholds will fall. Thresholds may fall for other reasons, too. If the government becomes less efficient at delivering selective incentives, or the opposition becomes more efficient, thresholds will decrease. The same result will obtain if individuals privately sympathetic to the opposition develop greater expressive needs.

A fall in individual thresholds will raise the propagation curve. Such

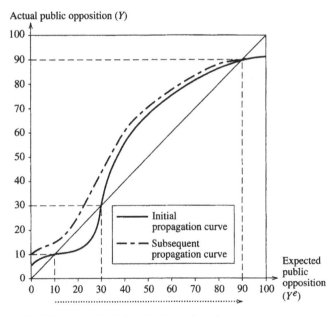

Figure 15.1 A fall in individual thresholds pushes the propagation curve upward, causing the incumbent equilibrium to vanish. Public opinion darts from 10 to 90.

a shift is illustrated by the broken curve in Figure 15.1. The shift destroys the incumbent equilibrium, leaving 90 as the only equilibrium. Public opinion then darts from 10 to 90, implying that 80 percent of the population abandons the government for the opposition. This explosive growth in the size of public opposition represents a revolution.

Small Events, Large Outcomes

The analysis could be carried on through diagrams.[1] The key points can be developed more simply, however, through stylized numerical examples. Imagine a ten-person society featuring the *threshold sequence*

A:
Individuals	a	b	c	d	e	f	g	h	i	j
Thresholds	0	20	20	30	40	50	60	70	80	100

Person a, whose threshold is 0, supports the opposition regardless of its size, just as person j always supports the government. The remaining eight people's preferences are sensitive to the expected size of the public opposition. Depending on its level, they will opt for one camp or the other. Initially, as in the geometric illustration, the opposition consists of 10 percent of the population, so $Y = 10$. Specifically, person a supports the opposition, and persons b through j support the government. Because individuals other than a have thresholds above 10, a public opposition of 10 percent is self-sustaining.

Suppose now that person b has an unpleasant encounter at some government ministry. Her alienation from the regime deepens, pushing her threshold down from 20 to 10. The threshold sequence becomes

A^1:
Individuals	a	b	c	d	e	f	g	h	i	j
Thresholds	0	10	20	30	40	50	60	70	80	100

The new threshold of b happens to equal the existing Y of 10. So she switches sides, revealing her decision by tossing an egg at the country's leader during an official rally. Y thus becomes 20. The new Y is not self-sustaining but self-augmenting, as it drives c into opposition. The higher Y of 30 then triggers a fourth defection, raising Y to 40. And the process continues until Y reaches 90—a new equilibrium. Now the first nine individuals are in opposition, with only j supporting the government. A slight shift in one individual's threshold has generated a *revolutionary bandwagon.*

Comparing A with A^1 reveals that an event that changes even a single threshold may destroy an equilibrium and precipitate a massive shift in public opinion. In the case at hand, the destroyed equilibrium happens to be the status quo.

Now consider sequence

B:

Individuals	a	b	c	d	e	f	g	h	i	j
Thresholds	0	20	30	30	40	50	60	70	80	100

It differs from A only in the threshold of c: 30 as opposed to 20. As in the previous illustration, let the threshold of b fall from 20 to 10. The resulting sequence is

B^1:

Individuals	a	b	c	d	e	f	g	h	i	j
Thresholds	0	10	30	30	40	50	60	70	80	100

Once again, the incumbent equilibrium of 10 becomes unsustainable, and Y rises to 20. But the opposition's growth stops there, for the new Y is self-sustaining. Some government supporters privately enjoy the sight of the leader's egg-splattered face, but none follows the egg thrower into public opposition. We see that a minor variation in thresholds may drastically alter the effect of a given perturbation. In particular, an event that causes a revolution in one setting may in a slightly different setting generate only a slip in the government's public support.

Neither private preferences nor the corresponding thresholds are common knowledge. A society can therefore come to the brink of a revolution without anyone realizing this, not even those with the power to unleash it. Under sequence A, for instance, person b need not recognize that she is capable of setting off a revolutionary bandwagon. Although she may sense that preference falsification is common, she cannot know whether the actual sequence is A or B.

In principle, such pluralistic ignorance can be mitigated through polls that accord their participants anonymity. But it is easier to offer participants anonymity than to convince them that their revealed preferences will remain anonymous and never be used against them. In any case, an outwardly popular government sustained by preference falsification has no interest in publicizing the fragility of its support, because this would inspire the disaffected to bring their antigovernment feelings into the open. On the contrary, such a government has an incentive to discourage independent polling.

The Inessentiality of Mass Discontent

Anything that shifts private opinion—for instance, an economic recession, interactions with other societies, or intergenerational replacement—may alter the threshold sequence. But whatever the underlying factors, the threshold sequence can move dramatically against the government without catalyzing a revolution. In sequence

C:	Individuals	a	b	c	d	e	f	g	h	i	j
	Thresholds	0	20	20	20	20	20	20	20	60	100

the average threshold is 30, possibly because most people despise the government. Yet $Y = 10$ remains an equilibrium. It is true, of course, that a revolution is more likely under C than under A. Sequence C features seven individuals with thresholds of 20, A only one.

The point remains that widespread antipathy toward the government is not sufficient to mobilize large numbers for revolutionary action. Antigovernment feelings can certainly bring a revolution within the realm of possibility, but other conditions must come together to set it off. So it is that a nineteenth-century Russian journal once declared: "No village has ever revolted merely because it was hungry."[2] For hungry people to revolt they must not only blame their misery on the government but believe that revolt is a remedy. If the opposition is minuscule, the expected cost of revolting is immense. A person who chooses to follow the call of his conscience will merely compound his misery—unless, of course, he derives immense satisfaction from expressing his antigovernment feelings.

By the same token, a revolution may break out in a society where private preferences, and therefore individual thresholds, tend to be relatively favorable to the government. It is necessary only for additions to the opposition to trigger further defections from the government's ranks. In other words, the threshold sequence must form a bandwagon that is mobile at the prevailing public opposition. Reconsider the sequence A^1, where the average threshold is 46, and C, where it is 30. Under A^1, public opposition darts from 10 to 90. Under *C*, it remains stuck at 10. In the latter case, public opposition would somehow have to reach 20 to get a bandwagon rolling.

A nineteenth-century socialist is reputed to have exclaimed to a friend handing coins to a beggar: "Don't delay the revolution!" The logic underlying this cry is shared by two of the most popular theories of revolution: the Marxian theory, which posits that social orders are overthrown as a result of discontent generated by epochal changes in forms of production and exchange,[3] and the relative deprivation theory, which holds that mass upheavals are fueled by frustration-inducing gaps between economic expectations and outcomes.[4] The proponents of these theories believe that mass discontent automatically leads to change-oriented political action. They thus overlook the interdependence of individual political choices. And they deny the significance of the distribution of discontent. Yet, as demonstrated by the comparison between A^1 and *C*, under the right conditions a single disaffected individual with a threshold of 10 may do more for a revolution than seven slightly less disaffected individuals with thresholds of 20.

Neither theory accords with the historical record. If the Marxian theory were correct, the first successful socialist takeover would not have occurred in semifeudal Russia. As for the theory of relative deprivation, it conflicts with evidence that deep economic crises do not necessarily generate heightened political agitation. As a case in point, between 1830 and 1960 the level of collective violence in France was uncorrelated with the degree of mass discontent.[5]

A related flaw of these two theories is that they treat mass discontent as a precondition of revolution. They assume, in effect, that for a mass upheaval to occur large numbers must first come to desire political change. In reality, a revolutionary bandwagon may help create the discontent that keeps it in motion. Switches from the government to the opposition may alert essentially content people to the government's failings; or they may make people who had been resigned to the status quo recognize the possibility of political change.

Not only is mass discontent inessential to start a revolution, but the early movers need not be among society's most disaffected members. Private preferences constitute only one determinant of individual political choices. Others are the probability of revolutionary success; the expected cost of failure and the expected reward to success; and the expressive cost of preference falsification. Highly disenchanted people may hold back if they consider the chances of being punished unduly high, or if they derive little utility from expressing themselves truthfully. Conversely, individuals with relatively comfortable lives may join the revolutionary vanguard if they happen to oppose the status quo and cannot bear the thought of remaining quiet. As will be shown in the next chapter, revolutionary leaders have not necessarily expected to be rewarded for their defiance, nor have they all expected their movements to succeed. Invariably, they have been individuals with unusually intense expressive needs.

The Role of Political Structure

Imagine now that some superpower has long been committed to keeping our government in power. Suddenly, the superpower rescinds its commitment. Both the expected cost of joining the opposition and, of course, individual thresholds are likely to fall. Let us say that every threshold between 10 and 90 drops by 10 units. If the preexisting threshold sequence were A, B, or C, the result would be a revolutionary jump in public opinion from 10 to 90. Suppose, however, that it is sequence

D:

Individuals	a	b	c	d	e	f	g	h	i	j
Thresholds	0	30	30	30	30	30	30	30	30	100

The structural shock turns D into

D^1:

Individuals	a	b	c	d	e	f	g	h	i	j
Thresholds	0	20	20	20	20	20	20	20	20	100

Fully four-fifths of the population are now willing to switch over to the opposition, but *only if someone else goes first*. No one does, leaving Y at 10.

A shift in international relations is among the types of change to which yet another popular theory of revolution, the structuralist theory, accords revolutionary significance. Theda Skocpol, a proponent of structuralism, argues that a revolution occurs when two conditions coalesce. First, a state's evolving relations with other states and local classes weaken its ability to maintain law and order; and second, the elites harmed by the situation are powerless to restore the status quo ante, yet strong enough to paralyze the government. Through their obstructionism the elites aggravate antielite sentiment, which sets in motion an uprising aimed at social transformation.[6] The suggested appeal of Skocpol's theory lies in its invocation of structural tendencies to explain shifts in the structure of political power. It does not depend on such "subjective" factors as beliefs, expectations, preferences, and goals, although these factors regularly seep into structuralist case studies. Structural theories are thus more "scientific," say their promoters, than theories that ascribe explanatory power to individual dispositions.

The argument here views structural factors as only part of the story.[7] A single person's reaction to an event of global importance might make all the difference between a massive uprising and a *latent bandwagon* that never takes off. So to suggest, as the structuralists do, that individuals are simply the passive bearers of deep-seated revolutionary forces is to overlook the potentially crucial importance of individual characteristics of little significance in and of themselves. It is always a conjunction of factors, many of them intrinsically unimportant and thus unobserved, that determines the flow of events. A major global event can produce drastically different outcomes in two settings that differ trivially. Structuralism and individualism are not, therefore, rival and mutually incompatible approaches to the study of social change. They are essential components of a single story.

To summarize thus far, anything that perturbs a society's threshold sequence may generate a political upheaval. Thresholds may move as a result of changes in private preferences, or shifts in the efficiencies of pressure groups, or both. Another possible precipitant is a rise in the opposition's expected size. Turn back to C, recalling that public opposition stands in equilibrium at 10. If person *a* were to convince even one of the people with thresholds of 20 (persons *b* through *h*) that he was not alone, his bold exaggeration would turn into a self-fulfilling prophecy.[8]

The overall argument depicts the individual member of society as both powerless to generate a revolution and yet potentially very powerful. The individual is powerless because a revolution requires the mobilization of large numbers, but potentially very powerful because under the right circumstances he might set off a chain reaction. Not that the individual can know precisely when he can make a difference. Although he may sense that his chances of sparking a wildfire are unusually great, he can never be certain about the consequences of his own opposition.

Poor Foresight . . .

We are prepared at last to explain why a long-standing regime that appears stable might collapse suddenly, catching everyone by surprise.

Individuals who become increasingly sympathetic to political change do not necessarily publicize their evolving dispositions. If the government enjoys widespread support and is thus very powerful, such individuals remain outwardly loyal to the status quo. In the process, they keep the government, outside observers, opposition leaders, and even one another in the dark as to the regime's vulnerability. They conceal the developing latent bandwagon that might topple the regime. They disguise the fact that the government's public support would collapse precipitously if there were even a slight growth in opposition. Sooner or later, an intrinsically minor event brings a few individuals to their boiling points. They take to the streets, unleashing the long-latent bandwagon. The opposition darts to power.

These dynamics are captured beautifully by the old Chinese saying, "A single spark can start a prairie fire."[9] Given the right combination of physical conditions, a normally ephemeral spark will ignite a blaze. Likewise, given the right combination of social conditions, an event that normally produces mere grumbling will touch off a revolutionary uprising.

. . . Excellent Hindsight

A successful revolution exposes but also exaggerates the tensions that produced it. On the one hand, it brings into the open genuine grievances that had been repressed out of fear. On the other, it makes people who were content with the old order embrace the new regime with apparent enthusiasm, possibly attributing their former public preferences solely to persecution.

Reconsider the threshold sequence

A^1:	Individuals	a	b	c	d	e	f	g	h	i	j
	Thresholds	0	10	20	30	40	50	60	70	80	100

The relatively high thresholds in A^1 are associated with private preferences more favorable to the government than to the opposition.[10] Person i is much more satisfied with the government than, say, person c. As such, she has little desire to join a movement aimed at toppling it. Remember that when public opposition explodes from 10 to 90, she is the last to jump on the revolutionary bandwagon. She changes her public preference only after the opposition snowballs into a crushing majority, making it imprudent to remain a government supporter.

Having made the switch, she has every reason to feign antipathy to the toppled government. She will not admit that she yearns for the status quo ante, because this would contradict her newly chosen public preference. Nor will she say that her change of heart occurred after the government's collapse, because this might render her declared sympathy for the revolution unconvincing. She has much to gain from claiming that she was very dissatisfied with the old order.

An unintended effect of such misrepresentation is to make it seem that the toppled government enjoyed even less genuine support than it actually did. The illusion is rooted in the very phenomenon responsible for making the revolution a surprise: preference falsification. Having made everyone dismiss the probability of revolution, preference falsification now conceals the forces that were working against it. One consequence of postrevolutionary preference falsification is thus to make it even less comprehensible why the revolution was unforeseen.

The historians of a revolution may appreciate the biases that afflict postrevolutionary accounts of prerevolutionary dispositions without being able to measure the significance of the biases. Consider the sequence

C^1:	Individuals	a	b	c	d	e	f	g	h	i	j
	Thresholds	0	10	20	20	20	20	20	20	60	100

Like A^1, C^1 drives Y from 10 to 90, implying that nine of the ten individuals have an incentive to claim that they despised the prerevolutionary regime. If thresholds below 50 reflect private support for a revolution, and those above 50 private satisfaction with the status quo, eight of the nine would be telling the truth, the one liar being i, whose threshold is 60. It follows from the same assumption that if the threshold sequence were A^1 four of the nine (f through i) would be lying. Given that thresholds are not public knowledge, the key implication here is that historians may have difficulty determining whether the prerevolutionary sequence was A or C—or for that matter, whether the postrevolutionary sequence is A^1 or C^1.

If a revolution brings into view both real and simulated grievances against the toppled government, and if the two types are often practically indistinguishable, public discourse will offer historians reasons in abundance why society had to overthrow its old order. From these reasons almost any writer will be able to construct an explanation for the observed eruption. Preference falsification is thus a prime reason why accounts of revolution, whether journalistic or scholarly, typically give revolutions the appearance of inevitability, even when they seemed anything but inevitable until they occurred. Preference falsification contributes, in other words, to making our hindsight better than our foresight.

Cognitive Biases and the Interpretation of Revolutions

Preference falsification on the part of revolutionary actors interacts with the cognitive limitations of the interpreters of revolutions. The mind of a researcher, like that of anyone else, is severely limited in its ability to handle information. It is thus forced to use judgmental heuristics in trying to interpret, estimate, and infer. Two heuristics introduced in earlier chapters are especially relevant here: the availability heuristic and the representativeness heuristic.[11]

The availability heuristic comes into play because after a revolution's occurrence, information consistent with revolution gains salience and information inconsistent with revolution loses salience. The information absorbed by observers will depend, of course, on the models they carry in their heads. Historians who subscribe to different theories of revolution are apt to notice, and to consider significant, separate data sets.

Marxist historians, noticing that there were many strikes in the decades preceding the Russian Revolution of 1917, infer that a proletarian revolution was in formation.[12] They tend not to notice that in the decade before the revolution the incidence of strikes was minuscule compared with the previous decade, or that the war generated a wave of pro-tzarist sentiment, or that large segments of the masses were apathetic.[13] For another illustration, consider the relative-deprivation explanation for the Iranian Revolution, which is that the uprising was fueled by disappointments caused by the post-1975 decline in Iran's oil revenues.[14] Those who favor this explanation fail to appreciate that throughout the shah's long reign Iran was never without groups who felt relatively deprived. Nor do these observers accord significance to the absence of revolutions in oil-poor Turkey, Brazil, and India, among other countries where certain groups suffered severely from the oil shocks of the 1970s.

The availability heuristic also makes historians exaggerate the fore-knowledge of revolutionary actors. Might proper training overcome this bias in historical interpretation? In controlled experiments trained subjects manage to reduce, but not eliminate, the bias. Like their un-trained counterparts, they continue to overestimate what they them-selves knew. They also continue overestimating what others could have known. Exhibiting the illusion known in cognitive psychology as the I-knew-it-would-happen fallacy, they keep portraying unantic-ipated events as inevitable, foreseeable, and actually foreseen.[15] The relevant implication here is that understanding the workings of the human mind will not, by itself, immunize historians against overesti-mating the foresight of revolutionary actors. To overcome the bias an awareness of the logic of preference falsification is also needed. It is important to understand that preference falsification creates fictitious grievances while masking real ones, that it hinders prediction, and finally, that it accords intrinsically insignificant events potentially mo-mentous significance.

Unfortunately, efforts to overcome distortions rooted in the avail-ability heuristic can be frustrated by the representativeness heuristic, because the latter conflicts with the notion that small events may pro-duce great outcomes. The representativeness heuristic focuses the at-tention of historians on great forces such as massive disappointments and epochal shifts in economic structures. It keeps them from appre-ciating how small forces, such as misjudgment on the part of a ruler or a string of fortuitous circumstances, might explain why one country blew up while another remained stable. By the logic of representativeness, a small event is unrepresentative of a great outcome, and so the two should not be related causally. Accordingly, if Iran experienced a revolution while Turkey remained stable, the reason must be that some great force, absent in the latter, was at work in the former.

Among the lessons of this chapter is that in interpreting social change we need to be on guard against the biases caused by the availability and representativeness heuristics. We need to recognize that transformations of public opinion generate information that would not have been available in advance. And we need to realize that where individual decisions are interdependent, small events can have great consequences. If one way to avoid being misled by our mental heuristics is to become aware of conditions under which they produce errors, another is to become familiar with events that have defied their logic. The next chapter will present examples of such events. Specifically, it will show that, for reasons rooted in preference falsification, some of the great revolutions of modern history have perplexed people who based their predictions or explanations on the availability and representativeness heuristics.

16

The Fall of Communism and Other Sudden Overturns

"Our jaws cannot drop any lower," exclaimed Radio Free Europe one day in late 1989. It was commenting on the collapse of Eastern Europe's communist regimes.[1] In a matter of weeks entrenched communist regimes had been overthrown in one country after another and persecuted dissidents catapulted into high office. Even the most seasoned observers of the region were astonished.

The stunned included champions of the view that communist totalitarianism is far more stable than ordinary authoritarianism.[2] "It has to be conceded," wrote a proponent of this view in early 1990, "that those of us who distinguish between the two non-democratic types of government underestimated the decay of Communist countries and expected the collapse of totalitarianism to take longer than has actually turned out to be the case."[3] Another acknowledged her bewilderment through the title of a new book: *The Withering Away of the Totalitarian State . . . And Other Surprises.*[4]

Also amazed were specialists who had rejected the concept of an immobile region. In 1987 the American Academy of Arts and Sciences had invited a dozen such specialists to prepare interpretive essays on East European developments. As the *Daedalus* issue featuring the essays went to press, the uprisings took off, prompting many authors to change "whole sentences and paragraphs in what were once thought to be completed essays."[5] *Daedalus* editor Stephen Graubard remarks in his preface to the issue that even before the last-minute revisions, the essays offered insights into the stirrings that were transforming the region. But he concedes that neither he nor his essayists foresaw what was to come.[6]

Wise statesmen, discerning diplomats, and gifted journalists were among those caught off guard, as were futurologists. John Naisbitt's *Megatrends*, which sold eight million copies in the early 1980s, does not predict the fall of communism.[7] As the *Economist* observed even before the East European Revolution had run its course, 1989 turned out to be a year when "the most quixotic optimists" were repeatedly "proved too cautious."[8]

Since the fall of East European communism, some scholars, while recognizing that it caught the world by surprise, and while admitting that they themselves were among the stunned, have argued that the collapse could have been predicted, if only the right model of revolution had been available and widely understood.[9] Challenging this view, I argue in the present chapter that systematic processes rooted in preference falsification kept us from foreseeing the uprisings of 1989. I show, moreover, that the ranks of the amazed included people with everything to gain or lose from the fall of communism, people with unusually good access to information, and even people with deep insight into the communist system. Amazement was universal because factors now seen as obvious revolutionary triggers, like Gorbachev's various initiatives, did not seem so significant at the time.

This chapter also takes on three additional tasks. I seek to show that in toppling communism public opinion followed the explosive pattern described in the previous chapter. In addition, I investigate whether there have been other unanticipated political revolutions. Finally, I present evidence that revolutions create new incentives to engage in preference falsification. Specifically, revolutions alter the character of these incentives, inducing some people to become more truthful and others less so.

An Amazed Half-Continent

In "The Power of the Powerless," Václav Havel recognized that East European communism was anything but invincible. It might be toppled, he wrote, by a "social movement," an "explosion of civil unrest," or a "sharp conflict inside an apparently monolithic power structure."[10] Yet he steered clear of speculation on the timing of the collapse. His essay is replete with statements about the unpredictability of political change, although it ends on a cautiously optimistic note: "What if [the 'brighter future'] has been here for a long time already, and only our own blindness and weakness [have] prevented us from seeing it around us and within us, and kept us from developing it?"[11]

Eight years later Havel himself would exhibit "blindness" to events that were ushering in a "brighter future." In 1986, he commented on a Prague crowd's rousing welcome to Gorbachev: "I feel sad; this nation of ours never learns. How many times has it put all its faith in some external force which, it believed, would solve its problems? . . . And yet here we are again, making exactly the same mistake. They seem to think that Gorbachev has come to liberate them from Husák!"[12] In late 1988, with less than a year to go, Havel was unsure about the direction of events: "Maybe [the Movement for Civil Liberties] will quickly become an integral feature of our country's life, albeit one not particularly beloved of the regime . . . Perhaps it will remain for the time being merely the seed of something that will bear fruit in the dim and distant future. It is equally possible that the entire 'matter' will be stamped on hard . . ."[13]

Other Czechoslovak dissidents were just as unprepared for the revolution. In November 1989, when Jan Urban suggested that the opposition contest the elections scheduled for June 1991, his friends ridiculed him as a utopian dreamer.[14] Within a matter of days, the government that Urban's friends considered unchallengeable was gone.

In neighboring Poland a few months before the revolution, negotiations were under way between the communist regime and Solidarity, the trade union that had been demanding political pluralism. To near-universal surprise, the regime agreed in April 1989 to hold elections for a pluralistic parliament. In elections scheduled for June noncommunists would be permitted to contest all 100 Senate seats and 161 of the 460 Assembly seats. Exceeding the wildest expectations, Solidarity won 260 of the 261 seats it was allowed to seek. Stunned by the enormity of this victory, Solidarity officials worried that the electorate's raised hopes would force them to make bold moves, which would then provoke a Soviet reaction or make the Polish leadership resort to violence. The significant point is that neither the government nor Solidarity was prepared for such a lopsided result. The April accord was designed to give Solidarity a voice in Parliament, not to substantiate its claim to being *the* voice of the Polish people.[15]

From the April accord in Poland to the final anticommunist uprising in Romania in December, journalistic accounts invariably painted the picture of an amazed half-continent. Four months after the breaching of the Berlin Wall the Allensbach Institute systematically investigated what had been foreseen. It asked a broad sample of East Germans: "A year ago did you expect such a peaceful revolution?" Only 5 percent answered in the affirmative, although 18 percent answered "yes, but not that fast." Fully 76 percent indicated that they had been totally surprised.[16] These figures are all the more remarkable given the human tendency to exaggerate foreknowledge. In view of this tendency, if East Germans had been asked a year *before* the revolution "Do you expect a revolution in a year's time?" the percentage of unqualified negative answers would undoubtedly have been even higher.[17]

Church members played a key role in initiating the demonstrations that were to topple the East German regime. Yet in the 1990 survey negative answers are statistically unrelated to church attendance. In other words, a churchgoer was not less likely to have been surprised than a nonchurchgoer. Evidently the most outspoken East Germans had no better foresight, on average, than their less outspoken compatriots.

The events that sealed the fate of East German communism took off in late summer when thousands of East German vacationers in Hungary took advantage of relaxed border controls to turn their trips into permanent departures for West Germany. In the ensuing days the East German government acceded to a series of face-saving arrangements under which the vacationers could depart for the West, but only after first returning home. Each new concession prompted further waves of emigrants, however, confuting the government's expectation that the exodus would quickly taper off.[18] The government was not alone in failing to anticipate where events were headed. Thousands of East German citizens rushed to join the exodus precisely because they considered their chances of reaching the West extraordinarily good. Had they known that the Berlin Wall was about to come down, few would have left in such haste, leaving behind almost all their possessions.

It might be said that some very knowledgeable observers of the communist bloc *had* predicted its disintegration before the century was out. As early as 1969, for instance, the Soviet dissident Andrei Amalrik wrote in a tract entitled *Will the Soviet Union Survive until 1984?* that the Russian Empire would break up within a decade and a half. Although it is tempting to credit Amalrik with exemplary foresight, a rereading of his famous essay shows that he expected the Soviet Empire to meet its end following a devastating war with China, not through a string of popular upheavals. In fact, he stated that the Soviet system of government had left people too demoralized and too dependent on authority to allow a spontaneous uprising.[19] So Amalrik did not really foresee the events of 1989. Like a broken watch that tells the correct time every twelve hours, he got the timing of the first crack in the empire essentially right, but on the basis of a spurious forecast of events.

To reiterate a point made earlier, I am not suggesting that the East European explosion came as a *total* surprise to everyone. A small number of commentators, including Havel, had prophesied that the revolution, when it finally arrived, would be swift and remarkably bloodless. Another writer who sensed the possibility of change was Vladimir Tismaneanu, a Romanian professor living in the United States. A year before the collapse of the Romanian regime, he depicted it as "probably the most vulnerable" in Eastern Europe. Sensing an "all-pervasive discontent," he observed that the Braşov riots of 1987, when thousands of citizens took to the streets, signaled that "uncontrollable violence may flare up in Romania."[20] Tismaneanu did not place the Romanian uprising in the context of a regionwide upheaval. Nor did he predict that Romania would be the last Soviet satellite to overthrow its government. It is remarkable nonetheless that he diagnosed the Romanian regime's vulnerability. Like Havel, he succeeded where most other observers failed, because he understood the hidden weaknesses of communism.

Although the collapse of the post–World War II political order of Eastern Europe stunned the world, in hindsight it appears as the inevitable consequence of a multitude of factors. In each of the six countries the leadership was generally despised, lofty economic promises remained unfulfilled, and freedoms taken for granted elsewhere existed only on paper. But if the revolution was indeed inevitable, why was it not foreseen? Why did so many people overlook signs that now, after the fact, are so plainly visible?

Perestroika, Glasnost, and the Escalation of Mass Discontent

For decades, East Europeans cheered leaders they despised and kept quiet in the face of tyranny. Equally important, to prove their loyalty to communist rule, they turned on citizens who had the courage to express misgivings about the political status quo. Huge numbers of East Europeans were dissatisfied with their lives, yet most remained attached to socialist principles.

These arguments from earlier chapters have two immediate implications. First, the regimes of Eastern Europe were substantially more vulnerable than the subservience and quiescence of their populations made them seem. All along, millions were prepared to stand up in defiance if ever they sensed that they could do so safely. Second, even the support of those genuinely sympathetic to the status quo was rather thin. Although the impoverishment of public discourse kept them from seeing an alternative to socialism, their many grievances predisposed them to the promise of fundamental change. Were public discourse somehow to turn, they would probably awaken to the possibility of improving their lives.

But what would catalyze the process of revolutionary mobilization? With hindsight, the push came from the Soviet Union. In the mid-1980s festering economic problems, until then officially denied, convinced the top Soviet leadership to call for *perestroika* (restructuring) and *glasnost* (public openness). Repressed grievances burst into the open, including dissatisfaction with communist rule itself. And with Gorbachev's rise to the helm in 1985, the Soviet Union abandoned its policy of confrontation with the West.[21] In Eastern Europe these changes kindled hopes of greater independence and meaningful social reform. They also generated much new thinking.

The East German surveys discussed in Chapter 13 show that after 1985 East German attachment to socialism steadily deteriorated. By October 1989 only 15 percent of the surveyed trade school students endorsed the statement "I am a devoted citizen of the German Democratic Republic," down from 46 percent in 1983. Fully 60 percent endorsed it with reservations and 25 percent rejected it. In the same month as few as 3 percent continued to believe that "socialism will triumph throughout the world," down from 50 percent in 1984. Just 27 percent agreed with reservations and a whopping 70 percent disagreed.[22] The contrast between the figures for 1989 and those for 1983–84 is striking. It points to a ballooning of discontent in the second half of the decade.

The surveys of official public opinion institutes in Hungary and Czechoslovakia tell a similar story. By 1987, Hungarians characterizing socialism as unsuccessful outnumbered those characterizing it as successful by 72 percentage points, up from 18 points four years earlier. For the capitalist economy, meanwhile, the corresponding difference moved in the opposite direction, from 75 to 21.[23] In the mid-1980s, therefore, vast numbers of Hungarians lost faith in socialism and accepted the superiority of capitalism. In Czechoslovakia, meanwhile, the percentage who believed that socialist living standards would eventually surpass the standards of the capitalist West fell from 50 percent in 1983 to 26 percent in mid-1989.[24] In both Hungary and Czechoslovakia answers to various specific questions are consistent with the results reported here. They reveal increasingly widespread disillusionment with socialism.

Should It Have Been Obvious that a Revolution Lay Ahead?

Did the initiatives of Gorbachev and the ensuing mass disillusionment provide clear signals of the coming revolution? It is tempting to draw this inference, but remember that the surveys just reported were available only to top communist officials. Remember, too, that Havel dismissed a Czechoslovak crowd's jubilation over Gorbachev as a sign of naïveté. He was hardly alone in his pessimism. Even if Gorbachev wanted to liberate Eastern Europe, a popular argument went, it was not obvious that he could. Surely the military would insist on retaining the Soviet Union's strategic buffer against an attack from the West.

Nor was this the only obstacle to liberation. Economic troubles and ethnic tensions within the Soviet Union could provide the pretext for a conservative coup. There was always the precedent of Khrushchev, toppled in 1964. Around the time that Havel was exuding pessimism, a joke was making the rounds in Prague: "What is the difference between Gorbachev and Dubček [the deposed leader of the 1968 Prague Spring]?" The answer: "None—except Gorbachev doesn't know it yet."[25] Significantly, in the fall of 1989 Moscow was rife with rumors of an impending coup.[26] Some observers expected Gorbachev to survive, but only by reversing course and becoming increasingly repressive. An old Soviet joke gives expression to the underlying thinking. Stalin leaves his heirs in the Party two envelopes. One is labeled, "In case of trouble, open this." Trouble arises and the envelope is ceremoniously opened. Its message reads: "Blame me." The other envelope is labeled, "In case of more trouble, open this." More trouble comes and the second envelope is opened: "Do as I did."[27]

In support of their prediction that conservative elements in the leadership would ultimately prevail, pessimists invoked the conservatism of the Soviet people. Observing that the masses tended to be deeply suspicious of Gorbachev's intentions, they inferred that Gorbachev could not count on them for protection against a conservative challenger.

As Gorbachev was trying to restructure the Soviet Union, Poland was testing the limits of its freedom from Moscow. The struggle to legalize Solidarity had already given the country a taste of pluralism, and government censorship was being relaxed in fits and starts. Everyone recognized that these developments enjoyed Gorbachev's approval. Yet few informed people put much faith in Gorbachev's ability to complete the liberation of Eastern Europe, and it was not even clear that he intended to try. "Dissidents throughout Europe," wrote the *Economist* in mid-1987, sounded "sceptical" when talking about Gorbachev.[28] Plenty of evidence fueled their doubts. For instance, Gorbachev did not prevent the East German regime from falsifying the results of local elections held in the spring of 1989, or from endorsing China's Tiananmen Square massacre that summer, or from using force to disperse small demonstrations against these acts.[29]

Prior to the actual revolution it was thus anything but obvious that the Soviet Union would welcome, or even tolerate, attempts to overthrow the communist regimes of its Warsaw Pact allies. Statements, events, and trends that in retrospect appear as signs of an imminent overturn coexisted with many signs of political inertia. Some of Gorbachev's actions did indeed suggest that he wanted to reconfigure the

Soviet Union's relations with its satellites. But there were many reasons to expect his efforts to end in failure.

Since the uprisings of 1989, however, many have come to believe that Gorbachev *engineered* the liberation of Eastern Europe. In reality, he was a master at putting the best face on developments that had pushed past him. In the fall of 1989 there were many reports that events were going much further and faster than he wanted.[30] He was reportedly willing to permit moves toward democracy, provided the communists were not humiliated and East European military ties to the Soviet Union were preserved. Like other world leaders, he was afraid of disturbing Europe's hard-won peace. His idea was to promote revisionist leaders committed to his vision of a socialism based on law and respect for the individual. By no means did he want, nor was he trying, to end communist rule in Eastern Europe.[31] Yet when the peoples of Eastern Europe grabbed political power, pushed the communists aside, and moved to leave the Warsaw Pact, Gorbachev accepted reality and gave his blessing to events generated by forces beyond his control. One is reminded of the horseman who, thrown from his horse, explains with a smile that he has "dismounted."

The point remains that Gorbachev's initiatives fueled expectations of a freer Eastern Europe and reduced the perceived risk of challenging the status quo. His actions made millions of East Europeans increasingly willing to demand political change publicly. In terms of the argument in Chapter 15, his initiatives lowered individual revolutionary thresholds, making it ever easier to set in motion a revolutionary bandwagon. But because of the imperfect observability of thresholds no one could see that a revolution was in the making, not even Gorbachev himself.

Turning Points

What specific events set the bandwagon in motion? Attempting to answer this question is akin to identifying the spark that ignited a prairie fire or the cough responsible for a flu epidemic. There were many turning points in the East European Revolution, any one of which might have derailed it.

One came in early October, when the East German leadership refrained from cracking down on demonstrators. On October 7 Gorbachev was in Berlin for celebrations marking the fortieth anniversary of the German Democratic Republic. With reporters looking on, crowds started chanting, "Gorby! Gorby!" and police went into action with their clubs to silence what was obviously a call for local reforms. The episode, which many East Germans watched on West German television, alerted disgruntled citizens to the existence of groups prepared to protest publicly. At the same time, the government's weak response revealed its vulnerability. New Forum, an opposition group founded just weeks before by disillusioned ex-communists, called for a peaceful protest in Leipzig on October 9. Stories began to circulate of an imminent "Tiananmen Square solution," and of hospital beds being emptied to make room for expected new arrivals from Leipzig. The stories were not baseless, for the Politburo had discussed using live ammunition against the marchers. Erich Honecker, the Party leader, apparently favored a crackdown but lost the vote by a slim margin. Yet the feeling that the regime would respond brutally was so widespread that several prominent citizens appealed for restraint and moderation.[32] A participant in the demonstration of October 9, one of the founders of New Forum, remembers: "In the event, we escaped bloodshed. But it was not known at the time that we would. There was a real, objective threat of violence."[33] Another demonstrator recalls: "There was a terrible feeling that day. No one knew whether we would come out alive. After that day, we started believing that one could demonstrate peacefully."[34]

It has been estimated that 70,000 citizens marched on October 9. The peacefulness of that demonstration encouraged more East German citizens to join the protests. In Leipzig itself, mass demonstrations were held every Monday. The number of participants rose to around 450,000 by November 6, the last Monday before the breaching of the Berlin Wall.[35] Along the way, the regime tried to stem the tide through concessions, but the swelling crowds began to make increasingly bold demands. With the fall of the Berlin Wall, the German Democratic Republic effectively ceased to exist, and in less than a year it was reincorporated into a unified German state.[36]

Another turning point came on October 25. Two months earlier a Solidarity official had formed Poland's first noncommunist government since the 1940s, following the Communist Party's stunning defeat at the polls. An aide to Gorbachev had declined comment on the grounds that events in Poland were its own business.[37] The communists were in retreat in Hungary, too. In meetings with dissident groups the Hungarian Communist Party had endorsed free parliamentary elections. Then, sensing that its candidates would do poorly running under the banner of communism, it had transformed itself into the Hungarian Socialist Party.[38] Never before had ruling communists formally abandoned communism. With the world wondering whether the Soviet Union had reached the limits of its tolerance, Gorbachev declared on October 25 that his country had no right to interfere in the affairs of its East European neighbors. Defining this position as "the Sinatra doctrine," his spokesman jokingly asked reporters whether they knew the Frank Sinatra song "I Did It My Way." He went on, "Hungary and Poland are doing it their way." Using the Western term for the previous Soviet commitment to keep Warsaw Pact governments in communist hands, he added: "I think the Brezhnev doctrine is dead."[39] Coming on the heels of communist retreats in Poland and Hungary, these comments again signaled that Gorbachev would not try to silence East European dissent.

If one effect of this signal was to embolden the opposition movements of Eastern Europe, another must have been to discourage the region's governments from resorting to violence unilaterally. This is not to say that the uprisings would have petered out in the absence of Gorbachev's October 25 statement. By the time Gorbachev renounced the Soviet Union's right to intervene, opposition movements in Poland, East Germany, and Hungary already commanded mass support, and it is unclear that anything short of massive brutality would have broken their momentum and restored the status quo ante. Nonetheless, some incumbent communist leaders were seriously considering a military solution, and the proclamation of the Sinatra doctrine may well have tipped the balance against the use of force. Had even one government resorted to force at this stage, the result might have been a series of protracted civil wars.

Just as we cannot be certain that a delay in announcing the new Soviet doctrine would have altered the course of history, we will never know whether the East German regime's restraint on October 9 had a significant impact on subsequent events. What can be said is that if the hard-liners in the Politburo had prevailed, the opposition's growth would have slowed, and later demonstrations would probably not have stayed peaceful. The same historical significance can be attributed to the restraint shown by the soldiers on duty during the demonstration and by individual demonstrators. In the tense atmosphere of the demonstration a shot fired in panic or a stone thrown in excitement could have sparked a violent confrontation. An extraordinary conjunction of individual choices kept the uprising peaceful and prevented the revolution from being sidetracked.

The Domino Effect

With events in the region receiving enormous media coverage, demonstrations in one country inspired demonstrations elsewhere. In early November Sofia was shaken by its first antigovernment demonstration in four decades as several thousand Bulgarians marched on the National Assembly. Within a week, on the very day throngs broke through the Berlin Wall, Todor Zhivkov's thirty-five years of leadership collapsed, and his successor began talking of radical reforms.

Up to that time Czechoslovakia's communist government had yielded little to its own public opposition. Conscious of developments elsewhere, it had simply promised economic reforms and made minor concessions on travel and religion. These retreats encouraged the mushrooming crowds to ask for more. On November 24, after Alexander Dubček addressed a crowd of 350,000 in his first public speech since 1968, the Communist Party declared a leadership shake-up, only to face a larger rally of people shouting, "Shame!" The new government tried to placate the demonstrators by vowing to punish the commandant of the paramilitary forces that had roughed up protesters a week earlier. Unimpressed, the opposition leaders labeled the announced changes "cosmetic" and promised to redouble their pressure. They called a general strike for November 27, whose success led the Communist Party to capitulate within hours to the opposition's major demands, including an end to its monopoly on political power.[40] "Not since the Paris crowd discovered that the dreaded Bastille contained only a handful of prisoners and a few terrified soldiers has a citadel fallen with such ease," wrote the *Economist* a few days later. "They just had to say boo."[41]

This brings us back, once again, to Havel's 1979 essay. He predicted there that when the greengrocers decided they had had enough, communism would fall like a house of cards. So it turned out. When the masses took to the streets, the support for the Czechoslovak government vanished. The mobilization process followed the patterns of East Germany and Bulgaria. Emboldened by signals from the Soviet Union and the successes of opposition movements elsewhere, a few thousand people stood up in defiance, joining the tiny core of long-persecuted activists. In so doing they encouraged additional citizens to drop their masks, which then impelled more onlookers to jump in. Before long fear changed sides. Where people had been afraid to oppose the regime, they came to fear being caught defending it. Party members rushed to burn their cards, asserting that they had always been reformists at heart. Top officials, sensing that they might be made to pay for resisting change and for any violence, hastened to accept the opposition's demands, only to be confronted with bolder ones yet.

Had the communist leadership shown greater resistance, the transfer of power would not have been so swift, and certainly not so peaceful. A remarkable aspect of the East European Revolution is that, with the partial exception of Romania, the communist establishment simply melted away in the face of growing public opposition. Indeed, as a transfer of power appeared increasingly likely, many state officials crossed over to the opposition. This is highly significant, for a defection from the inner establishment provides a strong indicator of the prevailing political winds. A Politburo member distancing himself from the Party leader does more to expose the regime's vulnerability than a greengrocer who stops displaying a Marxist slogan.

In the model of the last chapter the perceived strength of public opposition was measured by Y, the share of society publicly in opposition. This variable treats all individuals equally. With ten individuals, each carries a weight of 10 percent. In reality, as I have just argued, people differ in their contributions to the perceived strength of the opposition. So a more realistic measure of perceived strength would be some *unequally weighted* indicator of public opposition, where the weights correlate with levels of relative influence. Such a weighted measure would assign a Politburo member more weight than a greengrocer, and the latter more weight than a nameless prisoner in solitary confinement. Were this refinement introduced into the model, the central argument would remain unaffected. With public preferences still interdependent, there would remain the possibility of an unobserved latent bandwagon.[42]

Some of the officials who distanced themselves from the government in late 1989 may at heart have disliked communism. Many others undoubtedly acted for opportunistic reasons rather than out of conviction. Sensing the imminent collapse of the old order, they abandoned it in hopes of securing a place in the order about to be born. A few officials chose to resist, but the speed of the anticommunist mobilization gave them insufficient time to coordinate a reaction. Had the mobilization proceeded more slowly, they might have managed to mount a credible, effective response.[43]

In the days following the fall of Czechoslovak communism, a banner in Prague read: "Poland—10 years, Hungary—10 months, East Germany—10 weeks, Czechoslovakia—10 days."[44] Underlying the implied acceleration is the fact that each successful challenge to communism lowered the perceived risk of dissent in the countries still under communist rule. This relaxation generated a *domino effect*, with a bandwagon in one country touching off even speedier bandwagons elsewhere. Three interrelated factors helped line up the dominos. First, the successes of the early mobilizations helped the citizens of still-dormant countries recognize the vulnerability of their own regimes. Second, the successful mobilizations raised the reputational utility that could be anticipated from joining the opposition early. And finally, in focusing attention on the failures of communism, the mobilizations caused private preferences to move against the status quo.[45]

Had the Prague banner been prepared a few weeks later, it might have added "Romania—10 hours." As the Czechoslovak uprising neared its climax, the executive committee of the Romanian Communist Party was busy reelecting Nicolae Ceauşescu as President and interrupting his acceptance speech with standing ovations. Three weeks later protests that broke out in the western provinces were brutally put down by the security forces. Confident that he could prevent a replay of the events that had brought down other regimes, Ceauşescu went on a state visit to Iran, but the protests intensified. Upon his return he organized a rally to denounce the "counterrevolutionaries," but when he started to speak he was booed, and ritual chants of *"Ceauşescu si poporul!"* (Ceauşescu and the people!) changed to

"Ceauşescu dictatorul!" (Ceauşescu the dictator!). Television showed the look of shock on his face, and the Romanian revolt was on. The consequent change of regime turned out to be bloodier than the previous five, as the security units responsible for the earlier week's massacre fought back. Ceauşescu tried to escape, but he was caught and summarily executed.[46]

Yet again, the world watched a nation jump suddenly from quiescence and subservience to turbulence and defiance. As the year ended, commentators were still marveling at the speed with which the East European political landscape had changed. Long-persecuted dissidents now occupied high government positions. In Czechoslovakia, for instance, Havel was president, Dubček chairman of the Federal Assembly, and Jiří Dienstbier, a Charter 77 signatory serving time as a coal stoker, foreign minister. Nothing symbolizes the speed of the transformation better than the fact that a few hours after being named foreign minister Dienstbier had to rush back to stoke his boiler, as there had not been enough time to replace him.[47]

The Unavoidability of Amazement

It bears repeating that, in spite of massive evidence that the fall of communism was unanticipated, to many analysts it now seems as though the transformation could have been predicted.[48] Wasn't it clear that the economic failures of communism had sown the seeds of a massive revolt? Wasn't it self-evident that the East Europeans were just waiting for an opportunity to topple their despised dictators? Didn't the severe problems of the Soviet Union necessitate its withdrawal from Eastern Europe, to concentrate its resources on economic reforms?

Yet as we have seen, warning signs of the revolution remained cloudy until it was all over. Moreover, the imperfect observability of private preferences and revolutionary thresholds concealed the latent bandwagons in formation and made it difficult to appreciate the revolutionary significance of critical developments. Because of widespread preference falsification, and because the determinants of public preferences could not be identified with any semblance of certainty, no one could tell where events were headed.

My argument in Chapter 15 was not tied, of course, to the particularities of Eastern Europe. Indeed, 1989 was hardly the first time a major social uprising came as a surprise. Other unanticipated revolutions include the French Revolution of 1789, the Russian Revolution of February 1917, and the Iranian Revolution of 1978–79. In each of these cases, I shall argue briefly,[49] preference falsification was a key factor in the observed predictive failures.

The French Revolution

The French Revolution of 1789 shocked its victims, observers, and even the rioters who helped bring it about. Tocqueville reports that on the eve of the revolution Louis XVI had no idea that a violent eruption was in the making—let alone that he was about to lose his throne and his head. The king saw in the middle class, which was to form the backbone of the insurgence, his strongest base of support.[50] For their part, the *philosophes*—whose criticisms of the status quo would later be cited as the prime cause of the revolution—did not even dream of revolution. As a historian suggests, they would not "even have understood the idea."[51] True, they advocated a change in outlook and less dependence on tradition. But not until the revolution would they begin to favor fundamental institutional reforms.[52]

Yet in retrospect it is easy to find signs of the impending revolution. "Though it took the world by surprise," writes Tocqueville, "it was the inevitable outcome of a long period of gestation, the abrupt and violent conclusion of a process in which six generations played an intermittent part."[53] Indeed, prior to 1789 many groups in France had reasons to resent the status quo. The cloth merchants faced increasing competition, seasonal laborers lacked job security, soldiers felt underpaid—and the list goes on. From time to time, moreover, disenchanted groups took to the street in protest. Generally, however, they respected the rules of protest laid down by watchful authorities.[54] Riots were thus considered no more of a threat to the monarchy than screaming stadium crowds are to the Fifth Republic. What no one appreciated was that the preservation of order depended vitally on enforcement of the established rules of protest. Everyone saw that the monarchy commanded the support of public opinion and that most Frenchmen respected its rules even in letting off steam. No one saw that multitudes were prepared to rise against it if ever they felt they could do so safely, and it was even less clear that sincere monarchists would then be afraid to put up a defense.

Another sign of the coming revolution was that weakening discipline was undermining the Royal Army's ability to protect the regime. In June 1788 a riot broke out in Grenoble, and the units called to restore order were attacked by a rock-throwing mob; some units refrained from firing on the crowd. As the fateful month of July 1789 approached, there were many additional indications of the unreliability of the army and of dissatisfaction within its ranks. But not all developments in the military pointed to the regime's vulnerability. Right up to the revolution, some critical units continued performing in a disciplined manner.[55]

That the government became less repressive, suggests Tocqueville, is what sealed the monarchy's fate. Significantly, the revolution drew much of its strength from districts where "the freedom and wealth of the peasants had long been better assured" than elsewhere.[56] In the same vein, another historian observes that under the influence of the democratic ideas in the air the monarchy had "lost the will to repress."[57] These insights fit into the argument developed here. Relatively free peasants would have had relatively low thresholds for joining antigovernment protests. And democratic ideas would have lowered revolutionary thresholds throughout French society.

The Iranian Revolution

In September 1977, only sixteen months before the collapse of the Iranian monarchy, the CIA found Iran to be an island of stability within a sea of turbulence. The demonstrations that were to culminate in the shah's departure were in progress, but as the CIA saw it, these were minor disturbances that the government could easily suppress. Every other major intelligence service also expected the shah to pull through, even as the demonstrations grew by leaps and bounds. It is revealing that all the great powers supported him almost to the end.[58]

The shah and his entourage displayed no better foresight. In May 1978, eight months before the end, the Empress Farah first heard a name that she would soon find impossible to forget. "For heaven's sake," she asked, "who is this Khomeini?"[59] In June 1978, according to inside accounts, the shah continued to believe that the demonstra-

tors were fanatics who could never gain broad support.[60] His perception was shared by the leaders of Tudeh, the pro-Soviet Communist
Party, who were accustomed to viewing religion as the "opiate of the
masses."[61] Most amazing, perhaps, is that Khomeini himself doubted
that the shah could be toppled. While telling the media that the monarchy was about to collapse, to his close associates he was confiding
serious reservations. In the spring of 1978 he feared that the shah
would somehow put down the opposition.[62] It is significant that as late
as December 1978 Khomeini's lieutenants were looking for a country
that would accept him upon the expiration of his French visa in April
1979.[63] As it turned out, within weeks a tumultuous crowd welcomed
him in Tehran.

The list of scholars caught off guard by the turn of events includes,
a historian notes, "political scientists who interviewed both government and oppositional figures; economists who wrote of serious economic problems; and anthropologists, sociologists, and historians
who looked at and listened to many classes of people, urban and rural,
including clerics."[64] The list even includes scholars who sided with the
religious opposition. Hamid Algar, a professor of Islamic studies at
Berkeley, had long understood that the Shi'i clergy posed a threat to
the shah's rule. Yet as the uprising that would topple the shah got
under way, he failed to foresee what was to come.[65]

There is much evidence that the looming revolution was obscured
by extensive preference falsification. Four years before the revolution,
when the shah formed a political party, prominent Iranians rushed to
join it, though in many cases grudgingly. Some high-level bureaucrats
were critical of the sumptuous celebrations of the 2500th anniversary
of the Persian monarchy, but they expressed their opinions only to
family and close friends.[66] And until the eve of the revolution, numerous clerics who were to achieve prominence under the Islamic regime were restrained in their public criticisms of the shah. Some even
served in his administration.[67] Such examples illustrate why the sim-
mering trouble was hardly noticed.

As in France two centuries earlier, the uprising appears to have been
instigated by a lightening of official repression. In the years preceding
the revolution President Jimmy Carter was promoting human rights
as a central objective of U.S. foreign policy. To prevent the appearance
of caving in to pressure, the shah took some measures on his own

initiative: more freedom for the press and open military trials.[68] Regardless of the intrinsic merits of these measures, they probably benefited the opposition. If a government is widely despised, greater opportunities for public criticism will help make this known, thereby encouraging more people to side openly with the opposition. Also significant no doubt was the shah's vacillation with regard to the use of force against the growing crowds. Inasmuch as vacillation is seen as a sign of weakness, it reduces the perceived risk of joining the opposition.

The Russian Revolution of February 1917 and Unsuccessful Uprisings against Communism

The very revolution that prepared the ground for the first communist regime in history was a scarcely foreseen event.[69] Weeks before the revolution of February 1917, Lenin told an audience in Switzerland that older men like himself would not live to see Russia's great explosion.[70] It is revealing that until he came to power Lenin gave little thought to the characteristics of an actual socialist economy. The Bolsheviks and Mensheviks stationed in St. Petersburg were also unprepared for the fall of the tzar,[71] as were foreign diplomats. Just three days before the tzar was overthrown the British ambassador cabled London: "Some disorders occurred to-day, but nothing serious."[72] Nor did the tzar and his family realize what was happening.[73] Two days before the end the tzarina Alexandra had this to say about the general strike in the capital: "This is a hooligan movement. Young people run and shout that there is no bread, simply to create excitement, along with workers who prevent others from working. If the weather were very cold they would all probably stay home. But all this will pass and become calm, if only the Duma [the parliament] will behave itself."[74]

There were, of course, the precedents of the French Revolution and of Russia's own revolution in 1905. And it was widely known that many Russians harbored grievances against the regime. The peasants were hungry for land, and the urban working class felt exploited. But the potential revolutionaries were divided.[75] Equally important, the capital featured a huge garrison to help the police quell disturbances. True, the soldiers were disgruntled, but when had they been content?

And even if most Russians would welcome a change in regime, who among them would take the lead in revolting? In 1848 Bismarck had managed to avert a German revolution by retaining the support of the army. Why, people asked, shouldn't the same strategy work for the tzar?[76]

As it happened, the uprising was ignited by a strategic error on the part of the tzar that was rendered fatal by a series of coincidences. The St. Petersburg regiments normally responsible for protecting the regime were at the front in early 1917, and most of their replacements were new recruits attuned to the civilian mood. The new regiments fell apart upon contact with the crowds.[77] But what brought the crowds into the street in the first place? On February 23, the day the uprising began, many residents of St. Petersburg were standing in food queues, because of rumored shortages. Some twenty thousand workers were in the streets after being locked out of a large industrial complex over a wage dispute. Hundreds of off-duty soldiers were outdoors, looking for distraction. And as the day went on, multitudes of workers left their factories early to march in celebration of Women's Day.[78] The combined crowd quickly turned into a self-reinforcing mob. It toppled the Romanov dynasty in four days, and before the year was over communists had gained full control of the government. Preference falsification contributed to the speed of the associated shifts in public opinion. As we shall see shortly, the leaders of the new communist regime understood this very well.

Marxist scholarship did not anticipate that the world's first communist takeover would occur in, of all places, economically backward Russia. Nor did Marxist scholarship—or, for that matter, non-Marxist scholarship—foresee the mid-century uprisings in communist Eastern Europe. "The Hungarian uprising of October 1956 was a dramatic, sudden explosion, apparently not organized beforehand by a revolutionary center; neither outsiders nor the participants had anticipated anything like the irresistible revolutionary dynamism that would sweep the country." Thus begins a monograph on Hungary's failed attempt to overthrow communism.[79] Entitled *The Unexpected Revolution*, it is replete with evidence of widespread preference falsification right up to the uprising. Many leading players in the mobilization remained docile and submissive until the uprising, often hiding their grievances even from family members.[80]

The Prague Spring of 1968 offers another example of an unforeseen challenge to communism. In 1967, recalls Havel, the entire Czechoslovak nation was behaving like the Good Soldier Švejk, accommodating itself to the regime's demands. "Who would have believed . . . that a year later this recently apathetic, skeptical, and demoralized society would stand up with such courage and intelligence to a foreign power!" "And," he continues, "who would have suspected that, after scarcely a year had gone by, this same society would, as swiftly as the wind blows, lapse back into a state of deep demoralization far worse than its original one!"[81]

Triumphs of Truth?

The unsuccessful anticommunist uprisings of Eastern Europe resulted in the defeat of candor. In each case, millions had to resume living a lie. But were the successful uprisings triumphs of truth? Timothy Garton Ash, an eyewitness to the mobilizations in Poland, Hungary, East Germany, and Czechoslovakia, characterizes 1989 as Eastern Europe's "year of truth."[82] Ash's designation is accurate insofar as it captures the end of feigned support for communism. But it obscures the push the revolution got from preference falsification on the part of people content with the status quo. As noncommunists threw off their masks in joy and relief, many genuine communists slipped on masks of their own—masks depicting them as former preference falsifiers thrilled to be speaking their minds after years of silent resentment. In Czechoslovakia, for instance, just one month after the Communist Party ceded its monopoly of power, the same legislature that had given the communist regime its unanimous support voted unanimously to make Havel president.[83]

It is true, of course, that the flowering of anticommunist public discourse exposed the official ideology more clearly than before as a web of sophistries, distortions, and myths. It awakened millions of dormant minds, confronting citizens with the conflicts between the pragmatic and theoretical layers of their beliefs. This is to say neither that the thoughts of every East European suddenly became internally consistent nor that Marxist thinking abruptly ceased. It is to suggest that the transformation of public discourse accompanying the political overturn opened many minds to previously unthought possibilities.

"Everything," remarked a Hungarian a year after the revolution, "has become so strange. A year ago, the Communists ran the country. Today, you can't find a Communist anywhere."[84] Indeed, East European preference falsification had turned into a shield for people afraid to admit their yearnings for the status quo ante. Some systematic evidence comes from the first postrevolutionary elections in Hungary and Czechoslovakia. In each country, the party of the former communists did substantially better than predicted by preelection polls based on face-to-face interviews.[85]

In the mid-1990s it is too early to tell whether preference falsification in reverse will generate a sustained hunt for hypocrites, though there have been efforts to examine the communist archives for names of informers and collaborators.[86] Massive campaigns of repression and indoctrination did follow various other revolutions. Invariably, the targets included the revolutionaries themselves. The revolutionary regime in France was obsessed with tearing the mask of mendacity off the faces of all Frenchmen. Thousands were charged with privately wishing to restore old privileges. Many of the accused, including such leaders as Danton and Robespierre, were sent to the guillotine as traitors. Ironically, the postrevolutionary war on hypocrisy provided its own justification. Precisely because of it, millions of French citizens with much to gain from a counterrevolution chose to appear as ardent supporters of revolutionary objectives.[87] Under Stalin, the Bolshevik regime engineered one of the worst calamities of the twentieth century, wiping out more than ten million people, often under the pretext of punishing duplicity. Almost all of Lenin's closest comrades were executed as counterrevolutionaries in disguise.[88] Finally, the victims of Iran's Islamic regime have included thousands who, before victory seemed assured, risked their lives by participating in antishah demonstrations. And immense efforts have been made to control how people think and act.[89]

How to explain such campaigns? And how, specifically, to explain that revolutionaries figure prominently among their targets? Some of the most popular theories of revolution are unequipped to answer these questions. Both the Marxian theory and the theory of relative deprivation suggest that individuals rise against an established order when they become convinced that a new one would serve them better. By implication, a revolutionary regime might gain security from terrorizing and indoctrinating its active opponents. It would have no reason, however, to target its own supporters.

The theory of revolution based on the dual preference model suggests the following explanation for the commonness of postrevolutionary repression. Revolutionary leaders recognize the ubiquity of preference falsification. They thus suspect that their supporters include many would-be turncoats—people who would quickly turn against the regime were the political climate to change. Reconsider the threshold sequence

A^1:

Individuals	a	b	c	d	e	f	g	h	i	j
Thresholds	0	10	20	30	40	50	60	70	80	100

As we saw earlier, A^1 drives the size of the public opposition to 90. The last person to jump on the revolutionary bandwagon is person *i*. Privately *i* greatly prefers the old regime to the new, so she would rejoin the antirevolutionary camp if the pressures against doing so were to abate. In so doing, she could easily trigger a *counterrevolutionary bandwagon*.

For a demonstration, suppose that the revolutionary regime eases its pressure on the citizenry, because, say, divisions within the new leadership render it indecisive. The threshold sequence becomes

A^2:

Individuals	a	b	c	d	e	f	g	h	i	j
Thresholds	0	21	31	41	51	61	71	81	91	100

Under A^2 a prorevolutionary public opinion of 90 becomes unsustainable, and the size of the revolutionary camp falls all the way back to 10. The shift from A^1 to A^2 thus transforms overwhelming support *for* the revolution into crushing support *against* it.

This illustration demonstrates why revolutionary regimes, including ones committed to human liberties, often turn repressive. Their leaders sense that if they grant their constituents broad expressive freedoms, the revolution may lose sufficient public support to spark a counterrevolution. To alleviate the danger, they begin repressing the very people who brought them to power.

The leaders of the Iranian Revolution had well-founded reasons to fear that many of those who helped make the revolution would disapprove of forced Islamization. The demonstrations that brought down the shah united clerics and Westernized intellectuals, national-ists and pro-Soviet communists, wealthy industrialists and bazaar merchants, women veiled and unveiled.[90] Those who marched in the streets shouting "Death to the shah" and "Allah is great" included people who had prospered under the shah and had everything to lose from a theocratic order. Even the mullahs were divided on the scope and means of Islamization.[91] All these factors pointed to the possibility of some counterrevolution.

This is not to say that in the aftermath of a revolution the counterrevolutionary potential will be assessed accurately. Postrevolutionary preference falsification may exaggerate the people's commitment to the revolution. Nevertheless, until the former regime's one-time popularity and the suddenness of its collapse recede from memory, many, including leaders of the revolutionary regime, will consider a counterrevolution within the realm of possibility.[92]

Soon after the Iranian Revolution, the leftist Mojahedin Party set out to destroy the nascent theocracy.[93] The fears that drove the Islamic regime's repression and indoctrination campaigns were not, therefore, entirely imagined.

Crowds and Leaders

"In default of a Napoleon, another would have filled his place." So claimed Friedrich Engels in one of his most famous sentences.[94] He meant that when historical trends bring a society to the brink of a major transformation, the leadership required to accomplish the change will always be forthcoming. This view, shared by Marx, is difficult to accept. For one thing, the emergence of a great leader depends on many complex factors—biological, psychological, and social. Because no one knows precisely how these factors come together, we cannot be sure that when society becomes ripe for change a revolutionary leader will always be available. For another, there is no guarantee that when a great leader does arrive on the scene the proponents of change will be the beneficiary. The leader might choose to join the political establishment.

Given that Marx and Engels saw political revolutions as the work of grand historical forces, one might expect communist revolutionaries to have deemphasized the role of leadership. Yet the successful ones have accorded it a vital role. Rejecting the doctrine of historical inevitability, Lenin maintained that successful revolutionary mobilization depends on sound political strategy and on inculcating workers with a revolutionary consciousness.[95]

To recognize the importance of leadership is not to endorse the "great man" theory of history, which ascribes a huge influence to exceptional individuals. Generations of revolutionary leaders might come and go before fundamental change becomes possible. This suggestion is in line with Tocqueville's views on the role of leadership in the French Revolution. He observes that the ideas that turned the middle classes against the king came to them largely from above— from the *philosophes,* the aristocrats, and surprisingly in retrospect, the king and his ministers. He maintains, moreover, that revolutionary leaders are likely to preach to deaf ears until people are ready to accept change.[96]

What, precisely, do revolutionary leaders do? First of all, they expose the incumbent regime's vulnerability. Publicizing hidden discontent in an effort to raise the perceived probability of a revolutionary uprising, they foster the belief that a vast majority privately wants change. A leader can never know, of course, the exact distribution of private preferences. His task is akin to that of an entrepreneur who, sensing that his new product has market potential, sets out to maximize his sales. Just as the entrepreneur discovers the actual demand for his product as the market unfolds, the revolutionary leader improves his knowledge of private opinion in the course of his political struggle.

Remember that society can come close to a revolution without this being recognized. Ordinary citizens will know their own private preferences and possibly those of their relatives and close friends. But such limited information does not provide a reliable base for estimating the wider distribution. Revolutionary leaders are unusually skilled at acquiring and interpreting the relevant information. We lack a complete explanation as to why the pertinent skills are distributed unevenly across individuals, but that is no reason to deny that differences exist. After all, we do not quite know how to account for variations in mechanical ability, yet we do not pretend that it is distributed uniformly.

In the years preceding the Iranian Revolution the Ayatollah Khomeini and other opposition leaders played a crucial role in creating the impression that the shah's genuine support was thin. In Eastern Europe an analogous role was played by dissidents who kept alive the possibility of a sharp turn in public opinion. They promoted the view that communist power rested on widespread preference falsification. Through calculated acts of defiance, moreover, they showed that the people were not of one voice even in public. When, after many decades, circumstances became ripe for an overturn, the dissidents formed the base on which the anticommunist opposition rose.

Another role of revolutionary leaders is to mold private preferences. To this end, they find wrongs in the existing order and drum into people's consciousness the advantages of an alternative. Insofar as they are successful, the effect is a fall in revolutionary thresholds. Khomeini did a brilliant job of convincing a wide spectrum of Iranians that they would do better under Islamic rule. He managed to be all things to all people: to the devout, an idol smasher; to the downtrodden, a deliverer of dignity; to the poor, an egalitarian redistributionist; and to the Marxist, a democrat who would allow them to prepare for their own revolution.

Finally, leaders enhance the advantages of joining the public opposition. Through means ranging from social events to prayer meetings to physical intimidation, they try to lighten the reputational costs of dissent. Every revolutionary movement also serves as a support network for the regime's declared opponents. The support is often coupled with a threat to members of the government camp: if the movement succeeds, you may be punished. As the Iranian Revolution gained momentum Khomeini made it clear that he would seek to punish those who stood in the revolution's way. His warning helped convince workers to go on strike as the antishah opposition swelled.

Some revolutionary leaders expect to obtain handsome rewards in the event their movement succeeds. But one must not exaggerate the role of such motives as fame, political power, and pecuniary gain. After all, many successful revolutionaries have not expected to succeed. And in many cases, they could have done quite well if, at the start of their careers, when chances of a revolution must have seemed remote, they had chosen to collaborate with the prevailing regime. Very often revolutionary leaders are substantially motivated by the need to speak out against some perceived injustice or inefficiency.

Two years before the founding of Charter 77, Václav Havel sent his government an open letter that pointed to crises hidden behind Czechoslovakia's apparent tranquility. A decade later, when asked why he took such a risk, he replied:

> The letter, on the primary level, was a kind of autotherapy: I had no idea what would happen next, but it was worth the risk. I regained my balance and my self-confidence. I felt I could stand up straight again, and that no one could accuse me any longer of not doing anything, of just looking on in silence at the miserable state of affairs. I could breathe more easily because I had not tried to stifle the truth inside me. I had stopped waiting for the world to improve and exercised my right to intervene in that world, or at least to express my opinion about it.[97]

In addition to a strong need for self-respect, Havel also had, of course, a phenomenal ability to distinguish between public and private opinion. Many great political leaders have united these two qualities.

Revolutionary leaders seldom operate alone. Ordinarily, they are the most outspoken and resourceful members of an organized public opposition. Organizations vary, however, in terms of their tightness and effectiveness. In making sense of why a society does or does not experience a revolt, it helps to consider, therefore, the factors governing its patterns of political organization.[98] Yet we must guard against overemphasizing the role of organization at the expense of the role of the unorganized crowd. A small difference in the resources at an organized opposition's disposal may make all the difference in the outcome of its efforts.[99] Where a small pressure group fails to activate a bandwagon, one slightly better organized, or slightly larger, might.

A notable aspect of the East European Revolution is that in some of the six countries the uprisings featured no leaders of great prominence. For Poland, one thinks of Lech Wałęsa, and for Czechoslovakia, Havel. No one of such stature comes to mind for Hungary, East Germany, Bulgaria, or Romania. The dissident organizations in the latter four countries did not direct the mobilizations in their countries the way Khomeini masterminded the revolt against the shah. Many of the demonstrations that toppled communism were initiated by loosely organized, even unorganized, groups composed largely of citizens with no previous history of activism. The early demonstrators were people simply fed up with communist mismanagement; sensing that the risk of demonstrating had fallen a bit, or angry as never before, they needed to make a public statement. Nevertheless, dissident activists did play an important role in ending communist rule. By exposing the flaws, hypocrisy, and vulnerability of communism through years of agitation, they laid the groundwork for the uprisings of 1989. Specifically, they helped put in place latent bandwagons that a combination of fortuitous circumstances would eventually push into motion.

The Predictability of Unpredictability

A complex array of trends, events, and decisions thus determines a regime's fate. Some of the relevant factors, like private opinion and revolutionary thresholds, are only imperfectly observable. Herein lies a fundamental obstacle to predicting political revolutions.

Because the imperfect observability of private variables is a universal feature, we can expect to be surprised again and again. In the future, as in the past, seemingly tranquil societies will burst aflame with little warning, toppling regimes considered invincible.

The general argument applies to a much broader set of contexts than revolutions that topple national governments. A specific law, regulation, policy, norm, or custom can be abruptly abandoned when people who have helped sustain it suddenly discover a common desire for change. So it is that long-protectionist nations suddenly embrace trade liberalization; fashions appear and disappear inexplicably; and in a matter of years deep-seated prejudices become dangerous to vent. The same phenomenon of abrupt and unforeseen change is also observed in collectivities narrower than entire nations. Academic departments, corporate managements, and social organizations sometimes change direction at astonishing speed, following long periods of continuity that lulled everyone into considering them frozen. The explanation for the sudden shift will often be found in a bandwagon process that alters the character of preference falsification.

The imperfectly observable factors that make it difficult to forecast revolutions impart unpredictability also to the broader process of social evolution. Moreover, these factors interact with other poorly observable factors to compound the difficulties of controlling and explaining social trends. The next chapter will develop these points. It will also revisit an issue introduced in Chapter 6: preference falsification as a source of social inefficiency.

17

The Hidden Complexities of Social Evolution

One of the most enduring splits in scholarly thought concerns the orderliness of what we call the "social order." On one side are traditions that treat social relationships as simple, continuous, harmonious, predictable, controllable, and efficient. On the other are traditions that recognize and seek to explain complexity, discontinuity, disharmony, unpredictability, uncontrollability, and inefficiency. The theory of general economic equilibrium, which draws inspiration from Newtonian physics, epitomizes the former class. Examples of the latter include evolutionary economics[1] and the emerging discipline of complexity.[2]

The arguments developed in this book are in tune with the latter set of traditions. Unforeseen breaks in public opinion are consistent with the idea, common to many evolutionary theories, including some theories of biological evolution,[3] that invisible phenomena may have enormous consequences. The book's other evolutionary themes include the persistent inefficiencies caused by collective conservatism and the tensions fueled by incongruities between public and private opinion.

The purpose of this chapter is to extend and knit together the evolutionary themes of past chapters with an eye to generating further lessons for historical interpretation and social forecasting. I first introduce several complications into the basic framework, highlighting factors that make private preferences somewhat autonomous from public discourse, and actual public policies somewhat autonomous from public opinion. As in earlier contexts, it turns out that changes in one variable may have disproportionate effects on other variables. Turning attention to the circularities of the model, I explore the inefficiencies they produce and the added difficulties they pose for prediction and control. Among my key points is that discontinuities, unintended outcomes, and inefficiencies flow from a coherent social process. The whole chapter demonstrates, from a broader perspective than earlier chapters, that one can understand the complexities of social evolution without being able to pinpoint the causes of particular historical outcomes.

Small Events and the Evolution of Private Preferences

A political scientist observes that in the voting booth a voter "goes through the straightforward mental calculations of deciding whether the country is in an economic recession or war, and if it is not, votes for the incumbent."[4] In this view, a voter first asks himself how he is doing relative to some standard, and then, depending on what he finds, decides whether to support change or stability. Such a characterization of the voter's choice mechanism may seem to contradict the emphasis I have given to the role of public discourse in molding individual private preferences. Actually, there is no conflict, for individual perceptions are not autonomous. In the months leading up to the U.S. presidential election of 1992 voters were bombarded with reports of a deepening recession, whereas in reality the recession was over and signs of a recovery were multiplying.[5] That the election took place in an atmosphere of gloom and doom was doubtless a factor in the defeat of the incumbent president, George Bush.

Not that private preferences are independent of personal experiences. All else equal, an unemployed voter was less likely to vote for Bush than was someone holding a secure job. Significantly, Bush suffered one of his sharpest losses relative to 1988 in California, which on election day had the second highest unemployment rate in the country.[6] Yet the relationship between personal experience and political orientation is never simple. If an aerospace technician is unemployed, to what extent is her situation an inevitable result of an event she had welcomed, the end of the Cold War? And if the responsibility belongs partly to the government, is the main culprit the Republican president or the Democratic-controlled Congress? Such questions have no easy answers. In trying to determine her own stake in the election, our technician will look for clues in political commentaries and opinion polls.

The outcome of her search will depend partly on fortuitous circumstances unrelated to the presidential choice. If the only talk show that she finds time to watch is one in which the speakers are uniformly hostile to Bush, she is more likely to blame him than if she catches a generally sympathetic show. Imagine that she ends up voting Democratic. If we know everything about her, including the reasons why she watched one show rather than another, we could have anticipated her vote. In practice, of course, we never have access to such details. We can observe major happenings like her job loss but not the small events that shape her perceptions. To an observer, therefore, her vote is neither fully explicable nor practically predictable. It is, or will be, determined partly by visible forces—the hardships of unemployment, the anti-Bush tone of public discourse—and partly by invisible forces. Just as biologists cannot explain every genetic mutation or predict precisely how a gene pool will evolve, social observers can never unlock all the mysteries of the evolution of private preferences.

The Impact of Shifts in Private Preferences on the Evolution of Public Opinion

Small events, in altering private preferences, may also affect public preferences. Moreover, the consequent shifts in public opinion may turn out to be disproportionately large or small. This is not a new point. We have already seen how minor changes in a regime's private support might trigger a revolutionary shift in public opinion. But more can be learned from additional scenarios.[7]

Consider, then, a ten-person society where an inverse relationship exists between private preferences and the corresponding individual thresholds. Specifically, every individual's threshold equals 100 minus the value of his private preference. Such a relationship might reflect, of course, the utility of expressive honesty. A person with a high private preference will start supporting the option 100 over the option 0 at a lower public opinion than would an otherwise identical person with a low private preference.

Given this setup, a descending sequence of private preferences implies an ascending sequence of thresholds. Here is an example:

	Private preferences	80	70	70	60	50	45	40	40	25	20
E:	Individuals	a	b	c	d	e	f	g	h	i	j
	Thresholds	20	30	30	40	50	55	60	60	75	80

Initially, let us say, the expected public opinion is 50. Given this expectation, persons a through e support the option 100, because their thresholds are at or below 50; and f through j support the option 0. The prevailing expectation is thus self-confirming. It is, as we say, an equilibrium.

Sometime later, person e becomes slightly more sympathetic to option 0. Specifically, his private preference falls to 45, raising his threshold to 55. Under this new configuration, E, with its top row omitted, becomes

	Individuals	a	b	c	d	e	f	g	h	i	j
E^1:	Thresholds	20	30	30	40	55	55	60	60	75	80

The expected public opinion of 50 is no longer self-confirming. It generates an actual public opinion of 40, which constitutes a new equilibrium. At the new equilibrium persons a through d support 100, and the remaining six support 0.

Returning to E, consider a different small change in a single individual's private preference: a rise in f's private preference from 45 to 50. The change lowers f's threshold to 50, and the adjusted threshold sequence becomes

	Individuals	a	b	c	d	e	f	g	h	i	j
E^2:	Thresholds	20	30	30	40	50	50	60	60	75	80

As with the preceding scenario, the prevailing expectation of 50 becomes self-falsifying. But here the consequence is a huge rise in public opinion to 100.

What needs recognition is that public opinion may be enormously sensitive to movements in individual private preferences. Where a tiny decline in one private preference would lower it, a tiny rise in another might raise it substantially. Yet such possibilities arise only under very special conditions. Under a wide variety of circumstances, even enormous changes in private preferences will leave public opinion undisturbed. Go back to E, and suppose that the private preferences of nine individuals rise by various amounts. The threshold sequence becomes

E^3:	Individuals	a	b	c	d	e	f	g	h	i	j
	Thresholds	0	0	0	0	0	55	55	55	55	55

Though cumulatively huge, the private changes will not trigger public switches, and public opinion will remain at 50.

These illustrations establish that, depending on particularities of the threshold sequence, a given shift in private opinion may affect public opinion slightly, affect it greatly, or leave it unaffected. The rich variety of possibilities is linked, of course, to preference falsification. On issues where people do not hide their sentiments, all shifts in private opinion, however large or small, get reflected in public opinion. On sensitive issues, however, private and public opinion may well grow apart.

The evolution of public opinion may or may not be sensitive to the timing of the changes in individual private preferences. In the last scenario, it does not matter whether the changes that turn E into E^3 come simultaneously or sequentially. And if sequential, the precise sequencing of the changes is immaterial. Neither observation applies, however, to the changes considered previously: the rise in e's threshold and the fall in that of f. If these two shifts were to come simultaneously, the thresholds of e and f would get transposed,[8] leaving public opinion unchanged. If instead they were to come sequentially, there would be two possible outcomes. If the first change were a rise in e's threshold, public opinion would settle at 40, and the subsequent fall in f's threshold would leave public opinion undisturbed. But if the changes were to come in reverse order, public opinion would dart to 100, and then remain there. In each case, the self-amplifying reactions to the first change would render the second inconsequential. We see that the timing of private changes can be critical to the course of public opinion.[9]

Nothing I have just said negates the significance of public discourse as a shaper of private beliefs and preferences. Recognizing that private preferences are not *completely* dependent on public discourse, I have shown that under some conditions a streak of independent thought or some personal experience may trigger important changes.

The Autonomy of Public Policy

If our private preferences exhibit some independence from public discourse, one reason is that we learn from our experiences. Another is that our preconceptions distort what we recognize and remember. Still another is that the correspondence between public discourse and political outcomes is imperfect.

Up to this point, I have abstracted from the last source of independence by treating political outcomes—implemented policies and adopted institutions—as perfect reflections of public opinion. I have presumed, in effect, that if public opinion moves from 50 to 40, the relevant political choices will follow suit. Missing from this simple formulation is the hurly-burly of politics—the disorder generated, on the one hand, by procedural factors like legislative loopholes and the quirks of election laws, and on the other, personal factors like the ambitions of individual politicians and executive irresponsibility. In reality, political procedures and flesh-and-blood politicians complicate the relationship between public opinion and political outcomes.[10]

An example of a procedural constraint is given by rules that inhibit small departures from the status quo.[11] The U.S. Congress might consider a proposal to extend the presidential term from four years to six, but not one that calls for a half-year extension. In terms of our spatial metaphor, it is as though Congress could not consider policy proposals within 15 units of the status quo. Under such a rule, if public opinion and the implemented policy were both 50, and public opinion were then to fall to 40, Congress could not entertain a motion to lower the policy to 40. It could, of course, consider and adopt a bigger change, like a reduction to 35.

Another possible source of divergence between a legislature's policy choices and public opinion is the fact that to stay in office politicians pay special attention to public opinion in their own districts. If members of Congress vote in accordance with the predominant public preference in their own districts, their collective decisions will not necessarily reflect national public opinion. For an illustration, suppose that 40 percent of society supports 100 and the remaining 60 percent supports 0. At the national level, therefore, mean public opinion is 40. There are two districts of equal size and equal legislative representation, in each of which public opinion mirrors that of the wider population. If the representatives honor the expressed wishes of the majorities in their districts, they will both support 0. And they will thus produce a legislative opinion of 0, causing their policy choice to differ from national public opinion by 40 units.

As public opinion evolves, then, the political system may either dampen or amplify its demands. What are the consequences for the evolution of private knowledge and preferences? If private changes were driven solely by public discourse, procedural limits on the political system's responsiveness to public opinion would have no lasting consequences. In practice, however, individuals also learn from actual political decisions, so procedural limits may put the evolution of private variables onto new paths. Like any influence on private variables, a policy shift that is autonomous from public discourse will normally play no major evolutionary role. Yet for reasons that need no repetition, the shift's impact could be huge.

Creative and Self-Serving Interpretations

I turn now to personal factors that make actual political choices differ from public opinion.

We entrust the implementation of our expressed wishes to legislators, bureaucrats, judges, and other officials. Such functionaries are generally expected to abide by the orders they receive, even ones in conflict with their own private or public preferences. In practice, however, they commonly pursue policies that deviate from their mandates.

One source of deviation is that officials receive directives through symbols subject to interpretation—votes, words, statistics, images. Their directives thus leave room for discretion. The problem is compounded when the relevant functionaries form a hierarchy, with those at the bottom receiving their orders through chains of intermediaries. With members of a chain inadvertently distorting their directives, orders communicated to the last member can differ from those heard by the first. Experiments suggest that the cumulative transformation can be substantial. In a classic experiment, the drawing of an owl, when replicated successively by eighteen individuals, turned into a picture of a cat.[12]

Some verbal instructions are intended to remain in force indefinitely, as when a school superintendent's directive on how to handle cheating is meant to guide teachers until further notice. Such a directive is committed to memory, to be retrieved whenever needed. But memory is not perfectly reduplicative. At each recall its substance is condensed, elaborated, and distorted.[13]

Certain distortions can be checked by putting instructions into writing. But written communication does not prevent all distortions, for it is first committed to memory, if only for a few seconds, before it is retrieved for application. In any case, there is another source of distortion that is independent of the form of communication. However detailed, a blueprint for action cannot cover all possible contingencies, because imagining the future consumes valuable time. Nor can a blueprint articulate the rationale behind each of its specifications, for communication is costly. Inevitably, therefore, functionaries face situations requiring them to infer intentions from incomplete and only partially justified specifications. Must rule A be enforced in circumstances already covered by B? What constitutes an "emergency," and when one arises how much may one restrict freedoms C and D? Faced with such questions, functionaries may find a blueprint riddled with gaps and ambiguities.[14] In trying to follow the blueprint they may, therefore, have to engage in *creative interpretation*. Their choices will be constrained, of course, by public discourse, context, and precedents. Ordinarily, however, such factors will leave them many options.

Another form of deviation is a conscious abuse of authority, which may be called a *self-serving interpretation*. Unlike creative interpretations, which are generated by the cognitive limitations of society's functionaries, self-serving interpretations are made possible by the limitations of the people they are mandated to serve. No society can devise a separate word to describe every object, nuance, phenomenon, or condition. The resulting linguistic imprecisions enable functionaries to pretend that they abided by their instructions, when they know they should have acted differently.[15]

When functionaries have abused their authority, this will not necessarily be obvious. This is partly because the observers of their actions are bound to overlook some relevant relationships. Suppose that a corrupt customs officer waives an import duty required by the law. In and of itself, the transgression lowers tariff revenue. It so happens that an economic boom raises imports, increasing tariff revenue sufficiently to offset the fall caused by the illegal exemption. Observers who overlook the connection between tariff revenue and aggregate growth will have no reason to suspect any wrongdoing.

In principle, self-serving interpretations are preventable through monitoring. But monitors are themselves functionaries, and the problem of monitoring the monitors is ultimately insoluble. Ordinary individuals may help monitor the functionaries with whom they come in contact, as when citizens report graft to the police. Such voluntary monitoring tends, however, to be unreliable. Because public opinion need not coincide with any particular individual's private preference, someone who observes a betrayal of public opinion may have a personal incentive to keep quiet. And even if he finds the betrayal offensive, he may want to avoid the personal cost of making a report.

In violating their mandates, functionaries alter the policy experiments to which their constituents get exposed. Functionaries thus influence how private preferences evolve, possibly with cascading consequences for public variables. This point qualifies the notion that political power flows from public opinion. Yet, although policy deviations on the part of functionaries are common, few have profound and enduring consequences. Many deviations cancel one another, as when some teachers apply a disciplinary code too strictly and others too permissively, to yield the right implementation on average. And in any case, even large deviations may leave public opinion unaffected.

Hidden Circularities

When a change in one variable within a system influences another, the effect may occur through a linear chain of adjustments, as when a change in *a* transforms *b*, the change in *b* transforms *c*, and the change in *c* transforms *d*. Alternatively, the effect may involve a circular chain, as when *a* transforms *b*, *b* transforms *c*, *c* transforms *a*, and so on indefinitely. This book has focused on several relationships of the latter type. I have just proposed, for example, that a self-serving interpretation of public opinion may alter private knowledge and, hence, private opinion; that the modifications in private opinion may reshape public opinion; and that the new public opinion may restart the whole process by pressuring the political system to make further policy changes. A basic difference between linear and circular relationships is that in the latter small shocks may be self-amplifying.[16]

The principal circularities discussed in this book appear in Figure 17.1. The left side of the figure represents the realm of understandings, perceptions, judgments, and feelings. The broken boxes around its two main variables, private knowledge and private opinion, indicate that they are essentially unobservable. The right side of the figure represents the realm of politics. Its variables are in solid boxes, for they are relatively observable. The numbered arrows capture the major circularities. *I* represents the influence of private opinion on politics; *IIa* the reciprocal influence of public opinion and public discourse on the underlying private knowledge; and finally, *IIb* and *IIc* the feedback from the consequences of actual political choices to private knowledge. All the numbered arrows are broken, to indicate that they represent relationships that are only imperfectly observable.

The figure bears upon a long-standing controversy concerning the evolutionary role of ideas. The fount of social change, say many intellectual historians and cultural anthropologists, generally lies in the realm of ideas. By this logic, historical explanation ordinarily must begin with an account of what people were thinking. Other scholars, including many Marxists, treat economic structure as "base" and ideas as "superstructure." Social change flows, in their view, from the institutions that make up the economic structure. Sound historical explanation requires, first and foremost, attention to the evolution of economic institutions. The former position gives absolute priority to people's inner worlds (left side of the figure); the latter gives priority to people's outer worlds (right side). One maintains, for example, that the capitalist spirit creates capitalism; the other claims that capitalism creates the capitalist spirit.

Each of these views exhibits what has been called the "fallacy of absolute priority."[17] This is the notion that any causal series must have an absolute first term. It implies, for instance, that the relationship between chicken and egg must start with either one or the other. Yet by allowing for circularity, and thus treating each entity as both a source and a product, we gain a better understanding of the relationship. Similarly, we achieve a more realistic appreciation of the social order once we see that there is no permanent base and no permanent superstructure. Institutions are both causing and caused, and the same goes for ideas.

To identify a circular process is not to deny the usefulness of studying its components. One learns much from examining how the flaws of communism generated mass disillusionment, and also from studying how intellectual currents shaped East European perceptions. But such focused analyses should be treated as complementary components of a single evolutionary investigation, not as rival explanations.

At any given time, of course, one component of a circular relationship may override all others. In terms of Figure 17.1, in late 1989 the dominant force in East European politics was effect *I*, which took the form of a mushrooming of public dissent. Also operative was effect *IIa,* in that the associated transformation of public discourse made millions reconsider their convictions about socialism. But cognitive

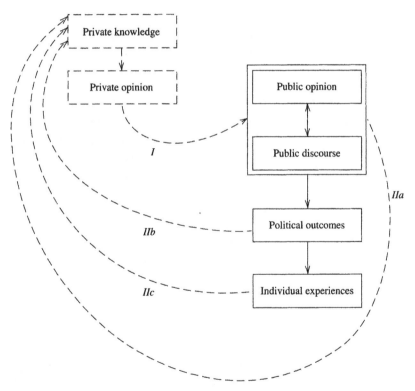

Figure 17.1 The hidden circularities of social evolution. The variables on the left are not directly observable; those on the right are.

adjustments can be slow, so they were still in progress when communism already lay in ruins.

Discontinuous Change

The observation that the components of our circular relationship may, at any given time, operate at different speeds brings us to yet another prominent evolutionary theme: discontinuous change. As the communist regime of Czechoslovakia teetered on the brink of collapse, Václav Havel remarked: "History has begun to develop very quickly in this country. In a country that has had 20 years of timelessness, now we have this fantastic speed."[18] In the exuberance of the moment, Havel probably did not realize that he had entered a long-standing controversy over the possibility of evolutionary breaks. Enshrined on the title page of Alfred Marshall's influential *Principles of Economics* is the motto *natura non facit saltum*—nature does not make leaps.[19] Popularized earlier by Leibniz, this motto proposes that evolution always proceeds through small, continuous changes.

"Evolution" is often used in the sense of gradual change. This meaning of the term drew support from Charles Darwin's theory of biological evolution, commonly interpreted as saying that species emerge and disappear through the slow and steady effects of biological competition.[20] Yet Darwin's theory also fostered another meaning: change governed by mutation and selection. The second meaning is not necessarily consistent with the first.[21] Some biological theories show that mutations and natural selection produce continuous *and* discontinuous changes. These theories posit successions of "punctuated" ecological equilibria—stable states that give way, over short time periods, to new stable states.[22] They thus make sense of the gaps many paleontologists find in fossil records.[23] And they explain why mass extinctions appear to have been much more frequent and more rapid than scientists had once imagined.[24]

Like modern biology, some contemporary social theories treat continuous and discontinuous changes as part of a single, unified process. In Joel Mokyr's theory of technological evolution numerous small innovations set the stage for technological breakthroughs.[25] And in the theory of technological competition developed by Brian Arthur and Paul David, a technology may spread gradually or rapidly, depending on various interactions. Technological choices may remain fixed for long periods punctuated by episodes of vast adaptation.[26]

In the social theory of this book, too, continuous and discontinuous changes coexist. In fact, they are causally related. Small events spread over a long period—new personal experiences, communication failures, policy distortions—may suddenly destabilize the political status quo, generating revolutionary transformations in public opinion, public discourse, and the social order. Political discontinuities are thus consistent with the continuous evolution of individual characteristics. A revolution does not require prior breaks in private knowledge and opinion. Nor need it be followed by abrupt changes in private variables.

That public political outcomes can be in rapid flux against a background of slowly changing individual characteristics was recognized in the late nineteenth century by Gustave Le Bon. Crowds, he observed, possess a "conservative spirit" and are "the most obstinate maintainers of traditional ideas," yet occasionally they shed their immobility with "startling suddenness" and overthrow venerable institutions.[27] The suddenness, he went on, is only a "superficial effect, behind which must be sought a preliminary and preparatory action of long duration."[28] Le Bon thus sensed that unobserved continuities may be a source of observed discontinuities. He offered no analytical framework, however, to elucidate why developments pregnant with momentous consequences might fail to catch attention.

This book's distinction between private and public selves suggests the missing explanation. Nothing in my argument precludes, I hasten to note, abrupt changes in private knowledge or opinion. There can also be discontinuities in the private realm, as when a leap in unemployment turns private opinion sharply against the prevailing economic system. When private discontinuities occur, however, they will not necessarily generate public ones. I have illustrated how thresholds can move against the status quo without producing an overt demand for change.

There are conditions, of course, under which public and private discontinuities come in quick succession. In the course of a revolution that brings a sharp turn in public discourse, long-settled issues become the focus of attention, and everyone gets exposed to reformist arguments. Public discontinuities are followed, therefore, by private discontinuities. Critical to such an outcome is that few members of any given society think deeply on fundamental issues of the social order. People whose views are governed chiefly by social proof ordinarily lack a capacity for mental resistance to new social demands.

It has been observed that our beliefs are strongest when they have been mildly attacked, for then we have become aware of their vulnerability and learned how to counter criticisms. Prior exposure to mild objections thus produces resistance to later persuasion, which then blocks sharp changes in private knowledge and preferences.[29] By implication, beliefs whose counterarguments were unthought are easier to change than ones whose counterarguments, while treated as unthinkable, have enjoyed at least some public exposure. When a revolution challenges many established beliefs, the ones to succumb first may thus be those that had enjoyed the *greatest* protection from public challenges.

Unconstructed and Unintended Social Outcomes

The possibility of discontinuous social change implies that individual perceptions, experiences, and choices may have disproportionately significant social consequences. And the existence of hidden circular relationships implies that changes may occur through imperfectly observed channels. These two observations yield a pair of additional implications. First, insofar as social outcomes result from interactions among individual actions, collective responses, and preexisting social structures, no person or group will deserve full credit for an unfolding outcome. Observed social outcomes are bound to be *unconstructed*. Second, no one can reliably imagine all long-term consequences of any given choice. There will be social outcomes that were *unintended*.

The new points are illustrated by the long transformation that resulted in Europe's secularization. Centuries after the transformation began, a fairly sincere consensus now exists in favor of limiting ecclesiastical political power. It would be wrong, however, to hold past promoters of secularization responsible for pathways to the present, for prevailing forms of government, or for current attitudes toward religion. Although one can identify outstanding efforts, influential writings, forceful personalities, and critical events, no person or group bears responsibility, or deserves credit, for everything accomplished in the name of secularization. Europeans who promoted a new world-view—by fighting, for example, to free schoolbooks of theological perspectives—have undoubtedly left a mark on Europe's social evolution. But an ideological revolution is never the product of political activists alone. The spread of new ideas is determined partly, if not substantially, by the diverse communications that form ordinary public discourse. Neither these communications nor the consequent development of public discourse can be controlled with precision. It is one thing to sense that an agenda's success depends on the evolution of public discourse, quite another to direct the evolution.

Lest the obstacles to controlling a complex social process seem obvious, it is worth noting that the point has never enjoyed universal acceptance. The annals of social thought are replete with explanations that attribute social institutions to the imaginations and designs of identifiable individuals. Abbé Dubois, an influential contributor to Indian history, considered the caste system a conscious creation of wise lawmakers. He once characterized it as "the *chef-d'oeuvre,* the happiest effort, of Indian legislation."[30] In the United States, some textbooks present American history as the unfolding of a splendid plan laid out by the country's founders. There are also arguments that trace evils like war and poverty to such entities as the CIA and the "corporate establishment."

Such "constructivist" explanations contain several fallacies. The first is that the gainers and losers from a social outcome constitute fixed categories. In fact, individuals may move across categories. For example, a person who feels threatened by a proposed policy may happily discover, during implementation, that it gives him many advantages. A second fallacy of constructivism is its treatment of the masses as either helpless victims of evil designs or the fortunate beneficiaries of wisdom and compassion. In reality, the masses contribute to phenomena that affect them, including the harmful. The lower castes played a role in the caste system's persistence, if only by helping to punish code-breakers. The third fallacy is the notion that the promoters of an outcome must desire its realization. People may promote outcomes they privately fear, and whatever they end up constructing may be by-products of their efforts to maintain prudent reputations. Finally, it is fallacious to treat social actors as infinitely knowledgeable about social conditions and possibilities. Actors seeking particular ends can never be certain about the reactions they will generate, and so they cannot pursue fail-proof strategies.[31]

If a social outcome is the work of a small group, with the rest of society merely watching, the group may justifiably be credited with the good in the outcome and blamed for the bad. But if everyone has contributed to the outcome—some by imagining it, others by proposing and justifying it, still others by concealing their misgivings—no one is free of responsibility. As I argued in Chapter 9, the victims, even if they intended no harm to themselves, are co-constructors of their own victimization.

Where some outcomes are created by groups wider than the teams that pursued them consciously and willingly, others are the unanticipated by-products of actions taken for different ends. Christopher Columbus went looking for India and found a continent blocking the way. Medieval Christendom, seeking to keep Jews out of agriculture, forced them to specialize in commerce and banking; their descendants benefited disproportionately from subsequent economic transformations. What differentiates such consequences from an unconstructed outcome is that they were not intended by anyone. The Christians who restricted the economic options of Jews had no intention of giving later Jews a head start in the economy of the future. Nor did the Jews who honored the restrictions do so for the benefit of their great-grandchildren. They did so for immediate survival. By contrast, the communist governments of Eastern Europe included individuals genuinely committed to central economic planning. That cowed citizens contributed to the creation of a planned economy does not negate the fact that others did so consciously and willingly.

The root reason for unintended consequences is that the choices we make on one issue impinge on issues we have been treating as unrelated, and possibly also on matters not yet recognized as issues. For the Christians who restricted Jewish occupational choices the goal was keeping agriculture in Christian hands. The distributional implications for the industrial economy of the future were no source of concern. As it turned out, industrialization raised the value of commercial and financial skills, causing the agricultural restrictions to lose significance.

Throughout history seekers of glory have claimed credit for the unintended by-products of their actions. And there have always been observers prepared to recognize spurious claims of accomplishment, even to bestow laurels on individuals innocent of self-glorification. There are history books that credit leaders of the Protestant Reformation with laying the groundwork for the modern economy. Yet many fought to restore the simplicity and fraternity of an imagined past. It so happened that their attacks on ecclesiastical corruption weakened the authority of the Church, thereby accelerating the very developments they tried to reverse. Although their work did indeed set the stage for the Industrial Revolution, the benefit was unintended.[32]

That social evolution involves unconstructed and unintended outcomes is entirely consistent with calculated, purposeful human action. Underlying all social outcomes—anticipated and unanticipated, planned and unplanned, wanted and unwanted—are multitudes of individual decisions, each undertaken in response to inner drives and outer incentives. This much has been frequently noted.[33] A couple of points may be added. First, preference falsification distorts the corpus of public knowledge about the unintended outcomes we observe. This is because preference falsifiers ordinarily refrain from divulging the unalloyed truth about their motivations. They do not announce that their positions were motivated partly, if not largely, by reputational concerns. The second point hinges on the fact that our categories of thought are generally those of public discourse. Often, therefore, our lack of foresight with regard to unintended consequences is a collectively generated limitation.

Concealed Inefficiency

If social outcomes may be unintended and unconstructed, they can leave potential benefits unachieved or produce net losses. This claim goes against the all-too-common view that whatever exists is necessarily optimal. One variant of such unbridled optimism lies in economics. Some schools of economics hold that prices, outputs, and institutions, or at least ones that show persistence, must represent efficient solutions to processes of optimization and equilibration. The argument presupposes, of course, that selection pressures are quick to weed out any inefficiencies, as when high-price firms succumb to competition without delay. Seldom, however, do its exponents check whether the invoked selection pressures are truly strong enough to maintain efficiency.[34]

For all its inclinations to see efficiency, economics is also the fountainhead of an argument pointing to the inevitability of various inefficiencies. Mancur Olson's *Logic of Collective Action* shows that free riding, the tendency to avoid paying for benefits available to payers and nonpayers alike, results in the undersupply of collective goods like parks and clean air.[35] The theory does not appeal to preference falsification. Within Olson's framework it may be common knowledge that an entire community wants a park, and also that the community's joint willingness to pay outweighs the expected cost. Nevertheless, in the absence of appropriate "selective incentives," no one will contribute, and the park will remain unbuilt.

Preference falsification is itself a form of free riding, for it is undertaken to avoid the personal cost of achieving a desirable social outcome. As such, it is another basic source of inefficiency. If everyone wants a change of regime, yet no one says so, the unanimously disliked political status quo will persist. Where preference falsification differs from Olsonian free riding is that both its practice and its consequences may remain hidden. Indeed, the actual desire for change can exceed the apparent desire, and the produced inefficiencies need not be recognized. It might be said that discerning individuals will sense the commonness of preference falsification. True, but the very pressures that breed preference falsification may keep such insights unexpressed.

In Chapter 6, I demonstrated that preference falsification breeds inefficiency by preventing change. But preference falsification may lower social welfare even when it *promotes* change. To keep things simple, suppose that in each period a perfect correspondence exists between public opinion and the policy option that gets implemented. Also, let a person's intrinsic utility equal $100 - |Y - x|$, where Y represents public opinion and x his private preference. According to this formulation, intrinsic utility is a declining function of the distance between one's own private preference and the public opinion that determines society's actual policy choice.

Against this background, reconsider the society represented earlier by E. I have added a row that gives each individual's intrinsic utility when public opinion, and thus the implemented policy, is 50. And I have omitted the row containing the thresholds.

Private preferences	80	70	70	60	50	45	40	40	25	20
E: Individuals	a	b	c	d	e	f	g	h	i	j
Intrinsic utilities	70	80	80	90	100	95	90	90	75	70

If we aggregate intrinsic utility for all ten individuals, we find *social intrinsic utility* to be 840.

After some time, f's private preference rises to 50, and E becomes E^2. We have already seen that public opinion will dart to 100. The last row in E^2 below gives each individual's intrinsic utility when public opinion is 100.

Private preferences	80	70	70	60	50	50	40	40	25	20
E^2: Individuals	a	b	c	d	e	f	g	h	i	j
Intrinsic utilities	80	70	70	60	50	50	40	40	25	20

At the new equilibrium, social intrinsic utility is 505. A slight change in one person's private preference has caused our measure of social intrinsic utility to slip from 840 to 505. Had the policy remained at 50, the measure would have risen slightly, from 840 to 845.

Without information about the reputational and expressive components of individual utilities, one cannot say whether the policy shift is socially inefficient. Yet the calculations do establish the possibility of such an outcome, for changes in intrinsic utility could easily swamp those in reputational and expressive utility. Remember from Chapter 2 that when the number of decision makers is large, preference revelation decisions are effectively independent of intrinsic utility considerations—simply because individuals expect their influence on the policy outcome to be insignificant. Even if the intrinsic effects of a policy are enormous, members of society may base their pertinent public preferences solely on reputational and expressive considerations.

The key lesson here is that policy changes need not be for the better. Under some circumstances, society will be much worse off. Moreover, an efficiency-lowering change may be highly durable. Just as an abandoned social policy need not have been inefficient, the persistence of a policy does not prove that it is efficient.[36] In the demonstration just given, inefficiency arises from the *hyperflexibility* of public opinion. A small change in a single person's disposition makes him switch sides, altering everyone's political incentives. The new incentives then drive public opinion to 100. Under other circumstances, inefficiency will stem from the *hypoflexibility* of public opinion—its unresponsiveness to changes in private preferences. Imagine that, with public opinion at 100, contacts with an outside society transform E^2 into

E^4:

Private preferences	5	5	5	5	5	5	5	5	5	5
Individuals	a	b	c	d	e	f	g	h	i	j
Thresholds	95	95	95	95	95	95	95	95	95	95
Intrinsic utilities	5	5	5	5	5	5	5	5	5	5

The threshold row indicates that even with such a dramatic change, public opinion and society's public choice will both remain stuck at 100. In the process, we see from the last row, social intrinsic utility will plunge to 50.

When adjustments lower social intrinsic utility, everyone may be a loser. The last example offers a case in point. Often, however, there will be some gainers. For instance, if society were to undergo the move from E to E^2, person a would benefit from the consequent 50-unit policy jump.[37]

Where there are both gainers and losers, the former may compensate the latter, so that no one is left worse off. The possibility of compensation is sometimes used to justify social changes that affect members of society differentially. In practice, however, losers rarely receive sufficient compensation, if they receive any at all. Ordinarily, political changes end up harming many individuals. Even where noted, this fact is usually left unexplained. A basic reason for the rarity of compensatory transfers is preference falsification. The conformist pressures of public opinion induce the harmed individuals to refrain from pressing for compensation, lest they damage their reputations. An American who pretends to support racial quotas will give away his true feelings if he demands compensation for the costs that he expects to endure. By leaving his claims unexpressed, he hides what he knows about the costs of affirmative action, thereby reducing his risk of being charged with racism.

Political changes driven by public opinion can thus worsen social welfare, and the created inefficiencies may persist indefinitely. Even where, moreover, the gains of some individuals swamp the losses of others, preference falsification may keep the losers from demanding compensation—to say nothing of securing it.

The Imperfections of Social Evolution

If one recently debunked view of biological evolution is that species come and go gradually, another is that the struggle for survival always favors the relatively fit. Now it appears that fitness is neither necessary for survival nor sufficient. Although there are forces that benefit species well adapted to their environments, biological outcomes are also shaped by chance and contingency.[38] If mammals have outlived dinosaurs, observes Stephen Jay Gould, the reason is not that they drove their rivals into extinction by eating their eggs. Dinosaurs probably disappeared because of a rare extraterrestrial impact. For millions of years prior to the impact, mammals lived in a world dominated by dinosaurs. That world could have persisted much longer, delaying the rise of human consciousness.[39]

Like biological evolution, social evolution is influenced by chance and contingency, in addition, of course, to genuine desires. Just as improbable stresses may destroy a species superbly adapted to common circumstances, so too intrinsically improbable contingencies may limit the political effectiveness of deeply felt and very widespread needs. Contingencies may maintain, even expand, gaps between private and public opinion. Social evolution does not always bring progress, if by that one means increasingly satisfying social policies and institutions. It is an imperfect process that generates happiness and sadness, triumphs and defeats, rises as well as declines in efficiency. The next chapter illustrates this point by reviewing the history of American race relations from slavery to the present—a longer perspective than that offered in Chapters 9 and 14.

18

From Slavery to Affirmative Action

A quarter-century before the American Civil War, Tocqueville predicted that the United States would never free itself of interracial conflict.[1] As the twentieth century draws to a close, events have yet to prove him wrong. Although there have been new beginnings and periods of relative optimism, the United States remains a race-conscious society. Huge numbers of Americans harbor overt or covert racial grievances.

The sources of racial tension have varied. In Tocqueville's time, the fundamental impediment to harmony was that the law permitted the enslavement of blacks. From the prohibition of slavery in the 1860s to the Civil Rights Act of 1964, frustrations were driven by the persistence of various forms of segregation and discrimination. For a brief period thereafter, additional resentments emerged from the realization that equality of opportunity does not necessarily produce equality of results. Finally, since the early 1970s, new stresses have arisen from efforts to engineer equality of results through special rights for blacks as a group.

The metamorphosis of the United States from a country that oppresses blacks into one that gives many blacks special privileges illustrates the themes developed in Chapter 17. The transformation occurred in stages, and transitions across stages were rapid. At each step of the way, some Americans consciously pursued the impending changes, yet their successes depended on social forces beyond their control. Certain developments, including the abolition of slavery and the advent of affirmative action, had unintended consequences. Government officials biased outcomes through their responses to shifts in public opinion. Finally, and most crucially for our purposes, preference falsification was a basic determinant of the observed patterns.

The account here is neither chronological nor exhaustive. Structured thematically, it focuses on a few critical episodes. It is followed by brief observations about an analogous transformation in India: the establishment of official quotas as a means of providing relief to the untouchables and other "backward" groups.

The Sudden Fall of American Slavery

We begin with the nineteenth-century struggle over American slavery. It is often argued that slavery was not only immoral but also economically unviable.[2] In this view, the Civil War was fought to rid the United States of an inherently unprofitable institution. Moreover, the South could not have won, because its slave-based economy was inferior to the economy of the North. Facts uncovered by economic historians paint a more complex picture. "Free" per capita income in the South grew faster between 1840 and 1860 than per capita income in the North. And the slaves who gave the South its economic edge were generally well nourished by prevailing standards.[3] Such findings indicate that, even if slavery could not have persisted forever, at the start of the Civil War it was not on the verge of collapse. For all slavery's injustices, it could have remained, for a while longer, the backbone of the southern economy.

Precisely because slavery was *not* doomed to fail, the outcome of the abolitionist drive was by no means clear in advance. Slave prices reached record highs in the 1850s—a strong indication that slavery was considered secure.[4] In the electoral contests of the early 1850s antislavery candidates fared poorly. Furthermore, at no point during the 1850s did the fragile abolitionist coalition, which had to compete for attention with movements against Catholics and the foreign-born, gain a decisive edge over the supporters of slavery. The 1860 election finally brought to the White House someone opposed to the expansion of slavery and destined to become a "great emancipator," but with less than 40 percent of the popular vote. A shift of just 18,239 votes in four states (less than one-half of one percent of the northern ballots cast) would have wiped out Abraham Lincoln's electoral majority.[5]

The closeness of Lincoln's victory suggests that small events might have halted the abolitionist advance. An awkwardly timed scandal or natural disaster might have resulted in his defeat. His campaign, like the abolitionist movement, drew strength, of course, from the conscious and systematic efforts of groups opposed to slavery. Still, Lincoln's ultimate success depended critically on a turn in public opinion. In the North, some politicians promoted such a turn by denouncing their rivals as "southern lackeys." Eminent writers pitched in by heaping scorn on northerners who, though critical of southern institutions in private, refused to condemn them in public.[6] The triumph of such attempts at making it imprudent to support slavery rested on millions of interdependent individual choices. Given the possibility of multiple equilibria in contexts featuring interdependence, there is no reason why victory *had* to come in the 1860s.

A complementary reason why public opinion might have remained favorable to slavery is that slaveowners and their allies took countermeasures to discourage public dissent. At first they ridiculed anyone who dared even to question the merits of slavery.[7] Then, as abolitionism gained an expanding presence in public discourse, they sought to stigmatize the abolitionists as dangerous fanatics. Wherever they could, moreover, they banned antislavery literature and harassed abolitionist writers.[8] The slaveowners had an immediate stake in retaining the support of public opinion: preserving the market value of slaves. Like the abolitionists, they understood that apprehensions about the morality or permanence of slavery would provoke a massive sell-off of slaves, depressing slave prices and sending the southern economy into a tailspin.[9]

For many decades pressures against abolitionists kept the antislavery movement minuscule. At its inception in 1831 the New England Anti-Slavery Society was able to enlist only a dozen members, for people sympathetic to black emancipation generally preferred to keep their sentiments private.[10] If public opinion eventually turned, the reason was not that the supporters of slavery lacked the economic resources to put up an effective resistance. Nor was it that the abolitionists succeeded in making slavery seem unprofitable. The scales of public opinion started to tip as the abolitionists achieved ideological gains. In particular, public opinion shifted as abolitionist leaders made slavery appear un-Christian, thus convincing a growing number of Americans that to support slavery was to court divine punishment.[11]

We can never uncover, of course, the full story of the shift in private opinion, nor that of the subsequent shift in public opinion. For all we know, an unlikely event or a strategic error on behalf of the antislavery cause could have made a huge difference.

What might have happened had Lincoln lost the election? Granted that counterfactual exploration is speculative, the fall of American slavery would probably have been delayed. Moreover, antislavery movements elsewhere in the world would have been undermined, along with various struggles to extend democratic rights to the lower classes. "The momentum for liberal reform would have been replaced," suggests Robert Fogel, "by a drive for aristocratic privilege under the flags of paternalism and the preservation of order."[12] Equally significant, had the Confederacy of the southern states been able to establish itself peacefully, it might well have become a major international power. It would certainly have enjoyed a formidable source of revenue. From a small sales tax on cotton alone, it could have raised, mostly at the expense of foreign buyers, a sum much greater than the entire federal budget at the start of the Civil War. Using the revenue, the Confederacy could have built a strong military machine and financed antidemocratic forces throughout the world. In addition, by exploiting its monopoly of raw cotton, it could have destabilized its enemies—including New England, home to an expanding textile industry. Such developments might have overwhelmed the abolitionist drive.[13]

The Unionist leaders of the North were anything but unaware of the Confederacy's huge economic potential. For many, in fact, this potential provided the impetus for fighting the Civil War. They pursued the emancipation of slaves not as an end in itself, but as a means of countering a geopolitical threat.[14] Northerners tended to be tolerant of slavery when it posed no danger to the regional balance of power.[15] Nor, one should recognize, did the whites of the North generally intend to treat emancipated blacks as their equals. In 1858, during one of his famous debates with Stephen Douglas, Lincoln was charged with believing that God endowed "the negro" with equality. Conceding that differences between the races "will probably forever forbid their living together upon a footing of perfect equality," he declared: "I have no purpose to introduce political and social equality between the white and black races." Having repudiated Douglas's charge, he went on to say that, although he would guarantee blacks the rights established in the Declaration of Independence, he would not give them all the rights held by whites.[16] Lincoln's qualified egalitarianism was by no means unrepresentative of abolitionist opinion. Few abolitionists expressed a desire to incorporate freed blacks into white society, and even fewer showed an appreciation for black culture.[17]

The foregoing account illustrates several themes developed in the previous chapter. The fall of slavery was largely unanticipated. Both the proponents and the opponents of slavery sensed that public opinion on the matter could reach a very different equilibrium than the one in place. And it was widely understood that the persistence of the incumbent equilibrium depended critically on the nature and extent of preference falsification.

Further Breaks in the Evolution of American Race Relations

The subsequent developments in American race relations, some of which were reviewed in earlier chapters, would scarcely have been possible without the demise of slavery. But not all of its consequences were planned—which illustrates yet another theme of the previous chapter. Few abolitionists intended to set the United States on the road to color-blind government. Most would have found Martin Luther King's dream alarming, if not offensive. And they certainly did not wish to give blacks compensatory entitlements. In the 1860s the racial quotas of our own time were not even an issue.

Nor do modern developments represent the realization of principles built into the original constitution of 1787. The original constitution uses the term "equality" only in relation to the rights of states. Contrary to current conventional wisdom, it does not declare that "all men are created equal."[18] In the *Federalist Papers,* written in defense of the Constitution, James Madison pointed to the dangers arising from "the unequal and various distribution of property," but this was the only explicit reference to equality in the whole series.[19]

A decade earlier, the Declaration of Independence had proclaimed the equality of "all men" as a "self-evident" truth. Yet some of its signatories, including Thomas Jefferson, continued to hold slaves. To the modern mind-set, there is a manifest contradiction here. To deny a person, let alone an entire race, the right of liberty is to reject universal equality. How, then, could the founders have considered human equality self-evident? The simple answer is that they believed in the equality of all *white* Americans.[20] And the prevailing public discourse segmented the rights of whites from those of nonwhites, so one could reflect on equality without being reminded of slavery. It helped that other societies displayed analogous splits. Indeed, nowhere did people have much trouble justifying lesser rights for "foreigners" or "heathens," even as they demanded broader liberties for themselves.[21]

Whatever the intentions of its preparers, the Declaration of Independence did not qualify the term "all men," as it might have. Many decades later, the omission allowed opponents of slavery to invoke its authority in pressing their case. Lincoln's proposal to give blacks the rights established in the Declaration constituted, despite his qualifications, a step toward removing the contradiction between the reality of racial inequality and the literal meaning of the equality of "all men." Soon after the contradiction gained public attention, the Constitution was amended to rewrite the terms of citizenship. It was transformed, in the words of a historian, "into a document that could not conceivably have been ratified, and could hardly have been proposed," a century earlier.[22]

For all its historical significance, however, the constitutional revision of the mid-nineteenth century denied black Americans the comfort and benefits of full equality with whites. It put in place a narrow conception of individual "equality before the law": Americans could still enjoy different rights, yet the law would now provide equal treatment to all those with the same rights.[23] It would take another century for the norm to become "equality of opportunity"—the opening of all economic, social, and political contests to everyone, regardless of skin color. In the meantime, blacks continued to live as second-class citizens. Especially in the South, they were segregated from whites, disfranchised, excluded from elite schools, and denied many government services. "Jim Crow," the term associated with this new system, was supported by laws, regulations, and social understandings.[24] The oppressive structures endured in part because they encouraged individual blacks to seek the protection of whites in exchange for loyal service and customary deference. There is a critical circularity here. Racial discrimination increased black dependency on whites, which then helped preserve a division of labor and a race etiquette that reinforced the perception of black inferiority.[25]

Although many black Americans resented the prevailing race etiquette, few opted to vent their anger in public.[26] Among those who refused to accept a subordinate status was the novelist Richard Wright. Growing up in the South, he would often "act straight and human." He recalls, however, that his own behavior was atypical. Resentful blacks almost always feigned acceptance of their inferior positions.[27] Whites, too, had incentives to keep their reservations to themselves. To achieve social acceptance, advance professionally, and succeed in politics, they often had to accommodate, if not actively promote, racial segregation and discrimination.

Whether black or white, violators of the prevailing race etiquette faced penalties ranging from raised eyebrows to lynching. Even some blacks helped punish people pursuing equal rights. As late as 1960, when four college students in Greensboro, North Carolina, sought to register their disapproval of Woolworth's policy of refusing lunch counter service to blacks, they were rebuked by a black employee. Blaming "their kind" for perpetuating black inferiority, she told the students: "That's why we can't get any place today, because of people like you, rabble-rousers, troublemakers. . . . This counter is reserved for white people, it always has been, and you are well aware of that. So why don't you go on out and stop making trouble."[28]

A century after the Civil War, Jim Crow was finally overthrown through the Civil Rights Act of 1964, which marked a new turning point in American race relations. Around that time, Presidents Kennedy and Johnson took the first official steps in regard to affirmative action. The term was initially used to connote special efforts to ensure *equal treatment* for historically disadvantaged groups. Kennedy's Executive Order to government contractors, where the term made its first appearance, specified that employers were to "take affirmative action to ensure that the applicants are employed, and that employees are treated during employment *without* regard to race, creed, color, or national origin."[29] Although the pressures created by Kennedy's order immediately prompted some contractors to accord special breaks to blacks, simply to forestall the appearance of racial bias, the government did not yet insist on "equality of results." Public opinion was still moving in favor of eliminating the social significance of race, not yet in favor of replacing one set of racial criteria by another. Within a few years, however, affirmative action evolved into an insistence on ensuring equality of results as opposed to equality of opportunity. By the early 1970s, the government was promoting statistical parity for socially approved groups in a color-conscious, rather than color-blind, manner. The new goal was quickly extended, moreover, to an ever-widening set of domains.

In view of the emphasis in earlier chapters on the possibility of evolutionary breaks, it is significant that certain major shifts in American race relations occurred at great speed. In the space of a single decade, the 1960s, the United States traveled from government-supported discrimination against blacks to the prohibition of all color-based discrimination, and from there to government-promoted discrimination in favor of blacks. In the words of one observer, the federal government moved to "positions that would have been unthinkably radical only a few years before."[30] The reason why such transitions could be so rapid is that public opinion may undergo huge shifts with startling suddenness. Having remained behind private opinion, public opinion may jump ahead of its private counterpart over a short period of time.

A century earlier, the fall of slavery had come equally quickly. "It is remarkable," writes Fogel, "how rapidly, by historical standards, the institution of slavery gave way before the abolitionist onslaught, once the ideological campaign gained momentum."[31] Indeed, it took just a few decades of concerted agitation to outlaw an institution that had been part of human civilization for millennia. As we have seen, changes in the character of preference falsification played a critical role in the demise of slavery.

Interactions between Public Opinion and Government Policy

Were the described evolutionary patterns shaped solely by the hidden hand of small events? Or are they attributable partly to the visible hand of government? The record shows that the government has not been an entirely passive player in the evolution of public opinion. Although officials have been responsive to public opinion, from time to time they have stepped ahead of it, either intentionally or unintentionally. Their transgressions have accentuated, accelerated, and sometimes reoriented the prevailing trends in public opinion. Thus the relationship between public opinion and government policy has been circular. It has exhibited the pattern described in Chapter 17.

An example of a government action that mattered to subsequent developments is the founders' failure to specify what they meant by the equality of "all men." Counteracting unintended consequences arose from an 1873 decision of five Lincoln-appointed Supreme Court justices, all committed opponents of slavery. The decision concerned Louisiana's right to pass a law allowing a corporation to monopolize the local meat business. In ruling that such an issue falls under state jurisdiction, the justices inadvertently gave ammunition to southern politicians seeking to evade new federal restrictions on discrimination.[32] For almost a century thereafter the precedent provided the Jim Crow system a legal basis, and it helped keep public opinion opposed to color-blind government.

At each stage of the historical transformation, there were, to be sure, people who consciously fought for the impending institutional changes. In the decades preceding the Civil War, for example, there existed abolitionists who favored a color-blind society. In the mid-1960s, likewise, the crowds that demonstrated against racism included activists whose eyes were set on compensatory programs for blacks. Yet the goals of such "extremists" did not yet enjoy the consent of public opinion. Just as most abolitionists were opposed to the principle that came to be known as equality of opportunity, so a century later, around the time of the Civil Rights Act, most civil rights leaders stood against color-coded programs, at least in public.[33] It would be a mistake, however, to credit advocates of the unfolding racial policies with *engineering* the subsequent turns in public opinion. Countless Americans opposed to quotas helped shift public opinion in favor of quota-generating policies. They did so through various forms of preference falsification aimed at covering themselves against charges of racism.

Government agencies contributed to the transformation of public opinion by legitimizing policies to which private opinion was strongly opposed. Most important, through a series of decisions in the 1970s the Supreme Court permitted quota-fostering policies, even quotas themselves. In *Griggs v. Duke Power Co.* (1971), for instance, it unanimously adopted the "disparate impact" theory of discrimination as the central principle of official antidiscrimination policy. It thus allowed evidence of racial imbalance to be treated as proof of discrimination, even in the absence of any indication of discriminatory intent. Thereafter, companies found themselves burdened with proving their innocence of bias. As a precaution, many responded by making racial balance an objective of their employment practices. Another key decision was *Weber v. Kaiser Aluminum* (1976), which upheld a company's discrimination against a white applicant. In effect, the court established that members of the majority are not entitled to legal protection against discrimination: only members of minorities recognized as disadvantaged are so entitled. Yet another landmark case was *Regents of the University of California v. Bakke* (1978). While striking down an absolute racial quota, *Bakke* confirmed the legality of color-coded preferential admission schemes, thus making it more difficult to challenge affirmative action on constitutional grounds.[34] This case served as a powerful reminder, moreover, of the reorientation of public opinion in favor of race-conscious policies.

Agencies established to monitor employment practices, like the Equal Employment Opportunity Commission (EEOC), contributed to keeping public opinion favorable to racial quotas. By virtue of their power to file charges of racial discrimination, such agencies made employers reluctant to challenge the prevailing policies in public, lest criticisms provoke investigations or be construed as evidence of bias.[35] And, as with decisions of the Supreme Court, their activities reinforced the perception of a public opinion strongly supportive of special rights for particular minorities, thus making Americans ever more reluctant to voice misgivings about color-coded discrimination.

In helping to promote a color-conscious agenda, government agencies and other political players engaged in many creative interpretations of the law. Specifically, they made judgment calls and addressed ambiguities in a manner generally partial to the view that double standards are essential to black progress. Some have also engaged in self-serving interpretations of the law. An example lies in the Republican Party's participation in efforts to create more black-majority and

Hispanic-majority voting districts. Most Republican strategists have understood that the required gerrymandering would pervert the Voting Rights Act of 1965, whose intent was to protect individual access to the ballot, not to concentrate the electoral power of certain groups.[36] They suspected, moreover, that color-coded districts would generate racially segregated electorates, analogous to those of South Africa under apartheid. Still, they supported the gerrymandering in a ploy to establish heavily white districts partial to Republicans.

The creative and self-serving interpretations that extended race consciousness took place against a backdrop of enormous private opposition to double standards. As shown in Chapter 9, a quarter-century after the start of affirmative action most Americans still reject the goal of equalizing results. The government's racial agenda has never been fundamentally inconsistent, however, with public opinion. To escape the stigma of racism, skeptics have tended to mute, soften, and qualify their open criticisms, so public opposition to the basic agenda has remained minimal.

Where decisions of the federal government, like those of the Supreme Court and the EEOC, helped shape public opinion, the effects were felt partly through the actions of lower-level officials. In effect, policies crafted in the top reaches of the Washington bureaucracy enabled or induced other officials to carry out decisions that did not yet enjoy the support of public opinion, let alone private opinion. Widespread implementation then helped transform public opinion, through its effect on individual perceptions.

Mid- and low-level officials—not to mention most high-level officials—usually refrain from jumping substantially ahead of public opinion, except where it is clear that they will not be held accountable. Only when it is understood that their superiors have issued unambiguous orders will they exhibit a willingness to enforce controversial directives, for then they can do so without appearing personally responsible.

An illustration lies in the history of the judiciary's response to the Supreme Court's landmark decision on school desegregation, *Brown v. Board of Education* (1954). In allowing local officials wide discretion, *Brown* made them personally responsible for their enforcement decisions. Consequently, where white public opinion ran strongly against desegregation, as in the South, most judges required only cosmetic changes in school practices. Southern school boards contained, of course, some people sympathetic to the spirit of *Brown*. Generally through private channels, many of them encouraged the judiciary to issue an unequivocal order requiring immediate desegregation. Yet in public they maintained an appearance of sympathy for continued segregation; some went so far as to petition for a postponement of desegregation efforts.[37] The key point is that the practical influence of the Supreme Court's famous 1954 decision was muted, and its impact on public opinion delayed, because it gave local decision makers too much choice.

During a brief period in the 1960s the Supreme Court's position on school desegregation became unequivocal, and the federal government started to withhold funds from schools that were in violation of racial balance guidelines. Many local judges responded by implementing *Brown* more rigorously, because they could now insist on desegregation without seeming to favor it personally. Subsequently, as public opinion and the national political leadership became increasingly opposed to mandatory school desegregation, local judges felt increasingly vulnerable, and the rigor of their implementation waned.[38]

The record of efforts to desegregate public schools thus demonstrates that public opinion interacts with government policy, and also that high-level decisions have the greatest impact when they give lower officials little choice. The record also shows that preference falsification on the part of both government officials and ordinary citizens can affect the impact of official decisions.

The Role of Efficiency in the Evolution of American Race Relations

Like other major social changes, every transformation in American race relations has created both gainers and losers. Have the gains always outweighed the losses? And have the institutions adopted at each stage of the evolutionary process dominated all the prevailing alternatives? For conclusive answers to such questions one would need to know, for each stage, the private preferences of all Americans. So heavy a requirement can obviously never be met. What can be established is that social efficiency—in the sense of Chapter 17—has not been the only engine of change.

In discussing the caste system's deleterious effects on Indian economic performance, I made the point that heredity-based barriers to occupational choice result in production losses through the misallocation of labor. Such barriers result in further losses, of course, insofar as they are perceived as an affront to one's own or others' humanity. The knowledge that some groups enjoy lesser rights by birth can in itself be a source of discomfort, humiliation, resentment, and anger.

If this reasoning is correct, can one infer that the transformations that culminated in the Civil Rights Act of 1964 were all driven by social efficiency considerations? Not at all. If efficiency was indeed the sole engine of change, why did it take a whole century to get from the fall of slavery to the color-blind agenda of 1964? And what accounts for the rise of Jim Crow? An attempt to answer such questions would show, at the very least, that if efficiency was a factor in the evolution of American race relations, it was not always the dominant one.

In any case, if we were to accept the efficiency of color blindness as the driving force behind the Civil Rights Act, what would we make of the color-conscious programs that followed? There have been few attempts to estimate the economic costs of affirmative action, which, given that it is risky even to raise the issue of costs, is not surprising. According to one rough estimate, however, the cumulative costs of the quotas established under the rubric of affirmative action, including the indirect costs, have depressed the gross national product by about four percentage points.[39] Although the figure might overstate the loss, even so large a loss could be viewed as the price of greater racial integration. There is no indication, however, that the American nation has been willing to pay such a price. On the contrary, American private opinion has always been solidly against racial quotas. Also relevant is that the abandonment of color blindness has attenuated the interracial goodwill of the 1960s and created mounting resentments. Though mostly unexpressed, the resentments may be setting the stage for a tragic interracial confrontation.[40]

Private preferences with regard to race relations are not fixed in stone, of course. They are shaped partly by public opinion and public discourse. It is possible, therefore, for private opinion to become increasingly supportive of the new color consciousness. Just as white Americans once accepted slavery as natural, and just as Indians indoctrinated themselves with an ideology that sanctifies their segmentation into castes, Americans may yet internalize the principle of group rights. Such a transformation has already taken place on a small scale, as discussed in Chapter 14. If the acceptance of group rights were to spread, affirmative action would gain private acceptance, thus becoming more efficient. But the rise in efficiency would be a *result* of the prevailing racial policies, not their *cause*. In any case, the required cognitive adjustments would probably not run their course quickly. Because attitudes on race relations are formed partly through personal experience, it could take decades, if not centuries, for group rights to capture widespread private support. In the meantime, the United States would remain vulnerable to a social explosion.

The Metamorphosis of India's Caste System

American preference falsification on matters of race has an analogue in contemporary Indian attitudes toward caste. Over the past two centuries caste distinctions have declined in significance as a determinant of social status, and the customary caste barriers now enjoy somewhat less private support than they did in the past. The senescent system has come to coexist, however, with an extensive affirmative action scheme that gives various "backward" groups preferential treatment in employment, schooling, and political representation.[41] There is scant public opposition to affirmative action itself, although specific quotas are a constant source of public controversy and social tension. Yet it is known that many Indians, particularly among the educated, privately worry about the resurgence of caste consciousness. I shall end the chapter with a few remarks on the transformation of the caste system, with an emphasis on drawing parallels to the evolutionary themes highlighted in the preceding discussion of American race relations.

The old caste system began weakening through urbanization and the cultural impact of the West. Indians who came in touch with the outside world were less likely than their culturally sheltered ancestors to accept the impurity of the untouchables as self-evident. And if they lived in a metropolis where they had to walk on crowded sidewalks and ride crammed buses, they could not avoid, as their village-dwelling ancestors could, physical contact with the ritually impure. With such factors breeding skepticism about various aspects of the caste system, even about the system itself, early in this century influential Indian intellectuals joined forces to eliminate the system's most egregious features. Their efforts bore fruit in the constitution of independent India, which carries a provision to alleviate caste-based inequalities through "protective discrimination" in favor of the untouchables and certain other historically oppressed groups. The framers of the Indian constitution saw protective discrimination as a measure to be discarded in about a decade, after which the backward groups would have to compete for positions without special concessions.[42]

A half-century later, not only does protective discrimination continue unabated but it covers more than three-fourths of all Indians. Half of all government jobs are allocated on the basis of caste quotas, and to enlarge their shares groups ranging from primitive tribes to religious converts are trying to outdo one another with tales of relative backwardness.[43] Protective discrimination has thus turned into a spoils system that treats past sufferings, real or contrived, as a badge of permanent privilege. Within each protected group, reserved positions are going, however, generally to those least in need of special breaks, so few of the worst victims of caste are benefiting from the entitlements instituted on their behalf.

Like the American civil rights victories of the 1960s, India's anti-caste movement has thus had some unintended consequences. The founders of modern India, though by no means averse to forced redistribution, did not envision a society in which a growing share of government jobs would be tied to caste identity. They did not want the principle of merit discarded. They did not seek to accentuate the historical divisions of Indian society. They did not wish to make groups in the middle or top tiers of the caste hierarchy draw benefits from a program designed to bring relief to groups horribly stigmatized and terribly impoverished. Although some early leaders, including Mahatma Gandhi, were content with certain elements of the caste system, they wanted to reduce its economic, political, and social significance, not to reinvigorate its importance in daily life. None foresaw the social dynamics that would make caste quotas politically unassailable. Most would probably be horrified to witness affirmative action in its present form. They would be startled that affirmative action exerts so great a hold over public opinion that when, in 1990, Parliament heard a proposal to widen the scope of protective discrimination, no party would express opposition. "Only one or two MPs dared to speak honestly," recalls an observer.[44]

It is not clear that the economy as a whole has gained from protective discrimination. Caste-based occupational barriers were falling anyway at its introduction, and the instituted job quotas have depressed a broad array of work standards. Commissions set up to investigate the causes of railway problems have attributed many accidents to protective discrimination, especially in promotions.[45]

As with affirmative action in the United States, the transformation of the caste system appears to have been guided by much more than efficiency. The two experiences with protective discrimination illustrate yet another property of social evolution: multiple equilibria. They thus demonstrate how public opinion can jump from one extreme to another, rearranging the sets of winners and losers. They show, finally, that preference falsification is a two-edged sword, a weapon that can protect or harm anyone. It may shield Brahmans from market competition, or it can serve to compress their market opportunities. It can protect white workers against competition from more productive blacks, or black workers against competition from better qualified whites.

19

Preference Falsification and Social Analysis

At the end of this inquiry into the mechanisms whereby preference falsification shapes decisions, knowledge, and patterns of change, it is appropriate to consider how the argument enriches, limits, and proposes to reorient social analysis. Accordingly, this chapter undertakes four interrelated tasks.

First, it highlights the ways in which the dual preference model serves to integrate disciplines and scholarly traditions often viewed as mutually incompatible paths to social understanding. I show how the model links traditions that focus on social structure with ones that emphasize individual choice. Drawing on properties of the model, I stress that structuralist and individualistic traditions should be viewed as complementary components of social analysis.

The second point of the chapter is that in illuminating past events and delineating future possibilities, the dual preference model also identifies certain limitations of scientific analysis. In particular, the model proposes that on sensitive issues pressures that breed preference falsification inevitably constrain what can be explained and predicted.

The chapter's third task is to explore the measurability of preference falsification. To this end, it presents techniques for identifying and quantifying hidden perceptions, resentments, fears, and aspirations— some developed by anthropologists, others by opinion scholars. I argue that the techniques can be put to new uses in improving—up to a point, of course—our capacity to explain and predict social evolution.

Finally, I address the matter of refutability. Can the arguments be disproved? What tests may be used to establish their significance or insignificance? Because concepts such as concealment, cognitive limitations, small events, complexity, and unpredictability have played essential roles, the last task should be of special interest to readers inclined to deny scientific status to theories that involve poorly observable variables.

Connecting Past and Present

The "march of science," wrote Henri Poincaré, is simultaneously "towards unity and simplicity" and "towards variety and complexity." On the one hand, "new relations are continually being discovered between objects which seemed destined to remain forever unconnected; scattered facts cease to be strangers to each other and tend to be marshalled into an imposing synthesis." On the other hand, "we are continually perceiving details ever more varied in the phenomena we know, where our crude senses used to be unable to detect any lack of unity." Both processes, Poincaré went on, are critical to the cumulation of useful knowledge.[1]

Most historians tend to specialize in the "variety and complexity" component of knowledge creation, with many denying the possibility, and some even the desirability, of "unity and simplicity." To be sure, the chronicling of the past is valuable in its own right. Satisfying our innate curiosity, it enriches our lives. But the causal links among historical details do not speak for themselves. Nor do details make clear why the past matters to the present. Absent a mechanism to account for the past's influence, Ottoman history would be irrelevant to interpreting the reforms of the Turkish Republic. To make a valid connection between, say, eighteenth-century Ottoman education and modern Turkish thought, one must specify a chain of causal links stretching over three centuries. Without such a chain, the connection would imply influence *at a distance*—an impossibility.

This book has developed a series of interrelated mechanisms that connect the past with the present. In doing so, it has simultaneously served both the ends of "unity and simplicity" and those of "variety and complexity." With regard to the first pair of objectives, the overall model incorporates just a few relationships, all derived from a small set of variables. The relationships form a coherent whole, so they provide a unified explanation for phenomena that tend to be analyzed within separate academic specialties. They allow one to connect, for instance, a society's intellectual development (the domain of intellectual history) with the transformation of its economic institutions (the province of economic history). With regard to the latter pair of objectives, the argument shows how a given mechanism may account for substantively very different outcomes, such as persistent dictatorship and stable democracy, or beliefs in human equality and beliefs in natural differences. The argument thus helps account for the richness of human history.

In making sense of historical variety, I have attached much weight to small events. The book thus provides a rationale, apart from benefits like the quenching of curiosity, for the documentation of historical particulars. It shows that some details of the past may have made a crucial difference to subsequent developments.

Like history, anthropology documents the diversity of human civilization. Specifically, it identifies cross-cultural variations in beliefs, values, mores, and institutions. And it demonstrates how people tend to regard their own cultural forms as natural, however unnatural these may seem to outsiders. Yet anthropology has tended to shun the task of developing a coherent framework for explaining how cultural differences develop, grow, and abate. But without such a framework, more and more accounts of cultural diversity, however carefully supported by observation, impose a growing burden on the human capacity to learn and remember. Readers of anthropological description are bound, after all, by the same cognitive limitations that make us all seek guidance from our respective cultures. Precisely because of the limitations that make culture so essential, it is imperative to bring simplifying and unifying social theories into the task of interpreting cultural diversity.

Deconstructionists with a penchant for "decanonizing," "dephallicizing," and "dehegemonizing" might respond that social theories reflect the biases of their developers.[2] True enough. A given event may be observed from multiple vantage points, and the perspectives of investigators inevitably reflect their personal backgrounds, circumstances, and interests. But the choice is not between imperfect theory and no theory at all. Even the anthropological procedure of "thick description," with its meticulous attention to detail, variation, and nuance, involves interpretation.[3] A statement delivered in a hushed voice means one thing in a quiet restaurant, another in a hospital ward bearing the sign, "Please Be Quiet." In discriminating among such meanings anthropologists regularly draw on their preconceptions about human nature, social interactions, and the cultures that they are studying. Likewise, historians draw on their "historical sense" to fill in gaps in the available documentary evidence.[4] They rely, for instance, on their general knowledge about past expectations, apprehensions, and perceptions—knowledge subject to error and distortion. In practice, therefore, there is no such thing as atheoretical or pretheoretical description. Try as we might to report events simply as they are, we cannot escape the influence of our personal biases.

The real choice is between, on the one hand, loose and implicit theorizing, and on the other, tight and explicit theorizing. The latter form offers several advantages. First, it makes it easier to separate bad theories from good ones. Second, it lays out exactly what is being assumed and asserted, thus facilitating critical scrutiny. And third, it allows one to segregate universal phenomena from culture-specific details. In regard to the final advantage, once the universal elements in an event or trend have been identified and connected, they can be used to specify what is predictable. Suppose, for example, that we discover that many Egyptian women are veiling themselves in order to escape fundamentalist censure. On the basis of the theory in this book, we would categorize the finding as one specific manifestation of a general phenomenon that afflicts diverse societies. And in the process we would become sensitized to possible social implications. We would become attuned, for instance, to the existence of a hidden potential for revolt against fundamentalist Islam, and also to the reasons why a mass reaction, were it to occur, would probably come as a surprise.

Structure and Choice

Social scientists who do recognize the uses of explicit theorizing are divided on the social significance of individual choice and social structure. On one side are "rationalists," "behaviorists," and "individualists," who view the logic of individual choice as the key to comprehending the social order. For them, choice is all-important, and social structures are the alterable consequences of conscious personal decisions. On the other side are "structuralists," who consider individual choices less important than the constraints within which choices are made. People's important decisions are generally fixed, they say, by the social order.[5] It has been remarked that, where the structuralist notices "the bounding of political activity by social structure," the individualist sees "political decision making within these bounds." Accordingly, in studying a cattle herd the former focuses on "the fence around the cattle," the latter on "the activity of the cattle within the bounds of the fence."[6]

Neither the structuralists nor the individualists fabricate what they report observing. Constraints and decision making are both facts of life. It is wrong, however, to give absolute priority to one factor or the other. Structures do not have absolute priority, because the constraints they incorporate are never fixed in stone. In Eastern Europe, even as formidable a constraint as the communist monopoly of power proved impermanent because of millions of individual decisions to say "enough." By the same token, individual choice does not have absolute priority, because social constraints may make the outcome of a choice process practically a foregone conclusion. For decades, Romanians had the option of protesting against repression, but only at the expense of possibly very costly reprisals.

Both choice and structure can be critical, and each shapes the other. The social sciences must explain how the two elements interact. The theory presented in earlier chapters contributes to the task by explaining, through a framework grounded in individual choice, the evolution of the social pressures that constrain individual public preferences. It thus serves to integrate the individualist and structuralist traditions, showing that they are not at all incompatible. Not all constraints, one might observe, take the form of social pressure. Constitutions, laws, and regulations limit our feasible options; political rules make inherited policies hard to change; and ideologies make certain options difficult to accept. But all such constraints are *created* and *sustained* by social pressures, which are produced by individual choices. We see again that structuralism and individualism serve complementary ends.

Individualism has developed a bad name in certain academic circles, partly because many of its practitioners treat the individual as a monad. But in making the individual the unit of analysis one need not ignore the social factors that shape personal dispositions. The model in this book shows, as do assorted others, that methodological individualism is not the same thing as methodological monadism.

In some scholarly circles, of course, the assumption that the individual is a "windowless monad" is viewed not as a weakness but as a source of analytical power. There do exist many useful studies that rest on monadism. Especially in short-run contexts where private preferences are unlikely to undergo appreciable change, monadism provides an analytically reasonable simplification. Nevertheless, deeper understandings can be achieved, and a wider set of phenomena explained, through a more realistic conception of the individual. This book has demonstrated how a model that treats the individual as a social product can yield insights into people's perceptions, theories, and myths. It has shown how cognitive constructs may outlive the external constraints on individual action. And it has considered how public discourse helps shape perceptions of self-interest.

The Limits of Social Knowledge

Now I turn to the second of the chapter's tasks: evaluation of the model's insights regarding the limits of social knowledge.

Ask a randomly selected social scientist to characterize the purpose of social science and you will probably hear the answer, "explanation and prediction." Such a response might seem to raise questions about the usefulness of a theory that exposes obstacles to social understanding and forecasting. Why ponder the limits of social knowledge when so much that is clearly knowable remains uninvestigated? And given all that we can still learn, is it not premature to accept scientific defeat?

Identifying the limits of knowledge is not a declaration of failure. It is itself a contribution to the pool of useful knowledge as well as a necessary step toward charting a realistic scientific agenda. In the words of Friedrich Hayek, "to act as if we possessed scientific knowledge enabling us to transcend [the absolute obstacles to the prediction of specific events] may itself become a serious obstacle to the advance of the human intellect."[7] Darwin did not obstruct or retard science by developing a theory that limits our ability to predict biological evolution. Producing a quantum leap in biological knowledge, he catalyzed research that has improved our capacity to control the evolution of particular species. The goal of all science, not just biology, should be to explain the explicable, predict the predictable, and equally important, separate the knowable from the unknowable.

Objectors should scan the major social trends of our time and ask themselves whether any have been accurately predicted and whether, even with the benefit of hindsight, any are understood fully. Do we comprehend exactly why the late twentieth century has seen a rise in religious fundamentalism, an intensification of nationalism, and the rise of East Asia as an economic giant? Who foresaw, back in the 1950s, that within three decades South Korea would be a major industrial exporter, secularism would be on the defense throughout the world, and ethnic warfare would have escalated? Even a cursory evaluation of the past record of the social sciences will show that, at least on politicized matters involving multitudes of decision makers, neither perfect prediction nor full explanation is the norm. As a practical matter, we do not have to choose between theories that produce complete knowledge and ones that generate only limited knowledge. The critical difference is that some theories deny or disguise their limitations whereas others make them explicit.

The limitations of the dual preference model stem from a combination of two factors. First, some of its elements are related to one another *nonlinearly,* which is to say that their sensitivities to each other and to outside shocks are variable. In a nonlinear system the consequences of a given perturbation can vary enormously. Depending on circumstances, the effects may be disproportionately large or small.[8] In the present context, nonlinearities are rooted in interdependencies among individual public preferences. They take the form of variations in the sensitivity of public opinion to the distribution of individual characteristics. For example, massive changes in private opinion may leave public opinion undisturbed, only to be followed by a tiny change that transforms public opinion radically. The second factor that limits the model's explanatory and predictive powers is that the interdependencies among public preferences are *imperfectly observable.* The joint effect of the two factors is to make it impossible to predict with certainty the consequences of any given political development.

Let us be clear about the roles of nonlinearity and imperfect observability. Absent preference falsification, which is the source of imperfect observability, we would always be aware of approaching discontinuities. We would notice, for instance, that an antigovernment bandwagon will begin rolling if just three more people become disillusioned with the political status quo. And absent interdependencies among public preferences, the source of nonlinearity, small changes in individual dispositions would not give rise to explosive changes in public opinion. Whereas an easily observed change in millions of people's commitment to the status quo might well cause a large shift in public opinion, an unnoticeable change in just a few people's feelings would produce at best a commensurately small shift. With both preference falsification and interdependencies, and therefore both imperfect observability and nonlinearity, effects can be both unforeseen and disproportionate.

The fact that an outcome was unforeseen does not imply that it must remain a complete mystery. With the benefit of hindsight, many unanticipated events are understood reasonably well. We know much about the frustrations that propel modern fundamentalisms, even though their rise was scarcely predicted. We know why and how the East Europeans toppled their communist regimes, even though the fall of the Berlin Wall amazed us all. The proposed theory explains, in a manner compatible with its own logic, why explanation is often easier than prediction.[9] A shift in public opinion brings to the surface information that is consistent with the shift, and it conceals information that is inconsistent. The problem is compounded, as we saw in Chapter 15, by the fact that information consistent with an event gets absorbed more readily than inconsistent information.

A model's ability to demonstrate why explanation may prove easier than prediction should not be taken lightly. In the social sciences the two concepts are often used interchangeably, as though a model that yields insights into the past must be equally good at predicting the future. In addition, retrospective accounts seldom make clear what actors actually knew and what they could have known. Frequently such accounts suggest that recorded events "had" to happen, failing to explain why, if so, they were not predicted. Many accounts of the East European Revolution make it seem to have been inevitable. They are all very misleading. If the old communist order were still in place, would we not be advancing persuasive reasons for the *permanence* of communism? Who would be paying serious attention to a suggestion that communism could easily fall? The truth is that if no revolution had occurred, few observers of Eastern Europe would consider the region's ongoing political stability a puzzle.

From the practical difficulties of social prediction some scholars infer that general social theories are essentially useless. We should confine ourselves to case studies, they say, without seeking to achieve conceptual unity. In the context of revolutions, for example, repeated predictive failures have made some social scientists question the usefulness of seeking a general theory of revolutions.[10] Such scholars deserve credit for noticing the commonness of predictive failures. They are wrong, however, to dismiss the possibility of general insights into the revolutionary process. The problem lies not with theorizing per se but with the type of theorizing that has dominated the social sciences. What we need is theorizing that accounts for its own limitations and that distinguishes between explanation and prediction. A theory that meets these two criteria can provide a coherent explanation for the observations that ostensibly prove the futility of searching for conceptual unity and generality.

Toward Improved Explanation and Prediction

To identify the limits of knowledge is not to say that we are doomed to *total* ignorance about the past or that unfolding events must always surprise us. The limits stem, I have said, not from the *un*observability of interdependencies among public preferences but, rather, from their *imperfect* observability. As previous chapters have explored, the signs of preference falsification are seldom fully hidden, and the pressures that inhibit sincere expression are often partially identifiable. Depending on the context, for instance, much relevant information may lie in the results of anonymous polls or in such sources as memoirs, diaries, confidential letters, deathbed confessions, and secret archives. One can often distinguish, therefore, between honest devotion and fear-driven obedience, and between genuine agreement and suppressed controversy.

Private information is generally harder to gather, it might be said, in countries where democratic freedoms are nonexistent or fragile than in countries with strong democratic traditions. In the former, the very forces that discourage sincerity also inhibit the collection of data on private opinion. Thus the communist regimes of Eastern Europe restricted poll taking. They used various means, moreover, to mislead the world about the extent of private opposition to communist rule. Nevertheless, most of us realized that the East European regimes enjoyed less genuine acceptance than, say, the Swedish form of government did among Swedes. What we could not know was the exact nature of private opinion, to say nothing of the precise distribution of revolutionary thresholds. It bears reemphasis that preference falsification poses a problem for social analysis with respect to democratic countries as well. Even where the right to express unpopular views enjoys legal protection, there exist sensitive issues on which people think twice before venturing an opinion in public. In the United States, race relations is such an issue.

Where sincere conversation is blocked—in Czechoslovakia on the communist monopoly of power, in Iran on Islamic rule, in India on caste, or in the United States on affirmative action—there generally exist signs of hidden opposition to positions that enjoy vast public support. One can identify, therefore, a potential for social explosion. One can also see indications that the distortions of public discourse are affecting, or have affected, private thinking. Notwithstanding its acknowledged limitations, the theory in this book thus enhances both explanation and prediction. It can improve our readings of history and alert us to future possibilities, though necessarily within bounds. Our understandings will always remain imperfect and our expectations subject to error.

In all polities, however democratic or undemocratic, there exist openly contested issues on which one can express a range of views without enduring significant penalties. On such issues public opinion will not make unforeseen jumps, except in response to a major shock that changes many minds simultaneously—an earthquake, say, that jolts millions into reconsidering the importance of strict building codes. Also, the evolution of public opinion can be explained without worrying much about interdependencies. It is on socially sensitive issues that preference falsification may sharply limit our predictive and explanatory capabilities. Yet even on such issues, I repeat, we are never totally in the dark. With respect to the past, we can understand the persistence and the consequences of repressive conditions. With respect to the future, we know where to look for the possibilities of sudden change.

The task of identifying instances of widespread preference falsification generally involves the consideration of data difficult to document and interpret. Prior to 1989 a scholar trying to demonstrate the pervasiveness of East European preference falsification might have invoked: (1) opinion surveys conducted by Western organizations on East European travelers; (2) the claims of dissidents; and (3) the observations of informed outside observers. All such data were discounted as biased. They could not be supplemented with credible opinion surveys, however, because the governments in power withheld the necessary permissions. Not that polling data were nonexistent. As we saw in Chapters 13 and 16, the communist regimes regularly conducted surveys. Before 1989, however, these surveys were kept outside the public domain. Now we understand, and then we had reason to suspect, that communist governments were secretive precisely because they recognized their private unpopularity. A regime that enjoys genuine legitimacy has no reason to keep its opinion surveys classified. Nor does it need to prohibit independent polling.

It might appear "unscientific" to assert, in the absence of systematic polling data, that a regime, institution, policy, or political agenda is privately unpopular. Yet the scientific ethos demands only that we gather the best data available and interpret our evidence in the light of sound theory. It does not require us to ignore problems on which data are relatively scarce or imperfect. In any case, the unavailability of good opinion data may itself be a sign of preference falsification. Just as it was significant to Sherlock Holmes that the dog did not bark, it was politically significant that, unlike West Germany, East Germany prohibited independent polling. In the same vein, it is highly significant that American universities, which teach thousands of courses on the social costs of contemporary white racism, offer few courses that are explicitly critical of affirmative action. Dogs that do not bark—untaught courses, unavailable survey data—may yield as much useful information as dogs that do.

In contexts where preference falsification is rampant, we often have little choice but to employ whatever data can be found, even inexact data. Whether we are interpreting the past or exploring future possibilities, we have to pay attention to the scattered perceptions of observers who seem well informed about happenings behind the public stage. Impressionistic accounts do not provide exact figures, but they can identify the existence of widespread discontent.[11] After repression eases or disappears, of course, the relevant database may improve appreciably. Since 1989 we have gained access to many secret surveys conducted over the years for the benefit of Eastern Europe's communist regimes.

Social predictions based on perceptions of preference falsification may suffer from a problem absent from historical explanation. Predictions interact with the phenomena they predict. A report that society is about to erupt may become self-fulfilling; or, by provoking the government to take precautionary measures, it may become self-negating. Such effects are not specific, however, to contexts where people are afraid to express themselves truthfully. Any social observation may alter the reality being observed.[12] An economist who predicts a recession may contribute to a recession that would not have occurred had he kept quiet. Reports of a candidate's invincibility may scare off her most qualified opponents, thus compounding her advantage.

Measuring Preference Falsification

To suggest that the concept of preference falsification can improve our predictive and explanatory capabilities is not to say, then, that it can be incorporated into social analysis without risk. A further problem, which brings me to the chapter's third task, concerns the imperfections of the available techniques for identifying and quantifying preference falsification. The latter problem does not necessarily point, I should note, to a flaw in the theory outlined in this book. Techniques for forming new databases rarely get developed until new theories establish their usefulness.[13] Methods for quantifying temperature were devised only after physicists crafted theories featuring temperature scales. And techniques for measuring monetary velocity emerged only after the concept became commonplace in economic texts.

When a theory precedes the measurement techniques needed to verify or use it, it will generally be harder to test in historical contexts than in contemporary ones. Evidence on the velocity of coinage in fourteenth-century Anatolia is not as reliable as information on the modern velocity of the Japanese yen. This is no reason, however, to spurn the concept of monetary velocity. Rather, one must simply use extra caution in Ottoman economic research. One can recognize the impediments to measuring early Ottoman velocity without denying the concept's scientific merits. Similarly, one can acknowledge the difficulties in measuring discrepancies between private and public opinion in the past without declaring the concept of preference falsification useless. The fact that no scientific opinion surveys were conducted during the American Civil War does not mean that the concept is of no help to research on the period.

There have been fruitful attempts to identify instances of preference falsification in the past, even the remote past. For example, some medievalists have developed a technique for determining concealed messages in old philosophical texts. It is based on the following principle. When an experienced writer expresses a view that goes against public opinion, there is strong reason to believe that he is sincere. When he conveys a view supportive of public opinion, however, one cannot rule out the possibility that he is trying to avoid punishment, especially if the view contradicts what he expressed elsewhere. Medieval philosophers wrote at a time when challenges to popular beliefs often brought retribution. Under the circumstances, they made it a practice to present their most original and potentially most controversial thoughts "between the lines," for the exclusive benefit of other independent thinkers. As Leo Strauss and others have documented, in the depths of a treatise an able writer would surreptitiously contradict an orthodox tenet that he had defended in many conspicuous passages, with an eye toward exposing his dissent to cultivated readers likely to be sympathetic, but also hiding it from unsophisticated readers likely to be offended. Careful readings of the works of Farabi, Maimonides, Ibn Khaldun, Hobbes, Spinoza, and other towering philosophers suggest that they tended to express their heretical views in relatively inconspicuous passages and in deliberately ambiguous terms, probably to escape persecution.[14]

Reading between the lines is not an infallible technique. But to reject it for this reason alone would be like denying emergency aid to a wounded sailor at sea on the grounds that he could get better treatment from a fully equipped hospital on shore. The value of any datum is contingent, as noted earlier, on what else is available. In any case, to presume that past writers had neither incentives nor the capacity to hide their true thoughts would contradict basic facts of human nature. It could also generate serious historical misinterpretations.

The point remains that in historical contexts one rarely has access to ideal data. If future historians are to have better data on our own age, systematic efforts must be made to collect data that distinguish, on the one hand, between private and public opinion, and on the other, between private knowledge and public discourse. The needed undertakings fall into two general categories: qualitative field research and quantitative surveys.

Work of the former sort would be performed by scholars trained in the techniques of thick description—establishing rapport with a community, selecting informants, keeping a diary, and so on. Living for a while in the community under investigation, they would try to win the community's trust in order to gain exposure to the perceptions, ideas, resentments, aspirations, and ambitions that its members tend to keep private. The research would thus capture differences between the community's life on stage and its life off stage. James Scott has shown how this can be done through fieldwork in rural Malaysia.[15] He has documented that poor peasants deliberately and routinely mislead landlords and government officials about their knowledge and dispositions. As mentioned in Chapter 10, Scott misconstrues his findings as implying that public discourse, however distorted, has no bearing on private knowledge. Still, his work testifies to the possibility of identifying the scope and extent of preference falsification on the part of subordinate groups.

Certain survey techniques for measuring preference falsification have already been developed. I shall discuss two, beginning with one of many tests developed by the Allensbach Institute. A representative Allensbach test is the "parking space test."[16] On the eve of the West German elections of 1976 a sample of prospective voters heard the following:

Someone drives into a strange city and can't find a parking space. He finally gets out of the car and asks a pedestrian, "Can you tell me, please, where I can find a place to park?" The pedestrian replies, "Ask somebody else, buddy!" and walks away. I should mention that the driver is wearing a political badge on his jacket. What do you think: which party did this badge support? What is your guess?

Only 14 percent of the respondents named the Social Democratic Party (SDP), as against 23 percent who named the Christian Democratic Union (CDU) and 21 percent who named communist parties. Interestingly, even the Christian Democratic respondents considered it riskier to express support for the CDU than for the SDP. These findings are consistent with the fact that in the same month a marked tendency existed for citizens who had voted Christian Democratic four years earlier to pretend they had not. Many individual Christian Democrats were refashioning their public selves because public opinion had turned against their private selves.

The second technique that I will discuss was developed, like the parking space test, to predict an electoral outcome. In the heat of an election campaign social pressures favoring one side or the other may give misleading signals regarding the outcome of the pending election. The induced preference falsification may bias preelection polls, especially if poll takers are suspected of dangerous partisan sympathies. As a case in point, a *Washington Post-ABC News* poll completed ten days before the Nicaraguan election of 1990 gave the Sandinista presidential candidate, Daniel Ortega, a lead of 16 percentage points over the UNO coalition candidate, Violeta Chamorro. Other polls gave Ortega an even wider lead. In the actual election, Chamorro came out ahead by 14 points. Yet, taking the projections at face value, many news organizations had interviewed Sandinista leaders just before the election to discuss how they would exploit their imminent victory. The only polls that turned out to be in the right ballpark were ones conducted by organizations linked, in fact or in people's imagination, to UNO.[17] Foreign news organizations had dismissed the latter polls as partisan. Consequently they were stunned by Chamorro's victory, much as they had been stunned a few months earlier by the fall of East European communism.[18]

An ingenious experiment run by Katherine Bischoping and Howard Schuman points to the source of confusion.[19] A few weeks before the election, they conducted 300 interviews, all administered identically, except for the type of pen used to record responses. In one-third of the interviews the interviewer used a pen featuring the red and black colors of the Sandinista Party and the inscription "DANIEL PRESIDENTE." In another third the interviewer used a pen featuring the blue and white colors of the opposition and the inscription "UNO." And in the remaining third the interviewer used a neutrally colored pen with no lettering. Interviewers did not draw attention to their pens or make claims about their own political sympathies. Yet the results show that the pens influenced the respondents. When the interviewer held a Sandinista pen the respondents voiced support for Ortega by a 26-point margin. Ortega also came out ahead in the neutral-pen condition, by 20 points. When the interviewer held a UNO pen, however, Chamorro was the winner by 12 points.

The UNO-pen condition thus came close to predicting the election outcome, whereas the Sandinista-pen condition replicated the highly inaccurate preelection polls. Remarkably, the neutral-pen condition generated a result similar to that of the Sandinista-pen condition. Bischoping and Schuman suggest that after a decade of Sandinista repression voters tended to view pollsters as progovernment activists unless clear signs existed to the contrary. Insofar as this intuition is correct, we have an explanation for the marked inaccuracy of the *Washington Post-ABC News* poll. Precisely because it was conducted by interviewers striving for a neutral image, respondents sympathetic to UNO considered it prudent to keep their private preferences concealed. Evidently it took interviewers with apparent UNO connections to give certain UNO sympathizers the courage to reveal their private preferences.[20]

Like the parking space test, the pen experiment identifies fears and sensitivities. It thus points to possible incongruities between public and private opinion. Because elections by secret ballot measure private opinion, polls undertaken to predict electoral outcomes will yield misleading forecasts unless the respondents feel comfortable expressing themselves honestly. Of course, interpreting a poll designed to overcome preference falsification is anything but a mechanical matter. It requires a sound understanding of political realities. An analyst ignorant of Nicaraguan politics may well have designated the source of fear as UNO, because it was the UNO pen, not the Sandinista pen, that registered a dramatically different outcome from the neutral pen. One needs to know the history of Sandinista rule to see that a pollster striving to appear neutral would usually be perceived as pro-Sandinista. A related point is that preference falsification, when identified, is not always self-explanatory. Analysts in agreement that an experiment has revealed widespread preference falsification might disagree on what is being concealed.

For all their ambiguities, however, experiments like the two just discussed also have uses outside of elections. They can be brought into broader studies of social stability, political evolution, and ideological change. But we must guard against excessive optimism, for, as noted in discussing the prospects for predicting revolutions, social observations interact with what is being observed. A poll designed to measure hidden opposition may generate more discontent by making people reflect on issues they had been ignoring. And a survey that uncovers a pattern of preference falsification may reinforce the perceived risk of nonconformism.

The measurement techniques that I have presented may be criticized on the grounds that they yield imprecise readings. It is true that pen experiments and parking space tests provide inexact readings of private opinion, preference falsification, and perceived social pressures. But I am not suggesting otherwise. Insisting that the determinants of political outcomes are *imperfectly* observable, I am arguing only that techniques exist to provide rough readings of the political climate and crude estimates of private variables. Techniques that yield more exact measurements may yet be developed. Barring the invention of an instrument for reading the individual mind, however, the techniques will never attain the precision of a microscope. In any case, not every domain of analysis requires the same precision. Just as the appropriate unit for measuring the distance between two stars is not the micron, we do not need to know private opinion exactly to uncover the existence of a latent revolutionary bandwagon. If in 1988 a variant of the pen experiment had been run in East Germany and the nature of the interviewer's pen had been found to make a huge difference, the finding would certainly have been informative. We would still not have known that the Berlin Wall would be breached in a year's time. But at least we would have obtained controlled evidence of a potential for mass revolt.

Another criticism of the measurement techniques that I have discussed might be that they do not offer standardized procedures for measuring hidden variables—procedures that can be applied more or less mechanically to every possible situation. Indeed, the parking space test was developed for a country where most adults own cars. It would not be as meaningful in an economically backward country. Perhaps standardized tests will someday be developed and put to regular use. But they will still need to be interpreted on a case by case basis. The results of pen experiments conducted in Mexico and Turkey could be meaningfully compared only in the light of information about social conditions in the two countries. Identical figures could signify widespread political fear in one country, customary politeness in the other.

The Possibility of Refutation

We come at last to the theory's potential refutability. Can the propositions and explanations offered herein be disproved? Can they be tested against alternative theories? The answer to these questions is a qualified yes. I start with the qualification.

In the social sciences, tests that can be imagined cannot always be performed. One cannot rerun the twentieth century to show that in the absence of preference falsification on the part of Soviet citizens communism would have collapsed long before it finally did. Nor can one rerun Indian history to demonstrate that if Indians had always been in close contact with other cultures there would have been no doctrine of karma.

In practice, therefore, we must often rely on natural experiments—strings of uncontrolled events that provide opportunities for investigating the plausibility of proposed theories. But natural experiments are seldom precise enough. Their power is often diminished by variations in factors that one would have wanted to hold fixed. As a result, no single natural experiment will rule out all alternative explanations. Inevitably, our evaluations of alternative theories must rely on how well they explain data from different sources and on how well they agree with our overall understanding of human civilization. This is one reason why I considered it critical to apply my argument to disparate cases—the caste system, communism, and American race relations.

The criteria that I have outlined are those Darwin used to establish the merits of his theory of biological evolution. Where physicists looked for experimental testing, he considered it sufficient and, in view of the constraints on biological testing, equally rigorous, to show that his theory explained, through a single set of mechanisms, data from fields as diverse as embryology, paleobotany, and zoogeography. Even in physics, long the quintessential experimental science, a common methodological view at present is that theories are more or less adequate depending on their consistency with the totality of human knowledge, or at least the totality of what is known in a particular discipline. The view, promoted most vigorously by Karl Popper, that science proceeds through conclusive refutations[21] has given way in some circles of physicists to a new view whose most effective expositor has been Thomas Kuhn.[22] Kuhn holds that science advances through the rise of new paradigms that expand the range of explicable phenomena.

The Kuhnian philosophy of science recognizes that an observation might admit more than one explanation. Take my claim that Americans refrain from criticizing affirmative action to forestall charges of racism. The data I offered to support the claim are also consistent with the notion that preference falsifiers are motivated by altruism, as opposed to fear. Indeed, it could be that preference falsifiers intend to shield the beneficiaries of affirmative action from discomforting truths, like the fact that costs fall on people who are both better qualified and less privileged. Fear and altruism are not, of course, mutually incompatible motives. But if one has to choose, the fear thesis will win, for it is consistent with more facts. Unlike the altruism thesis, it explains why it is extraordinarily difficult to forecast the outcomes of racially charged elections. And it explains why underprivileged whites tend not to object publicly to the breaks given to visibly privileged minorities.

The point remains that no single test will prove or disprove the dual preference model. Let me suggest, however, how some of the individual propositions advanced in the book could be refuted. If one or more of these propositions were to fail further empirical scrutiny, the foundations of the model, or its logic, would have to be reconsidered.

The proposition that *more revolutionary surprises are inevitable* (Chapter 15) could be debunked simply by building a model that predicts future revolutions. A string of successful forecasts as to the location and timing of future revolutions would suggest that preference falsification is not, contrary to what I have argued, an obstacle to refined prediction. Jack Goldstone maintains that, despite the impediments to observing private opinion, it is possible to identify the "objective conditions" for revolution.[23] If this is true, his demographic-structural model (or some other model) will yield accurate predictions of the form: "Country A will experience a mass uprising three years from now" or "Over the next decade countries B, C, and D will remain politically stable, while E and F will not." Of course if events were to invalidate such predictions, one could not jump to the conclusion that the source of error had to be preference falsification. Anything that conceals or constrains information about individual revolutionary motives may lead to predictive error. In addition to preference falsification, the possibilities include obstacles to observing the structural determinants of political loyalty and difficulties in assessing the political implications of known grievances.

So while continued predictive failures would discredit Goldstone's claim, it would not, by itself, validate the dual preference model. But note that I have not suggested only that there will be more revolutionary surprises. I have also proposed that such *surprises will occur in countries that are politically repressive.* In countries with strong democratic traditions, misgivings about the regime are expressed relatively freely. Therefore it is easy to gauge the prospects for their continued stability. By contrast, countries with weak democratic traditions severely limit our ability to track popular grievances against the political regime. If preference falsification is indeed the key factor in revolutionary surprises, such surprises will arise primarily in dictatorships and in weak or newly founded democracies. At the present time, the set includes most countries of Africa, the Arab world, the former Communist bloc, and China. In established democracies unanticipated overturns will be less momentous. They may entail electoral shifts like the stunning Republican takeover of the U.S. Congress in the midterm elections of 1994. And they will generally involve sensitive issues unrelated to the form of government. It is possible, if my argument is correct, for the United States to experience a sudden backlash against the color-coded social agenda of recent decades. At the same time the United States is less likely than, say, China or Saudi Arabia to experience an unanticipated mass reaction directed at its core institutions of government.

A central claim of this book is that *social policies and institutions evolve sometimes through slow and continuous adjustments and at other times through sudden, discontinuous jumps* (Chapters 15, 17). Were one to demonstrate that social evolution is always continuous—

by showing, say, that Russia has seen no sharp changes in its political institutions and economic policies—the presented model would become suspect.

Yet another claim has been that *in contexts featuring political discontinuities public and private opinion are often out of step* (Chapters 6, 15, 17). This claim can be refuted directly by contrasting the results of opinion surveys that differ in the anonymity they give respondents. And it can be refuted indirectly through techniques like the parking space test and the pen experiment. American policies concerning race relations have taken some sharp turns in the past, and the future will probably bring further discontinuities. If surveys reveal, contrary to indications provided in foregoing chapters, a persistent consistency between public and private opinion, the theory that I have developed would need to be reformulated.

One of the proposed links between private and public variables is that *public discourse helps shape private knowledge and private preferences* (Chapters 10–11). Specifically, private understandings and wants evolve differently in societies that differ in terms of public discourse. Indians who grow up in rural India will develop different worldviews than ones raised, say, in urban France. Such a prediction can be tested through any number of techniques that give respondents anonymity.

The very possibility of *preference falsification promotes efforts to encourage truthful expression and counterefforts to foster untruthfulness* (Chapters 3, 5). In the United States, for instance, the currently fashionable campus agendas include efforts to silence "politically incorrect" speech; and the opponents of these agendas have formed organizations that provide assistance to students and faculty accused of speech crimes. If campaigns concerning preference falsification were to lose prominence, then the empirical significance of my argument would come into question. There would be reason to suspect that preference falsification is not as great a social force as I have suggested.

Finally, the entire argument is based on the notion that *people derive utility from truthful expression, though in varying degrees that can differ across contexts* (Chapter 2). If variations in expressive need are indeed significant, persecuted dissenters will include people who, by dissenting, incur great material costs. If instead dissenters come primarily from among people who have little to lose from turning against the status quo, the model would have to be reconsidered. Expectational differences are an alternative, of course, to differences in expressive need. Dissenters could be people who tend to expect, for whatever reason, that public opinion is about to turn. Fortunately, one can test the relative significance of expectations and expressive need. If expectational differences are important, dissidents will prove more successful at predicting revolutions than nondissidents. The argument developed here suggests that revolutions will surprise dissidents along with everyone else.

Living a Lie: The Future

The history of every society offers opportunities for testing the foregoing propositions. Unfolding events will doubtless present diverse additional opportunities. Especially if sustained efforts are made to collect refined data, there should be no shortage of cases loaded with lessons on the dynamics and consequences of preference falsification. Further studies would allow the theory of this book to be enhanced and extended.

There is no way to foresee all the ways in which future instances of preference falsification will make a difference. But one can identify broad areas of ongoing human conflict where the phenomenon will probably continue to play a large role. Throughout the world, nationalist, irredentist, and tribalist movements are pressuring individuals to assert differentiating identities. In so doing, they are raising fears, hostilities, and countermovements among threatened groups. Religious fundamentalisms are pursuing analogous goals with similar effects, invariably in reaction to real or imagined secular threats to religious freedom. Another huge battleground involves gender roles and family structure. Various participants in conflict over these issues, from militant feminists to cultural conservatives, are striving to make it imprudent to defend ideas or behaviors to which they object. Economic distribution constitutes yet another issue for which preference falsification is a major factor. On matters ranging from land reform to social security, pressures exist to make people misrepresent their dispositions. Finally, especially in economically underdeveloped regions, struggles over development strategy are generating heavy social pressures to limit public discourse.

In each of these areas and many others, future patterns of preference falsification will have enduring legacies. They will foster political stability, accentuate social trends, create winners and losers, and shape the evolution of human knowledge.

Notes

Index

Notes

1. The Significance of Preference Falsification

1. Some of the relevant factors are weighed by Sissela Bok, *Lying: Moral Choice in Public and Private Life* (New York: Pantheon, 1978), especially chap. 16; and Bok, *Secrets: On the Ethics of Concealment and Revelation* (New York: Pantheon, 1983).

2. Cecil Roth, *A History of the Marranos*, 4th ed. (New York: Hermon Press, 1974), chaps. 1–2. See also Perez Zagorin, *Ways of Lying: Dissimulation, Persecution, and Conformity in Early Modern Europe* (Cambridge, Mass.: Harvard University Press, 1990), chap. 3.

3. Zagorin, *Ways of Lying*, chap. 7. Quotations at pp. 137–138.

4. Nikki Keddie, "Symbol and Sincerity in Islam," *Studia Islamica*, 19 (1963): 27–63, especially pp. 51–52.

5. Gustave E. von Grunebaum, *Medieval Islam: A Study in Cultural Orientation*, 2nd ed. (Chicago: University of Chicago Press, 1953), pp. 191, 354.

6. See, for example, 'Allamah Sayyid Muhammed Husayn Tabataba'i, *Shi'ite Islam*, trans. and ed. Seyyed Hossein Nasr (Albany, N.Y.: SUNY Press, 1975), pp. 223–225. For general commentary on modern trends, see Hamid Enayat, *Modern Islamic Political Thought* (Austin: University of Texas Press, 1982), pp. 175–181; and Abdulaziz A. Sachedina, "Activist Shi'ism in Iran, Iraq, and Lebanon," in *Fundamentalisms Observed*, ed. Martin E. Marty and R. Scott Appleby (Chicago: University of Chicago Press, 1991), pp. 403–456, especially pp. 433–437.

7. Mohammed Heikal, *Iran: The Untold Story* (New York: Pantheon, 1982; British ed., 1981), p. 86.

8. Bernard Lewis, *The Emergence of Modern Turkey*, 2nd ed. (London: Oxford University Press, 1968), pp. 401–424; and Binnaz Toprak, *Islam and Political Development in Turkey* (Leiden: E. J. Brill, 1981), chaps. 1–2.

9. *Economist*, July 27, 1991, p. 21; and Randy Shilts, "The Nasty Business of 'Outing,'" *Los Angeles Times*, August 7, 1991, p. B11. For accounts of the episodes by a homosexual activist, see Michelangelo Signorile, *Queer in America: Sex, the Media, and the Closets of Power* (New York: Random House, 1993), chaps. 5–7.

10. The distinction was made by John Scagliotti, a gay activist, in an interview with Alexander Cockburn, incorporated into the latter's "False Fronts Can't Always Be Left Standing," *Los Angeles Times*, August 8, 1991, p. B11.

11. For a defense of the intermediate position, see Mark Blasius, "An Ethos of Lesbian and Gay Existence," *Political Theory*, 20 (November 1992): 642–671. Various facets of the controversy are discussed by Larry Gross, *Contested Closets: The Politics and Ethics of Outing* (Minneapolis: University of Minnesota Press, 1993).

12. Richard A. Posner, *Sex and Reason* (Cambridge, Mass.: Harvard University Press, 1992), pp. 291–309. See also Edward O. Laumann, John H. Gagnon, Robert T. Michael, and Stuart Michaels, *The Social Organization of Sexuality: Sexual Practices in the United States* (Chicago: University of Chicago Press, 1994), especially pp. 287–290.

13. Priscilla Painton, "The Shrinking Ten Percent," *Time*, April 26, 1993, pp. 27–29.

14. Betty Cuniberti, "The Fine Art of the D.C. Newsleak," *Los Angeles Times*, August 9, 1987, pt. 6, pp. 1, 10–11.

15. Stephen Hess, *The Government/Press Connection: Press Officers and Their Offices* (Washington, D.C.: Brookings Institution, 1984), pp. 78–81. Hess's seventh chapter is devoted entirely to "leaks and other informal communications."

16. David A. Gergen, "Secrecy Means Big Things Get Little Thought," *Los Angeles Times*, November 27, 1986, pt. 2, p. 7.

17. Niccolò Machiavelli, *The Prince*, trans. and ed. Thomas G. Bergin (Northbrook, Ill.: AHM Publishing, 1947; orig. Italian ed., 1532).

18. Dilip Hiro, *Iran under the Ayatollahs* (London: Routledge & Kegan Paul, 1985), p. 108.

19. William B. Quandt, *Camp David: Peacemaking and Politics* (Washington, D.C.: Brookings Institution, 1986), especially p. 219.

20. In most contexts, a related consideration would be that social outcomes can change more rapidly than the personal characteristics that support individual decisions. If the early steps of an investigation require treating something as fixed, better that it be what is in fact relatively stable. See Ekkehart Schlicht, *Isolation and Aggregation in Economics* (Berlin: Springer-Verlag, 1985), especially chap. 2.

2. Private and Public Preferences

1. The point is developed by James M. Buchanan and Gordon Tullock, *The Calculus of Consent: Logical Foundations of Constitutional Democracy* (Ann Arbor: University of Michigan Press, 1962), pt. 2.

2. Amartya Sen, "The Impossibility of a Paretian Liberal," *Journal of Political Economy*, 78 (January/February 1970): 152–157; and Sen, "Liberty, Unanimity, and Rights," *Economica*, 43 (August 1976): 217–245. See also James M. Buchanan, "Politics and Meddlesome Preferences," in *Smoking and Society: Toward a More Balanced Assessment*, ed. Robert D. Tollison (Lexington, Mass.: Lexington Books, 1985), pp. 335–342.

3. Hannah Arendt, *The Human Condition* (Chicago: University of Chicago Press, 1958), especially pt. 2.

4. Jerome H. Barkow, Leda Cosmides, and John Tooby, eds., *The Adapted Mind: Evolutionary Psychology and the Generation of Culture* (New York: Oxford University Press, 1992), especially pts. 1–3, 8.

5. Jerome H. Barkow, "Beneath New Culture Is Old Psychology: Gossip and Social Stratification," in Barkow, Cosmides, and Tooby, *Adapted Mind*, pp. 627–637.

6. F. A. Hayek, *The Fatal Conceit: The Errors of Socialism* (Chicago: University of Chicago Press, 1989; orig. pub., 1988); and James M. Buchanan, *The Economics and the Ethics of Constitutional Order* (Ann Arbor: University of Michigan Press, 1991).

7. Barkow, "Beneath New Culture Is Old Psychology."

8. Erving Goffman, *The Presentation of Self in Everyday Life* (Woodstock, N.Y.: Overlook Press, 1973; orig. ed., 1959).

9. Forerunners of this research include Gabriel Tarde, *The Laws of Imitation*, trans. Elsie C. Parsons (New York: Henry Holt, 1903; first French ed., 1890); and Gustave Le Bon, *The Crowd: A Study of the Popular Mind* (Atlanta: Cherokee Publishing Co., 1982; first French ed., 1895). For a critical survey of the entire literature, see Serge Moscovici, "Social Influence and Conformity," in *The Handbook of Social Psychology*, 3rd ed., vol. 2, ed. Gardner Lindzey and Elliot Aronson (New York: Random House, 1985), pp. 347–412.

10. The most prominent of these early studies is Muzafer Sherif, "A Study of Some Social Factors in Perception," *Archives of Psychology*, 27, no. 187 (1935).

11. Solomon E. Asch, "Effects of Group Pressure upon the Modification and Distortion of Judgments," in *Groups, Leadership, and Men*, ed. Harold Guetzkow (New York: Russell and Russell, 1963; first ed., 1951),

pp. 177–190. Further details may be found in Asch, "Studies of Independence and Conformity: I. A Minority of One against a Unanimous Majority," *Psychological Monographs*, 70, no. 416 (1956).

12. Morton Deutsch and Harold B. Gerard, "A Study of Normative and Informational Social Influences upon Individual Judgment," *Journal of Abnormal and Social Psychology*, 51 (November 1955): 629–636.

13. Lee Ross, Günter Bierbrauer, and Susan Hoffman, "The Role of Attribution Processes in Conformity and Dissent: Revisiting the Asch Situation," *American Psychologist*, 31 (February 1976): 148–157.

14. James E. Dittes and Harold H. Kelley, "Effects of Different Conditions of Acceptance upon Conformity to Group Norms," *Journal of Abnormal and Social Psychology*, 53 (July 1956): 100–107; Michael Argyle, "Social Pressure in Public and Private Situations," *Journal of Abnormal and Social Psychology*, 54 (March 1957): 172–175; and Bertram H. Raven, "Social Influence on Opinions and the Communication of Related Content," *Journal of Abnormal and Social Psychology*, 58 (January 1959): 119–128.

15. Jerry B. Harvey, *The Abilene Paradox and Other Meditations in Management* (Lexington, Mass.: Lexington Books, 1988), chap. 7.

16. Stanley Milgram, *Obedience to Authority: An Experimental View* (New York: Harper & Row, 1974), chaps. 2–3. The experiment was carried out in 1960–1963.

17. Ibid., pp. 32–43, 59–62.

18. Richard I. Borden, "Audience Influence," in *Psychology of Group Influence*, ed. Paul B. Paulus (Hillsdale, N.J.: Lawrence Erlbaum, 1980), pp. 99–131.

19. Kurt W. Back and Morton D. Bogdanoff, "Plasma Lipid Responses to Leadership, Conformity, and Deviation," in *Psychobiological Approaches to Social Behavior*, ed. P. Herbert Leiderman and David Shapiro (Stanford: Stanford University Press, 1964), pp. 24–42.

20. This argument is analogous to the observation, put forth by Anthony Downs, *An Economic Theory of Democracy* (New York: Harper & Row, 1957), that one vote is unlikely to change the outcome in a national election. Downs goes on to suggest that voters have little incentive to vote. Putting aside the paradox that people do nonetheless vote, I would point out that while national elections are held infrequently, in between elections individuals routinely respond to social pressures to express preferences on a wide variety of matters.

21. Asch, "Effects of Group Pressure," pp. 185–187.

22. Milgram, *Obedience to Authority*, pp. 116–121.

23. Ronald Friend, Yvonne Rafferty, and Dana Bramel, "A Puzzling

Misinterpretation of the Asch 'Conformity' Study," *European Journal of Social Psychology,* 20 (January–February 1990): 29–44.

24. Jon Elster, *Sour Grapes: Studies in the Subversion of Rationality* (Cambridge: Cambridge University Press, 1983), p. 67.

25. Sigmund Freud, *The Ego and the Id,* trans. James Strachey (New York: W. W. Norton, 1961; first German ed., 1923); Gordon W. Allport, *Personality: A Psychological Interpretation* (New York: Henry Holt, 1937); Erich Fromm, *Man for Himself: An Inquiry into the Psychology of Ethics* (New York: Fawcett Premier, 1975; first ed., 1947); and Abraham H. Maslow, *Motivation and Personality,* 3rd ed. (New York: Harper & Row, 1987; first ed., 1954), especially chaps. 11–13.

26. Sigmund Freud, *Civilization and Its Discontents,* trans. James Strachey (New York: W. W. Norton, 1961; first German ed., 1930).

27. For much evidence, see Karen Horney, *Neurosis and Human Growth: The Struggle toward Self-Realization* (New York: W. W. Norton, 1950).

28. Richard Totman, *Social Causes of Illness* (New York: Pantheon, 1979).

29. See, for instance, Yaşar Kemal, *Memed My Hawk,* trans. Edouard Roditi (New York: Pantheon, 1961; orig. Turkish ed., 1955).

30. For two statements to this effect, one by an economist and the other by a sociologist, see Gary Becker, *The Economic Approach to Human Behavior* (Chicago: University of Chicago Press, 1976), especially pt. 1; and John F. Scott, *Internalization of Norms: A Sociological Theory of Moral Commitment* (Englewood Cliffs, N.J.: Prentice-Hall, 1971), especially pp. 35–38. I was led to the latter reference by Barrington Moore, Jr., *Injustice: The Social Bases of Obedience and Revolt* (White Plains, N.Y.: M. E. Sharpe, 1978), p. 102. On pp. 89–108 of his book, Moore provides a lucid analysis of "moral autonomy," a concept related to what I have identified as self-assertion. His analysis complements the present discussion.

31. For elaboration on this point, see James Q. Wilson, *The Moral Sense* (New York: Free Press, 1993), especially chaps. 1, 10.

32. H. G. Creel, *Confucius and the Chinese Way* (New York: Harper Torchbooks, 1960; orig. ed., 1949), p. 130.

33. To record this algebraically, let U represent total utility, and I, R, and E its three components. In terms of this notation, $U = I + R + E$. The first component, intrinsic utility, depends on society's decision, d. In turn, society's decision is a function of the individual's own public preference, y, and of those of all other individuals, $y-$. Thus, $I = I(d)$, where $d = d(y, y-)$. The second component of total utility, reputational utility,

depends simply on the individual's choice of a public preference: $R = R(y)$. Finally, expressive utility depends on the discrepancy between the individual's private and public preferences: $E = E(x, y)$.

34. R could have discontinuities and multiple modes, which is likely in the presence of multiple pressure groups. These possibilities receive attention in later chapters.

35. Robert H. Frank, *Passions within Reason: The Strategic Role of the Emotions* (New York: W. W. Norton, 1988).

36. Goffman, *Presentation of Self.* See also Robert J. Edelmann, *The Psychology of Embarrassment* (Chichester, U.K.: John Wiley, 1987).

37. Maureen Dowd, "Masters of the Sound Bite Cede Match to Gorbachev," *New York Times,* June 2, 1990, p. 5.

38. Fred E. Karch, "Blushing," *Psychoanalytic Review,* 58 (Spring 1971): 37–50. See also Edelmann, *The Psychology of Embarrassment,* especially chaps. 4, 6; and Gershen Kaufman, *The Psychology of Shame: Theory and Treatment of Shame-Based Syndromes* (New York: Springer Publishing Co., 1989), pt. 1.

39. *Economist,* December 23, 1989, p. 55.

40. Cited by Perez Zagorin, *Ways of Lying: Dissimulation, Persecution, and Conformity in Early Modern Europe* (Cambridge, Mass.: Harvard University Press, 1990), p. 8.

41. Herbert A. Simon, "Rational Choice and the Structure of the Environment," *Psychological Review,* 63 (March 1956): 129–138; and Simon, *Reason in Human Affairs* (Stanford: Stanford University Press, 1983).

42. An illuminating critique of the concept is provided by G. Peter Penz, *Consumer Sovereignty and Human Interests* (Cambridge: Cambridge University Press, 1986). The notion that decision makers are sovereign underlies the principle of "revealed preference," which many researchers use to deduce individual private preferences from individual actions. In contexts where reputational utility is significant, individual actions "reveal" the combined impact of several factors. And the reputational advantages of preference falsification may well swamp the benefits of making one's private preference public.

43. Harvey Leibenstein, "Bandwagon, Snob, and Veblen Effects in the Theory of Consumers' Demand," *Quarterly Journal of Economics,* 64 (May 1950): 183–207; and Robert H. Frank, *Choosing the Right Pond: Human Behavior and the Quest for Status* (New York: Oxford University Press, 1985).

44. Albert O. Hirschman, *Exit, Voice, and Loyalty: Responses to De-*

cline in Firms, Organizations, and States (Cambridge, Mass.: Harvard University Press, 1970).

45. Plato, *The Republic,* trans. Francis M. Cornford (New York: Oxford University Press, 1945; first Greek ed., 4th c. B.C.E.), chap. 13.

46. Adam Smith, *A Theory of Moral Sentiments* (Oxford: Clarendon Press, 1976; first ed., 1759), especially pt. 3, chap. 3. Modern treatments of Smith's two-way decomposition are offered by Howard Margolis, *Selfishness, Altruism, and Rationality* (Cambridge: Cambridge University Press, 1982); and Geoffrey Brennan and Loren Lomasky, "The Impartial Spectator Goes to Washington: Toward a Smithian Theory of Electoral Behavior," *Economics and Philosophy,* 1 (October 1985): 189–211.

47. Immanuel Kant, *Groundwork of the Metaphysic of Morals,* trans. H. J. Paton as *The Moral Law* (New York: Barnes and Noble, 1950; first German ed., 1785), especially chap. 2.

48. Sigmund Freud, *Beyond the Pleasure Principle,* trans. James Strachey (New York: W. W. Norton, 1961; first German ed., 1922). The id, wholly unconscious, embodies the individual's selfish impulses. The ego, wholly conscious, is his instrument of learning and adaptation. The partly subconscious superego constitutes his conscience.

49. Jon Elster, *Ulysses and the Sirens: Studies in Rationality and Irrationality* (Cambridge: Cambridge University Press, 1979); and Thomas Schelling, *Choice and Consequence: The Perspectives of an Errant Economist* (Cambridge, Mass.: Harvard University Press, 1984), especially essays 2–4.

50. Stuart Hampshire, *Morality and Conflict* (Cambridge, Mass.: Harvard University Press, 1983).

51. As quoted by Marshall G. S. Hodgson, *The Venture of Islam: Conscience and History in a World Civilization,* vol. 1: *The Classical Age of Islam* (Chicago: University of Chicago Press, 1974), p. 401.

3. Private Opinion, Public Opinion

1. The term comes from Stephen Hilgartner and Charles L. Bosk, "The Rise and Fall of Social Problems: A Public Arenas Model," *American Journal of Sociology,* 94 (July 1988): 53–78. This article contains many useful insights on the evolution of political agendas.

2. Giovanni Sartori, *Democratic Theory* (Detroit: Wayne State University Press, 1962; Italian ed., 1958), pp. 252–257. Political activity can also diminish the incentive to produce.

3. Edward G. Carmines and James A. Stimson, *Issue Evolution: Race*

and the Transformation of American Politics (Princeton: Princeton University Press, 1989), p. 5.

4. Norbert Elias, *The Civilizing Process*, vol. 1: *The History of Manners* and vol. 2: *Power and Civility*, trans. Edmund Jephcott (New York: Pantheon, 1982; German ed., 1939).

5. John Zaller and Stanley Feldman, "A Simple Theory of the Survey Response: Questions versus Revealing Preferences," *American Journal of Political Science*, 36 (August 1992): 579–616.

6. Mancur Olson, *The Logic of Collective Action: Public Goods and the Theory of Groups* (Cambridge, Mass.: Harvard University Press, 1965).

7. George J. Stigler, "Free Riders and Collective Action: An Appendix to Theories of Economic Regulation," *Bell Journal of Economic and Management Science*, 5 (Autumn 1974): 359–365.

8. For additional explanations and informed critiques of the entire literature, see Russell Hardin, *Collective Action* (Baltimore: Johns Hopkins University Press, 1982); Todd Sandler, *Collective Action: Theory and Applications* (Ann Arbor: University of Michigan Press, 1992); and Mark I. Lichbach, *The Cooperator's Dilemma* (Ann Arbor: University of Michigan Press, 1995).

9. Gerald Marwell and Ruth E. Ames, "Economists Free Ride, Does Anyone Else?: Experiments on the Provision of Public Goods, IV," *Journal of Public Economics*, 15 (June 1981): 295–310; and Robyn M. Dawes, "Social Dilemmas, Economic Self-Interest, and Evolutionary Theory," in *Frontiers of Mathematical Psychology: Essays in Honor of Clyde Coombs*, ed. Donald R. Brown and J. E. Keith Smith (New York: Springer Verlag, 1991): 53–79. For insightful interpretations of such experiments, see Robert H. Frank, *Passions within Reason: The Strategic Role of the Emotions* (New York: W. W. Norton, 1988); and James Q. Wilson, *The Moral Sense* (New York: Free Press, 1993).

10. R. Mark Isaac, Kenneth F. McCue, and Charles R. Plott, "Public Goods Provision in an Experimental Environment," *Journal of Public Economics*, 26 (February 1985): 51–74; and R. Mark Isaac and James M. Walker, "Communication and Free-Riding Behavior: The Voluntary Contribution Mechanism," *Economic Inquiry*, 26 (October 1988): 585–608.

11. Steven E. Finkel, Edward N. Muller, and Karl-Dieter Opp, "Personal Influence, Collective Rationality, and Mass Political Action," *American Political Science Review*, 83 (September 1989): 885–903.

12. For an attempt at solving this puzzle, see Albert O. Hirschman,

Shifting Involvements: Private Interest and Public Action (Princeton: Princeton University Press, 1982).

13. Finkel, Muller, and Opp, "Personal Influence."

14. W. Russell Neuman, *The Paradox of Mass Politics: Knowledge and Opinion in the American Electorate* (Cambridge, Mass.: Harvard University Press, 1986).

15. James Madison, "The Federalist no. 10" (1787), in *The Federalist,* ed. Jacob E. Cooke (Middletown, Conn.: Wesleyan University Press, 1961), p. 57.

16. Laurence H. Tribe, *Abortion: The Clash of Absolutes* (New York: W. W. Norton, 1990).

17. The last point and some others are developed by Bernard Manin, "On Legitimacy and Political Deliberation," trans. Elly Stein and Jane Mansbridge, *Political Theory,* 15 (August 1987): 355–357 (French ed., 1985). Additional insights are offered by Michael Hechter, *Principles of Group Solidarity* (Berkeley: University of California Press, 1987).

18. David B. Truman, *The Governmental Process: Political Interests and Public Opinion,* 2nd ed. (New York: Alfred A. Knopf, 1971), especially pt. 1.

19. Niccolò Machiavelli, *The Prince,* trans. and ed. Thomas G. Bergin (Northbrook, Ill.: AHM Publishing, 1947; orig. Italian ed., 1532), chap. 19.

20. David Hume, *A Treatise of Human Nature,* ed. L. A. Selby-Bigge (Oxford: Clarendon Press, 1896; orig. ed., 1739/1740), p. 39.

21. The term *mass opinion* may be used to convey the generic concept.

22. Elisabeth Noelle-Neumann, *The Spiral of Silence: Public Opinion—Our Social Skin* (Chicago: University of Chicago Press, 1984; German ed., 1980), p. 97.

23. Gustave Le Bon, *The Crowd: A Study of the Popular Mind* (Atlanta: Cherokee Publishing Co., 1982; first French ed., 1895).

24. For two critical surveys of the history of this idea, see Serge Moscovici, *The Age of the Crowd: A Historical Treatise on Mass Psychology,* trans. J. C. Whitehouse (Cambridge: Cambridge University Press, 1985; French ed., 1981); and J. S. McClelland, *The Crowd and the Mob: From Plato to Canetti* (London: Unwin Hyman, 1989).

25. In formal terms, $\max [R(0), R(100)] > E(x, x)$ for each nonactivist.

26. For a presentation that admits such differences, see Timur Kuran, "Sparks and Prairie Fires: A Theory of Unanticipated Political Revolution," *Public Choice,* 61 (April 1989): 41–74.

27. There are several variants of this principle. For an influential one, see William H. Riker, _The Theory of Political Coalitions_ (New Haven: Yale University Press, 1962).

4. The Dynamics of Public Opinion

1. Pamela Oliver, "Rewards and Punishments as Selective Incentives for Collective Action: Theoretical Investigations," _American Journal of Sociology,_ 85 (May 1980): 1356–1375.

2. I have borrowed the idea of putting transformations of the standard maxim to pedagogical use from Robert Sugden, "Review of _The Economics of Conformism_ by Stephen R. G. Jones," _Economic Journal,_ 95 (June 1985): 502–504.

3. Perez Zagorin, _Ways of Lying: Dissimulation, Persecution, and Conformity in Early Modern Europe_ (Cambridge, Mass.: Harvard University Press, 1990), p. 42.

4. Intracommunal compliance efforts are explored more fully by Douglas Heckathorn, "Collective Sanctions and Compliance Norms: A Formal Theory of Group-Mediated Social Control," _American Sociological Review,_ 55 (June 1990): 366–384.

5. Another reason why the initially weaker group may gain dominance over the initially stronger rival is that it might be motivated to invest more in the competition. See Jack Hirshleifer, "The Paradox of Power," _Economics and Politics,_ 3 (November 1991): 177–200.

6. For an N-person society whose members are indexed by i, the propagation curve satisfies the equation

$$T(Y) = \left(\frac{100}{N}\right)\sum_{i=1}^{N} \underline{t}^{i},$$

where $\underline{t}^{i}$ is 1 if $t^{i} \leq Y$ and 0 if $t^{i} > Y$.

7. Formally, public opinion is given by $Y = T(Y^{e})$. It is in equilibrium when $Y = Y^{e}$.

8. Alexis de Tocqueville, _Democracy in America,_ vol. 1, ed. Henry Reeve, Francis Bowen, and Phillips Bradley (New York: Alfred A. Knopf, 1989; orig. French ed., 1835), p. 263 (emphasis added).

9. My depiction of instability bears the influence of Alfred Marshall's classic description, although his metaphor was different. See his _Principles of Economics: An Introductory Volume,_ 8th ed. (London: Macmillan, 1936), pp. 806–807.

10. Timothy J. Kehoe, "Multiplicity of Equilibria and Comparative

Statics," *Quarterly Journal of Economics,* 100 (February 1985): 119–147.

11. For more on why economists have tended to shun the study of multiple equilibria, see W. Brian Arthur, "Positive Feedbacks in the Economy," *Scientific American,* 262 (February 1990): 92–99.

12. The bandwagon phenomenon has received attention under various other terms, including snowballing, the domino effect, the herd effect, critical mass, and tipping. A superb introduction is provided by Thomas C. Schelling, *Micromotives and Macrobehavior* (New York: Norton, 1978), especially chap. 4. Other important contributions include: Mark Granovetter, "Threshold Models of Collective Behavior," *American Journal of Sociology,* 83 (May 1978): 1420–1443; Stephen R. G. Jones, *The Economics of Conformism* (New York: Basil Blackwell, 1984); Paul David, "Some New Standards for the Economics of Standardization in the Information Age," in *Economic Policy and Technological Performance,* ed. Partha Dasgupta and Paul Stoneman (Cambridge: Cambridge University Press, 1987), pp. 206–239; W. Brian Arthur, "Self-Reinforcing Mechanisms in Economics," in *The Economy as an Evolving Complex System,* ed. Philip W. Anderson, Kenneth J. Arrow, and David Pines (Redwood City, Calif.: Addison-Wesley, 1988), pp. 9–31; Ulrich Witt, "The Evolution of Economic Institutions as a Propagation Process," *Public Choice,* 62 (August 1989): 155–172; James S. Coleman, *Foundations of Social Theory* (Cambridge, Mass.: Harvard University Press, 1990), chap. 9; and Sushil Bikchandani, David Hirshleifer, and Ivo Welsh, "A Theory of Fads, Fashion, Custom, and Cultural Change as Informational Cascades," *Journal of Political Economy,* 100 (October 1992): 992–1026. The model under consideration here appeared in its earliest form in Timur Kuran, "Chameleon Voters and Public Choice," *Public Choice,* 53 (1987): 53–78.

13. Pamela Oliver, Gerald Marwell, and Ruy Teixeira, "A Theory of Critical Mass. I. Interdependence, Group Heterogeneity, and the Production of Collective Action," *American Journal of Sociology,* 91 (November 1985): 522–556.

14. V. S. Naipaul, *India: A Wounded Civilization* (New York: Vintage Books, 1978; orig. ed., 1977), p. 146.

15. Catherine Marsh, "Back on the Bandwagon: The Effect of Opinion Polls on Public Opinion," *British Journal of Political Science,* 15 (January 1984): 51–74.

16. The term is drawn from W. Brian Arthur, "Competing Technologies, Increasing Returns, and Lock-In by Historical Events," *Economic Journal,* 99 (March 1989): 119.

17. See Amos Tversky and Daniel Kahneman, "Judgment under Uncertainty: Heuristics and Biases," *Science,* 185 (September 1974): 1124–1131; and Richard Nisbett and Lee Ross, *Human Inference: Strategies and Shortcomings of Social Judgment* (Englewood Cliffs, N.J.: Prentice-Hall, 1980), pp. 24–28, 115–122.

18. Another heuristic, the "availability heuristic" that will be introduced in Chapter 10, sometimes works at cross-purposes with the representativeness heuristic. An event that is "small" for most observers may receive inordinate attention from an observer for whom the event happens to be salient and, hence, "available." A reporter trying to explain the decline of an automobile company may ascribe greater significance to one bad personal experience with the automobile than to a consumer report based on a huge sample.

19. Michael Wheeler, *Lies, Damn Lies, and Statistics: The Manipulation of Public Opinion in America* (New York: Liveright, 1976); Robert B. Cialdini, *Influence: How and Why People Agree to Things* (New York: William Morrow, 1984); Benjamin Ginsberg, *The Captive Public: How Mass Opinion Promotes State Power* (New York: Basic Books, 1986), especially chap. 3; and George F. Bishop, "Manipulation and Control of People's Responses to Public Opinion Polls: An Orwellian Experiment in 1984," in *The Orwellian Moment: Hindsight and Foresight in the Post-1984 World,* ed. Robert L. Savage, James Combs, and Dan Nimmo (Fayetteville: University of Arkansas Press, 1989), pp. 119–129.

20. Eugene Borgida and Richard E. Nisbett, "The Differential Impact of Abstract vs. Concrete Information on Decisions," *Journal of Applied Social Psychology,* 7 (July–September 1977): 258–271. For other relevant experiments, see Daniel Kahneman and Amos Tversky, "Subjective Probability: A Judgment of Representativeness," *Cognitive Psychology,* 3 (July 1972): 430–454.

21. See Nisbett and Ross, *Human Inference,* chap. 4.

22. Under the term "impression of universality," the concept was introduced by Floyd Henry Allport, *Social Psychology* (Boston: Houghton Mifflin, 1924), pp. 305–309. The term "pluralistic ignorance" was first used by Richard Louis Schanck, "A Study of a Community and Its Groups and Institutions Conceived of as Behavior of Individuals," *Psychological Monographs,* 43-2 (1932): 101.

23. Hubert J. O'Gorman, "Pluralistic Ignorance and White Estimates of White Support for Racial Segregation," *Public Opinion Quarterly,* 39 (Fall 1975): 313–330. See also Hubert J. O'Gorman with Stephen L. Garry, "Pluralistic Ignorance—A Replication and Extension," *Public Opinion Quarterly,* 40 (Winter 1976–77): 449–458.

24. Gunnar Myrdal, *Against the Stream: Critical Essays on Economics* (New York: Pantheon, 1973), p. 303.

25. Detlev J. K. Peukert, *Inside Nazi Germany: Conformity, Opposition, and Racism in Everyday Life*, trans. Richard Deveson (New Haven: Yale University Press, 1987; German ed., 1982), p. 239.

26. Bella M. DePaulo, Miron Zuckerman, and Robert Rosenthal, "Humans as Lie Detectors," *Journal of Communication*, 30 (Spring 1980): 129–139; and Zuckerman, DePaulo, and Rosenthal, "Verbal and Nonverbal Communication of Deception," in *Advances in Experimental Social Psychology*, vol. 14, ed. Leonard Berkowitz (New York: Academic Press, 1981), pp. 1–59. For an interpretation of the evidence, see Robert H. Frank, *Passions within Reason: The Strategic Role of the Emotions* (New York: W. W. Norton, 1988), chap. 7.

27. Arthur G. Miller, Barry Gillen, Charles Schenker, and Shirley Radlove, "Perception of Obedience to Authority," *Proceedings of the 81st Annual Convention of the American Psychological Association*, 8, pt. 1 (1973): 127–128.

28. This experiment, conducted in the early 1970s by Günter Bierbrauer, is described by Nisbett and Ross, *Human Inference*, pp. 121–122.

29. Lee Ross, "The Intuitive Psychologist and His Shortcomings," in *Advances in Experimental Social Psychology*, vol. 10, ed. Leonard Berkowitz (New York: Academic Press, 1977), pp. 173–220. For a survey of the pertinent research, see Michael Ross and Garth O. Fletcher, "Attribution and Social Perception," in *The Handbook of Social Psychology*, 3rd ed., vol. 2, ed. Gardner Lindzey and Elliott Aronson (New York: Random House, 1985), pp. 73–122.

30. For an influential statement of this principle, see Harold H. Kelley, "Attribution Theory in Social Psychology," in *Nebraska Symposium on Motivation*, ed. David Levine (Lincoln: University of Nebraska Press, 1967), pp. 192–238. Kelley's theory is discussed in detail by Ross and Fletcher, "Attribution and Social Perception." The foundations for Kelley's theory were laid by Fritz Heider, *The Psychology of Interpersonal Relations* (New York: Wiley, 1958).

5. Institutional Sources of Preference Falsification

1. For more on these common distinctions, see Giovanni Sartori, *The Theory of Democracy Revisited* (Chatham, N.J.: Chatham House Publishers, 1987), chap. 2.

2. Frank R. Strong, "Fifty Years of 'Clear and Present Danger': From Schenck to Brandenburg—and Beyond" (1969), in *Free Speech and As-*

sociation: The Supreme Court and the First Amendment, ed. Philip B. Kurland (Chicago: University of Chicago Press, 1975), pp. 302–341.

3. Samuel A. Stouffer, *Communism, Conformity, and Civil Liberties: A Cross-Section of the Nation Speaks Its Mind* (Garden City, N.Y.: Doubleday, 1955), pp. 39–46. Many other surveys offered similar results. For an overview, see Herbert McClosky and Alida Brill, *Dimensions of Tolerance: What Americans Believe about Civil Liberties* (New York: Russell Sage, 1983), pp. 74–77.

4. Clyde Z. Nunn, Harry J. Crockett, Jr., and J. Allen Williams, Jr., *Tolerance for Nonconformity* (San Francisco: Jossey-Bass, 1978), p. 43. The third chapter of this book contains much additional data. See also John Mueller, "Trends in Political Tolerance," *Public Opinion Quarterly,* 52 (Spring 1988): 1–25.

5. McClosky and Brill, *Dimensions of Tolerance,* pp. 54–56, 62–64.

6. Herbert McClosky and John Zaller, *The American Ethos: Public Attitudes toward Capitalism and Democracy* (Cambridge, Mass.: Harvard University Press, 1984), pp. 36–37.

7. McClosky and Brill, *Dimensions of Tolerance,* p. 82.

8. Nat Hentoff, *Free Speech for Me—But Not for Thee: How the American Left and Right Relentlessly Censor Each Other* (New York: HarperCollins, 1992).

9. For commentary on the feminist drive against pornography, see Donald Alexander Downs, *The New Politics of Pornography* (Chicago: University of Chicago Press, 1989); and Ronald Dworkin, "Two Concepts of Liberty," in *Isaiah Berlin: A Celebration,* ed. Edna and Avishai Margalit (Chicago: University of Chicago Press, 1991), pp. 100–109.

10. Alexis de Tocqueville, *Democracy in America,* ed. Henry Reeve, Francis Bowen, and Phillips Bradley, 2 vols. (New York: Alfred A. Knopf, 1989; first French ed., 1835), especially vol. 1, pp. 254–270, and vol. 2, pp. 316–321.

11. John Stuart Mill, *On Liberty* (Indianapolis: Hackett Publishing Co., 1978; orig. ed., 1859), especially chap. 4.

12. Douglas Maurice MacDowell, *The Oxford Classical Dictionary,* 2nd ed., ed. N. G. L. Hammond and H. H. Scullard (Oxford: Clarendon Press, 1970), pp. 762–763; and M. I. Finley, *Politics in the Ancient World* (Cambridge: Cambridge University Press, 1983), pp. 53–55.

13. Paul L. Montgomery, "French Students Teach Chirac on the Streets," *Los Angeles Times,* December 14, 1986, p. V-2.

14. Maura Dolan, "Reagan Record on Parks Gets Mixed Marks," *Los Angeles Times,* June 21, 1988, pp. 1, 3, 19.

15. The last point is developed by Charles E. Lindblom, *Politics and*

Markets: The World's Political-Economic Systems (New York: Basic Books, 1977), chap. 9.

16. Robert A. Dahl, *A Preface to Democratic Theory* (Chicago: University of Chicago Press, 1956), p. 125.

17. The observation that electoral competition offers a limited menu of choices lies at the heart of a literature initiated by Harold Hotelling, "Stability in Competition," *Economic Journal*, 39 (March 1929): 41–57, and brought to maturity by Anthony Downs, *An Economic Theory of Democracy* (New York: Harper & Row, 1957). The theory has been refined to accommodate factors that keep the platforms of rival candidates from becoming entirely similar. See, for instance, James S. Coleman, "Internal Processes Governing Party Positions in Elections," *Public Choice*, 11 (Fall 1971): 35–60.

18. Alexis de Tocqueville, *The Old Régime and the French Revolution*, trans. Stuart Gilbert (Garden City, N.Y.: Doubleday, 1955; orig. French ed., 1856), p. xi.

19. *New York Times*, January 6, 1989, p. A13.

20. Carole Pateman, *Participation and Democratic Theory* (Cambridge: Cambridge University Press, 1970), chap. 2.

21. Even if it were closed, a sufficient number of individuals would first have to plead publicly for the vote.

22. Shaul Bakhash, "The Politics of Land, Law, and Social Justice in Iran," *Middle East Journal*, 43 (Spring 1989): 186–201.

23. Julius G. Getman, Stephen B. Goldberg, and Jeanne B. Herman, *Union Representation Elections: Law and Reality* (New York: Russell Sage, 1976), especially chap. 6.

24. John Stuart Mill, *Representative Government* (London: Longmans, Green, and Co., 1919; orig. ed., 1861), p. 81.

25. Mill, *On Liberty*, chap. 4.

26. Mill, *Representative Government*, pp. 84–85.

27. The point has also been made by Alan Ryan, "Two Concepts of Politics and Democracy: James and John Stuart Mill," in *Machiavelli and the Nature of Political Thought*, ed. Martin Fleisher (New York: Atheneum, 1972), sect. 3.

28. For an elaboration, see Preston King, *Toleration* (New York: St. Martin's Press, 1976), chap. 1.

29. José Ortega y Gasset, *The Revolt of the Masses*, trans. Anthony Kerrigan (Notre Dame, Ind.: University of Notre Dame Press, 1985; orig. Spanish ed., 1929), p. 65.

30. McClosky and Brill, *Dimensions of Tolerance*, p. 16.

31. This argument is developed and supported empirically by Dank-

wart A. Rustow, "Transitions to Democracy: Toward a Dynamic Model," *Comparative Politics*, 2 (April 1970): 337–363. An influential variant of the argument is by Bernard Crick, *In Defense of Politics*, 2nd ed. (Chicago: University of Chicago Press, 1972), especially chap. 1.

32. Perry Miller, *Errand into the Wilderness* (Cambridge, Mass.: Harvard University Press, 1956), pp. 143–144. By way of McClosky and Zaller, *The American Ethos*, p. 22.

33. For evidence in support of this interpretation, see Daniel J. Boorstin, *The Americans: The Colonial Experience* (New York: Random House, 1958), pts. 1–4.

34. James Madison, "The Federalist no. 51" (1788), in *The Federalist*, ed. Jacob E. Cooke (Middletown, Conn.: Wesleyan University Press, 1961), p. 349. The Madisonian strategy is discussed and critiqued by Dahl, *A Preface to Democratic Theory*, especially chap. 1.

35. Sartori, *The Theory of Democracy Revisited*, p. 90.

36. Hugh Roberts, "From Radical Mission to Equivocal Ambition: The Expansion and Manipulation of Algerian Islamism, 1979–1992," in *Accounting for Fundamentalisms: The Dynamic Character of Movements*, ed. Martin E. Marty and R. Scott Appleby (Chicago: University of Chicago Press, 1994), pp. 428–489.

6. Collective Conservatism

1. This theme is developed in works surveyed by Timur Kuran, "The Tenacious Past: Theories of Personal and Collective Conservatism," *Journal of Economic Behavior and Organization*, 10 (September 1988): 143–171; and Paul A. David, "Path Dependence: Putting the Past in the Future of Economics," Institute for Mathematical Studies in the Social Sciences Technical Report no. 533, Stanford University, November 1988.

2. Albert O. Hirschman, *Exit, Voice, and Loyalty: Responses to Decline in Firms, Organizations, and States* (Cambridge, Mass.: Harvard University Press, 1970).

3. Mancur Olson, *The Rise and Decline of Nations: Economic Growth, Stagflation, and Social Rigidities* (New Haven: Yale University Press, 1982).

4. The attribution of an equal likelihood to all possibilities is arbitrary, but it is reasonable in the absence of a rationale for introducing differences. Also, it has the virtue of making clear what is being assumed.

5. Formally, the measure can be defined as follows. Let Y^* denote the established equilibrium and Y^{-h} the average public opinion in the absence of memory. In terms of this notation, the role of history in the persistence

of Y^* is given as $C(Y^*) = |Y^* - Y^{-h}|/(Y^{max} - Y^{min})$, where the denominator gives the difference between the maximum and minimum possible values of mean public opinion. For two related measures, see Timur Kuran, "Preference Falsification, Policy Continuity, and Collective Conservatism," *Economic Journal,* 97 (September 1987): 642–665.

6. In mathematical terms, the evolution of public opinion forms a nonergodic process, as opposed to an ergodic one whereby every small event is annulled by later small events. See W. Brian Arthur, "Competing Technologies, Increasing Returns, and Lock-In by Historical Events," *Economic Journal,* 99 (March 1989): 116–131.

7. F. M. Cornford, *Microcosmographia Academica, Being a Guide for the Young Academic Politician,* 2nd ed. (Cambridge: Bowes & Bowes, 1922), p. 4.

8. Jerry B. Harvey, "The Abilene Paradox: The Management of Agreement," *Organizational Dynamics,* 3 (Summer 1974): 63–80.

9. Elisabeth Noelle-Neumann, *The Spiral of Silence: Public Opinion—Our Social Skin* (Chicago: University of Chicago Press, 1984; first German ed., 1980).

10. Friedrich A. Hayek, *The Constitution of Liberty* (Chicago: University of Chicago Press, 1960), pp. 395–411.

11. For an exposition of Pareto's efficiency criterion, see T. C. Koopmans, *Three Essays on the State of Economic Science* (New York: McGraw Hill, 1956), pp. 41–66.

12. For a fuller exposition, see Donald Wittman, "Why Democracies Produce Efficient Results," *Journal of Political Economy,* 97 (December 1989): 1395–1424.

13. George F. Hourani, "The Basis of Authority of Consensus in Sunnite Islam," *Studia Islamica,* 21 (1964): 13–60.

14. On the history of this proverb, see George Boas, *Vox Populi: Essays in the History of an Idea* (Baltimore: Johns Hopkins Press, 1969), chap. 1.

15. Noelle-Neumann, *Spiral of Silence,* p. 175.

7. The Obstinacy of Communism

1. For a survey of the dissident literature, see H. Gordon Skilling, *"Samizdat" and an Independent Society in Central and Eastern Europe* (Columbus: Ohio State University Press, 1989).

2. The words of Leon Trotsky, cited by Hannah Arendt, *The Origins of Totalitarianism,* 2nd ed. (New York: Meridian, 1958), p. 307.

3. Alexander Solzhenitsyn, "The Smatterers," in Solzhenitsyn et al.,

From Under the Rubble, trans. A. M. Brock et al. (Boston: Little, Brown, 1975; orig. Russian ed., 1974), p. 275.

4. Ibid., p. 276 (emphasis in original).

5. Václav Havel, "The Power of the Powerless," in Havel et al., *The Power of the Powerless: Citizens against the State in Central-Eastern Europe,* ed. John Keane, trans. Paul Wilson (Armonk, N.Y.: M. E. Sharpe, 1985; orig. Czech ed., 1979), pp. 27–28.

6. Amanda Haight, *Anna Akhmatova: A Poetic Pilgrimage* (New York: Oxford University Press, 1976), chaps. 3–4; and *Encyclopaedia Britannica,* 15th ed., vol. 1 (1987), p. 190.

7. Aleksander Wat, *My Century: The Odyssey of a Polish Intellectual,* trans. Richard Lourie (New York: W. W. Norton, 1990; orig. Polish ed., 1977), p. 101.

8. For an account of the campaign against Pasternak, see Ronald Hingley, *Pasternak: A Biography* (New York: Alfred A. Knopf, 1983), chap. 10.

9. H. Gordon Skilling, *Charter 77 and Human Rights in Czechoslovakia* (London: George Allen and Unwin, 1981). See also Timothy Garton Ash, *The Uses of Adversity: Essays on the Fate of Central Europe* (New York: Random House, 1989; orig. publ., 1983–1989), especially pp. 61–70.

10. Krzysztof Nowak, "Covert Repressiveness and the Stability of a Political System: Poland at the End of the Seventies," *Social Research,* 55 (Spring/Summer 1988): 189 (emphasis omitted).

11. Leszek Kołakowski, *Main Currents of Marxism: Its Origin, Growth, and Dissolution,* vol. 3, trans. P. S. Falla (Oxford: Clarendon Press, 1978), p. 91.

12. Jiří Ruml, "Who Really Is Isolated?" in Havel et al., *Power of the Powerless,* p. 180.

13. Jane Kramer, "Letter from Europe," *New Yorker,* May 25, 1992, p. 43.

14. Havel, "Power of the Powerless," p. 39 (emphasis in original).

15. Ibid.

16. Ibid., p. 37.

17. Timothy Garton Ash, "Eastern Europe: The Year of Truth," *New York Review of Books,* February 15, 1990, p. 18 (emphasis in original).

18. Authoritative accounts include Roy A. Medvedev, *Let History Judge: The Origins and Consequences of Stalinism,* trans. Colleen Taylor (New York: Vintage, 1973; orig. Russian ed., 1968); Robert Conquest, *The Great Terror: A Reassessment* (New York: Oxford University Press,

1990); and Zbigniew K. Brzezinski, *The Soviet Bloc: Unity and Conflict* (Cambridge, Mass.: Harvard University Press, 1960).

19. Nowak, "Covert Repressiveness," p. 193.

20. Czesław Miłosz, *The Captive Mind*, trans. Jane Zielonko (New York: Alfred A. Knopf, 1953; orig. Polish ed., 1951), p. 54.

21. Quoted by Robert Conquest, *Tyrants and Typewriters: Communiqués from the Struggle for Truth* (Lexington, Mass.: Lexington Books, 1989), p. 90.

22. Miłosz, *Captive Mind*, especially pp. 43, 61.

23. See Nowak, "Covert Repressiveness"; and Helena Flam, "Fear, Loyalty, and Greedy Corporate Actors" (unpublished paper, University of Konstanz, 1992).

24. Nowak, "Covert Repressiveness," p. 187.

25. László Bruszt, " 'Without Us but for Us'? Political Orientation in Hungary in the Period of Late Paternalism," *Social Research, 55* (Spring/Summer 1988): table 3. The figures for the Western countries are from 1978.

26. Miłosz, *Captive Mind*, p. 24.

27. Quoted in Jan Vladislav, "Encounters with History or *Une Education Sentimentale* 1938–68," in *The Prague Spring: A Mixed Legacy*, ed. Jiří Pehe (New York: Freedom House, 1988), p. 12. Poem translated by A. G. Brain.

28. Václav Havel, *Disturbing the Peace: A Conversation with Karel Hvížďala*, trans. Paul Wilson (New York: Alfred A. Knopf, 1990; orig. Czech ed., 1986), p. 138.

29. This point is developed at length by Vladimir Tismaneanu, *Reinventing Politics: Eastern Europe from Stalin to Havel* (New York: Free Press, 1992), chaps. 4–5.

8. The Ominous Perseverance of the Caste System

1. Mark Fineman, "Lynchings over Caste Stir India," *Los Angeles Times*, April 12, 1991, pp. A1, 18; and W. P. S. Sidhu, "Medieval Murders," *India Today*, April 30, 1991, pp. 122–125.

2. M. N. Srinivas, *Social Change in Modern India* (Berkeley: University of California Press, 1971); Louis Dumont, *Homo Hierarchicus: The Caste System and Its Implications*, rev. ed., trans. Mark Sainsbury, Dumont, and Basia Gulati (Chicago: University of Chicago Press, 1980, orig. French ed., 1966); and Marc Galanter, *Competing Equalities: Law and*

the Backward Classes in India (Berkeley: University of California Press, 1984).

3. J. H. Hutton, Caste in India: Its Nature, Function, and Origins, 4th ed. (Bombay: Oxford University Press, 1963), pp. 64–67, 130, and Appendix A. Estimates go as high as 30 percent.

4. Ibid., chap. 6; and Dumont, Homo Hierarchicus, chaps. 4–6.

5. Dumont, Homo Hierarchicus, especially pp. 46–49, 202–208; Hutton, Caste in India, chaps. 6–7 and Appendix A; Barrington Moore, Jr., Injustice: The Social Bases of Obedience and Revolt (White Plains, N.Y.: M. E. Sharpe, 1978), pp. 55–64; and L. S. S. O'Malley, Indian Caste Customs (Cambridge: Cambridge University Press, 1932), chap. 8.

6. O'Malley, Indian Caste Customs, p. 141.

7. Hutton, Caste in India, p. 121.

8. Imtiaz Ahmad, ed., Caste and Social Stratification among Muslims in India (New Delhi: Manohar, 1978), especially articles by M. K. A. Siddiqui and Ranjit K. Bhattacharya.

9. Deepak Lal, The Hindu Equilibrium, vol. 1: Cultural Stability and Economic Stagnation, India c. 1500 B.C.–A.D. 1980 (Oxford: Clarendon Press, 1988), chap. 3.

10. The practice is noted by O'Malley, Indian Caste Customs, p. 142.

11. Max Weber, The Religion of India: The Sociology of Hinduism and Buddhism, trans. and ed. Hans H. Gerth and Don Martindale (New York: Free Press, 1958; orig. German ed., 1916–17), p. 112. Another such argument is provided by Angus Maddison, Class Structure and Economic Growth: India and Pakistan since the Moghuls (New York: W. W. Norton, 1971), especially pp. 24–29.

12. Jawaharlal Nehru, The Discovery of India, ed. Robert I. Crane (New York: Doubleday, 1959; orig. ed., 1946), especially sect. 4.7 and chap. 5; quote, p. 126.

13. M. N. Srinivas, "The Role of Caste in India: Present and Future," Reviews in Anthropology, 7 (Fall 1980): 415–430. Also see Dumont, Homo Hierarchicus, chap. 10.

14. Hutton, Caste in India, p. 123.

15. According to Lal, Hindu Equilibrium, vol. 1, chaps. 2–3, the system originated during the Aryan invasion of India, beginning around 1500 B.C.E. The preexisting division of labor among priests, warriors, and merchants generated conflicting claims for status, which found expression in various behavioral restrictions. As the Aryans formed agricultural settlements, they faced the problem of maintaining an adequate supply of labor. In response, they enslaved their indigenous enemies and put them to work as cultivators. The shudras are the descendants of these

slaves. Eventually, the shudras were emancipated and incorporated into the nascent Aryan caste system. Untouchability arose much later as the Aryans came into contact with various aboriginal tribes. The Aryans' desire to gain full control over the land produced a sustained and often violent campaign to keep these aborigines out of Aryan society. Another thesis traces the origins of caste to an attempt on the part of the relatively successful occupational groupings to limit their ranks. See Mancur Olson, *The Rise and Decline of Nations: Economic Growth, Stagflation, and Social Rigidities* (New Haven: Yale University Press, 1982), pp. 156–161.

16. Michael Moffatt, *An Untouchable Community in South India: Structure and Consensus* (Princeton: Princeton University Press, 1979), p. 7, n. 1.

17. Hutton, *Caste in India*, chap. 7.

18. V. S. Naipaul, *India: A Wounded Civilization* (New York: Vintage Books, 1977), p. 188.

19. On the enforcement of caste etiquette, see Thomas A. Zwicker, "Morality and Etiquette in the Reproduction of Hierarchical Caste Relations in South Asia," M.A. thesis, University of Pennsylvania, 1984.

20. This argument is developed by George A. Akerlof, "The Economics of Caste and of the Rat Race and Other Woeful Tales," *Quarterly Journal of Economics*, 90 (November 1976): 599–618. Akerlof's argument was anticipated by Weber, *Religion of India*, p. 19.

21. On the operation of village assemblies, see Dumont, *Homo Hierarchicus*, chap. 8; and Hutton, *Caste in India*, chap. 7.

22. Joseph A. Schumpeter, "Social Classes in an Ethnically Homogeneous Environment," in his *Imperialism and Social Classes*, trans. Heinz Norden (New York: Augustus Kelley, 1951; orig. ed., 1927), p. 145.

23. Srinivas, *Social Change in Modern India*, pp. 100–106.

9. The Unwanted Spread of Affirmative Action

1. Michael Oreskes, "American Politics Loses Way as Polls Displace Leadership," *New York Times*, March 18, 1990, pp. A1, 22. The series continued to March 22.

2. See, for example, Richard D. Lamm, "The Politics of Sensitivities: Critical Policy Issues Fester under Fear of Offending," *Los Angeles Times*, May 28, 1988, pt. 2, p. 8; Michael Ross, "U.S. Lawmakers Toss in Towel in Frustration," *Los Angeles Times*, April 13, 1992, pp. A1, 16–17; and Timothy E. Wirth, "It's Not Enough to Throw Bums Out," *Los Angeles Times*, June 17, 1992, p. B11.

3. "Serious Times, Trivial Politics," *New York Times*, March 25, 1990, sect. 4, p. 18.

4. Shelby Steele, *The Content of Our Character: A New Vision of Race in America* (New York: St. Martin's, 1990), p. x.

5. Richard G. Niemi, John Mueller, and Tom W. Smith, *Trends in Public Opinion: A Compendium of Survey Data* (New York: Greenwood Press, 1989), chap. 8. The figures come from table 8.3. See also Howard Schuman, Charlotte Steeh, and Laurence Bobo, *Racial Attitudes in America: Trends and Interpretations* (Cambridge, Mass.: Harvard University Press, 1985), chap. 3.

6. Arlene F. Saluter, *Marital Status and Living Arrangements: March 1991* (Washington, D.C.: U.S. Government Printing Office, 1992), table E.

7. Jack Citrin, Donald Philip Green, and David O. Sears, "White Reactions to Black Candidates: When Does Race Matter?" *Public Opinion Quarterly*, 54 (Spring 1990): 74–96.

8. Lee Sigelman and Susan Welch, *Black Americans' Views of Racial Inequality: The Dream Deferred* (Cambridge: Cambridge University Press, 1991), p. 131.

9. Ibid., p. 129.

10. *Responsive Community*, 2 (Spring 1992), p. 82.

11. Andrew Hacker, *Two Nations: Black and White, Separate, Hostile, Unequal* (New York: Charles Scribner's Sons, 1992), pp. 4, passim. See also Jonathan Rieder, *Canarsie: The Jews and Italians of Brooklyn Against Liberalism* (Cambridge, Mass.: Harvard University Press, 1985), especially chaps. 3–5.

12. According to a 1986 survey by Michigan's Institute for Social Research, three out of four whites consider it "likely" or "somewhat likely" that they will be denied a position in favor of an equally or less qualified black. As reported by Dinesh D'Souza, *Illiberal Education: The Politics of Race and Sex on Campus* (New York: Free Press, 1991), p. 131.

13. Worker resentment is documented and analyzed by Frederick R. Lynch, *Invisible Victims: White Males and the Crisis of Affirmative Action* (New York: Greenwood Press, 1989). The pervasiveness of resentment turned up in focus-group sessions conducted in 1985 by a Democratic polling firm. According to the ensuing report, "The special status of blacks is perceived by almost all [members of the groups] as a serious obstacle to their personal advancement. Indeed, discrimination against whites has become a well-assimilated and ready explanation for their status, vulnerability and failures." As quoted by Thomas Byrne Edsall

and Mary D. Edsall, *Chain Reaction: The Impact of Race, Rights, and Taxes on American Politics* (New York: W. W. Norton, 1991), p. 182.

14. Paul M. Sniderman and Thomas Piazza, *The Scar of Race* (Cambridge, Mass.: Harvard University Press, 1993).

15. Ibid., pp. 69–78.

16. Ibid., pp. 102–104.

17. Benjamin I. Page and Robert Y. Shapiro, *The Rational Public: Fifty Years of Trends in Americans' Policy Preferences* (Chicago: University of Chicago Press, 1992), especially chap. 3.

18. Edsall and Edsall, *Chain Reaction*, especially chaps. 9–11.

19. *Economist*, November 30, 1991, pp. 47–48.

20. Terry Eastland, "In This White House, Principle Is Just the Politics of the Day," *Los Angeles Times*, December 19, 1990, p. B11.

21. Patrick Thomas, "The Persistent 'Gnat' that Louisiana Can't Get Out of Its Face," *Los Angeles Times*, October 14, 1990, p. M1.

22. Andrew Rosenthal, "Broad Disparities in Votes and Polls Raising Questions," *New York Times*, November 9, 1989, pp. A1, B14; and J. Phillip Thompson, "David Dinkins' Victory in New York City: The Decline of the Democratic Party Organization and the Strengthening of Black Politics," *PS: Political Science and Politics*, 23 (June 1990): 145–148.

23. Excerpts from speech reprinted in David J. Garrow, *Bearing the Cross: Martin Luther King, Jr., and the Southern Christian Leadership Conference* (New York: William Morrow, 1986), pp. 283–284.

24. James P. Smith and Finis R. Welch, "Black Economic Progress since Myrdal," *Journal of Economic Literature*, 27 (June 1989): 519–564.

25. Deborah J. Carter and Reginald Wilson, *Minorities in Higher Education* (Washington, D.C.: American Council on Education, December 1989), p. 20.

26. Smith and Welch, "Black Economic Progress," pp. 552–557. See also Jonathan S. Leonard, "The Impact of Affirmative Action Regulation and Equal Employment Law on Black Employment," *Journal of Economic Perspectives*, 4 (Fall 1990): 47–63.

27. Richard B. Freeman, *Black Elite: The New Market for Highly Educated Black Americans* (New York: McGraw Hill, 1976), p. 34.

28. Thomas Sowell, *Education: Assumptions versus History* (Stanford: Hoover Institution Press, 1986), pp. 81–89.

29. Thomas Sowell, *Civil Rights: Rhetoric or Reality?* (New York: William Morrow, 1984), pp. 49–50.

30. Edsall and Edsall, *Chain Reaction,* table 11.3.

31. These statistics are drawn from Robin Williams, Jr., and Gerald David Jaynes, eds., *A Common Destiny: Blacks and American Society* (Washington, D.C.: National Academy Press, 1989).

32. Stephen L. Carter, *Reflections of an Affirmative Action Baby* (New York: Basic Books, 1991); Richard A. Epstein, *Forbidden Grounds: The Case against Employment Discrimination Laws* (Cambridge, Mass.: Harvard University Press, 1992); Nathan Glazer, *Affirmative Discrimination: Ethnic Inequality and Public Policy* (Cambridge, Mass.: Harvard University Press, 1987; orig. pub., 1975); Glenn C. Loury, "Why Should We Care about Group Inequality," *Social Philosophy and Policy,* 5 (Autumn 1987): 249-271; Stephen Coate and Loury, "Will Affirmative-Action Policies Eliminate Negative Stereotypes," *American Economic Review,* 83 (December 1993): 1220-1240; Sowell, *Civil Rights;* Steele, *Content of Our Character;* and William Julius Wilson, *The Truly Disadvantaged: The Inner City, the Underclass, and Public Policy* (Chicago: University of Chicago Press, 1987).

33. Gertrude Ezorsky, *Racism and Justice: The Case for Affirmative Action* (Ithaca: Cornell University Press, 1991).

34. U.S. Department of Labor, Office of Policy Planning and Research, *The Negro Family: The Case for National Action* (Washington, D.C.: Government Printing Office, 1965).

35. Ibid., pp. 47–48.

36. E. Franklin Frazier, *The Negro Family in the United States* (Chicago: University of Chicago Press, 1939).

37. Herbert G. Gutman, *The Black Family in Slavery and Freedom, 1750–1925* (New York: Pantheon, 1976).

38. The quotes are drawn from Lee Rainwater and William L. Yancey, *The Moynihan Report and the Politics of Controversy* (Cambridge, Mass.: MIT Press, 1967), pp. 172–173, 259.

39. As cited by Glenn C. Loury, "The Family, the Nation, and Senator Moynihan," *Commentary,* June 1986, p. 22. Loury's article contains many further details and a rich interpretation.

40. Rainwater and Yancey, *Moynihan Report,* pp. 247–248, 256.

41. William Ryan, "Savage Discovery: The Moynihan Report," *Nation,* November 22, 1965, pp. 380–384. Quotes drawn from an abridged reprint in Rainwater and Yancey, *Moynihan Report,* pp. 458, 464.

42. Ibid., pp. 259–260.

43. Daniel Patrick Moynihan, *Family and Nation: The Godkin Lectures, Harvard University* (San Diego: Harcourt Brace Jovanovich, 1986), p. 36.

44. Hacker, *Two Nations,* p. 68.

45. Glenn C. Loury, "The Family as Context for Delinquency Prevention: Demographic Trends and Political Realities," in *From Children to Citizens,* vol. 3, ed. James Q. Wilson and Glenn C. Loury (New York: Springer-Verlag, 1985), 3–26.

46. Jim Sleeper, *The Closest of Strangers: Liberalism and the Politics of Race in New York* (New York: W. W. Norton, 1990), pp. 253–254.

47. Ellen Goodman, "And He Serves to Free Long-Buried Feelings," *Los Angeles Times,* January 18, 1985, pt. 2, p. 5.

48. Hacker, *Two Nations,* p. 192.

49. Goodman, "And He Serves to Free Long-Buried Feelings."

50. Ellen Goodman, "Polite Silence All Around While the Monsters Prowl," *International Herald Tribune,* December 13, 1991, p. 7.

51. Morton Hunt, *Profiles of Social Research: The Scientific Study of Human Interactions* (New York: Sage, 1985), p. 84–92. For Coleman's own account of the episode, see his remarks in *Footnotes,* 17 (January 1989): 4–5.

52. Thomas B. Rosenstiel, "Paper's Editorial Sparks Racial Uproar in Philadelphia," *Los Angeles Times,* December 20, 1990, p. A32.

53. See Carter, *Reflections,* chaps. 5–8; and Glenn C. Loury, "The Problem of Ideology and Political Discourse among Afro-Americans" (unpublished manuscript chapter, Harvard University, 1986).

54. As quoted by Carter, *Reflections,* p. 108.

55. Alphonso Pinkney, *The Myth of Black Progress* (New York: Cambridge University Press, 1984), pp. 14–15.

56. Carter, *Reflections,* pp. 111–112.

57. Sleeper, *Closest of Strangers,* especially pp. 80–85.

58. Linda S. Lichter, "Who Speaks for Black America?" *Public Opinion* (August/September 1985), pp. 41–44.

59. All these points are developed with respect to Jesse Jackson's presidential candidacy by Adolph L. Reed, Jr., *The Jesse Jackson Phenomenon: The Crisis of Purpose in Afro-American Politics* (New Haven: Yale University Press, 1986).

10. Public Discourse and Private Knowledge

1. For an overview of Leibniz's work, see Bertrand Russell, *A History of Western Philosophy* (New York: Simon and Schuster, 1945), pp. 581–596.

2. The most influential modern defense of the fixed-preference as-

sumption is George J. Stigler and Gary Becker, "De Gustibus Non Est Disputandum," *American Economic Review,* 67 (March 1977): 76–90.

3. The inspiration for this distinction comes from Viktor Vanberg and James M. Buchanan, "Interests and Theories in Constitutional Choice," *Journal of Theoretical Politics,* 1 (January 1989): 49–62. Diverse other scholars have recognized the plasticity of human knowledge and preferences. See, for instance, Norbert Elias, *Power and Civility,* trans. Edmund Jephcott (New York: Pantheon, 1982; orig. German ed., 1939); Edward Shils, *Tradition* (Chicago: University of Chicago Press, 1981); S. Ryan Johansson, "The Computer Paradigm and the Role of Cultural Information in Social Systems," *Historical Methods,* 21 (Fall 1988): 172–188; Randall Bartlett, *Economics and Power: An Inquiry into Human Relations and Markets* (Cambridge: Cambridge University Press, 1989), chap. 9; and James S. Coleman, *Foundations of Social Theory* (Cambridge, Mass.: Harvard University Press, 1990), especially chaps. 10–12.

4. Herbert A. Simon, *Reason in Human Affairs* (Stanford: Stanford University Press, 1983).

5. The seminal papers on heuristics may be found in Daniel Kahneman, Paul Slovic, and Amos Tversky, eds., *Judgment under Uncertainty: Heuristics and Biases* (Cambridge: Cambridge University Press, 1982; chaps. orig. pub. 1971–1982). An overview is provided by Richard Nisbett and Lee Ross, *Human Inference: Strategies and Shortcomings of Social Judgment* (Englewood Cliffs, N.J.: Prentice-Hall, 1980). Anthony Pratkanis and Elliot Aronson observe that heuristics are most likely to be used under one or more of the following conditions: we do not have time to think carefully about an issue; we are too overloaded with information to process it fully; the issues at stake are unimportant; we have little other information on which to base a decision; and a given heuristic comes quickly to mind. See their *Age of Propaganda: The Everyday Use and Abuse of Persuasion* (New York: W. H. Freeman, 1991), p. 121.

6. Two outstanding studies are John H. Holland, Keith J. Holyoak, Richard E. Nisbett, and Paul R. Thagard, *Induction: Processes of Inference, Learning, and Discovery* (Cambridge, Mass.: MIT Press, 1986); and Howard Margolis, *Patterns, Thinking, and Cognition: A Theory of Judgment* (Chicago: University of Chicago Press, 1987). For studies concerned specifically with models pertaining to political issues, see Richard R. Lau and David O. Sears, eds., *Political Cognition: The 19th Annual Carnegie Symposium on Cognition* (Hillsdale, N.J.: Lawrence Erlbaum, 1986).

7. Nisbett and Ross, *Human Inference,* p. 245. See also George Mandler, *Mind and Emotion* (New York: John Wiley, 1975).

8. John Zaller and Stanley Feldman, "A Simple Theory of the Survey

Response: Answering Questions versus Revealing Preferences," *American Journal of Political Science,* 36 (August 1992): 579–616.

9. Daniel Kahneman and Amos Tversky, "Choices, Values, and Frames," *American Psychologist,* 39 (April 1984): 341–350.

10. Alexis de Tocqueville, *Democracy in America,* vol. 2, ed. Henry Reeve, Francis Bowen, and Phillips Bradley (New York: Alfred A. Knopf, 1989; orig. French ed., 1835), p. 8.

11. Albert Bandura, *Social Learning Theory* (Englewood Cliffs, N.J.: Prentice-Hall, 1977).

12. This point is developed at length by Gordon Tullock, *Toward a Mathematics of Politics* (Ann Arbor: University of Michigan Press, 1967), chaps. 7–8; and Hannah Arendt, "Lying in Politics," in her *Crises of the Republic* (New York: Harcourt Brace Jovanovich, 1972), pp. 1–47.

13. Niccolò Machiavelli, *The Prince,* trans. and ed. Thomas G. Bergin (Northbrook, Ill.: AHM Publishing, 1947; orig. Italian ed., 1532), chap. 18.

14. I have drawn here on Russell, *History of Western Philosophy,* p. 510.

15. The more things change, the more they stay the same.

16. The thesis that long-standing patterns of thought regulate the dissemination of ideas is developed by Albert O. Hirschman, *The Rhetoric of Reaction: Perversity, Futility, Jeopardy* (Cambridge, Mass.: Harvard University Press, 1991).

17. Plato, *The Republic,* trans. Francis M. Cornford (New York: Oxford University Press, 1945; first Greek ed., 4th c. B.C.E.), chap. 10. See also Sissela Bok, *Lying: Moral Choice in Public and Private Life* (New York: Pantheon, 1978), chap. 12; and Kaushik Basu, "Bad Advice," *Economic and Political Weekly,* March 7–14, 1992, pp. 525–530.

18. For an overview of contemporary censorship, see Kevin Boyle, ed., *Article Nineteen: Information, Freedom, and Censorship* (New York: Times Books, 1988).

19. The proposition was developed by Walter Lippmann, *Public Opinion* (New York: Harcourt, Brace and Company, 1922). Later variants include Joseph A. Schumpeter, *Capitalism, Socialism, and Democracy,* 3rd ed. (New York: Harper & Row, 1942), chaps. 20–23; and Anthony Downs, *An Economic Theory of Democracy* (New York: Harper & Row, 1957), chaps. 11–13. For a survey of the pertinent research, see Donald R. Kinder and David O. Sears, "Public Opinion and Political Action," in *The Handbook of Social Psychology,* 3rd ed., vol. 2, ed. Gardner Lindzey and Elliot Aronson (New York: Random House, 1985), pp. 659–741.

20. W. Russell Neuman, *The Paradox of Mass Politics: Knowledge and Opinion in the American Electorate* (Cambridge, Mass.: Harvard University Press, 1986), p. 15.

21. Ibid., pp. 14–22.

22. "The American Public's Knowledge of the U.S. Constitution: A National Survey of Public Awareness and Personal Opinion" (San Francisco: Hearst Corporation, n.d.), p. 13.

23. This argument is developed by Neuman, *Paradox of Mass Politics*.

24. The underlying normative principle is developed by Harold H. Kelley, "Attribution Theory in Social Psychology," in *Nebraska Symposium on Motivation*, ed. David Levine (Lincoln: University of Nebraska Press, 1967), pp. 192–238.

25. The terminology comes from Coleman, *Foundations*.

26. The term "social proof" comes from Robert B. Cialdini, *Influence: The New Psychology of Modern Persuasion* (New York: Quill, 1984), chap. 4.

27. James Madison, "The Federalist no. 49" (1788), in *The Federalist*, ed. Jacob E. Cooke (Middletown, Conn.: Wesleyan University Press, 1961), p. 340.

28. Bernard Lewis, *History Remembered, Recovered, Invented* (Princeton: Princeton University Press, 1975); and David Lowenthal, *The Past Is a Foreign Country* (Cambridge: Cambridge University Press, 1985).

29. Joseph Schacht, *The Origins of Muhammadan Jurisprudence*, 3rd ed. (London: Oxford University Press, 1959). Pseudoepigraphy has also been a common practice in other religions. For references, see the sources cited in the preceding note.

30. As quoted by Elisabeth Noelle-Neumann, *The Spiral of Silence: Public Opinion—Our Social Skin* (Chicago: University of Chicago Press, 1984; orig. German ed., 1980), p. 66.

31. For insights into the scholarly uses of consensual verification techniques, see Thomas S. Kuhn, *The Structure of Scientific Revolutions*, 2nd ed. (Chicago: University of Chicago Press, 1970); and Thomas Sowell, *Knowledge and Decisions* (New York: Basic Books, 1980).

32. Pratkanis and Aronson, *Age of Propaganda*, pp. 134–139.

33. David Hackett Fischer, *Historians' Fallacies: Toward a Logic of Historical Thought* (London: Routledge & Kegan Paul, 1971), p. 302.

34. Amos Tversky and Daniel Kahneman, "Availability: A Heuristic for Judging Frequency and Probability," in *Judgment under Uncertainty*, ed. Kahneman, Slovic, and Tversky, pp. 163–178. See also Shelley E. Taylor, "The Availability Bias in Social Perception and Interaction," in

Judgment under Uncertainty, ed. Kahneman, Slovic, and Tversky, pp. 190–200.

35. Everett M. Rogers and James W. Dearing, "Agenda-Setting Research: Where Has It Been, Where Is It Going?" in *Communication Yearbook* 11, ed. James A. Anderson (Beverly Hills, Calif.: Sage Publications, 1988), pp. 555–594.

36. Lynn Hasher, David Goldstein, and Thomas Toppino, "Frequency and the Conference of Referential Validity," *Journal of Verbal Learning and Verbal Behavior,* 16 (February 1977): 107–112.

37. Marian Schwartz, "Repetition and Rated Truth Value of Statements," *American Journal of Psychology,* 95 (Fall 1982): 393–407.

38. This illustration bears the influence of Erich Fromm, *Escape from Freedom* (New York: Avon Books, 1969; orig. ed., 1941), pp. 208–230.

39. Joseph Harriss, *The Tallest Tower: Eiffel and the Belle Époque* (Boston: Houghton Mifflin, 1975), pp. 19–23.

40. George Bishop, "Manipulation and Control of People's Responses to Public Opinion Polls: An Orwellian Experiment in 1984," in *The Orwellian Moment: Hindsight and Foresight in the Post-1984 World,* ed. Robert L. Savage, James Combs, and Dan Nimmo (Fayetteville: University of Arkansas Press, 1989), pp. 119–129.

41. J. St. B. T. Evans and P. C. Wason, "Rationalization in a Reasoning Task," *British Journal of Psychology,* 67 (November 1976): 479–486. See also P. N. Johnson-Laird and P. C. Wason, "A Theoretical Analysis of Insight into a Reasoning Task," in their *Thinking: Readings in Cognitive Science* (Cambridge: Cambridge University Press, 1977), pp. 143–157; and Margolis, *Patterns, Thinking, and Cognition,* especially chap. 1.

42. This point is developed by Noelle-Neumann, *Spiral of Silence,* chap. 23.

43. Daniel Lerner, *The Passing of Traditional Society: Modernizing the Middle East* (New York: Free Press, 1958).

44. Ronald Heiner, "The Origin of Predictable Behavior," *American Economic Review,* 73 (September 1983): 560–595.

45. Neuman, *Paradox of Mass Politics,* pp. 61–64.

46. Nisbett and Ross, *Human Inference,* chap. 8.

47. K. R. L. Hall, "Perceiving and Naming a Series of Figures," *Quarterly Journal of Experimental Psychology,* 2 (November 1950): 153–162.

48. Charles G. Lord, Lee Ross, and Mark R. Lepper, "Biased Assimilation and Attitude Polarization: The Effects of Prior Theories on Subsequently Considered Evidence," *Journal of Personality and Social Psychology,* 37 (November 1979): 2098–2109.

49. Much evidence as to the perception of spurious patterns is offered

by Thomas Gilovich, *How We Know What Isn't So: The Fallibility of Human Reason in Everyday Life* (New York: Free Press, 1991).

50. David O. Sears, Richard R. Lau, Tom R. Tyler, and Harris M. Allen, Jr., "Self-Interest vs. Symbolic Politics in Policy Attitudes and Presidential Voting," *American Political Science Review,* 74 (September 1980): 670–684; and Lau, Thad A. Brown, and Sears, "Self-Interest and Civilians' Attitudes toward the Vietnam War," *Public Opinion Quarterly,* 42 (Winter 1978): 464–483.

51. Neuman, *Paradox of Mass Politics,* p. 69.

52. Joseph P. Kalt and Mark A. Zupan, "Capture and Ideology in the Economic Theory of Politics," *American Economic Review,* 74 (June 1984): 279–300.

53. James C. Scott, *Domination and the Arts of Resistance: Hidden Transcripts* (New Haven: Yale University Press, 1990). The quote is from p. 110 (emphasis in original).

54. Sharon S. Brehm and Jack W. Brehm, *Psychological Reactance: A Theory of Freedom and Control* (New York: Academic Press, 1981).

11. The Unthinkable and the Unthought

1. Mohammed Arkoun, "Émergences et Problèmes dans le Monde Musulman Contemporain (1960–1985)," *Islamochristiana,* 12 (1986): 158–159.

2. For recent examples, see Fazlur Rahman, *Islam and Modernity: Transformation of an Intellectual Tradition* (Chicago: University of Chicago Press, 1982); and William Montgomery Watt, *Islamic Fundamentalism and Modernity* (London: Routledge, 1988).

3. Edward E. Jones and Richard E. Nisbett, "The Actor and the Observer: Divergent Perceptions of the Causes of Behavior," in *Attribution: Perceiving the Causes of Behavior,* ed. Jones et al. (Morristown, N.J.: General Learning Press, 1972), pp. 79–94. For a survey of related research, see Edward E. Jones, "How Do People Perceive the Causes of Behavior?" *American Scientist,* 64 (May-June 1976): 300–305.

4. Richard Nisbett and Lee Ross, *Human Inference: Strategies and Shortcomings of Social Judgment* (Englewood Cliffs, N.J.: Prentice-Hall, 1980), chap. 9.

5. For some complementary insights, see Daniel B. Klein, "If Government Is So Villainous, How Come Government Officials Don't Seem Like Villains," *Economics and Philosophy,* 10 (April 1994): 91–106.

6. Leon Festinger, *A Theory of Cognitive Dissonance* (Stanford:

Stanford University Press, 1957). For extensions of Festinger's theory, see George A. Akerlof and William T. Dickens, "The Economic Consequences of Cognitive Dissonance," *American Economic Review*, 72 (June 1982): 307–319; Ekkehart Schlicht, "Cognitive Dissonance in Economics," *Gesellschaft für Wirtschafts- und Sozialwissenschaften*, 141 (1984): 61–81; and Matthew Rabin, "Cognitive Dissonance and Social Change," *Journal of Economic Behavior and Organization*, 23 (March 1994): 177–194.

7. Festinger, *Theory of Cognitive Dissonance*, chaps. 4–5.

8. Ibid., chaps. 6–7.

9. Michael Polanyi, *The Tacit Dimension* (Gloucester, Mass.: Peter Smith, 1983; orig. ed., 1966), p. 61.

10. Bernard Cohen, *The Press and Foreign Policy* (Princeton: Princeton University Press, 1963); Maxwell E. McCombs and Donald L. Shaw, "The Agenda-Setting Function of the Media," *Public Opinion Quarterly*, 36 (Summer 1972): 176–187; and G. Ray Funkhouser, "The Issues of the Sixties: An Exploratory Study in the Dynamics of Public Opinion," *Public Opinion Quarterly*, 37 (Spring 1973): 62–75.

11. John H. Holland, Keith J. Holyoak, Richard E. Nisbett, and Paul Thagard, *Induction: Processes of Inference, Learning, and Discovery*. Cambridge, Mass.: MIT Press, 1986.

12. Thomas Kuhn, *The Structure of Scientific Revolutions*, 2nd ed. (Chicago: University of Chicago Press, 1970).

13. Howard Margolis, *Patterns, Thinking, and Cognition: A Theory of Judgment* (Chicago: University of Chicago Press, 1987), chaps. 11–13.

14. Except, perhaps, for a threshold at an extreme.

15. With or without any memory loss, public opinion remains at 100. The difference between the two figures is 0, which corresponds to 0 percent of the range of public opinion.

16. Walter Bagehot, *Physics and Politics* (Boston: Beacon Press, 1956; orig. ed. 1884), p. 26.

17. W. Brian Arthur, "Self-Reinforcing Mechanisms in Economics," in *The Economy as an Evolving Complex System*, ed. Philip W. Anderson, Kenneth J. Arrow, and David Pines (Redwood City, Calif.: Addison-Wesley, 1988), pp. 9–31.

18. Sushil Bikchandani, David Hirshleifer, and Ivo Welsh, "A Theory of Fads, Fashion, Custom, and Cultural Change as Informational Cascades," *Journal of Political Economy*, 100 (October 1992): 992–1026.

19. George A. Akerlof, "A Theory of Social Custom, of Which Unemployment May Be One Consequence," *Quarterly Journal of Economics*, 94 (June 1980): 749–775.

12. The Caste Ethic of Submission

1. K. S. Mathur, "Hindu Values of Life: Karma and Dharma" (1964), in *Religion in India,* ed. T. N. Madan (Delhi: Oxford University Press, 1991), pp. 63–77.

2. R. S. Khare, *The Untouchable as Himself: Ideology, Identity, and Pragmatism among the Lucknow Chamars* (Cambridge: Cambridge University Press, 1984).

3. Joan P. Mencher, "The Caste System Upside Down, or the Not-So-Mysterious East," *Current Anthropology,* 15 (December 1974): 469–493.

4. Mark Juergensmeyer, "What if the Untouchables Don't Believe in Untouchability?" *Bulletin of Concerned Asian Scholars,* 12 (January–March 1980): 24.

5. M. N. Srinivas, *The Remembered Village* (Los Angeles: University of California Press, 1976), p. 182.

6. Khare, *Untouchable as Himself,* pp. 7–8, passim.

7. Juergensmeyer, "What if the Untouchables," p. 25.

8. Michael Moffatt, *An Untouchable Community in South India: Structure and Consensus* (Princeton: Princeton University Press, 1979); and Hazari, *Untouchable: The Autobiography of an Indian Outcaste* (London: Pall Mall Press, 1969), especially chaps. 1, 5; and James M. Freeman, *Untouchable: An Indian Life History* (Stanford: Stanford University Press, 1979), passim. For an enlightening discussion and additional references, see Barrington Moore, Jr., *Injustice: The Social Bases of Obedience and Revolt* (White Plains, N.Y.: M. E. Sharpe, 1978), pp. 55–64.

9. Quoted by L. S. S. O'Malley, *Indian Caste Customs* (London: Cambridge University Press, 1932), p. 138.

10. Hazari, *Untouchable,* p. 11.

11. Max Weber, *The Religion of India: The Sociology of Hinduism and Buddhism,* trans. and ed. Hans H. Gerth and Don Martindale (New York: Free Press, 1958; orig. German ed., 1916–17), especially pp. 117–123.

12. Hazari, *Untouchable,* p. 65.

13. G. S. Ghurye, *Caste, Class, and Occupation,* 4th ed. (Bombay: Popular Book Depot, 1961), chap. 9, especially pp. 218–221.

14. J. H. Hutton, *Caste in India: Its Nature, Function, and Origins,* 4th ed. (Bombay: Oxford University Press, 1963), p. 47.

15. For an account of early European research on caste, see Bernard

S. Cohn, "Notes on the History of the Study of Indian Society and Culture," in *Structure and Change in Indian Society,* ed. Milton Singer and Bernard S. Cohn (New York: Wenner-Gren Foundation for Anthropological Research, 1968), pp. 3–28. It has been argued that European scholarship standardized Hindu ideology and elevated the significance of such concepts as caste and reincarnation. By this account, elaborated by Ashis Nandy, *The Intimate Enemy: Loss and Recovery of Self under Colonialism* (Delhi: Oxford University Press, 1983), the British helped construct the caste-centered worldview and also promoted the solidification of historically fluid caste distinctions. These claims are implausible. First of all, few of the Indians whom European researchers identified as sharing the Hindu worldview had prior contact with the British. Second, a disproportionate share of those who had some prior contact, like the British-educated elites, became leading *anti*caste activists. Third, if Indians were easily brainwashed by the British, it is highly unlikely that until then their minds were immune to the pressures of their own culture. Finally, a cadre of rulers cannot reshape a nation's thought patterns at will. Anticaste reformists who have sought to emancipate the untouchables from the grip of "brahman ideology" know this through experience. As noted by Khare, *Untouchable as Himself,* especially chap. 7, their campaigns against the caste ethic have encountered resistance from the very people they wanted to help.

16. Vivekanand Jha, "Stages in the History of Untouchables," *Indian Historical Review,* 2 (July 1975): 14–31.

17. Gary S. Becker, *The Economics of Discrimination,* 2nd ed. (Chicago: University of Chicago Press, 1971).

18. Louis Dumont, *Homo Hierarchicus: The Caste System and Its Implications,* rev. ed., trans. Mark Sainsbury, Dumont, and Basia Gulati (Chicago: University of Chicago Press, 1980, orig. French ed., 1966), especially pp. 8–11.

19. A notable exception in the context of caste is Thomas A. Zwicker, "Morality and Etiquette in the Reproduction of Hierarchical Caste Relations in South Asia," M.A. thesis, University of Pennsylvania, 1984.

20. For two variants of the Marxian thesis, see Narmadeshwar Prasad, *The Myth of the Caste System* (Patna: Samjna Prakashan, 1957); and Gerald D. Berreman, "The Brahmanical View of Caste: Louis Dumont's *Homo Hierarchicus,*" *Contributions to Indian Sociology,* new ser. 5 (December 1971): 16–23.

21. Marx's pertinent passages are presented and interpreted by Jon Elster, *Making Sense of Marx* (Cambridge: Cambridge University Press, 1985), chap. 8. Elster develops this theory of ideology in his *Sour Grapes:*

Studies in the Subversion of Rationality (Cambridge: Cambridge University Press, 1983), chaps. 3–4, drawing on Paul Veyne, *Le Pain et le Cirque* (Paris: Seuil, 1976).

22. For a short history of the anticaste movement, see Eleanor Zelliot, "Untouchability," in *Encyclopedia of Asian History,* vol. 4 (New York: Charles Scribner's Sons, 1988), 169–171. Detailed accounts are offered by M. N. Srinivas, *Social Change in Modern India* (Berkeley: University of California Press, 1971); and Marc Galanter, *Competing Equalities: Law and the Backward Classes in India* (Berkeley: University of California Press, 1984).

13. The Blind Spots of Communism

1. Hannah Arendt, *The Origins of Totalitarianism,* 2nd ed. (New York: World Publishing, 1958), chaps. 11–13; and George Orwell, *1984* (New York: Harcourt Brace Jovanovich, 1961; orig. ed., 1949).

2. Alexander Solzhenitsyn, "As Breathing and Consciousness Return," in Solzhenitsyn et al., *From Under the Rubble,* trans. A. M. Brock et al. (Boston: Little, Brown, 1975; orig. Russian ed., 1974), p. 4.

3. Ibid., p. 15 (emphasis in original).

4. Alexander Solzhenitsyn, *Rebuilding Russia: Reflections and Tentative Proposals,* trans. Alexis Klimoff (New York: Farrar, Straus and Giroux, 1991; orig. Russian ed., 1990), p. 34.

5. V. I. Lenin, *State and Revolution* (New York: International Publishers, 1932; orig. Russian ed., 1917), especially sect. 1.4 and chap. 5.

6. Karl Marx, *A Contribution to the Critique of Political Economy,* vol. 29 of his and Frederick Engels's *Collected Works* (New York: International Publishers, 1987; orig. German ed., 1859), p. 263.

7. Geoffrey A. Hosking, "Memory in a Totalitarian Society: The Case of the Soviet Union," in *Memory: History, Culture, and the Mind,* ed. Thomas Butler (Oxford: Basil Blackwell, 1989), p. 115. The rest of the essay contains concrete examples of the rewriting of history.

8. Milan Kundera, *A Book on Laughter and Forgetting,* trans. Michael Henry Heim (New York: Penguin Books, 1981), p. 3. As quoted by Jeffrey C. Goldfarb, *Beyond Glasnost: The Post-Totalitarian Mind* (Chicago: University of Chicago Press, 1989), pp. 109–110.

9. Elemér Hankiss, "The 'Second Society': Is There an Alternative Social Model Emerging in Contemporary Hungary?" *Social Research,* 55 (Spring/Summer 1988), p. 28.

10. Daniil Granin, as quoted by David Wedgwood Benn, *Persuasion and Soviet Politics* (Oxford: Basil Blackwell, 1989), p. 195.

11. Miroslav Kusý, "Chartism and 'Real Socialism,' " in Václav Havel et al., *The Power of the Powerless: Citizens against the State in Central-Eastern Europe,* ed. John Keane, trans. Paul Wilson (Armonk, N.Y.: M. E. Sharpe, 1985; orig. Czech ed., 1979), pp. 158–159.

12. Robert C. Tucker, *Political Culture and Leadership in Soviet Russia* (New York: W. W. Norton, 1987), pp. 142–143.

13. Piotr Wierzbicki, "A Treatise on Ticks" (orig. Polish ed., 1979), in *Poland: Genesis of a Revolution,* ed. Abraham Brumberg (New York: Random House, 1983), pp. 206–207.

14. For evidence from the Soviet Union, see James W. Riordan, "The Revolution from Below: The Role of Letters to the Editor under *Perestroika,*" *Coexistence,* 27 (December 1990): 269–272.

15. This point is developed by Giuseppe di Palma, "Legitimation from the Top to Civil Society: Politico-Cultural Change in Eastern Europe," *World Politics,* 44 (October 1991), especially pp. 55–63.

16. Zhores A. Medvedev, *The Rise and Fall of T. D. Lysenko,* trans. I. Michael Lerner (New York: Columbia University Press, 1969), chaps. 2–3, 10.

17. C. Banc and Alan Dundes, *You Call This Living?: A Collection of East European Political Jokes* (Athens: University of Georgia Press, 1990), pp. 65, 86.

18. Igor Kon, "The Psychology of Social Inertia" (orig. Russian ed., 1988), *Social Sciences,* 20 (1989): 60–74. Quotation at p. 63.

19. Gennadii Batyagin, TASS, June 28, 1989. Quoted by Elizabeth Teague, "Perestroika and the Soviet Worker," *Government and Opposition,* 25 (Spring 1990): 192.

20. Ibid., pp. 191–211.

21. Personal interview, Leipzig, December 6, 1991.

22. Jiří Otava, "Public Opinion Research in Czechoslovakia," *Social Research,* 55 (Spring–Summer 1988): 249. Every issue of the Czechoslovak government's official bulletin on public opinion stated: "We remind all researchers that this bulletin is not meant for the public, which means not even for your friends and acquaintances, but serves exclusively as internal material for poll-takers and those who collaborate with us" (p. 251, n. 2). For similar evidence from the Soviet Union, see David Wedgwood Benn, *Persuasion and Soviet Politics* (Oxford: Basil Blackwell, 1989), especially chap. 4.

23. Walter Friedrich and Hartmut Griese, *Jugend und Jugendforschung in der DDR: Gesellschaftspolitische Situationen, Sozialisation und Mentalitätsentwicklung in den achtziger Jahren* (Opladen: Leske & Budrich, 1991), pp. 139, 145.

24. These surveys were based on face-to-face interviews, which calls for caution in interpreting the absolute figures. The trends are meaningful, for the methodology did not change. But they could partly reflect the diminution of fear.

25. Figures compiled in 1991 by Gallup-Hungary, Budapest, from *Jel kép*, the limited-circulation magazine of the Hungarian Institute of Public Opinion.

26. Classified survey of September 9, 1983. From the archives of the Public Opinion Research Institute, Prague.

27. Benn, *Persuasion and Soviet Politics*, p. 142.

28. Preference falsification cannot be ruled out as a contributor to these results.

29. Ibid., pp. 153–154.

30. Henry O. Hart, "The Tables Turned: If East Europeans Could Vote," *Public Opinion*, 6 (October/November 1983): 53–57. The surveys reported by Hart cover Czechoslovakia, Hungary, Poland, Romania, and Bulgaria.

31. Marek Ziółkowski, "Individuals and the Social System: Values, Perceptions, and Behavioral Strategies," *Social Research*, 55 (Spring/Summer 1988): 139–177. The reported figures are drawn from pp. 153–154.

32. László Bruszt, " 'Without Us but for Us'? Political Orientation in Hungary in the Period of Late Paternalism," *Social Research*, 55 (Spring/Summer 1988): 43–76. The figures are from pp. 70, 72, and 75.

33. Elisabeth Noelle-Neumann, "The German Revolution: The Historic Experiment of the Division and Unification of a Nation as Reflected in Survey Findings," *International Journal of Public Opinion Research*, 3 (Autumn 1991): 248, table 4. The East German survey was conducted in February and March 1990, the West German survey in December 1989.

34. Ibid., p. 258, table 9. The East German survey was conducted in March 1990; the West German survey, two months later.

35. Association for Independent Social Analysis, *Czechoslovakia—January 1990 (Survey Report)*, March 1990, mimeo, table 4.

36. *Democracy, Economic Reform, and Western Assistance: Data Tables* (New York: Freedom House, 1991), table 154.

37. *Barometer of Privatization*, Szonda Ipsos, Budapest, October 1991, pp. 27–31.

38. Hans Aage, "Popular Attitudes and *Perestroika*," *Soviet Studies*, 43 (January 1991), especially pp. 8, 10. With respect to the Soviet Union,

at least one survey finds attitudes toward free markets to be only mildly less permissive than in the United States. See Robert J. Shiller, Maxim Boycko, and Vladimir Korobov, "Popular Attitudes toward Free Markets: The Soviet Union and the United States Compared," *American Economic Review,* 81 (June 1991): 385–400.

39. Vladimir Tismaneanu, *The Crisis of Marxist Ideology in Eastern Europe: The Poverty of Utopia* (London: Routledge, 1988), especially chap. 4; and Leszek Kołakowski, *Main Currents of Marxism: Its Origin, Growth, and Dissolution,* vol. 3, trans. P. S. Falla (Oxford: Clarendon Press, 1978), especially chap. 13.

40. Vladimir Tismaneanu, *Reinventing Politics: Eastern Europe from Stalin to Havel* (New York: Free Press, 1992), pp. 67–80.

41. Ibid., pp. 90–106.

42. Adam Michnik, *Letters from Prison and Other Essays,* trans. Maya Latynski (Berkeley: University of California Press, 1985; orig. Polish eds., 1973–1984), especially pp. 133–198.

43. Tismaneanu, *Reinventing Politics,* pp. 175–191.

44. The unrealistic stands of communist revisionism are identified by John Clark and Aaron Wildavsky, *The Moral Collapse of Communism: Poland as a Cautionary Tale* (San Francisco: ICS Press, 1990), especially chap. 3.

45. János Mátyás Kovács, "From Reformation to Transformation: Limits to Liberalism in Hungarian Economic Thought," *East European Politics and Societies,* 5 (Winter 1991): 41–72. Quotation at p. 47.

46. Václav Klaus and Tomáš Ježek, "Social Criticism, False Liberalism, and Recent Changes in Czechoslovakia," *East European Politics and Societies,* 5 (Winter 1991): 26–40.

47. János Kornai, "The Hungarian Reform Process: Visions, Hopes, and Reality," *Journal of Economic Literature,* 24 (December 1986): 1728–1730.

48. Andrei D. Sakharov, *Progress, Coexistence, and Intellectual Freedom,* trans. *New York Times* (New York: W. W. Norton, 1968), pp. 72, 78.

49. Hankiss, "The 'Second Society'." See also Di Palma, "Legitimation from the Top," pp. 64–67.

50. Vladimir Shlapentokh, *Soviet Public Opinion and Ideology: Mythology and Pragmatism in Interaction* (New York: Praeger, 1986); and Shlapentokh, *Public and Private Life of the Soviet People: Changing Values in Post-Stalin Russia* (New York: Oxford University Press, 1989).

51. For an analysis of Western writings sympathetic to communism,

see Paul Hollander, *Political Pilgrims: Travels of Western Intellectuals to the Soviet Union, China, and Cuba, 1928–1978* (New York: Oxford University Press, 1981).

52. Jan Winiecki, *Resistance to Change in the Soviet Economic System: A Property Rights Approach* (London: Routledge, 1991), especially chaps. 1 and 2.

53. János Kornai, "Individual Freedom and Reform of the Socialist Economy," *European Economic Review*, 32 (March 1988): 259–262.

14. The Unfading Specter of White Racism

1. From a report of the Committee on Admissions and Enrollment, Academic Senate, University of California, *Freshman Admissions at Berkeley: A Policy for the 1990s and Beyond*. As recorded by Andrew Hacker, "Affirmative Action: The New Look," *New York Review of Books*, October 12, 1989, table A.

2. John Bunzel, "Affirmative Action: How It 'Works' at UC Berkeley," *Public Interest*, no. 93 (Fall 1988): 120.

3. Colleges rarely release ethnically disaggregated figures on the qualifications of their enrolled students, so overall figures are unavailable. What is available is information on the averages across all SAT takers, including ones who did not enter college. In 1991–92, the white averages on the verbal and mathematics sections were 442 and 491, and the corresponding black averages were 352 and 385. College Entrance Examination Board, *National Report on College-Bound Seniors* (Princeton: CEEB, 1992).

4. Terry Eastland and William J. Bennett, *Counting by Race: Equality from the Founding Fathers to Bakke and Weber* (New York: Basic Books, 1979), pp. 8–9.

5. James Crouse and Dale Trusheim, *The Case against the SAT* (Chicago: University of Chicago Press, 1988), especially chaps. 5, 8.

6. See statements recorded by Glynn Custred, "Onward to Adequacy," *Academic Questions*, 3 (Summer 1990): 64.

7. *Affirmative Action Newsletter*, Harvard University, Office of the Assistant to the President, Fall 1989. Quoted by Dinesh D'Souza, *Illiberal Education: The Politics of Race and Sex on Campus* (New York: Free Press, 1991), p. 220.

8. Stephen R. Barnett, "Who Gets In? A Troubling Policy," *Los Angeles Times*, June 11, 1992, p. B13. The enrollment figures at other University of California campuses show similar discrepancies. See the *Economist*, September 17, 1994, p. 28.

9. *Economist,* February 16, 1991, p. 22. For many additional examples, see Stephen L. Carter, *Reflections of an Affirmative Action Baby* (New York: Basic Books, 1991), chap. 8; and D'Souza, *Illiberal Education,* chap. 5. For a defense of campus speech codes, see Stanley Fish, *There's No Such Thing as Free Speech . . . And It's a Good Thing, Too* (New York: Oxford University Press, 1994), chap. 8.

10. Sensitivity programs are debated in Paul Berman, ed., *Debating P.C.: The Controversy over Political Correctness on College Campuses* (New York: Laurel, 1992).

11. D'Souza, *Illiberal Education,* pp. 215–218.

12. This theme is developed by Shelby Steele, *The Content of Our Character: A New Vision of Race in America* (New York: St. Martin's Press, 1990).

13. Suffering slights will not, by itself, prevent anyone from learning. Many minorities have advanced, and have even outperformed the majority, in societies accustomed to looking down on them. See Thomas Sowell, *Ethnic America: A History* (New York: Basic Books, 1981).

14. For examples see Charles J. Sykes, *The Hollow Men: Politics and Corruption in Higher Education* (Washington, D.C.: Regnery Gateway, 1990), p. 202; and Andrew Hacker, *Two Nations: Black and White, Separate, Hostile, Unequal* (New York: Charles Scribner's Sons, 1992), p. 159.

15. Much evidence is offered by Sykes, *Hollow Men.*

16. Christopher Shea, "Penn Report Faults Campus Police for Response to Students' Taking Papers," *Chronicle of Higher Education,* August 4, 1993, p. A27; and Shea, "Penn Won't Punish Black Students Who Threw Away Campus Papers," *Chronicle of Higher Education,* September 22, 1993, p. A35.

17. The perceptual shift is discussed by Hacker, *Two Nations,* chap. 10.

18. *Sources: Diversity Initiatives in Higher Education* (Washington, D.C.: American Council on Education, 1993).

19. Marcia Ascher, *Ethnomathematics: A Multicultural View of Mathematical Ideas* (Pacific Grove, Calif.: Brooks/Cole, 1991). See also the observations of Glenn M. Ricketts, "Multiculturalism Mobilizes," *Academic Questions,* 3 (Summer 1990): 57.

20. The logic and objectives of multiculturalism are outlined by Henry Louis Gates, Jr., *Loose Canons: Notes on the Culture Wars* (New York: Oxford University Press, 1992; orig. publ., 1985–1991). Critical accounts include Arthur M. Schlesinger, Jr., *The Disuniting of America: Reflections on a Multicultural Society* (Knoxville, Tenn.: Whittle Books, 1991); Diane

Ravitch, "Multiculturalism: E Pluribus Plures," *American Scholar,* 59 (Summer 1990): 337–354; and Gary B. Nash, "The Great Multicultural Debate," *Contention,* 1 (Spring 1992): 1–28.

21. D'Souza, *Illiberal Education,* chap. 3.

22. As cited in ibid., p. 8.

23. William A. Henry III, "Upside Down in the Groves of Academe," *Time,* April 1, 1991, p. 66.

24. D'Souza, *Illiberal Education,* pp. 148–151, 194–197; David P. Bryden, "It Ain't What They Teach, It's the Way They Teach It," *Public Interest,* no. 102 (Spring 1991): 44–45; and Chester E. Finn, "The Campus: 'An Island of Repression in a Sea of Freedom,' " *Commentary,* 88 (September 1989): 19.

25. Denise K. Magner, "When Whites Teach Black Studies: Controversy at Iowa State Dramatizes a Sensitive Issue on College Campuses," *Chronicle of Higher Education,* December 1, 1993, p. A19.

26. "Delaware U. Goes PC," *Washington Times,* June 14, 1991, p. F2.

27. Allan Bloom, *The Closing of the American Mind: How Higher Education Has Failed Democracy and Impoverished the Souls of Today's Students* (New York: Simon and Schuster, 1987), especially pp. 311, 324.

28. Richard Delgado, "The Imperial Scholar: Reflections on a Review of Civil Rights Literature," *University of Pennsylvania Law Review,* 132 (March 1984): 561–578.

29. Ibid., p. 577.

30. Mari Matsuda, "Affirmative Action and Legal Knowledge: Planting Seeds in Plowed-Up Ground," *Harvard Women's Law Journal,* 11 (Spring 1988): 1–17. Quotations at pp. 1, 4–5.

31. Quoted by Randall L. Kennedy, "Racial Critiques of Legal Academia," *Harvard Law Review,* 102 (June 1989): 1752.

32. Nash, "The Great Multicultural Debate," p. 17.

33. As reported by Kennedy, "Racial Critiques," pp. 1798–1800.

34. Carter, *Reflections,* pp. 1–2.

35. For further examples of exceptionally insightful analyses by outsiders, see Robert K. Merton, "Insiders and Outsiders: A Chapter in the Sociology of Knowledge," *American Journal of Sociology,* 77 (July 1972): 9–47. Merton provides a detailed evaluation of the principle that particular groups have monopolistic access to certain kinds of knowledge. See also Glenn C. Loury, "Self-Censorship in Public Discourse: A Theory of 'Political Correctness' and Related Phenomena," *Rationality and Society,* 6 (October 1994): 428–461.

36. Kennedy, "Racial Critiques," p. 1807.

37. James S. Coleman, "On the Self-Suppression of Academic Freedom," *Academic Questions*, 4 (Winter 1990–91): 17–22.

38. Ibid., p. 20.

39. Jason DeParle, "Talk of Government Being Out to Get Blacks Falls on More Attentive Ears," *New York Times*, October 29, 1990, p. B7.

40. John E. Chubb and Terry M. Moe, *Politics, Markets, and America's Schools* (Washington, D.C.: Brookings Institution, 1990), especially chap. 1.

41. David S. Crystal and Harold W. Stevenson, "Mothers' Perceptions of Children's Problems with Mathematics: A Cross-National Comparison," *Journal of Educational Psychology*, 83 (September 1991): 372–376.

42. See, for instance, T. R. Reid, "Miyazawa: Work Ethic Flags in U.S.," *Washington Post*, February 4, 1992, pp. A1, 11.

43. Steele, *Content of Our Character*, chap. 5. Quotations at pp. 78–80, emphasis in original. For a similar thesis, see Hacker, *Two Nations*, chap. 4.

44. Jim Sleeper, *The Closest of Strangers: Liberalism and the Politics of Race in New York* (New York: W. W. Norton, 1990), p. 34.

45. For its theoretical foundations, see Mancur Olson, *The Logic of Collective Action: Public Goods and the Theory of Groups* (Cambridge, Mass.: Harvard University Press, 1965).

46. James M. Buchanan and Gordon Tullock, *The Calculus of Consent: Logical Foundations of Constitutional Democracy* (Ann Arbor: University of Michigan Press, 1962), chaps. 10–11.

15. Unforeseen Political Revolutions

1. See Timur Kuran, "Sparks and Prairie Fires: A Theory of Unanticipated Political Revolution," *Public Choice*, 61 (April 1989): 41–74.

2. Cited by James DeNardo, *Power in Numbers: The Political Strategy of Protest and Rebellion* (Princeton: Princeton University Press, 1985), p. 17.

3. Karl Marx's most influential statement on the subject is in *A Contribution to the Critique of Political Economy*, ed. Maurice Dobb, trans. S. W. Ryazanskaya (New York: International Publishers, 1970; first German ed., 1859), pp. 20–21. Jon Elster, *Making Sense of Marx* (Cambridge: Cambridge University Press, 1985), pp. 428–446, critiques Marx's pertinent writings.

4. For two influential statements, see James C. Davies, "Toward a

Theory of Revolution," *American Sociological Review*, 27 (February 1962): 5–19; and Ted R. Gurr, *Why Men Rebel* (Princeton: Princeton University Press, 1970).

5. David Snyder and Charles Tilly, "Hardship and Collective Violence in France, 1830 to 1960," *American Sociological Review*, 37 (October 1972): 520–532; and Charles Tilly, Louise Tilly, and Richard Tilly, *The Rebellious Century: 1830–1930* (Cambridge, Mass.: Harvard University Press, 1975). For much additional evidence against the theory of relative deprivation, see Steven E. Finkel and James B. Rule, "Relative Deprivation and Related Psychological Theories of Civil Violence: A Critical Review," in *Research in Social Movements, Conflicts, and Change*, vol. 9, ed. Louis Kriesberg (Greenwich, Conn.: JAI Press, 1986), pp. 47–69.

6. Theda Skocpol, *States and Social Revolutions: A Comparative Analysis of France, Russia, and China* (Cambridge: Cambridge University Press, 1979). Another influential structural theory is the "demographic/structural theory" of Jack A. Goldstone, *Revolution and Rebellion in the Early Modern World* (Berkeley: University of California Press, 1991).

7. See also Mark I. Lichbach, *The Rebel's Dilemma* (Ann Arbor: University of Michigan Press, 1995). Lichbach's book contains a highly comprehensive critical survey of research on political revolutions.

8. Sequence C, like A, features two stable equilibria: 10 and 90. This is why expectations of the public opposition may influence its realization. By contrast, A^1 has a unique stable equilibrium at 90. Under A^1, expectations are practically immaterial. As long as public opposition is expected to be below 100, it will settle at 90.

9. As cited in Mao Tse-Tung, "A Single Spark Can Start a Prairie Fire" (1930) in *Selected Military Writings of Mao Tse-Tung* (Beijing: Foreign Languages Press, 1972), pp. 65–76.

10. Assuming, for the sake of illustration, that the individuals all have the same expressive needs.

11. See p. 166 for a definition of the former, p. 74 for a definition of the latter.

12. The standard Marxist explanation is critiqued by Martin Malia, *Comprendre la Révolution Russe* (Paris: Éditions du Seuil, 1980), pp. 91–93.

13. See William Henry Chamberlin, *The Russian Revolution, 1917–1921*, vol. 1 (New York: Macmillan, 1935), pp. 62–63; and Malia, *Comprendre la Révolution Russe*, pp. 92–93.

14. Thomas Walton, "Economic Development and Revolutionary Up-

heavals in Iran," *Cambridge Journal of Economics,* 4 (September 1980): 271–292.

15. Baruch Fischhoff, "Hindsight ≠ Foresight: The Effect of Outcome Knowledge on Judgment under Uncertainty," *Journal of Experimental Psychology: Human Perception and Performance,* 1 (August 1975): 288–299; and Baruch Fischhoff and Ruth Beyth, " 'I Knew It Would Happen'—Remembered Probabilities of Once Future Things," *Organizational Behavior and Human Performance,* 13 (February 1975): 1–16.

16. The Fall of Communism and Other Sudden Overturns

1. Bernard Gwertzman and Michael T. Kaufman, eds., *The Collapse of Communism, by the Correspondents of "The New York Times"* (New York: Times Books, 1990), p. vii.

2. For an early statement of this thesis, see Hannah Arendt, *The Origins of Totalitarianism,* 2nd ed. (New York: World Publishing, 1958), pt. 3. Arendt observed that communism weakens the interpersonal bonds rooted in family, community, religion, and profession. This, she went on to suggest, makes individuals terribly dependent on the state's goodwill, thus blocking the possibility of a mass mobilization.

3. Richard Pipes, "Gorbachev's Russia: Breakdown or Crackdown?" *Commentary,* March 1990, p. 16.

4. Jeane J. Kirkpatrick, *The Withering Away of the Totalitarian State . . . And Other Surprises* (Washington, D.C.: AEI Press, 1990). A decade earlier Kirkpatrick had proposed that the communist system was incapable of self-propelled evolution. See her "Dictatorships and Double Standards," *Commentary,* November 1979, pp. 34–45.

5. Stephen R. Graubard, "Preface to the Issue 'Eastern Europe . . . Central Europe . . . Europe,' " *Daedalus,* 119 (Winter 1990): vi.

6. Ibid., p. ii.

7. John Naisbitt, *Megatrends: Ten New Directions Transforming Our Lives* (New York: Warner Books, 1982).

8. *Economist,* November 18, 1989, p. 13.

9. See, for instance, Jack A. Goldstone, "Predicting Revolutions: Why We Could (and Should) Have Foreseen the Revolutions of 1989–1991 in the U.S.S.R. and Eastern Europe," *Contention,* 2 (Winter 1993): 127–152; Randall Collins, "Prediction in Macrosociology: The Case of the Soviet Collapse," *American Journal of Sociology,* 100 (May 1995): 1552–1593; and Susanne Lohmann, "The Dynamics of Informational Cascades: The Monday Demonstrations in Leipzig, East Germany, 1989–91,"

World Politics, 47 (October 1994): 42–101. Lohmann's analysis is largely consistent with the unpredictability of revolutions. Still, on page 91 of her paper she maintains that in 1989 East German political participation varied "in predictable ways."

10. Václav Havel, "The Power of the Powerless," in Havel et al., *The Power of the Powerless: Citizens against the State in Central-Eastern Europe,* ed. John Keane and trans. Paul Wilson (Armonk, N.Y.: M. E. Sharpe, 1985; orig. Czech ed., 1979), p. 42.

11. Ibid., pp. 87, 89, 96.

12. Václav Havel, "Meeting Gorbachev" (1987), in *Without Force or Lies: Voices from the Revolution of Central Europe in 1989–90,* ed. William M. Brinton and Alan Rinzler (San Francisco: Mercury House, 1990), pp. 266–267.

13. Václav Havel, "Cards on the Table" (1988), in *Without Force or Lies,* ed. Brinton and Rinzler, pp. 270–271.

14. Sidney Tarrow, " 'Aiming at a Moving Target': Social Science and the Recent Rebellions in Eastern Europe," *PS: Political Science and Politics,* 24 (March 1991): 12.

15. On the elections and the ensuing reactions, see the reports of John Taglibue, *New York Times,* June 3–6. The events leading up to the April accord have been chronicled and interpreted by Timothy Garton Ash, "Refolution: The Springtime of Two Nations," *New York Review of Books,* June 15, 1989, pp. 3–10. See also Elie Abel, *The Shattered Bloc: Behind the Upheaval in Eastern Europe* (Boston: Houghton Mifflin, 1990), chap. 4.

16. East German Survey of the Institut für Demoskopie Allensbach, February 17–March 15, 1990, Archive no. 4195 GEW.

17. In psychological experiments the I-knew-it-would-happen fallacy worsens over time. One would expect, therefore, the share of East Germans reporting that the explosion came as a surprise to decrease with the passage of time. Indeed, when asked in March 1991, a year after the first survey and sixteen months after the fall of East German communism, "Two years ago did you expect such a peaceful revolution," 7 percent answered "yes," and 33 percent "yes, but not that fast." The share responding that they were totally surprised was down to 54 percent (Allensbach Archives, Survey 5049). In March 1993, however, when a sample was asked, "Four years ago did you expect such a peaceful revolution," the first two figures fell back to 4 percent and 23 percent, respectively, and the share of the totally surprised rose to 70 percent (Allensbach Archives, Survey 5078). Interestingly, in 1991 the affirmative answers were substantially higher when the question was asked in the

form "If you think back two years from today, did you expect that the communist regime in the previous GDR would break down, or were you surprised by this?" Under this variant of the question, 20 percent said "yes," 47 percent "yes, but not that fast," and only 28 percent "I was surprised." The difference between the two variants is that the first asks whether the subjects expected communism to fall *peacefully,* the second merely whether they expected communism to fall. The latter variant of the question was not included in the surveys of 1990 and 1993.

18. For a compilation of pertinent reports from the *New York Times,* see Gwertzman and Kaufman, *The Collapse of Communism,* pp. 153–184. Eyewitness accounts include Timothy Garton Ash, "The German Revolution," *New York Review of Books,* December 21, 1989, pp. 14–19; and George Paul Csicsery, "The Siege of Nógrádi Street, Budapest, 1989," in *Without Force or Lies,* ed. Brinton and Rinzler, pp. 289–302.

19. Andrei Amalrik, *Will the Soviet Union Survive until 1984?* (New York: Harper & Row, 1970; orig. Russian ed., 1969), especially pp. 36–44.

20. Vladimir Tismaneanu, "Personal Power and Political Crisis in Romania," *Government and Opposition,* 24 (Spring 1989): 193–194.

21. For details, see Robert C. Tucker, *Political Culture and Leadership in Soviet Russia: From Lenin to Gorbachev* (New York: Norton, 1987), chap. 7.

22. Walter Friedrich and Hartmut Griese, *Jugend und Jugendforschung in der DDR: Gesellschaftspolitische Situationen, Sozialisation und Mentalitätsentwicklung in den achtziger Jahren* (Opladen: Leske & Budrich, 1991), pp. 139, 145.

23. Figures compiled in 1991 by Gallup-Hungary from *Jel kép.*

24. Correspondingly, the percentage believing that the trend favored the capitalist societies rose from 18 percent to 42 percent. Surveys of September 9, 1983, and June 14, 1989, from the archives of the Public Opinion Research Institute, Prague.

25. *Economist,* July 18, 1987, p. 45.

26. Z [Martin Malia], "To the Stalin Mausoleum," *Daedalus,* 119 (Winter 1990): 332.

27. Recorded by Daniel Bell, "As We Go into the Nineties: Some Outlines of the Twenty-First Century," *Dissent,* 37 (Spring 1990): 173.

28. *Economist,* July 18, 1987, p. 45.

29. Timothy Garton Ash, "Germany Unbound," *New York Review of Books,* November 22, 1990, p. 12.

30. In his own retrospective account, Gorbachev writes: "We did not realize immediately, of course, how far we had to go and what profound

changes were needed." See Mikhail Gorbachev, *The August Coup* (New York: HarperCollins, 1991), p. 104.

31. See Vladimir Tismaneanu, *Reinventing Politics: Eastern Europe from Stalin to Havel* (New York: Free Press, 1992), pp. 179–191.

32. Albert O. Hirschman, "Exit, Voice, and the Fate of the German Democratic Republic: An Essay in Conceptual History," *World Politics,* 45 (January 1993): 192; and Jens Reich, "Reflections on Becoming an East German Dissident, on Losing the Wall and a Country," in *Spring in Winter: The 1989 Revolutions,* ed. Gwyn Prins (Manchester: Manchester University Press, 1990), pp. 80–81.

33. Reich, "Reflections," p. 86.

34. Peter Voss in a personal interview, Leipzig, December 6, 1991.

35. Karl-Dieter Opp, "Spontaneous Revolutions: The Case of East Germany in 1989," in *German Unification and European Integration,* ed. Heinz Kurz (London: Edward Elgar, 1992), table 1. Analysts differ on whether the demonstrations grew monotonically. If the number of participants fell between two consecutive Mondays, the decline might have reflected shifting assessments of where events were headed.

36. For additional accounts and interpretations, see Ash, "The German Revolution"; Edith Anderson, "Town Mice and Country Mice," in *Without Force or Lies,* ed. Brinton and Rinzler, pp. 170-192; and the *New York Times* reports compiled in Gwertzman and Kaufman, *Collapse of Communism,* pp. 158–160, 166–184, and 216–222.

37. Bill Keller, "In Moscow, Tone Is a Studied Calm," *New York Times,* August 18, 1989, p. A6.

38. Henry Kamm,"Communist Party in Hungary Votes for Radical Shift," *New York Times,* October 8, 1989, pp. A1, A18. For a fuller account of the transformation, see Abel, *Shattered Bloc,* chap. 2.

39. Bill Keller, "Gorbachev, in Finland, Disavows Any Right of Regional Intervention," *New York Times,* October 26, 1989, pp. A1, A12.

40. For an eyewitness account of these events, see Timothy Garton Ash, "The Revolution of the Magic Lantern," *New York Review of Books,* January 18, 1990, pp. 42–51. See also Abel, *Shattered Bloc,* chap. 3.

41. *Economist,* December 2, 1989, p. 55.

42. See Timur Kuran, "Sparks and Prairie Fires: A Theory of Unanticipated Political Revolution," *Public Choice,* 61 (April 1989): 41–74.

43. The pace of events was doubtless a factor also in the failure of Soviet conservatives to block Eastern Europe's liberation. Had events moved more slowly, they might have had time to oust Gorbachev and order the Red Army into action.

44. "Czechoslovakia: The Velvet Revolution," *Uncaptive Minds,* 3 (January–February 1990): 11.

45. William H. Kaempfer and Anton D. Lowenberg, "Using Threshold Models to Explain International Relations," *Public Choice,* 73 (June 1992): 436.

46. For the *New York Times* reports of these events, see Gwertzman and Kaufman, *Collapse of Communism,* pp. 332–339. A detailed account is provided by Matei Calinescu and Vladimir Tismaneanu, "The 1989 Revolution and Romania's Future," *Problems of Communism,* 40 (January–April 1991): 42–59.

47. Jan Urban, "Czechoslovakia: The Power and Politics of Humiliation," in *Spring in Winter,* ed. Prins, p. 132.

48. See the references in note 9 in this chapter, and also J. F. Brown, *Surge to Freedom: The End of Communist Rule in Eastern Europe* (Durham, N.C.: Duke University Press, 1991); Mark Frankland, *The Patriots' Revolution: How Eastern Europe Toppled Communism and Won Its Freedom* (Chicago: Ivan R. Dee, 1992); and Sabrina R. Ramet, *Social Currents in Eastern Europe: The Sources and Meaning of the Great Transformation* (Durham, N.C.: Duke University Press, 1991).

49. For fuller and additional details, see Kuran, "Sparks and Prairie Fires."

50. Alexis de Tocqueville, *The Old Régime and the French Revolution,* trans. Stuart Gilbert (New York: Doubleday, 1955; first French ed., 1856), especially pp. 138–148.

51. William Doyle, *Origins of the French Revolution,* 2nd ed. (Oxford: Oxford University Press, 1988), p. 84.

52. Ibid., pp. 83–84.

53. Tocqueville, *Old Régime,* p. 20.

54. Richard Cobb, "The Beginning of the Revolutionary Crisis in Paris" (1967) and "Revolutionary Situations in France, 1789–1968" (1968), in his *A Second Identity: Essays on France and French History* (London: Oxford University Press, 1969), pp. 145–158, 267–281.

55. Samuel F. Scott, *The Response of the Royal Army to the French Revolution: The Role and Development of the Line Army, 1787–93* (Oxford: Clarendon Press, 1978), chap. 2, especially pp. 46–59.

56. Tocqueville, *Old Régime,* p. 175.

57. Cobb, "Revolutionary Situations," p. 272.

58. Fereydoun Hoveyda, *The Fall of the Shah,* trans. Roger Liddell (New York: Wyndham Books, 1980; orig. ed., 1979), pp. 15–17; and Marvin Zonis, "Iran: A Theory of Revolution from Accounts of the Revolution," *World Politics,* 35 (July 1983): 602.

59. Mohamed Heikal, *Iran: The Untold Story* (New York: Pantheon, 1982; orig. ed., 1981), p. 123.

60. Hoveyda, *Fall of the Shah,* pp. 35–38.

61. For this blunder, they were sacked in a meeting held in Prague. See Heikal, *Iran,* p. 156.

62. Shaul Bakhash, *The Reign of the Ayatollahs: Iran and the Islamic Revolution* (New York: Basic Books, 1984), p. 45.

63. Heikal, *Iran,* p. 157.

64. Nikki R. Keddie, "Can Revolutions Be Predicted; Can Their Causes Be Understood?" *Contention,* 1 (Winter 1992): 159–160.

65. Ibid., p. 160.

66. Hoveyda, *Fall of the Shah,* pp. 102–103, 117.

67. Bakhash, *Reign of the Ayatollahs,* pp. 41–42.

68. Ibid., pp. 13–14.

69. Much evidence is presented by Leopold Haimson, "The Problem of Social Stability in Urban Russia, 1905–1917," in *The Structure of Russian History: Interpretive Essays,* ed. Michael Cherniavsky (New York: Random House, 1970), pp. 341–380; and Hans Rogger, "Russia in 1914," *Journal of Contemporary History,* 1 (October 1966): 95–119. Each of these articles also presents an overview of the conflicting signs of stability and instability in pre-1917 Russia.

70. Leonard Schapiro, *The Russian Revolutions of 1917: The Origins of Modern Communism* (New York: Basic Books, 1984), p. 19.

71. Schapiro, *Russian Revolutions,* p. 39; and William Henry Chamberlin, *The Russian Revolution, 1917–1921,* vol. 1 (New York: Macmillan, 1935), p. 73.

72. Chamberlin, *Russian Revolution,* vol. 1, p. 76.

73. Ibid., pp. 73–77.

74. Ibid., p. 73.

75. Ibid., chap. 3.

76. On efforts to follow Bismarck's strategy, see Martin Malia, *Comprendre la Révolution Russe* (Paris: Éditions du Seuil, 1980), especially chap. 1. An additional component of this strategy was to make concessions to moderate the opposition, as when Alexander II emancipated the peasants.

77. Chamberlin, *Russian Revolution,* vol. 1, pp. 74–80; and Warren B. Walsh, "The Petrograd Garrison and the February Revolution of 1917," in *New Dimensions in Military History: An Anthology,* ed. Russell F. Weigley (San Rafael, Calif.: Presidio Press, 1975), pp. 267–269.

78. Chamberlin, *Russian Revolution,* vol. 1, p. 75; and Walsh, "Petrograd Garrison," pp. 267–273.

79. Paul Kecskemeti, *The Unexpected Revolution: Social Forces in the Hungarian Uprising* (Stanford: Stanford University Press, 1961), p. 1.

80. Ibid., pp. 60, 84–85.

81. Václav Havel, *Disturbing the Peace: A Conversation with Karel Hvížďala,* trans. Paul Wilson (New York: Alfred A. Knopf, 1990; orig. Czech ed., 1986), p. 109.

82. Timothy Garton Ash, "Eastern Europe: The Year of Truth," *New York Review of Books,* February 15, 1990, pp. 17–22.

83. Theodore Draper, "A New History of the Velvet Revolution," *New York Review of Books,* January 14, 1993, p. 18.

84. Quoted in Celestine Bohlen, "In Post-Communist Europe, Culture Takes a Fall," *Herald Tribune,* November 14, 1990, p. 1.

85. Information on Hungary provided by Adam Levendel, director of the Szonda Ipsos polling firm, during a December 13, 1991, interview in Budapest. Information on Czechoslovakia based on tables supplied by the Public Opinion Research Institute, Prague.

86. Adam Michnik, "An Embarrassing Anniversary," *New York Review of Books,* June 10, 1993, pp. 19–21.

87. Hannah Arendt, *On Revolution* (New York: Penguin, 1965; orig. ed., 1963), pp. 88–109.

88. Roy A. Medvedev, *Let History Judge: The Origins and Consequences of Stalinism,* trans. Colleen Taylor (New York: Vintage, 1973; orig. Russian ed., 1968), chaps. 2–8; and Robert Conquest, *The Great Terror: A Reassessment* (New York: Oxford University Press, 1990).

89. Bakhash, *Reign of the Ayatollahs,* especially chaps. 4, 9, 10.

90. Said Amir Arjomand, "Iran's Islamic Revolution in Comparative Perspective," *World Politics,* 38 (April 1986), especially pp. 392, 402.

91. Shahrough Akhavi, *Religion and Politics in Contemporary Iran: Clergy-State Relations in the Pahlavi Period* (Albany: State University of New York Press, 1980), pp. 168–180.

92. On the vulnerability of revolutionary regimes, see Stephen M. Walt, "Revolution and War," *World Politics,* 44 (April 1992): 321–368.

93. Bakhash, *Reign of the Ayatollahs,* pp. 219–224.

94. Friedrich Engels to Heinz Starkenburg, January 25, 1894. As quoted in Patrick Gardiner, *The Nature of Historical Explanation* (London: Oxford University Press, 1952), p. 100.

95. Vladimir Ilyich Lenin, "What Is to Be Done?" (1902), in *The Lenin Anthology,* ed. Robert C. Tucker (New York: Norton, 1975), pp. 12–114.

96. Tocqueville, *Old Régime,* p. 13.

97. Havel, *Disturbing the Peace,* p. 123. Similar sentiments are expressed on p. 144.

98. Charles Tilly, *From Mobilization to Revolution* (Reading, Mass.: Addison-Wesley, 1978).

99. Pamela E. Oliver, "Bringing the Crowd Back In: The Nonorganizational Elements of Social Movements," *Research in Social Movements, Conflict, and Change,* vol. 11, ed. Louis Kriesberg (Greenwich, Conn.: JAI Press, 1989), pp. 1–30. See also Sidney Tarrow, *Democracy and Disorder: Protest and Politics in Italy, 1965–1975* (Oxford: Clarendon Press, 1989).

17. The Hidden Complexities of Social Evolution

1. Richard R. Nelson and Sidney G. Winter, *An Evolutionary Theory of Economic Change* (Cambridge, Mass.: Harvard University Press, 1982); and Ulrich Witt, ed., *Evolutionary Economics* (Aldershot, U.K.: Edward Elgar, 1993).

2. W. Brian Arthur, *Increasing Returns and Path Dependence in the Economy* (Ann Arbor: University of Michigan Press, 1994); and M. Mitchell Waldrop, *Complexity: The Emerging Science at the Edge of Order and Chaos* (New York: Simon and Schuster, 1992).

3. Charles Darwin, *On the Origin of Species* (London: John Murray, 1859); and Stephen Jay Gould, *Wonderful Life: The Burgess Shale and the Nature of History* (New York: W. W. Norton, 1989).

4. W. Russell Neuman, *The Paradox of Mass Politics: Knowledge and Opinion in the American Electorate* (Cambridge, Mass.: Harvard University Press, 1986), p. 189.

5. Rance Crain, "Media Seers Clouding the Picture," *Advertising Age,* April 6, 1992, p. 25A; Robert A. Brusca, "Recession or Recovery?" *Challenge,* July–August 1992, pp. 4–15; and Robert D. Hershey, Jr., "This Just In: Recession Ended 21 Months Ago," *New York Times,* December 23, 1992, pp. D1, D3.

6. Bush's share of the vote declined by 19 percentage points in California, as against 15 percentage points nationally. In November 1992, California's unemployment rate stood at 9.3 percent, up from 4.8 percent in November 1988.

7. For a more technical presentation and further details, see Timur Kuran, "Cognitive Limitations and Preference Evolution," *Journal of Institutional and Theoretical Economics,* 147 (June 1991): 241–273.

8. The threshold of *e* would rise from 50 to 55, and that of *f* would fall from 55 to 50.

9. The changes could be ones that affect a single individual. Turn back to *E*, and assume that public opinion is in equilibrium at 50. If the threshold of *e* rises from 50 to 55, public opinion will dart to 100. Suppose now that this threshold falls back to 50, restoring *E*. Public opinion will remain stuck at 100.

10. This theme is developed at length in William H. Riker, *Liberalism against Populism: A Confrontation between the Theory of Democracy and the Theory of Social Choice* (San Francisco: W. H. Freeman, 1982). For many additional insights, see Thráinn Eggertsson, *Economic Behavior and Institutions* (New York: Cambridge University Press, 1990), chaps. 6–10.

11. Gordon Tullock, *Toward a Mathematics of Politics* (Ann Arbor: University of Michigan Press, 1967), chap. 3; and Kenneth A. Shepsle and Barry R. Weingast, "Structure-Induced Equilibrium and Legislative Choice," *Public Choice*, 37 (1981): 503–519.

12. F. C. Bartlett, *Remembering* (Cambridge: Cambridge University Press, 1932), especially chap. 8. For further evidence, see Nelson and Winter, *An Evolutionary Theory of Economic Change*, p. 112; and Ronald A. Heiner, "Imperfect Decisions and the Law: On the Evolution of Legal Precedent and Rules," *Journal of Legal Studies*, 15 (June 1986): 227–261.

13. Alan J. Parkin, *Memory and Amnesia: An Introduction* (Oxford: Basil Blackwell, 1987).

14. Herbert A. Simon, *Reason in Human Affairs* (Stanford: Stanford University Press, 1983), elaborates on obstacles to imagining contingencies, and Michael Polanyi, *The Tacit Dimension* (Gloucester, Mass.: Peter Smith, 1983; orig. ed., 1966), on those to articulating full justifications. Evidence pertaining to the enforcement and evolution of the law is offered by Ronald Dworkin, *Law's Empire* (Cambridge, Mass.: Harvard University Press, 1986); and Edward H. Levi, *An Introduction to Legal Reasoning* (Chicago: University of Chicago Press, 1948).

15. For evidence of self-serving interpretation on the part of judges, and many insights that complement those offered here, see Thomas J. Miceli and Metin Coşgel, "Reputation and Judicial Decision-Making," *Journal of Economic Behavior and Organization*, 23 (January 1994): 31–51.

16. Magoroh Maruyama, "The Second Cybernetics: Deviation-Amplifying Mutual Causal Processes," *American Scientist*, 51 (March 1963): 164–179.

17. David Hackett Fischer, *Historians' Fallacies: Toward a Logic of Historical Thought* (London: Routledge & Kegan Paul, 1971), p. 178.

18. R. W. Apple, Jr., "Opposition Calls for Vote and Gains Access to a More Open Press," _New York Times,_ November 29, 1989, p. A1.

19. Alfred Marshall, _Principles of Economics: An Introductory Volume,_ 8th ed. (London: Macmillan, 1936), p. iii.

20. Darwin, _Origin of Species._

21. Joel Mokyr, _The Lever of Riches: Technological Creativity and Economic Progress_ (New York: Oxford University Press, 1990), p. 273.

22. Niles Eldredge and Stephen Jay Gould, "Punctuated Equilibria: An Alternative to Phyletic Gradualism," in _Models in Paleobiology,_ ed. Thomas J. M. Schopf (San Francisco: Freeman, Cooper & Co., 1972), pp. 82–115; and Niles Eldredge, _Time Frames: The Evolution of Punctuated Equilibria_ (Princeton: Princeton University Press, 1985).

23. Gould, _Wonderful Life._

24. David M. Raup, _Extinction: Bad Genes or Bad Luck?_ (New York: W. W. Norton, 1991).

25. Mokyr, _Lever of Riches,_ pt. 4.

26. W. Brian Arthur, "Competing Technologies, Increasing Returns, and Lock-In by Historical Events," _Economic Journal,_ 99 (March 1989): 116–131; and Paul A. David, "The Hero and the Herd in Technological History: Reflections on Thomas Edison and the Battle of the Systems," in _Favorites of Fortune: Technology, Growth, and Economic Development since the Industrial Revolution,_ ed. Patrice Higonnet, David S. Landes, and Henry Rosovsky (Cambridge, Mass.: Harvard University Press, 1991), pp. 72–119.

27. Gustave Le Bon, _The Crowd: A Study of the Popular Mind_ (Atlanta: Cherokee Publishing Co., 1982; first French ed., 1895), pp. 65, 72.

28. Ibid., p. 68.

29. Anthony Pratkanis and Elliot Aronson, _Age of Propaganda: The Everyday Use and Abuse of Persuasion_ (New York: W. H. Freeman, 1992), pp. 206–215.

30. Abbé J. A. Dubois, _Hindu Manners, Customs, and Ceremonies,_ 3rd ed., trans. Henry K. Beauchamp (Oxford: Clarendon Press, 1906; first French ed., 1815), p. 28.

31. The last fallacy is the focus of F. A. Hayek's critique of constructivism. See his _Law, Legislation, and Liberty,_ vol. 1: _Rules and Order_ (Chicago: University of Chicago Press, 1973), chaps. 1 and 3.

32. R. H. Tawney, _Religion and the Rise of Capitalism_ (Gloucester, Mass.: Peter Smith, 1962; orig. ed., 1926), especially pp. 79–102.

33. Robert K. Merton, "The Unanticipated Consequences of Purposive Social Action," _American Sociological Review,_ 1 (December 1936): 894–904; Hayek, _Law, Legislation, and Liberty,_ vol. 1, chaps. 1 and 3; and

Raymond Boudon, *The Unintended Consequences of Social Action* (New York: St. Martin's Press, 1982; orig. French ed., 1977).

34. Mark Granovetter, "Economic Action and Social Structure: The Problem of Embeddedness," *American Journal of Sociology,* 91 (November 1985): 481–510; and Gregory Dow, "The Function of Authority in Transaction Cost Economics," *Journal of Economic Behavior and Organization,* 8 (March 1987): 13–38.

35. Mancur Olson, *The Logic of Collective Action: Public Goods and the Theory of Groups* (Cambridge, Mass.: Harvard University Press, 1965).

36. These implications are consistent with the historical interpretations of E. L. Jones, *Growth Recurring: Economic Change in World History* (Oxford: Clarendon Press, 1988).

37. Under E, a's intrinsic utility is $100 - |50 - 80| = 70$. With the shift to E^2, it becomes $100 - |100 - 80| = 80$.

38. Gould, *Wonderful Life;* and Raup, *Extinction.*

39. Gould, *Wonderful Life,* p. 318.

18. From Slavery to Affirmative Action

1. Alexis de Tocqueville, *Democracy in America,* vol. 2, ed. Henry Reeve, Francis Bowen, and Phillips Bradley (New York: Alfred A. Knopf, 1989; orig. French ed., 1835), chap. 18.

2. See, for instance, Jay R. Mandle, *Not Slave, Not Free: The African American Economic Experience since the Civil War* (Durham, N.C.: Duke University Press, 1992), chaps. 4–5.

3. Robert William Fogel, *Without Consent or Contract: The Rise and Fall of American Slavery* (New York: W. W. Norton, 1989), chaps. 4–5. The South did not compare well on all indices of material advancement. Intrauterine malnutrition was more common in the South than in the North, for example, because pregnant slaves had to keep working almost until childbirth.

4. Stanley L. Engerman, "Slavery and Emancipation in Comparative Perspective: A Look at Some Recent Debates," *Journal of Economic History,* 46 (June 1986): 327.

5. Fogel, *Without Consent or Contract,* pp. 322, 369, 382.

6. Ibid., pp. 328–329.

7. This campaign drew intellectual justification from a literature aimed at showing that blacks are naturally inferior to whites. See Stephen Jay Gould, *The Mismeasure of Man* (New York: W. W. Norton, 1981).

8. Russel B. Nye, *Fettered Freedom: Civil Liberties and the Slavery*

Controversy, 1830–1860 (East Lansing: Michigan State College Press, 1949), especially chaps. 3–5.

9. William W. Freehling, *Prelude to Civil War: The Nullification Controversy in South Carolina, 1816–1836* (New York: Harper & Row, 1966), p. 110.

10. Merton L. Dillon, *The Abolitionists: The Growth of a Dissenting Minority* (De Kalb: Northern Illinois University Press, 1974), p. 49.

11. Fogel, *Without Consent or Contract,* p. 326.

12. Ibid., pp. 413–414.

13. Ibid., pp. 414–416.

14. William H. Riker, *Liberalism against Populism: A Confrontation between the Theory of Democracy and the Theory of Social Choice* (San Francisco: W. H. Freeman, 1982), chap. 9; and Barry R. Weingast, "Institutions and Political Commitment: A New Political Economy of the American Civil War Era" (unpublished manuscript, Stanford University, 1994), pt. 4.

15. Don E. Fehrenbacher, *The Dred Scott Case: Its Significance in American Law and Politics* (New York: Oxford University Press, 1978), pp. 89–100.

16. J. R. Pole, *The Pursuit of Equality in American History* (Berkeley: University of California Press, 1978), pp. 148–149. For an interpretation of Lincoln's comments on equality, see David Zarefsky, *Lincoln, Douglas, and Slavery: In the Crucible of Public Debate* (Chicago: University of Chicago Press, 1990), pp. 78–80, 242–244.

17. George M. Frederickson, *The Black Image in the White Mind: The Debate on Afro-American Character and Destiny, 1817–1914* (New York: Harper & Row, 1971), chap. 1.

18. Stanley N. Katz, "The Strange Birth and Unlikely History of Constitutional Equality," *Journal of American History,* 75 (December 1988): 747–762.

19. James Madison, "The Federalist no. 10" (1787), in Alexander Hamilton, James Madison, and John Jay, *The Federalist Papers,* ed. Jacob E. Cooke (Middletown, Conn.: Wesleyan University Press, 1961; orig. pub., 1787–88), p. 59. I owe the observation to Pole, *Pursuit of Equality,* pp. 121–122.

20. Pole, *Pursuit of Equality,* pp. 13–26.

21. David Brion Davis, *The Problem of Slavery in Western Culture* (Ithaca: Cornell University Press, 1966), pt. 1; and Bernard Lewis, *Race and Slavery in the Middle East: An Historical Enquiry* (New York: Oxford University Press, 1990).

22. Pole, *Pursuit of Equality*, p. 117.

23. Katz, "Strange Birth," especially pp. 753–755. See also Pole, *Pursuit of Equality*, chaps. 6–7; and Terry Eastland and William J. Bennett, *Counting by Race: Equality from the Founding Fathers to* Bakke *and* Weber (New York: Basic Books, 1979), chaps. 2–3.

24. Eastland and Bennett, *Counting by Race*, chap. 5; Pole, *Pursuit of Equality*, chap. 7; and Robert Higgs, *Competition and Coercion: Blacks in the American Economy, 1865–1914* (Cambridge: Cambridge University Press, 1977).

25. A similar point is made, with a focus on tenancy relations in agriculture, by Lee J. Alston and Joseph P. Ferrie, "Social Control and Labor Relations in the American South before the Mechanization of the Cotton Harvest in the 1950s," *Journal of Institutional and Theoretical Economics*, 145 (March 1989): 133–157; and Lee J. Alston, "Race Etiquette in the South: The Role of Tenancy," in *Research in Economic History*, vol. 10, ed. Paul Uselding (Greenwich, Conn.: JAI Press, 1986), pp. 200–201.

26. Hortense Powdermaker, *After Freedom: A Cultural Study in the Deep South* (New York: Viking, 1939), especially chap. 16.

27. Richard Wright, *Black Boy: A Record of Childhood and Youth* (New York: Harper & Row, 1945), p. 253. As recorded in Mandle, *Not Slave, Not Free*, p. 62.

28. Dennis Chong, *Collective Action and the Civil Rights Movement* (Chicago: University of Chicago Press, 1991), p. 97.

29. Thomas Sowell, *Preferential Policies: An International Perspective* (New York: William Morrow, 1990), p. 126 (emphasis added). For the early history of affirmative action, see Nathan Glazer, *Affirmative Discrimination: Ethnic Inequality and Public Policy*, rev. ed. (Cambridge, Mass.: Harvard University Press, 1987), chaps. 2–4; and Herman Belz, *Equality Transformed: A Quarter-Century of Affirmative Action* (New Brunswick, N.J.: Transaction Publishers, 1992), chaps. 1–2.

30. Godfrey Hodgson, quoted in Chong, *Collective Action*, p. 224.

31. Fogel, *Without Consent or Contract*, p. 204.

32. Pole, *Pursuit of Equality*, pp. 178–180.

33. Belz, *Equality Transformed*, pp. 8–12.

34. For detailed accounts of these cases, see ibid., chaps. 2, 6–7.

35. Ibid., especially chap. 3.

36. Abigail M. Thernstrom, *Whose Votes Count? Affirmative Action and Minority Voting Rights* (Cambridge, Mass.: Harvard University Press, 1987).

37. J. W. Peltason, *Fifty-Eight Lonely Men: Southern Federal Judges and School Desegregation* (New York: Harcourt, Brace and World, 1961), pp. 12–14, 96–97.

38. D. Garth Taylor, *Public Opinion and Collective Action: The Boston School Desegregation Conflict* (Chicago: University of Chicago Press, 1986), chap. 6.

39. Peter Brimelow and Leslie Spencer, "When Quotas Replace Merit, Everybody Suffers," *Forbes,* February 15, 1993, pp. 80–102.

40. Timur Kuran, "Seeds of Racial Explosion," *Society,* 30 (September/October 1993): 55–67.

41. Marc Galanter, *Competing Equalities: Law and the Backward Classes in India* (Berkeley: University of California Press, 1984); André Béteille, *The Backward Classes in Contemporary India* (Delhi: Oxford University Press, 1992); and Thomas Sowell, *Preferential Policies: An International Perspective* (New York: William Morrow, 1990), especially pp. 91–103.

42. Béteille, *Backward Classes,* p. 74.

43. Dharma Kumar, "The Affirmative Action Debate in India," *Asian Survey,* 32 (March 1992): 290–302.

44. Ibid., p. 294.

45. Ibid., p. 301.

19. Preference Falsification and Social Analysis

1. Henri Poincaré, *Science and Hypothesis* (New York: Dover Publications, 1952; orig. French ed., 1902), p. 173.

2. Deconstructionism began with Jacques Derrida in the 1960s. A representative work of Derrida is *Writing and Difference,* trans. Alan Bass (Chicago: University of Chicago Press, 1978; first French ed., 1967). For a survey, see Christopher Norris, *Deconstruction: Theory and Practice,* rev. ed. (London: Routledge, 1991).

3. Clifford Geertz, "Thick Description: Toward an Interpretive Theory of Culture," in his *The Interpretation of Cultures* (New York: Basic Books, 1973), pp. 3–30.

4. Paul Veyne, *Writing History: Essay on Epistemology,* trans. Mina Moore-Rinvolucri (Middletown, Conn.: Wesleyan University Press, 1984; orig. French ed., 1971), pp. 151–153. For a similar perspective, see Edward Hallett Carr, *What Is History?* (New York: Alfred A. Knopf, 1962), especially chap. 1.

5. The former group is composed primarily of neoclassical economists. The latter features mostly sociologists and political scientists, but

also certain economists outside the neoclassical tradition. Several prominent works in the structuralist tradition were critiqued in Chapter 15.

6. Andrew S. McFarland, as quoted by Jon Elster, *Ulysses and the Sirens: Studies in Rationality and Irrationality* (Cambridge: Cambridge University Press, 1979), p. 113, n. 4. The third chapter of Elster's book offers a critique of structuralism.

7. F. A. Hayek, "The Pretence of Knowledge" (Nobel memorial lecture, 1974), in his *New Studies in Philosophy, Politics, Economics, and the History of Ideas* (Chicago: University of Chicago Press, 1978), p. 32.

8. In a linear system, by contrast, the sensitivity of a dependent variable to changes in an independent variable is constant. Minor variations might be accommodated, of course, through "noise"—the statistician's euphemism for chance events, data imperfections, and just plain ignorance.

9. There are theories that predict better than they explain. For example, the Ptolemaic theory of the universe is quite successful at predicting the movements of planets, but by modern standards its explanations are very inadequate. See Thomas S. Kuhn, *The Copernican Revolution: Planetary Astronomy in the Development of Western Thought* (Cambridge, Mass.: Harvard University Press, 1957).

10. See, for example, John Dunn, *Modern Revolutions: An Introduction to the Analysis of a Political Phenomenon*, 2nd ed. (New York: Cambridge University Press, 1989), pp. 2–3; and Valerie Bunce, "Democracy, Stalinism, and the Management of Uncertainty," in *Democracy and Political Transformation: Theories and East-Central European Realities,* ed. György Szoboszlai (Budapest: Hungarian Political Science Association, 1991), especially pp. 152–153.

11. A similar point is developed by Nancy Bermeo, "Surprise, Surprise: Lessons from 1989 and 1991," in *Liberalization and Democratization: Change in the Soviet Union and Eastern Europe,* ed. Bermeo (Baltimore: Johns Hopkins University Press, 1992), pp. 184–187.

12. Carr, *What Is History?,* pp. 90–91.

13. Imre Lakatos, "Falsification and the Methodology of Scientific Research Programmes" (1970), in his *The Methodology of Scientific Research Programmes* (Cambridge: Cambridge University Press, 1978), pp. 8–101.

14. Leo Strauss, *Persecution and the Art of Writing* (Glencoe, Ill.: Free Press, 1952); and Muhsin Mahdi, *Ibn Khaldun's Philosophy of History* (London: George Allen and Unwin, 1957), especially pp. 113–125.

15. James C. Scott, *Weapons of the Weak: Everyday Forms of Peasant Resistance* (New Haven: Yale University Press, 1985). See also Scott,

Domination and the Arts of Resistance: Hidden Transcripts (New Haven: Yale University Press, 1990).

16. Elisabeth Noelle-Neumann, *The Spiral of Silence—Our Social Skin* (Chicago: University of Chicago Press, 1984; first German ed., 1980), pp. 55–56.

17. Peter Miller, "Which Side Are You On? The 1990 Nicaraguan Poll Debacle," *Public Opinion Quarterly,* 55 (Summer 1991): 281–302. See also Stephen Schwartz, *A Strange Silence: The Emergence of Democracy in Nicaragua* (San Francisco: ICS Press, 1992), especially chaps. 4, 7.

18. Mark A. Uhlig, "Nicaraguan Opposition Routs Sandinistas; U.S. Pledges Aid, Tied to Orderly Turnover," *New York Times,* February 27, 1990, pp. A1, 12; and Norman Ornstein, "Why Polls Flopped in Nicaragua," *New York Times,* March 7, 1990, p. A25.

19. Katherine Bischoping and Howard Schuman, "Pens and Polls in Nicaragua: An Analysis of the 1990 Preelection Surveys," *American Journal of Political Science,* 36 (May 1992): 331–350.

20. For further insights on the pen experiment, see William A. Barnes, "Rereading the Nicaraguan Pre-Election Polls in the Light of the Election Results," in *The 1990 Elections in Nicaragua and Their Aftermath,* ed. Vanessa Castro and Gary Prevost (Lanham, Md.: Rowman and Littlefield, 1992), pp. 41–128.

21. Karl R. Popper, *Conjectures and Refutations: The Growth of Scientific Knowledge* (New York: Basic Books, 1962).

22. Thomas S. Kuhn, *The Structure of Scientific Revolutions,* 2nd ed. (Chicago: University of Chicago Press, 1970; first ed., 1962).

23. Jack A. Goldstone, "Predicting Revolutions: Why We Could (and Should) Have Foreseen the Revolutions of 1989–1991 in the U.S.S.R. and Eastern Europe," *Contention,* 2 (Winter 1993): 127–152.

Index